CultureShock!

A Survival Guide to Customs and Etiquette

Paris

Frances Gendlin

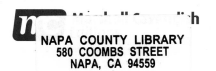

This 4th edition published in 2016

Published by Marshall Cavendish Editions
An imprint of Marshall Cavendish International (Asia) Private Limited
1 New Industrial Road, Singapore 536196

First published in 1998 by Times Editions Private Limited, reprinted in 1999, 2000, 2001;
2nd edition published by Marshall Cavendish Corporation in 2007, reprinted 2008. 3rd
edition published by Marshall Cavendish Corporation in 2011.

Other Marshall Cavendish Offices:
Marshall Cavendish Corporation. 99 White Plains Road, Tarrytown NY 10591-9001, USA ■
Marshall Cavendish International (Thailand) Co Ltd. 253 Asoke, 12th Flr, Sukhumvit 21 Road,
Klongtoey Nua, Wattana, Bangkok 10110, Thailand ■ Marshall Cavendish (Malaysia) Sdn
Bhd, Times Subang, Lot 46, Subang Hi-Tech Industrial Park, Batu Tiga, 40000 Shah Alam,
Selangor Darul Ehsan, Malaysia

Marshall Cavendish is a trademark of Times Publishing Limited

National Library Board, Singapore Cataloguing-in-Publication Data
Name(s): Gendlin, Frances. | Marshall Cavendish Editions, publisher.
Title: CultureShock! Paris : a survival guide to customs and etiquette / Frances
Gendlin.
Other title(s): Culture shock! Paris. | Paris. | Culture shock!
Description: Singapore : Marshall Cavendish Editions, 2016.
Identifier(s): OCN 944462198 | ISBN 978-981-4721-79-0 (paperback)
Subject(s): LCSH: Paris (France)--Guidebooks. | Paris (France)--Description and travel. |
Paris (France)--Social life and customs. | Etiquette—France--Paris.
Classification: LCC DC708 | DDC 914.436104--dc23

Printed in Singapore by Markono Print Media Pte Ltd

Photo Credits:
Black and white photos from Zeny Cieslikowski: pages xii, 7, 22, 32, 105, 165, 213,
222, 226, 233, 246, 267, 300; Photolibrary: pages xiii, 67, 78, 119, 141, 172, 283,
292, 312, 329; Dominique Bremond: 392-393. ■ Cover photo: Getty Images

All illustrations by TRIGG, except pages 20,23 (John Zaugg).

ABOUT THE SERIES

Culture shock is a state of disorientation that can come over anyone who has been thrust into unknown surroundings, away from one's comfort zone. *CultureShock!* is a series of trusted and reputed guides which has, for decades, been helping expatriates and long-term visitors to cushion the impact of culture shock whenever they move to a new country.

Written by people who have lived in the country and experienced culture shock themselves, the authors share all the information necessary for anyone to cope with these feelings of disorientation more effectively. The guides are written in a style that is easy to read and covers a range of topics that will arm readers with enough advice, hints and tips to make their lives as normal as possible again.

Each book is structured in the same manner. It begins with the first impressions that visitors will have of that city or country. To understand a culture, one must first understand the people—where they came from, who they are, the values and traditions they live by, as well as their customs and etiquette. This is covered in the first half of the book.

Then on with the practical aspects—how to settle in with the greatest of ease. Authors walk readers through topics such as how to find accommodation, get the utilities and telecommunications up and running, enrol the children in school and keep in the pink of health. But that's not all. Once the essentials are out of the way, venture out and try the food, enjoy more of the culture and travel to other areas. Then be immersed in the language of the country before discovering more about the business side of things.

To round off, snippets of basic information are offered before readers are 'tested' on customs and etiquette of the country. Useful words and phrases, a comprehensive resource guide and list of books for further research are also included for easy reference.

CONTENTS

FOREWORD

'Fluctuat nec mergitur—It tosses on the
waves but does not sink.'
—Paris motto

This book is designed for anyone who loves Paris. Loving Paris is not hard, as even cold statistics attest, for each year it is rated as the most visited city in the world. It's true that many world capitals have ardent admirers, but there seems to be something unique, something almost palpable about Paris that inspires love. It's not about you or me, this love, nor about anyone else; it is about the city itself and how being here makes us feel about our own lives. But why Paris? Certainly its charms are not unique. Rome is as historic and Venice as beautiful, Hong Kong is as bold and Marrakech as exotic. But somehow Paris has it all, including an ability to insinuate itself into our souls, demanding so much of us—and giving so much in return. Yet the spirit of this magnetic city is hard to convey: its impressions are so personal and its offerings so varied that each person who arrives for the first time ultimately seems to discover it anew. Perhaps it's best that way.

A tourist who comes to Paris for a week or two is fortunate, to be sure. There is so much atmosphere to soak up in the city's streets and there are historical monuments to stop and admire, outstanding works of art to appreciate and parks landscaped so beautifully that they take one's breath away. And what about the food and the wine? There are too many opportunities and not enough time. Yes, such visits are necessarily short, so before departure, before anything can be forgotten, people often jot down in the back of their guidebooks the museums to include for the next visit, a few restaurants to recommend to friends and which neighbourhoods remain to be explored. Unfortunately, these must be left until the next time.

So imagine, as many tourists do, actually living in Paris—having the Louvre nearby every day of the year and the world's temples of gastronomy to satisfy any culinary whim... how wonderful that must be! Fortunately, life here is as good as one imagines, even if few residents go to museums every day or—if they are at all concerned about their budgets—frequent restaurants on a daily basis. Yet Paris truly is a city in which it is ultimately better to live than visit—for the reasons above to be sure, but also for deeper, more lasting reasons that are understood little by little, as life in *la Ville Lumière* (the City of Light) unfolds. Immersion into any new culture takes some effort, but this is Paris after all, the most entrancing—and yes, romantic—city in the world and worth whatever effort it takes.

Think of the thousands who have come before who thought the same. Pablo Picasso painted his masterpiece *Guernica* while living on rue des Grands-Augustins, around the corner from rue Christine, where the American writer Gertrude Stein lived for a time. Farther north, at Square d'Orléans, the Polish composer Frédéric Chopin settled near his lover, writer George Sand. Artist Amadeo Modigliani, the 'king of Montparnasse', died young and broke in Paris, but composer Virgil Thompson (who claimed that if he had to starve to death, he would prefer to do it where the food was so good) found fame in time. Ultimately it was Ernest Hemingway who summed it up: "There is never any ending to Paris and the memory of each person who has lived in it differs from that of any other... Paris was always worth it and you received return for whatever you brought to it."

Actually, much about being in Paris is easy. It is easy to get around and to find out what is going on, no matter how deplorable your spoken French. The city has one of the most efficient public transportation systems in the world, reaching into every hidden nook you would want to explore. Everything you need or want is available somewhere within the city's confines. Both the Tourist Office and City Hall provide more information about the city than you would think possible—from brochures you can pick up to information on the Internet that is updated daily. In addition to museums, tours, monuments and interesting current events, you can find every sports facility and municipal pool, get advice on how to raise and educate healthy children, and even an explanation of why the city's water is so good. Descriptions of public gardens, suggested walks through historic neighbourhoods and schedules for cultural and entertaining events are available to visitors and residents alike. Shops sell guides, history books and restaurant critiques, and you can find directions to intriguing shops and compendiums of helpful advice from what is open on Sunday to what can be delivered to your door. There are also several locally produced English-language publications—and more on the Internet—to keep you updated on the area's events. Actually Paris may well be the most comprehensively covered city in the world.

So, what is it that takes an effort? It's moving. Moving to any new city, settling in, getting used to manoeuvering and finding the things you need when you descend upon a city not yet your own. Don't underestimate the time required to get your bearings, or to begin with, to cram the furniture you had shipped into a space that turns out to be too small. Or to deal with the fact that there is no hot water tap to hook up to the washing machine you brought from home. Or that the documents you were told to bring were not the right ones after all. Or that you cannot get a bank account without proof of domicile, but without a bank account you cannot get an apartment... These difficulties are wearying to be sure, but they can be overcome with dispatch—we hope—by using the information in this book.

USING THIS GUIDE

The first guidebook to Paris was published in 1685 and hundreds have been published since. Today, guidebooks for tourists recount the city's history and describe in their own ways its remarkable sights and sensations. In varying detail, they review restaurants and suggest hotels of all categories. Each tries to present the material in a more eye-catching manner than the others, and each has its own approach to capturing the glory of *la Ville Lumière*. All, however, have one thing in common: they are designed for people visiting for a short while, tourists who think that what they see in a week is what they would get every day of the year.

This book, although encompassing information for the short-term visitor, is different in approach. Its main purpose is to offer specific advice and assistance about daily life in Paris for those who are planning to stay longer, for people who have the time for byways rather than straight paths, for sojourners who want to get into the deeper Parisian life that is often hidden from the tourist's eye. Whether your stay is for a month or a year, the type of information you need for a successful stay is different—deeper and more detailed than that found in standard tourist guides: where and how to look for appropriate housing, how to manage finances, how to stay healthy and where to get fit, how to access the Internet and where to buy a computer, where to get a fun meal for your kids, etc. are just a few examples of basic information that should help you move with minimum discomfort into the Parisian scene.

Of course, there is a difference between learning how a city works and adapting yourself to its cultural rules. In Paris, this is what takes the real effort, requiring more adjustment than you might suspect. How much you want to adapt is up to you, for Paris is flexible above all. You can spend all your time with English speakers—some 100,000 live in the Greater Paris area—and learn just enough French to ask a grocer if the melons are ripe. Yet, if this is the route you choose, you'll never really feel at home. If you don't understand why your colleagues or new friends act as they do, you'll always be an outsider to them. This book will come in handy in this regard, with cultural tips, some do's and don'ts—and there are many of them—and even a quiz to see how many of the 'Paris Rules' you've absorbed.

Your success at this will depend for the most part on your expectations. Preconceived ideas about an unfamiliar society may not always prove true, and it's best not to assume that life in Paris will more or less be like life at home, except for the language—it isn't. Start from scratch and take Paris as it is, appreciate its remarkable beauty, explore its delicious novelty, enjoy its agreeable differences, cope with its difficulties and try to laugh (if only to yourself) when your own cultural assumptions collide head on with the differing assumptions of the French.

LIVING WELL

Parisians have long felt that they have mastered *l'art de vivre*—the art of living well. Tourists who stroll the length of the beautiful Champs-Elysées may get a whiff of the French traditions of elegance, culture and poise, but it is the total absorption of *l'art de vivre* that truly enriches the soul. It is the habits of everyday life—walking down the city's beautifully designed historic streets on your way to work, passing graceful apartment buildings and landscaped squares, shopping in the bustling markets, or lingering in the spring sunshine at a sidewalk café—that continually remind you of how gracious Parisian life can be. Watching a film under the summer stars at La Villette, hearing organ music soar to the high reaches of the Cathedral of Notre-Dame, or gathering with new Parisian friends at a neighbourhood bistro where you have become known as an *habitué* (regular customer)—these will remind you of the fullness of life in Paris as well. Make no mistake: appreciation of experience is what Paris is about, whether you are here for a day or a year. And this never stops as long as you are here. No, it doesn't stop, even amid the uncertainties that currently exist here and around the world.

Eventually you'll find your way—everyone does after a while. As your Parisian life unfolds, you'll come to discover which neighbourhood *fromagerie* (cheese store) is your favourite and which teller at the bank goes a little out of the way for you, and so you will be dealing less with strangers and more with people you know. You will walk down the streets and suddenly realise that those byways and hidden nooks are familiar, that they're become your own. The essence of your life will seem more vibrant, your conversation more animated, your days fuller. Now you will be developing your own *art de vivre*, keeping the best of your own culture and traditions while adding on those of the French. This is the beginning of *la belle vie*, the good life you could only imagine at first, but now coming true in ways you had not expected. And when these things happen, you'll understand—almost without thinking about it—that you're at home.

Be patient, for it will happen,with openness to new ideas, observation of life around you and even a little assistance. In this regard, we hope this book will help guide you and perhaps even keep you on course. *Bienvenue à Paris*. Welcome home.

ACKNOWLEDGEMENTS xi

This book was originally researched in 1996 and I had a lot of encouragement from long-time Parisians who knew more of the hidden and unusual than I did at the time. Colette and Claude Samama read every word of the manuscript and saw me through the project from beginning to end. My stalwart friend Jean Coyner offered invaluable advice, her humour often sorely needed. The late Jean and Warren Trabant loved Paris every day for their fifty years here, and conveyed that to me. And Virginia Crosby, who remained my closest ally, as for years we sailed through and around Paris, taking it all in. Thanks still go to legal and cultural consultant Jean Taquet, whose monthly report is always helpful, as well as to John Zaugg, who created the elegant maps in Chapter 2. To all of you I was grateful then and remain so now. *Je vous en suis très reconnaissante.*

Over the years we have updated information and have published new editions. This one, though—in both physical book and e-book formats—almost twenty years after the original book was published, brings you access to information that wasn't even dreamed of back then, with content updated, modernised, expanded. And even now, after all these years in Paris, I still needed some feedback on the new material created, so I relied once again especially on Jean Coyner, whose knowledge of Paris seems limitless. Of course, now as over the years, readers should understand that any mistakes herein are mine alone and not of anyone else.

A FEW NOTES ON FOREIGN WORDS

Throughout the book, foreign words are shown in italics, even those that have been assimilated into the English language and appear in the Oxford English Dictionary. This includes the word '*anglophone*', which is how the French refer to native English-speakers, and which is used here occasionally in the appropriate context. When listing services or shops (e.g., bakeries) in the vicinity, they are listed by *arrondissement*; where the services might be needed regardless of their location (e.g., churches), they are listed alphabetically. Where full addresses are given in the text, including the entire number of the *arrondissement* (e.g. 75012), the word Paris has been omitted; if writing to these addresses, be sure to include the city name.

DISCLAIMER

For a citizenry that resists change, Parisians must often be confounded these days. Change on all levels is on the air. Readers should understand that information here about regulations, addresses and Internet websites were current as of December 2015, to the best of our knowledge, but that doesn't mean they will be in another week or month. So, please note that the sites and links are informational only; most of the Internet sites listed have English language options, but the information there may not be a complete as in the French version. With all this streamlining and the current uncertainty in Paris, the author and publisher can bear no responsibility for any misunderstanding or inconvenience that might arise or for unexpected changes: in immigration laws (which seem always to be under review), closings, or even the sometimes unhelpful service, discrepancies in rates or prices, quality of products or accommodations, the disappearance of a shop, or the occasional bad meal (yes, even in Paris). Nor can we be responsible for websites that come and go or their own suggestions or recommendations which may be different than ours. As the French say, *"C'est la vie"*—that's life.

La Palette is a well-known café in Paris. Parisians flock to outdoor cafés as soon as the spring weather permits.

Paris as far as the eye can see—
a city awaits your exploration.

MAP OF FRANCE

IMPRESSIONS

CHAPTER 1

'If every soul left it one day and grass grew in the
pavements, it would still be Paris to me,
I'd want to live there.'
—Katherine Ann Porter

Do first impressions endure? Is love at first sight a reliable indicator for the future? Perhaps not, but then we wouldn't be talking about Paris. If Paris is the most visited city in the world, it is because those who pass through, again and again whenever they can, understand something that reaches their hearts as soon as their feet touch the first cobblestone or their eyes soar to the spire of a medieval church. Paris has something special, and what makes it so is plain to see.

Paris is, in fact, a city of impressions. When you first arrive, you can't help but take in the beauty right away, even if you can't quite define it—the open squares with charming cafés, the landscaped parks and verdant esplanades, the ancient palaces turned into museums, the gracious stone buildings vibrantly alive with pots of red geraniums on so many windowsills. And the colour of the sky—why does no one call it 'Paris blue'?

Then, as you look around, you notice that except for the Montparnasse Tower that looms large and rather out of sync, the city is of a human scale. It's just the right size for walkers. The boulevards are broad enough for several lanes of cars to zoom along, but the residential streets are narrower and welcoming to those who stroll, curving in unexpected directions and lined with small shops and outdoor tables that beckon you to stop for a moment to take it all in. The buildings are low—few extend beyond five stories—windows are tall and doorways are wide. Occasionally there's a door ajar, allowing you to peek in. You see a courtyard, perhaps. Or a bicycle propped against the wall. Sometimes there's a stone cherub looking down on you as you pass. Or an antique streetlight, curved and ornate, waiting for dusk. And just around the corner there's a church with a fountain, where a dog is splashing itself and everyone else along with it. Paris is constantly a surprise.

And suddenly you notice the noise, or at least, the quality of it. Paris is a city with some dignity, is it not? Certainly there are automobiles rushing about, but they rarely honk their horns, and some *métro* trains have only whooshing rubber wheels. There's no music intruding on your dinner in restaurants or in elevators, no one interrupting or shouting in stores. There's just a bustle and hum as the city works. And without thinking, you relax and take it down a notch yourself, hearing each sound for what it is.

Hungry, you stop at a fruit stand and browse through the artistically displayed produce: fresh, colourful and abundant fruit in season. Or you decide to drop in at a bistro and you choose one of the specials of the day written on a chalkboard propped up next to your table, the selections also in season and carefully prepared. Or perhaps you rest your feet at a café, where the waiter dressed in black allows you to sit with your coffee, accessing Wi-Fi or writing postcards until you're ready to take on the city once again.

And then you walk some more and finally back to your hotel. The concierge greets you quietly, but he asks you nothing about your day. He does not want to intrude on your privacy, on those thoughts that are swirling around in your head. You nod back and say "Good evening" in French, if you can. You understand though, that he is letting you know that he is there, ready to help if need be. But you are fine, if a little overwhelmed. A few minutes later, you have your shoes off, ready to run a bath and replay those hours that even now seem too short.

"Yes," you think, at the end of this first day awash with your first impressions, "Yes, I could live here, and quite well." And this is an impression that turns out to be true.

OVERVIEW

CHAPTER 2

'It is the only city in the world which
understands the world and itself.'
–Henry Adams

PAST AND PRESENT ENTWINED

Paris is, without a doubt, the most beautiful capital of the world, and it should well be. For more than a millennium, kings, emperors and presidents have devoted their patriotic, religious and imaginative energies to creating their capital. The result is Paris, a city of splendour unmatched on the world's stage. Yet it is a city designed to be lived in as well as admired, and it is the almost seamless weaving of the city's intricate history into everyday life that makes the Paris experience so rich.

It is hard not to think about Paris' history wherever you go. Every street name is a voice from the past, from rue Vercingétorix, which recalls the Celtic warrior who fought against the conquering Romans in 52 BC, to boulevard Haussmann, named after the man who, 150 years ago, designed much of the structure of Paris today. If you are stuck in traffic on the 36-km beltline highway, the *périphérique*, remember that your slow path traces the city's final fortress walls of almost 200 years ago. And as you stroll, plaques on buildings will remind you of historical events and the people who shaped them. Wherever you are, the saga of Paris is in plain view.

The Beginnings

It's hard to say when the city was 'founded'. A small band of Gauls called the Parisii lived in the hills of the Paris Basin as long ago as the 7th century BC and on what is now the Île-de-la-Cité from about 250 BC. From this island in the middle of the river Seine and surrounded by the rivers Oise, Aisne, Ourcq and the Marne, the Parisii plied a lucrative river trade by commanding a strategic stop for all travellers.

No wonder the Romans wanted it, taking it in 52 BC and staying some 400 years. They first established themselves on the island of the Parisii, then slowly expanded their city across the water to the south, into what is still called the Quartier Latin (named after the Latin-speaking students of the university quarter during the Middle Ages). North of the river was a marsh—a *marais*—and the trendy 21st century neighbourhood there still goes by that name, Le Marais.

Some 9,000 people lived in what was then called Lutetia, but by 212 AD, it was officially named Paris, after the displaced Parisii. Some ancient ruins from that time have survived, for example, those in the crypt in front of the Cathedral of Notre Dame and ruins in the Quartier Latin.

By the 3rd century AD, however, Christianity was spreading and the Pope sent his bishop Denis to Paris to convert the Gauls. To the displeasure of the Romans, he succeeded, so he and two fellow Christians were beheaded near the top of the region's highest hill, now called Montmartre or 'hill of martyrs'. Saint Denis became the patron saint of France.

The patron saint of Paris itself is Geneviève, a devout girl of the 5th century who convinced the Parisians to trust in the Christian God and saved the city from an onslaught of Attila the Hun in 451 AD. By then, the Romans had already lost control of the area and were replaced for 300 years by the Franks from Germania—a dynasty that fought among themselves but which managed to establish Francia as Christian once and for all, though not always peacefully, to say the least.

By the 9th century, Charlemagne (whose father Pépin III was the first of the Carolingians) was using harsh military conquest to expand the domain and to impose Christianity on the realm. He preferred the Germanic city of Aachen (Aix-la-Chapelle) to Paris, so Paris declined over the decades, suffering from neglect and invasions by Norse Vikings.

Notre Dame sits along the Seine, which curves leisurely through Paris.

Charlemagne's descendants fought amongst themselves as well, so just before the turn of the first Christian millennium the time was ripe in Paris for a new king to emerge. Thus came Hugues Capet who founded the Capetian Dynasty that lasted in direct male lineage for more than 300 years.

It's important to remember that the territory of Francia then did not correspond to the map of France today. At the time of Hugues Capet, it encompassed Paris and more or less what is now the region of Île de France. In fact, Gaul was a feudal society marked by regions, each with its own dialect, culture and governance. But as the centuries rolled on, and as the Capetians expanded their domains into these regions, Paris, with a population numbering about 20,000, grew in importance.

It was around 1163, at the time of the Capetians, that the construction of the Cathedral of Notre Dame began. It took about 150 years to be completed and still stands, as does the

Conciergerie, as part of the Palais Royal. (The Conciegerie became a prison during the French Revolution, but is now a national monument.) It was under the Capetians that the magnificent gothic Basilique Saint-Denis and the exquisite Sainte-Chapelle were built, and the Sorbonne founded in 1253. It was also under the Capetians—King Philippe-Auguste—that the fortress of the Louvre was built and the larger streets paved with stone. The city marketplace of Les Halles was also constructed under the Capetian reign. It remained on the same spot for some 800 years, but was razed in 1969 to make way for an enormous shopping and entertainment mall called, of course, Forum Les Halles.

Medieval Paris

But what was daily life like in this beautiful city we revere today? By the beginning of the 14th century, its population had reached more than 250,000, cramped in an area perhaps one-quarter of the city's size today. It may have had an awe-inspiring cathedral and other impressive churches and palaces, and it may have become a renowned centre of learning, but crowded and dank as most cities were at that time, Paris stank. The rich, of course, lived well regardless of the conditions, but with no indoor plumbing or underground sewers; with horses traversing the streets; rubbish piling up and trenches for excrement running open in the middle of many streets—life in the city was not easy for the masses. Houses were heated by fireplaces that smoked and built up soot inside and out; food spoiled quickly; and insects and bugs thrived in bedlinens, clothes and on the people themselves, who went mostly unwashed. In addition, disease was rampant. The Black Death (bubonic plague) that hit Europe in the mid-14th century took more than 25 million people, including some 70,000 in Paris, decimating its population and its economy.

And so came civil unrest and war. As the Capetians' direct male line died out, the English king figured he was next in line for the French throne—after all, it was the Normans (from Normandy in northern France) who, long before their 1066 conquest of England, had owned and ruled northern France.

Having lost much of their holdings, these 'Anglo-Normans' wanted them—and France—back. The French barons said "*non*" and put a Valois (a non-linear descendant of Hugues Capet) on the throne in Paris, beginning a dynasty that lasted about 250 years. Think of their rule however, and what comes to mind initially is the disastrous plague and a 116-year war against England.

It's hard now to imagine a war that could last so long, but the Hundred Years' War (1337–1453) saw decades of victories and defeats on both sides in brief skirmishes and major battles, intrigues and fluctuating allegiances. It saw Joan of Arc initially victorious at Orléans, then burnt at the stake by the English as a witch. It also saw Paris being occupied by the English for some 15 years, allowing Henry VI to be crowned king at Notre Dame. And finally, in 1437 it saw Paris retaken by the Valois king Charles VII, who ultimately regained the rest. And so, through the nascent nationalism that united the disparate regional forces to defeat the English, France started to become a nation with Paris as its major cultural and administrative force.

The Early Modern Age

The Valois dynasty lasted until 1589, reigning through the Reformation and the flowering of the Renaissance. In the century after the end of the war, Paris' population grew to about 400,000 and magnificent churches and mansions were built, including the Hôtel de Cluny, now the Museum of the Middle Ages. The Louvre began to be transformed into the magnificent palace of today, and French officially replaced Latin as the language for administrative and legal acts throughout the realm. The first printing press appeared and more people could read and write. Under François I—a poet and patron of the arts—Leonardo da Vinci came to France bringing with him the Mona Lisa, which visitors to the Louvre now flock to see. In fact, the bulk of the art in the Louvre today is from the collection of the Valois. François also established the Collège de France, the first humanist (non-religious) university, which is still going strong. Paris was a city of culture and learning under the last Valois kings.

By now, Parisians were solidly identifying themselves with the side of the river on which they resided. From the Middle Ages, the Right Bank (*rive droite*) became the mercantile focus of the city, because boats could moor easily, servicing the aristocrats who had settled near the palace of the Louvre. The Left Bank (*rive gauche*), home to the Sorbonne and other institutions of learning, was inhabited by artists and intellectuals. Till today, the modern city continues to divide itself thus, with headquarters of banks, the largest department stores and much of the city's major commerce clustered on the Right Bank, while the Left Bank holds the universities and artists' galleries in a vibrant atmosphere of creativity and ideas. And so the Paris of today is still somewhat reminiscent of the city under the Valois.

But it was also a city of persecutions and strife. In response to the harshness of Catholicism, the Huguenots (followers of the French reformer John Calvin), who spoke out against the Pope in Rome, began converting part of the French population, including Parisians. After fluctuating degrees of tolerance, Parisians witnessed the massacre of about 3,000 Protestant 'heretics' in Paris on Saint Bartholomew's Day in 1572. (All told, some 70,000 Huguenots were later slain.) Eventually—after intrigues and the assassination of King Henri III—Henri IV of Navarre was crowned king. Henri IV set out to build a more efficient town. In 1605, he began the construction of what is now called La Place des Vosges, near Place de la Bastille, which some say is the most beloved square in all of France. He also built the exclusive Place Dauphine and, to better connect the two banks, finished the Pont Neuf, which 400 years later, is still called the New Bridge.

Henri IV began the Bourbon dynasty, and the Catholic Bourbons—periodic uprisings and unrest aside—ruled for the next 200 years, until they were overthrown by the French Revolution. Wars were waged to extend the monarchy's realm, while the arts flourished in Paris, literacy increased for both men

"Paris is well worth a mass."

These were the famous words of the Huguenot Henri IV of Navarre who was crowned king only upon his conversion to Catholicism.

and women, literature and publishing expanded and the Luxembourg Palace (now the Sénat) was built.

We've all heard of Louis XIV, the 'Sun King' who abandoned crowded and filthy Paris in 1682 for his newly built opulent palace at Versailles, one of the most visited palaces in the world today. Paris had some 600,000 residents at that time, and although the streets were paved with stone and somewhat lit at night, and in spite of its expansion to the north and south, it was still a city of overcrowded slums. Despite such beautiful oases as the Place Vendôme and the Place des Victoires, and despite the flourishing of the arts and such amenities as the first true café, Procope (which still stands at the same spot today), the city hadn't changed much overall. Disease and crime were rampant, and so for the rich and powerful, it was best to be at Versailles.

The Revolution

And thus we come to poor ill-fated Louis XVI and his Austrian wife, the pampered and hated Marie Antoinette. Actually, by the end of the 17th century, the ideas of the liberal, anticlerical Enlightenment were taking hold, and Paris had assumed its place as the cultural centre of the Age of Reason. Learning and the arts were esteemed, and life was lovely— for individuals who could afford it. But in 1788, the French treasury was almost bankrupt, owing to costly wars (including the support of the American Revolution), the lavish lifestyle of the French royalty and a disastrous harvest. People were starving all across France. Unfortunately, Louis XVI, rather a simple, well-meaning man, only indecisive and conservative, yet ultimately willing to accept some reforms, did not react. And so, the Parisians decided that they had had enough: the Bastille—a prison near the present-day ultra modern Opéra National Paris Bastille—was taken. The active revolution had begun. Paris— and France—would never be the same.

"Let them eat cake."

It was during a bread shortage in Paris that Marie Antoinette is reputed to have uttered those famous words, "Let them eat cake". It's not clear if she really did so, but the populace blamed the Austrian-born queen for France's troubles, no matter that Louis himself might have been a scapegoat for the tyrannies and excesses of his predecessors.

All the regions of France came together in a meeting in Paris to pledge their allegience to a single, common nation. The Declaration of the Rights of Man and the Citizen was adopted. The country was divided into *départements* and in 1792, the First Republic declared the birth of La France. It wasn't an easy birth. Over the next five years, there were civil war and clashes with other European states. After a period of moderation and constitutional monarchy came the Reign of Terror led by the infamous Robespierre, during which some 17,000 'enemies of liberty' (including Louis and Marie-Antoinette) were beheaded by the guillotine. The major site of the executions was Place de la Révolution, now the beautiful and much more serene Place de la Concorde.

Napoléon

Despite the ensuing 75 years of instability and the revolutions of 1830 and 1840, which caused governments to swing from republic to empire to monarchy and then to republic, the legacy of the French Revolution was the power given to the citizens, who became—and remain—the country's dominant political force.

Napoleon, who seized power and had himself proclaimed Emperor, made lasting changes to France that are still felt today. In Paris, his legacy is seen everywhere. His successful military battles are honoured by street names— Iéna, Friedland, Wagram—and he has left his mark on the Madeleine Church, the Arc de Triomphe and the arcaded rue de Rivoli. He built the Pont des Arts and what is now the revitalised Canal Saint-Martin. He also systematised the city's districts by designating 12 *arrondissements* (they number 20 today) and even creating a uniform system for the numbering of buildings. He established the *lycée* educational system and most importantly, he devised a new civic legal code that was almost revolutionary in codifying the rule of law throughout the land. Military defeats brought all this to an end: the Russians entered Paris and Napoleon abdicated into exile on Elba. He returned to Paris for 100 days but was defeated once and for all by Wellington at the Battle of Waterloo.

A City of Unrest

With Napoleon's exile to the island of Sainte-Hélène, a series of unpopular governments ruled for the next 60 years, culminating finally in the 1871 establishment of a republic, once and for all. But it was a tumultuous period in teeming and seething Paris, whose population had now reached 900,000. First the Bourbons—two brothers of Louis XVI—took power one after the other, but they and Charles X, who was too reliant on the Church and too authoritarian, didn't last long. After a riot in which some 5,000 workers were killed ended the short-lived republic, Louis-Philippe ruled as the 'bourgeois monarch' from 1830–1848. However, intolerable conditions brought the city to bursting point, and explode it did.

By about 1848, the Industrial Revolution and the rise of science and reason were taking hold in Europe. Railroads were being built and ports expanded. French workers were flocking into the small city and its growing suburbs. Paris now held more than a million people, and it was still dark and dense, with warrens of narrow alleyways running with rats and filled with filth and disease. Fresh water was still rare and a crowded tenement stood directly in front of the Louvre. The streets were open sewers as in medieval times, the Seine was part of the sewer system and in 1848 alone, some 19,000 people died of cholera. Factories overworked their employees and there was a high rate of unemployment. Paris may have been the world capital of culture, but the air was polluted with smoke and soot, and crime was uncontrollable.

First came what was meant to be a peaceful demonstration near the Madeleine. But troops on the boulevard des Capucines (in the 8^e) started a riot by firing into the crowd. Revolution became the order of the day. Barricades shot up in the streets, the king abdicated and fled, and finally some 50,000 poverty-stricken citizens marched in protest in June. This was too much for the new conservative government, and in putting down the rebellion, some 1,500 Parisians were killed and another 5,000 deported.

As his name was known thoughout France, Louis Napoléon Bonaparte, Napoléon's nephew, was elected president in 1848. In 1852, he changed his mind and named himself Emperor

Napoléon III. It is true that Napoléon III's reign only lasted for 18 years—until war and another revolution terminated monarchy in France for good—but it was important, for much of the Paris that we see today was created during this period.

Imagine Paris then: workers from the countryside were streaming into the city and living conditions were untenable—the city simply couldn't be sustained. The Emperor knew something had to be done and asked his prefect, Baron Georges Haussmann to remake Paris into a 'new Rome'. Baron Haussmann went to work, demolishing the slums by relegating the poor to the eastern edges of the city and replacing the dark little alleyways with straight streets and broad avenues (so police could control any future uprisings of the masses). Apartment buildings that adhered to safety standards were constructed, as well as modern glass-and-iron public edifices. Open squares were created and landscaped, streets were paved with asphalt, and Haussmann brought Parisians into the sun with 5,000 acres of parks including the Bois de Boulogne and the Bois de Vincennes. He built hospitals and schools, dug an efficient 600-km underground sewer system and also constructed aqueducts and reservoirs that brought fresh water to all. Gas mains fuelled 15,000 street lamps, making the city safer after dark. None of this was easy: even today some people complain about Haussmann's destroying of old neighbourhoods and little local communities, but Paris was becoming more liveable, more modern—becoming one of the most successful cities.

But if Paris was beautiful and if sophistication and fashion ruled, the poor people had made few gains. There were also the wars. France had enough military successes under Napoléon III to erase the humiliation of Waterloo, but in 1870, a disastrous war was declared against Prussia, and that was the end of the Emperor, who abdicated into exile. Prussians were besieging the city, the people were hungry, cutting down trees on the Champs-Elysées for firewood just to keep warm. In the midst of this bombardment of Paris, revolution once again took hold, perhaps the bloodiest the Paris streets had ever seen.

The Paris Commune

The Paris workers had had enough. After the elected government had capitulated to the Prussians, they angrily forced the leaders to evacuate to Versailles, electing their own extremist council, the Commune, to run the city. Immediately it tried to impose reforms, including the abolition of the guillotine, the conversion of abandoned businesses into workers' cooperatives and a separation of church and state. But the Versailles government was not to be thwarted. After a few weeks, it retook Paris, street by street, neighbourhood by neighbourhood. (Owing to those open boulevards constructed by Haussmann just a few years before, it was hard to erect the barricades necessary to keep the 'Versaillais' at bay.) Atrocities and murders were committed on both sides, but the 'Versaillais' prevailed, slaughtering thousands of Communards. By the time it was all over, some 40,000 people had been arrested, 13,000 imprisoned or deported to Devil's Island and 20,000 left dead. Even after peace had been restored and the elected government returned to power, hard feelings and unrest lasted for decades, and the Commune is remembered till today.

The Belle Epoque

In spite of the upheavals and reshuffles under the Third Republic, Paris, with a population of some two million, seemed to glow. The torched Hôtel de Ville (City Hall) was rebuilt and old buildings began to be conserved and restored. The *métro* system was built, as was the beautiful basilica atop Montmartre—Sacré-Cœur. More open boulevards were constructed according to Haussmannian standards and theatres and gracious apartment buildings shot up. The staging of Expositions Universelles gave rise to the Trocadéro, the Grand Palais and the Petit Palais (now museums) and, of course, the Eiffel Tower. Impressionist painters, whose work can now be viewed at the Musée d'Orsay (which was then a railway station), emerged. The first department store, Au Bon Marché, opened in 1876, followed by Au Printemps. Literature thrived, theatres were packed and popular composers such as Camille Saint-Saëns, Claude Debussy and Maurice Ravel epitomised the cultural ethos of the time.

The Great War

However, World War I, known as the Great War, changed the face of Paris once again. Paris may have faced sporadic bombardment, but it was the aftermath of the war that had the greatest impact on the city. More than 1.5 million Frenchmen between the ages of 25 and 45 were killed and another million maimed during the long war. It was said that 'a generation was lost'. The birth rate plummeted, and women went to work in Paris. They also smoked in public, wore short skirts and were open about their love affairs (although they didn't get to vote until after World War II). Skilled workers were desperately needed to rebuild and modernise the city, but had disappeared. If previous influxes of workers into the city were from the French provinces, now Paris opened its doors to foreign immigrants, and they came by the thousands. Some new arrivals integrated themselves, but others formed their own ethnic enclaves within the city confines and beyond, many from France's North African holdings.

The 'crazy years' of the 1920s also saw foreign writers and artists flocking to Montparnasse, the new artistic *quartier*, and the entire Left Bank was populated by such lights as Ernest Hemingway, Pablo Picasso, James Joyce and Gertrude Stein. World War I may have ended with the Great Depression for the Americans, but the arts and high living in Paris still thrived—until Hitler made the city his own.

World War II

On 16 June 1940, Paris capitulated to Germany and the city was occupied by the Nazis. In May 1940, the population of Greater Paris stood at 3.5 million, but a month later it had diminished by more than half, those with resources to do so having fled. What was left in Paris, as one can imagine, were primarily the workers and the poor. A puppet government was set up in Vichy under the World War I hero Marshall Henri

Philippe Pétain, whose reputation for his collaborationist policies under the Nazis now has been revised. General Charles de Gaulle left for London, where he announced a government in exile, calling upon all 'Free French' to resist.

World War II is recent enough that the atrocities committed, the concentration camps and the deprivations need not be elaborated upon here. In Paris, life on the surface may have looked 'normal' with restaurants, nightclubs and theatres functioning (mostly for the occupiers), children playing in the parks and Parisians still going to church, but the newspapers were closed down and censorship and curfews established. Forbidden to own cars, Parisians crowded the *métro*, except on weekends when it was closed to them. Clocks were set to German time. Signs and restaurant menus appeared in German, and while the Germans lived well, Parisians were cold and hungry. But in the face of brutal repression and privations, executions for infractions of Nazi rules and a roundup and deportation of thousands of Jews by the Vichy government itself, there was nothing to do but endure, and clandestinely, to resist.

After D-Day on 6 June 1944 and the breakthrough of the German lines by the Allies, Paris rose up. Look around as you walk around Paris today and see the plaques remembering the brave French individuals who fought in the city's streets and died for La France. Stop on the corner of rue de Rivoli and rue Saint-Florentin, as you come out of the *métro*, where there are ten such plaques in a row, often covered by wreaths, and thank those heroes for having defied the Nazis' tanks right on that busy street. Finally, on 25 August 1944, after heavy fighting in the streets of Paris, General de Gaulle marched triumphant into the city, ready to take on the rebuilding of France.

From Then Until Now

It would be nice to say that all has been peaceful in Paris since then, but that wouldn't be true. For the next 12 years, the Fourth Republic (1946–1958) focused on rebuilding a country whose infrastructure had been destroyed by war. Hardship finally gave way to recovery, riding on the American-led Marshall Plan, combined with a French economic plan, and Paris seemed on its way to modernity. But the country's North African outposts, especially Algeria, wanted their independence, and a grizzly war (1954–1962) complete with massacres, torture and finally exodus, brought more than 500,000 colonists into France, notably Paris, where many were settled into dreary apartment blocks in residential suburbs. Sixty years and two generations later, these suburbs are openly and quite visibly seething with unrest.

Nonetheless, city life after the war began to shine. Intellectuals once again rose to the forefront—Jean-Paul Sartre, Simone de Beauvoir and Albert Camus frequented the cafés on the Left Bank, foreign writers again found Paris as their muse and the film industry gained prominence worldwide. *Haute cuisine* and *haute couture* rose to their greatest heights and Paris became a tourist Mecca once again. Not even the explosive student unrest of 1968 could dent the reputation of Paris; today Paris is the most visited city in the world.

Indeed, over the next several decades of the Fifth Republic (1958–), under presidents from both the Right and the Left, Paris continued to build, restore and modernise. Some streets were widened and the *péripherique* was built to alleviate the clogging of the roads brought on by the proliferation of cars. Historic buildings were restored and cleaned under a 1962 law. The poor neighbourhood of Beaubourg was replaced by the ultramodern art museum, the Centre Pompidou. The Tour Montparnasse that arose in the city centre reminded Paris that it didn't want such eyesores, and thus throughout the 1970s, the enormous, modern business-residential city of La Defense was built on the city's western edge. Its dominating Grande Arche was later constructed as part of President François Mitterrand's *Grands Projets* that envisioned urban revival and architectural modernity for a city whose cultural and economic position would be cemented in the European Union and beyond.

Mitterrand cleaned up those eastern slums to which the poor had retreated during the Haussmannian improvements. He also constructed a new science museum-park complex La

Villette on the site of the city's former slaughterhouse, as well as the huge Opéra Bastille. The Bibliothèque Nationale arose in the wasteland of the 13th *arrondissement*, an area that is becoming happily populated once again. More parks were landscaped and an ultramodern Finance Ministry building brightly commands the riverfront of the 12th *arrondissement*. The Louvre was restored to its former glory and modernised with a spectacular glass pyramid to welcome the millions of visitors who pass through every year.

Into a New Millennium

And now we are well into a new millennium, with the technological, social, and infrastructure improvements that make Paris easier every day to understand and more pleasant to live in. Which—make no mistake—it is. Of course, its long-time residents grumble daily about the state of their urban environment, with 2.3 million people in the city and another 10 million in the suburban surrounds. Talk about the traffic and the smog and the prices that continually rise!

Yet under these common surface concerns, all is not entirely well: political upheavals and new presidents both loved or hated (depending on with whom you're talking), high taxes, employment uncertainties, and despite the vigilance of the government, some unsettling—sometime terrifying—terrorist attacks that have now reached Paris itself, primarily by people from those faceless northern seething suburbs or others who have come to join them. Will something finally be done for descendants of those North African colonies, people who have French nationality, but who have been assimilated neither into society nor the workforce as 'true French'? In a formerly Catholic country with a revered separation of religion and state, how does one deal with the fact that some 9 per cent of the population is Muslim and that some 14 per cent of the Paris population is made up of foreigners? Of course, other European capitals—Amsterdam and Brussels, to name just two—are dealing with problems of the same sort and answers for them too are slow in forthcoming. In the meantime, uncertainty lies beneath the surface, bubbling up unexpectedly and unhappily as well, for France in particular,

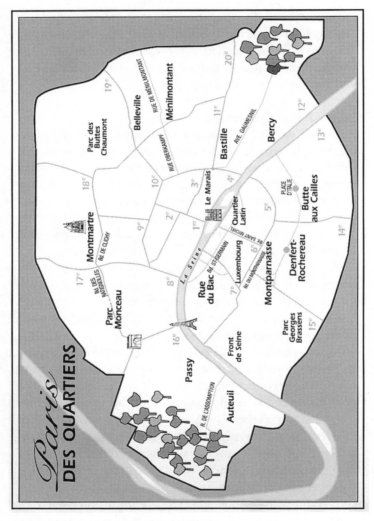

The *quartiers* and some landmarks of Paris.

with a culture that believes in rational solutions to most problems, it is at a loss when they do not appear. Protest marches call for solutions while cars are regularly burnt in the northern suburbs, and now the sporadic but devastating terrorist attacks, despite the extreme vigilance of the police.

Parisians—who love to talk about politics—have differing views on what should and can be done. Everyone agrees, though, that something has to change. One prominent current idea is to bring those faceless inner suburbs into the *arrondissement* system itself, expanding official Paris to become Métropole du Grand Paris, offering more services and benefits to areas and residents that have suffered without them. This would triple the population of Paris, something that should be considered by a new regional council that could coordinate the planning for a "greater Paris." For the moment, though, it is clear that the government has stepped up its vigilance to the highest level; at this writing a State of Emergency remains in effect, but the Parisians are going about their business every day, as usual.

So this is a time of some confusion as Paris strives to maintain its traditions while adapting to the modern world, greatly for the better, occasionally much for the worse. Changes are needed for traditional European societies that don't like change at all. But sometimes, as it is newly clear, adapting is forced upon them whether they like it or not. Yet the marvel of Paris is that the city, for the most part, is managing to hold on to its appreciated traditions while striving to meet the future, as it must. As for Parisians, despite it all, they are proud of how the history of their city melds into their comfortable modern surroundings and they know how fortunate they are. Their goal is to keep it that way.

PARIS NOW: THE CITY AS IT IS
Paris Overall

Still a small city as world capitals go, Paris encompasses no more than 80 sq km and is only about 12 km across. Although officially Paris is *intra-muros* (within the old city walls), Greater Paris today includes the outlying towns that border the *périphérique*. About two million people live intra-muros.

10 million more live in the suburbs, giving the metropolis a population of more than 12 million.

If Paris is the sum of its history, as any city is, it is also creating a new history as the days go by, changing its face and evolving into what this new millennium requires. Too much traffic in the city? Construct bicycle and bus lanes to encourage a reduced use of cars, or develop a tram line that circles the city edges, and provide 20,000 rental bikes for public use, docked in every neighbourhood. Add to this thousands of public electric rental cars as well. Not enough open space for the increasing population? Create a 3-km-long summer sandy "beach" along the riverfront, and offer recreational activities late into the night. And close much of the river's roadsides and create park-like settings, encouraging people to stroll. These are already accomplished and even the slightly inconvenienced car drivers don't complain anymore. Some areas not so pleasant? Upgrade the areas around the train stations, such as the Gare St-Lazare— and notice the difference in the commerce that comes in.

And more is in the Paris infrastructure wind. That enormous warren of shops at Les Halles is being upgraded and plans for the modernization of the Gare d'Austerlitz and its surroundings are underway. Additional residences for

Tulips appearing at the florists usually mean Spring is around the corner.

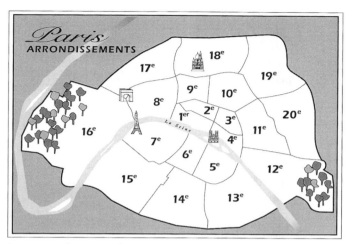

The 20 *arrondissements* of Paris.

students are being planned, and in general, there's a need for more affordable housing throughout the city. Although more than 5,000 apartments have been built in the past decade, future building might require changing zoning laws and reaching higher into the Paris sky. In this beautiful city, this is not popular option. Thus, with old neighbourhoods being gentrified, often forcing long-term residents out, Paris is considering another plan to determine fair market rates for apartments in certain vulnerable neighbourhoods as they come on the market, buy them itself, and then offer them again, subsidizing housing at a reasonable price.

For now, though, Paris still retains a very human scale. Buildings are low, few neighbourhood streets run straight, and there is always something unexpected, often delightful, to catch the eye. Thanks to Baron Haussmann 150 years ago (controversial as he was), Paris is an open city, characterised by ornate, spectacular squares and wide boulevards that converge at open junctions where residents do their shopping or sit at sidewalk cafés. Formally planned gardens and parks and casual, leafy squares dot the landscape; 100,000 trees line both narrow streets and wide boulevards; and two beautiful wooded parks, the Bois de Boulogne to the west and the Bois de Vincennes to the east, provide respite at Paris' flanks. Covered arcades and upgraded *passages* draw people to their attractions and shelter them from the rain. And the Seine, that marvellous river, flows through the city, joined from the northeast by the Canal Saint-Martin, itself crossed at intervals by little metallic bridges and partially by pleasant rows of trees.

Although the climate is fairly mild overall and Paris often shines gloriously in the sun, the city's uneven weather can bring problems in any season. In winter, the temperature may hover below freezing for weeks, with the wind howling down those wide boulevards and nipping at narrow corners. Rains make the river rise, sometimes closing the banks to traffic; occasionally there is snow. Spring, even well into the supposedly romantic April, is often unpleasantly grey and wet, but there are also splendid, almost warm, sunny days. True spring begins in May—the first signs are newly planted flower boxes on windowsills and the tables that begin to reappear outside cafés. By the time summer is in full swing late in July and August, the sometimes sweltering temperatures and high pollution drive Parisians out of town until the beginning of September, when they return in a burst of energy. This is an event in itself, known as *la rentrée*. September and October can be the best months, pleasantly sunny and warm.

The Layout

Since the time of Napoléon in the early 19th century, Paris has been divided into administrative zones called *arrondissements*. Originally there were 12, but in 1860 Napoléon III annexed outlying villages, doubling the population and creating more *arrondissements*, finally reaching the current 20. Each *arrondissement* has its *mairie* (town hall), its mayor and its *conseil d'administration d'arrondissement* (district council), which elects the mayor of Paris. Most of the bureaucratic business for residents is done at their local *mairie* and it is the best source for information about all public functions in the city.

The *arrondissements* begin at the core of Paris, the Île-de-la-Cité and move in an outward spiral, enlarging toward the periphery. City maps are arranged and numbered by *arrondissement*, from the 1er (*le premier*) to the 20e (*le vingtième*). Historically, the eastern parts of Paris were the factories and the workers' neighbourhoods, shabby and dense. The western parts—upwind from the unsanitary conditions and stench of industry—were the most aristocratic. Thus it was to the west that the nobles removed themselves after the 1789 revolution, and the west remains the most luxurious today. Nonetheless, the ambitious *Grands Projets* of the 1980s have upgraded the eastern *arrondissements* with modern public buildings, walkways and parks. Old buildings have also been refurbished, such that neighbourhoods are now trendy rather than squat —such as in the 12th at Bercy, and the 13th, around the Bibliothèque Nationale. Within the *arrondissements* are the *quartiers* (neighbourhoods) with their individual characteristics and tradition.

The Seine

The Seine, the 776-km river that winds so charmingly through Paris, may evoke romantic thoughts for many, but actually has been a working river since the time of the Celts. Today, from its 37 bridges—many of them noteworthy in themselves—you can look down and see barges hauling freight, as well as panoramic tourist boats and the pleasure craft passing through. Busy as It may be, the river is still magical at times, bringing thousands each summer to Paris Plage, the public beach set up on its banks, and for others romantic picnics. And, from where else can you see so many famous monuments—the Louvre, the Eiffel tower, Notre Dame? No wonder the banks of the Seine were listed as a UNESCO World Heritage Site in 1991. When you cross the river by foot, pay attention. The Seine is always worth a look.

Thinking about Place

Parisians live in every habitable square metre of space in their city, in spacious apartments overlooking leafy boulevards or tiny walk-up flats above neighbourhood stores. The *quartiers* can be airy and open, crowded and dense, or a succession of commercial streets that seem not to be a neighbourhood at all. Apartment buildings range from the graceful and traditional to the modern and faceless, down to the dilapidated and cheap. Some tranquil side streets have charming little houses and many large buildings look inward onto quiet courts; some must have windows with *double vitrage* (double glazing) to keep out the noise from the street. Some have lifts; many do not. Parisians live in them all.

If an area seems strictly for business, just look up and you will see a flowerpot on a ledge and a curtain waving in the breeze of an open window. If an area seems so noisy you cannot possibly imagine anyone living there, just wait until you see someone coming home from work with a briefcase in one hand and the evening's *baguette* in the other. And if an area seems absolutely perfect, be prepared to pay handsomely for that rare perfection.

The neighbourhood you choose for yourself will, of course, depend on your circumstances and your funds. Much will depend on the length of your stay, or if you have family in tow. A residential neighbourhood may not be important if you are single and your stay is only a few months, but a home near your workplace may be less important if your children need a park and proximity to a bilingual school. Much will also depend on your personal preferences: will you prefer living in the *banlieue* (suburbs) even if it requires the use of a car? Or would you prefer a lively area in the *centre ville* (city centre), where you can walk to work? Perhaps living in a dense *quartier* is acceptable if it is close to restaurants and exciting cultural activities? Remember that not all areas look residential, but Parisians and newcomers alike live in them.

It is true that despite the costs, foreigners continue to purchase apartments in Paris. The apartments in the inner *arrondissement*s are generally more traditional, with larger rooms, higher ceilings, sculpted mouldings, and prices to match. The more modern flats in the outer areas may be more affordable, but they may not have the charm one thinks of as typical Paris. Prices both for purchase and rent match location and amenities. When this book was written, foreigners were spending a median of €410,000 when purchasing traditional apartments in Paris. The most desirable apartments in the central Left Bank quarters could cost as much as €13,000 per square metre, while those in the outer *arrondissements* might average around €7,500. Currently, the Italians (right bank), Chinese (19^e), and Americans (6^e and 7^e) are the biggest groups of the foreign buyers, with the British (11^e) and Portuguese (5^e) close behind. Of course these are averages. Prices fluctuate according to the economy, and people buy what they can and where the can, and are generally happy with the result.

After deciding on your priorities, given the ever-present need for compromise, look carefully at each *quartier* you are considering. Are there open spaces in which to stroll, sidewalk cafés in which to relax, the kinds of shops you use, a park for children? Is there a *métro* stop nearby, and even better, a *correspondance*, meaning a junction of two different lines? Is there a major street artery nearby, but not too near? If you look at an apartment on a weekend, come back during the rush hour to get a realistic gauge of the traffic and noise. Look at the mix of people walking on the street, do some window-shopping... do everything you can to understand if this is the best place for you.

The River Islands

The Île-de-la-Cité, the oldest part of Paris, remains the sentimental heart of the city. *Kilomètre zéro*, the point from which French distances are measured, is a dial embedded in the square in front of the Cathedral of Notre-Dame. From its beginnings 2,000 years ago as home to the Celtic Parisii, the island has been an area of constant activity. Today, tourists congregate at Notre-Dame and Sainte-Chapelle, the Conciergerie and a memorial to the deported French of World War II. Parisians come to the Préfecture de Police, the Hôpital Hôtel Dieu and the Palais de Justice, built on the site where Roman governors and later the kings of France, once resided. Hardly a residential neighbourhood, there are nonetheless pockets of elegant apartments, especially north of Notre-Dame, along the quais and around the intimate Place Dauphine, an enchanting, tranquil triangle of brick and white stone dating from 1607.

Both the grandeur of the island and its apparent lack of neighbourhood character can be traced to the redevelopment of Baron Haussmann, who demolished a warren of slums and who brought order to the island while dispossessing its 20,000 residents. It is this centrality that makes the Île-de-la-Cité convenient, especially for a short stay. Bridges go directly into the 5e and 6e on the Left Bank and into the 1er and the 4e on the Right Bank. Even the *métro* stop on the island opens onto Place Lépine, the popular market for flowers and birds.

Just to the east is the Île Saint-Louis. Despite tourists who stroll down its main street, rue Saint-Louis-en-l'Île, the island remains peaceful and gracious. Although bridges connect it to both river banks and to the Île-de-la-Cité, the feeling of remove from modern life reminds one of how Paris must have looked 300 years ago.

Poplar trees shade the streets and the views of Paris from the quais are exceptional. Since development began only in the 17th century under Louis XIII, there is an architectural unity to the island, its harmonious, gracious buildings being of about the same width and height. The old *hôtels particuliers* (townhouses) and the large restored apartments still house affluent Parisians, and some foreigners have bought apartments to rent them to tourists for a well-deserved, often hefty price. Unfortunately, few long-term apartments are available, and when they are, their prices are steep, but the residents clearly think the Île Saint-Louis worth the price. For people who buy them only to rent them out privately, this may no longer be an entirely legal option.

First Arrondissement (1er)

Encompassing many tourist attractions such as the Louvre, the Tuileries gardens and the long rue de Rivoli, along with some of the city's most fashionable hotels, the 1st *arrondissement* is populated day and night, but not particularly by residents. From its beginnings, this has been among the most commercial area of the city; today, just a few streets away from the tourist attractions, financial and administrative offices continue to rule.

The atmosphere of the 1er is, in a sense, determined by the Louvre. To its east are the busy traffic junction of Châtelet, the former site of a dreaded prison, now home to several popular theatres, and Les Halles, the ancient marketplace transformed into an enormous shopping and cinema complex, Forum des Halles. Les Halles has extensive gardens, a cultural pavilion and a popular play facility for children, but its periphery is a hangout for young tourists and street entertainers. Les Halles has been undergoing a much-needed deep renovation and reconfiguration, but it remains open for business nonetheless.

Yet, typical of Paris, tucked just a few streets away is one of the most peaceful oases of the city—the quiet and romantic Jardins du Palais-Royal. Spacious old apartments nestle amidst discreet offices, and residents can still enjoy the sensation of being buffered from modernity while situated right in the heart of the city. An interesting neighbour is the lovely, circular Place des Victoires, home to fashion designers who occupy the harmonious 17th-century buildings. This may not be what one considers a real neighbourhood, but it has its attractions, including a variety of restaurants.

The royal heritage extends west of the Louvre. Kings lived at the Tuileries in a palace destroyed toward the end of the last century during the protests of the Paris Commune. What remains are the Jardins des Tuileries, one of Paris' most popular parks and the Orangerie, built in 1852 to preserve the royal fruit trees during the winters. Across the rue de Rivoli are both tourist shops and high-class enterprises of the type that once catered to the aristocrats who lived in the shadow of the king. Bordered on the west by the imposing Place de la Concorde, the size of a small town in itself, the area culminates nearby in the spectacular granite Place Vendôme, a royal square begun by Louis XIV in 1686, now home to exclusive banking establishments, prestigious jewellers, offices, a few plush apartments and the Hotel Ritz.

This remains the upscale end of the *arrondissement* and the apartments in the side streets and above the shops along rue du Rivoli can be comfortable and gracious; much depends on the shops below and where the tour buses stop. The parallel street, rue Saint-Honoré, is lined with shops and restaurants, and the charming modern Marché de Saint-Honoré has enlivened the place Saint-Honoré. Although little of this area is truly residential, it might be fun for a short stay.

Second Arrondissement (2e)

Extending the commercial centre of Paris, the tiny 2nd *arrondissement* contains La Bourse (Stock Exchange), financial offices of every type and nationality, airline offices, travel agencies and insurance companies. Cafés, cinemas and theatres keep the western edge alive well into the night. This is an area that is becoming more residential, as formerly rundown areas are being revitalised by a younger set of Parisians, and the area is becoming increasingly fashionable.

Toward the east are hundreds of factories and warehouses at the heart of Paris' clothing industry, culminating at cart- and traffic-jammed Sentier and Place du Caire. Except for streets near the fashion designer enclave of rue Etienne-Marcel and Place des Victoires and a few streets toward the east, there are only a few areas one would consider for a residence. Away from Place de l'Opéra, much of the area is deserted at night and on weekends, except for the broad avenues and the eastern boundary of boulevard Sébastopol. There is little open space and this is the least green area of the city.

The 2e, however, is the site of some of the city's famous *passages*—covered shopping arcades dating from the end of the 19th century. Several have been beautifully restored for upmarket shopping and dining—especially Galeries Vivienne and Panoramas, Passage Jouffroy and the linking Passage Verdeau, and Passage du Grand Cerf, which has a high glass roof—while others remain full of jumbled stores. For a variety in dining, rue Sainte-Anne is noted for its Japanese restaurants and shops. Here in the 2e too is one of Paris' important market streets, the pedestrian-only rue Montorgueil, an appealing combination of food emporia, *traiteurs* (take-out delicatessens) and terraced cafés. People used to come here only to do their shopping, but since refurbishment has spruced up the area and prices are still fairly reasonable, more people are calling this area home.

The Marais (3ᵉ and 4ᵉ)

The 3rd and 4th *arrondissements* are collectively known as the Marais, that ancient swampland that was once a visible part of the river basin of the Seine. As noted, it is the one of the oldest parts of the city, encompassing half of the Île-de-la-Cité; this was also the first part of the Right Bank that was inhabited—around the present-day rues des Blancs-Manteaux and Vieille-du-Temple—more than 1,000 years ago. Although not all parts of the Marais yet conform to the trendy image the name now evokes, this is certainly one of the most chic parts of town.

The Marais became popular with royalty and aristocrats about 400 years ago. Henri IV built the now-called Place des Vosges, the first royal square, which has been authentically restored to look much as it did in 1612: a square of almost identical, warm brick-and-stone townhouses with steep, pitched roofs, surrounding an exquisitely sculptured, symmetrical garden. From the 16th century, the southern part of the Marais had seen the building of *hôtels particuliers* for nobles and aristocrats, but in the 18th century, the area was abandoned when the court moved west toward Versailles. Sadly, with the vicissitudes of time and politics, the Marais declined.

How it has changed! Now one of the city's most colourful districts, the Marais benefitted from the 1962 Loi Malraux, which mandated the preservation of historic districts. Decrepit medieval streets and once-stately *hôtels particuliers* were refurbished without succumbing to the faceless modernisation suffered by other parts of the city at the time. Now this area is an unexpected delight of ever narrow, angled streets, low-rise buildings, and just one *métro* station, Saint-Paul on rue Saint-Antoine, the major shopping and transporation artery. Art galleries, fashion shops, nightspots and restaurants invigorate this good-natured district that is more and more in demand every day.

Although a Jewish community lived here until its expulsion from France in 1394, it is only since the last century that the influx of Eastern European Jews has given the quarter much of its character. Clustered around the 13th-century rue des

The famous café, Les Deux Magots, at place Saint-Germain-des-Prés, once frequented by such literary lights as Hemingway, Sartre and Simone de Beauvoir, among others.

Rosiers and rue des Ecouffes are kosher restaurants, bakeries, delicatessens and groceries. Some of these close on Friday afternoons and Saturday, but open again on Sunday, when the rest of the city is closed. With the upmarket boutiques and galleries open as well, this is a lively area every day.

The Marais has also become a major focus of Parisian gay life. Starting near Châtelet and moving east, gay nightspots and restaurants contribute to the area's eclectic 24-hour atmosphere. The bookshop, Les Mots à la Bouche, in rue Sainte-Croix-de-la-Bretonnerie is a central information point for this increasingly open and accepted community.

All in all, the part of the Marais that stretches west from Place de la Bastille to rue des Archives is a fun and somewhat affordable area in which to live. Comfortable apartments can be found in a range of prices, but parking in the crowded streets is scarce. Another residential area is the small *quartier* below rue Saint-Antoine. Buildings of homogeneous architecture line its sides, most of which are well maintained. There are just a few museums, some antique shops and the remnants of the medieval city wall that draw visitors.

Convenient shopping for both areas stretches along the rue de Rivoli, where it takes over from rue Saint-Antoine.

The 3ᵉ begins above the fashionable rue des Francs-Bourgeois, once the northern perimeter of the city walls, although here it is indistinguishable from the 4ᵉ. On rue Payenne, the Museum of the History of Paris was, in the 17th century, the *hôtel particulier* of the literary Marquise de Sévigné. This area declined when the nobles moved on, melding with the *quartier* farther north, toward what is now the wonderfully restored Place de la République. The surrounding area Itself is quickly coming up, happily replacing what had once been dilapidated and shabby—and is becoming known as the Haut Marais.

This northeastern corner (known as Temple) is where the Knights Templar in the 12th century settled after their return from the Crusades. Their Enclos du Temple was a powerful, fortified city containing a palace, a church and commerce, and it provided safety for workers and artisans within its walls. It is all long gone, even the tower in which Louis XVI was kept prisoner until his execution in 1793. When it was finally torn down by Napoléon, all that remained were the workers and tradesmen, and the area took on a rather shabby character, which it still retains in some spots.

It was precisely the inexpensive aspects of this sector that drew its present population. The post-World War I influx of Asians into the 3ᵉ constituted the first Chinese community in Paris; there is still an Asian presence around rues des Gravilliers and rue au Maire. At rue de Nazareth there is an important Jewish synagogue, as this was the Jewish community's centre before it moved south toward rue des Rosiers.

Until recently, one could have described much of this northern border as dull, but it is changing. Certainly the rag trade still extends here and some factories employ the immigrants who continue to come. But a new concept here may bring about new life. The rue Vertbois, nicknamed *la jeune rue*, is destined to transform itself into a street of gourmet shops and restaurants. At present it is struggling, but may well succeed in the end. And gentrification is slowly moving north on its own, up rue Charlot with its fashionable shops, around the covered Marché des Enfants Rouges, and around the pretty little Square du Temple. The total renovation of the huge Place de la Republique has also brought a once seedy area into the dynamic extension of the atmospheric Marais and this entire area will improve quite quickly. Certainly, the Place will continue to be a focal point for the *manifestations*—political protests of any sort that often spring up—but its huge plaza and raised terraces are now welcoming any day of the year.

Overall, foreigners do consider the traditional Marais as representing "old Paris," and apartments here—if any at all are available—can be quite pricey, and some older ones may be in need of renovation. But those who do find a home here consider it well worth the price. Look in Haut Marais, for there may be some more moderate prices, but probably, not for long.

The Latin Quarter and Saint-Germain (5^e and 6^e)

Encompassing the 5th *arrondissement* and by extension some of the 6th, the Quartier Latin is where many romantic images of Paris come true. This can be one of Paris' most exciting areas in which to live. Judging from the number of people—French and foreign alike—who day and night stroll the boulevards, explore the medieval streets, browse in the bookshops or frequent the cafés or cinemas, this ancient part of Paris is a most intriguing place to be.

The 5e is named for the medieval scholars who were required to speak to each other in Latin, but the part of the 6e that borders on the crowded boulevard Saint-Michel was also part of the Quartier Latin until Baron Haussmann widened the ancient Roman road and distanced an integral part of the quarter on the west.

Famous initially for the Sorbonne, founded in 1253 by Robert de Sorbon, the Latin Quarter is today an area of diverse intellectual endeavours. (Even the Sorbonne is just one part of the seventeen-school University of Paris system, much of which is spread throughout the city.) Here there are other educational institutions such as the Collège de France founded in the 16th century, several of the prestigious

Grandes Écoles, the famous lycées Louis-Le-Grand and Henri-IV and the Institut du Monde Arabe; various other institutions; a government ministry; museums; the impressive Islamic mosque; the Val-de-Grâce hospital; a botanical garden with a zoo; the oceanographic institute and an aquarium. Here too are important historical churches and, rising imposingly above the area's village-like streets, the famous Panthéon.

Fortunately for those who live in the area, though, the Latin Quarter remains agreeably residential. Its low buildings nestle securely amid the massive institutions that dominate its core. Along the narrow, medieval streets on both sides of the bisecting boulevard Saint-Germain, apartments of all types can be found—large and small, for long-term and short-term rentals—for this is an area that caters to faculty and students, a population that can come and go.

Rents and purchase prices may be high, especially for the larger apartments in the narrow streets north of Saint-Germain, heading toward the quais. South of the boulevard, going up into the winding hilly streets, the residential area may be slightly more affordable. Of course there are tourists here, particularly around the market street rue Mouffetard and at Place de la Contrescarpe, but somehow they do not intrude. The area that borders the 13^e is fairly inexpensive, lively and desirable as a result. Just about any street will do nicely here, but do not look for apartments in October, when the students return and are looking, too.

What draws tourists as well as locals—especially on and around the bordering boulevard St-Michel—are the international bookstores and music shops, offbeat boutiques, world-renowned jazz clubs and cabarets, an inviting mix of restaurants and cafés and a large selection of cinemas that show foreign and art films. Tourists congregate around Place Saint-Michel, where shops are fairly inexpensive and restaurants sometimes overpriced for the tourists. Nonetheless, this all contributes to the exuberant, youthful atmosphere that pervades the Quartier Latin.

The intellectual and artistic focus of the 5e becomes more sophisticated as one moves west toward Place Saint-Germain-des-Prés. Located here, where the Romans dedicated a temple to the goddess Isis, is the heart of the 6e—the 1,500-year-old site of Paris' first Christian church, now the Eglise Saint-Germain-des-Prés. This square is one of the most visited in Paris, and the crowds who come here every day of the year, whether to visit the ancient church or to sip a coffee across the street, experience all of Paris, then and now.

For centuries this area was just an extension of the Latin Quarter but is now more known for its place in the post-World War II scene. Existentialism and a liberated, intellectual life unfolded at this area—at the famous cafés, the Deux Magots and the Café de Flore, at the Brasserie Lipp and at the bookshop, La Hune (which finally was forced to close In 2014)—where Simone de Beauvoir and Jean-Paul Sartre held court. Jazz had long been hot nearby on rue Saint-Benoît. Today the cafés are the province of tourists, of the chic set coming to see and be seen, and of a few writers trying to soak up the atmosphere of the past.

This part of the *arrondissement* has it all. From Place de l'Odéon, past Mabillon, the well-trodden streets off the boulevard have antique shops, art galleries, cinemas, theatres, restaurants and cafés galore, upmarket boutiques, and markets at rue de Buci and near rue Mabillon. Toward the Seine, in the *quartier* Beaux-Arts, named for its prestigious arts school, the narrow, angled streets have low-rise 17th- and 18th-century buildings with apartments rented by both Parisians and foreigners—currently the most expensive residential niche.

This is certainly one of the most agreeable *quartiers* in the city. Between the relaxed 5^e on the east and the reserved 7^e on the west, housing here shares the character of its neighbours. It starts at a reasonable price along the east and gradually becomes extremely expensive the farther west one goes, particularly between boulevard Saint-Germain and the Seine. The atmosphere is unique, and it is one Parisians are fighting to preserve, although the battle seems lost. Local shops have moved out as rents have risen and impersonal giants such as Armani, Louis Vuitton and Cartier have taken their place.

Although the atmosphere may change from street to street, it doesn't change for the worse. Around Place Saint-Sulpice, with its fountained square and fashionable surrounds, and along the classy rue de Tournon, or rue de l'Odéon, the wide boulevard Raspail and rue Notre-Dame-des-Champs, the apartments are large, airy, and expensive. This holds true especially for buildings overlooking the spectacular Jardin du Luxembourg, one of the nation's most beloved public gardens and once the exquisite palace grounds of Marie de Médicis. This residential part of the *quartier* may be quieter in spots, but it picks up once again as the busy rue de Rennes reaches Montparnasse, where the atmosphere of quiet sophistication begins to disappear.

Seventh Arrondissement (7e)

Despite the tourists that stream constantly to the Eiffel Tower, Les Invalides and the Musée de Quai Branly, the 7e is one of the most tranquil areas of the city. The broad, leafy streets provide a haven for residents, for the government ministries and embassies that have moved into the 18th-century mansions of the aristocracy and for some erstwhile nobles who still live in their ancestral homes. This is 'old money' Paris. The presence of the Assemblée Nationale, UNESCO and the area's most famous official resident—the French prime minister—at the Hôtel Matignon, makes this the safest *arrondissement* in the city. And Paris is making it ever more desirable: Along the riverside *berges* there is a now a year-round pedestrian area with floating gardens, summer concerts, a stairway to connect the upper and lower areas, eating areas with terraces, cycling routes-and much more to bring people to enjoy the banks of the Seine.

Living here is extremely pleasant, with some parts seeming like a suburb in the city centre. In general, this is an open and airy *arrondissement*, with its widest border along the Seine and several long green stretches that bolster the feeling of luxury. The Champ-de-Mars, the longest grassy promenade in Paris, is a greensward stretching from the École Militaire to the Eiffel Tower, and the Esplanade des Invalides has a welcome green strip down to the river. A popular area for families with children, there are several small playgrounds and a sweetly hidden park at Square Récamier.

Apartments tend to be large, gracious and well-maintained.

Commerce clusters toward the edges of the 7e—to the east near rue du Bac and rue de Sèvres, and toward the west along rue Saint-Dominique and rue de Grenelle which have rows of clothing stores as well. Some of the city's best options for dining are in this *arrondissement*; otherwise there is little evening activity. Antique shops and galleries thrive in the compact area known as Le Carré Rive Gauche. Especially sought after by foreigners are the stylish rue du Bac area and other small streets throughout the *arrondissement*. Many provide commercial services, and on rue de Sèvres is the upscale department store and famous food hall, Le Bon Marché. The extensive market street, rue Cler, is conveniently near the old townhouses and modern apartment buildings of rue Bosquet and rue de Grenelle.

Eighth Arrondissement (8e)

The spectacular avenue des Champs-Elysées and the tourists who have taken it over dominate much of the 8th. Although a major overhaul of this 17th-century aristocratic promenade brought back a touch of its distinction after years of decline, its high rents are now affordable primarily for international chains and the hotels and restaurants that cater to the ubiquitous tourists. Despite the persistence of such traditional institutions as Fouquet's restaurant and the Lido Cabaret, this is one of the least Parisian parts of Paris.

This was not always the case. When the Tuileries Palace was burned down during the uprising of the Paris Commune in 1871 and the 1er dropped from aristocratic favour, this adjacent area took its place. Preferred by the upper classes since the area was laid out by the famous Le Nôtre during the time of Louis XIV, the rue du Faubourg Saint-Honoré was then a street of 18th-century townhouses belonging to wealthy Parisians, with gardens overlooking the still bucolic Champs-Elysées. But not today! Many of the old mansions are now occupied by embassies and offices, and the Palais de l'Elysée is the official residence of the president of France. Few of the old gems of apartments still exist, so when the corporate types go home for the evening, the side streets are left empty and dull. Yet elegance remains. Contributing both to the commercialisation and elegance of this eastern edge is the Golden Triangle of the *haute couture* salons of famous French and international designers, high-class shops of other sorts and some of Paris' finest purveyors of *haute* cuisine. Whatever is here will be of quality and grace. The Champs-Elysées is now closed to traffic one Sunday a month, bringing the beauty back to the Parisians once more.

Toward the eastern edges, along rue de Faubourg Saint-Honoré and rue Royale, are galleries and shops for gracious living—chinaware and home decorations, for example. And the Place de la Madeleine, dominated by its impressive Catholic church, is noted for its gourmet *traiteurs*, and Senderens, one of Paris' premier restaurants.

So, as one would expect, the people who do live in the 8e live very well. Around Place François-1er, tucked quietly toward the Seine and farther west at avenue George-V, well-kept buildings house a privileged few—primarily older, wealthy Parisians. The apartments are large and comfortable, but rarely available. These areas are fairly quiet, with high-class *traiteurs* and a few services catering to the rather sedate population.

Fortunately, the 8^e offers much more. The exquisite and formal Parc Monceau at its western edge, dating from the late 18th century, is one of the more desirable districts of Paris and coveted by both Parisians and newcomers. Here are wide streets, including avenue Hoche, rue de Monceau and the residential end of the long boulevard Malesherbes, plus small, inviting side streets abutting the park. Apartments are plush and airy, with high ceilings, floor-to-ceiling windows, and upmarket prices. In general, the sophisticated atmosphere of the Parc Monceau area and its proximity to the markets and services of the 17e make it a coveted place to live.

Ninth Arrondissement (9e)

The dense, southwestern edge of the 9th *arrondissement* is home to the famous Opéra Garnier, two prestigious Belle Epoque department stores, shops, cinemas, theatres, and banks. It is always crowded and always on the go. Restaurants of all levels line the boulevards, the broad streets that aerate one of the few areas of the city that has limited residential desirability and few open spaces to provide relief from the stress of urban life.

The 9^e appears fickle. Moving east from the Grands Boulevards and just out of the tourists' line of sight, the *arrondissement* seems to have a fitful character. A Jewish community lives around rue Richer, its Sephardic kosher restaurants and Middle Eastern shops incongruously situated near the famous Folies Bergères. Rue Cadet is the area's market street, and the only bit of green in this otherwise colourless commercial portion is the small Square Montholon. Farther north, however, the atmosphere becomes more agreeable, although it can change in character from street to street. Winding up toward the Place Saint-Georges is a long-time artists' quarter that once linked sophisticated Paris to the village of Montmartre in the north. Here too is a section built around 1820, known as the Nouvelle Athènes, which became fashionable after the construction of the church of Notre-Dame-de-Lorette. Today one still finds pleasant streets amid the uninspired, and although many of the old buildings have been taken over by offices, others offer well-maintained apartments. Place Gustave-Toudouze and a triangular space on rue Henri-Monnier are little oases lined with small shops and cafés, and the Square Alex Biscarre is a hidden touch of green. At the northwest is the refreshing Place Adolphe-Max, a square surrounding a small park and playground, but just beyond is boulevard de Clichy, which can be rather seedy. Indeed, as it heads toward Pigalle, which attracts tourists to the Moulin Rouge (just across the boulevard in the 18th), the atmosphere can vary from the traditional charm of rue des Martyrs (that stretches pleasantly up into the 18th), to the at times decidedly uncomfortable. Yet Pigalle, too, is on the move, trying to spruce itself up, with some new restaurants and boutiques coming in.

In the 9^e are some of the most reasonable rents and purchase prices in the city. If you are attracted by the prices, the varied nightlife toward the northern edges, or even by the international mix of population that is trickling down from

Montmartre, choose carefully, as almost every street has its own atmosphere. And prices are rising here, just slightly so far, as more people are having to look outside the centre, while still keeping central, nonetheless.

Tenth Arrondissement (10ᵉ)

Much of the 10th *arrondissement* is truly drab. Unfortunately close together and dominating most of the area, the Gare du Nord and the Gare de l'Est exist in the atmosphere that train stations generate, and their railroad yards cut through the entire northern part of the district. Much of the housing around here is working-class and rather uninspired. People come for the low prices, to visit several important hospitals, to frequent some theatres and museums. They also come to the rue de Paradis (known for its china shops) and the ancient church St-Vincent-de Paul, to Passage Brady for Indian restaurants and goods, and to the glass-roofed Passage du Prado, but they have not come for the neighbourhood. This held true all the way to Place de la République, but its recent total renovation may well soon bring a new atmosphere to its surrounds.

Toward the busy rue du Faubourg Poissonnière, however, is an area that was once home to prosperous Parisians who wanted to live north of the city in homes with gardens and fresh air. Now some of the old buildings are being restored and some affordable possibilities can be found. Close to rue d'Enghien there are still areas to avoid at night, but this should gradually change.

Toward the east, however, is where the *arrondissement* deserves increasing respect. The Canal Saint-Martin opens up the area, and refurbishment has made the area around the quai de Valmy area one to consider seriously for housing—if anything is available. The cobblestone strip is shaded by plane trees, arched footbridges cross at intervals and the quais are lined with graceful, 19th-century apartment buildings, bright cafés and shops. On Sundays the Quai de Valmy and the Quai de Jemmapes see no cars, leaving them calm for pedestrians and cyclists. Nearby, check out the eastern surrounds of the lovely Jardin Villemin, despite their proximity to Gare de l'Est. This area is sought out by young Parisians who are attracted to its animated, somewhat Bohemian atmosphere, openness, and reasonable prices. This also holds true for the areas toward the south that border on parts of the lively 11th and the 3rd *arrondissements*. Rue du Faubourg du Temple, for instance, that runs through both *arrondissements*—and despite being somewhat scruffy—sees some good restaurants and nightspots and a well-trod dance hall.

Bastille to Nation (11ᵉ and 12ᵉ)

One of the most up-and-coming areas of eastern Paris, the southern strip of the 11th *arrondissement* and the adjacent northern area of the 12th are much in demand. Starting at Place de la Bastille and stretching to the enormous Place de la Nation, this former furniture craftsmen's suburb of Faubourg Saint-Antoine is on the move. Prices may still be somewhat moderate in areas, though on the rise, as formerly shabby neighbourhoods are spruced up. Only pockets of the old proletarian atmosphere can still be found, distressing those who fear that the area is becoming too homogeneous and losing its village feel. Most people seem to agree, however, that the youthful, electric atmosphere is bringing a new energy to eastern Paris.

It begins at Place de la Bastille, which, from 14 July 1789 (Bastille Day) to the mid-20th century (site of the student uprising of 1968), was known for protest and resistance. Now, however, it is an engaging, open area that is dominated on the east by the Opéra Bastille, one of Mitterrand's *Grands Projets*. In the south reappears the Canal Saint-Martin, which had gone underground at rue du Faubourg du Temple, flowing below the broad, green boulevard Richard Lenoir. In summer, sunbathers—old and young, gay and straight—sit on the canal's landscaped and cobblestone banks and watch boats slowly pass through the lock to the Seine. The rest of the square is taken by chic terraced cafés—never a dull moment here.

Actually the area is mixed in spirit, partly by habit, partly by design. A few established artisans and furniture makers still inhabit the *cours* (courtyards) and *passages* on the sides of the vibrant rue du Faubourg Saint-Antoine, but others are slowly disappearing as redevelopment raises rents and forces them out. Replacing them are bistros, cafés and shops that draw enormous—sometimes quite voluble—crowds, plus the new businesses, galleries and the consulting and high-tech firms that appeal to young professionals. The major streets of rue de Charonne and rue de la Roquette are connected by the cobblestone rue de Lappe (once known for prostitutes and pimps), rue des Taillandiers and rue Keller, a centre for the gay community.

Old warehouses converted into lofts, restored buildings and new apartment blocks make for an eclectic mix. The park-like setting on the wide boulevard Richard Lenoir hosts one of Paris' most well-attended markets on Thursdays and Sundays, with cafés for a social visit, as well. As in the Marais, gentrification is expanding northwards as older buildings are restored and retail activities expanded. Pleasingly, the rue Oberkampf and Rue Jean-Pierre Timbaud are among the most successfully reconquered and desirable—with cafés, restaurants, and nightspots—and this renewed atmosphere extends itself to Place de la République, although not quite yet to the northeastern border with Belleville in the 20e.

To the south of rue du Faubourg Saint-Antoine, in the 12e, the life of the cours and passages continues. Just a few streets away however, the bustling crowds and exotic aromas of Place d'Aligre take hold. The covered Marché Beauvau gives over to an inexpensive, international extravaganza that spills out into rue d'Aligre and over to rue de Charenton. Owing to its proximity to Gare de Lyon, which opened Paris to southern Europe and then to Africa, this has long been a varied area, changing once again with the influx of young, professional Parisians. Although housing blocks intrude on the otherwise low-rise residential *quartier*, the neighbourhood spirit persists.

Modigliani arrived in Paris in 1906 and first stayed in Montmartre before moving to Montparnasse. Tubercular and drug-addicted, he was even known as the 'king of Montparnasse'. Two films have been made about Modigliani's life: Jacques Becker's *Les Amants de Montparnasse* and Mick Davis' *Modigliani*, starring Andy Garcia and French actress Elsa Zylberstein.

Almost a secret in the eastern area of the *arrondissement* is the Allée Vivaldi, a hidden greensward surrounded by modern offices and residences. Across an arched footbridge, the open Jardin de Reuilly has gardens, playgrounds filled with children, and a grassy expanse; it too is surrounded by unobtrusive, modern housing. To the northwest of the garden, connected by a footbridge, is the Promenade Plantée, a landscaped, 4.5-km path on a former elevated railroad bed. How welcome is this bucolic promenade that originates at the Bastille and how interesting the arched vaults below, now called the Viaduc des Arts! Its galleries and artisans' ateliers welcome visitors into what is becoming a lively, upmarket area, despite its proximity to the Gare de Lyon.

The *quartiers* of Picpus, Bel-Air and Daumesnil at avenue de Saint-Mandé and below have long been a solid, unpretentious, residential district. Increasingly as this area is revitalised with new shops, offices and housing, it will be even more in demand.

To the south, the former wine warehouse district of Bercy was once isolated from the rest of Paris by the train yards of the Gare de Lyon. No longer! Bercy, one of the dynamic *Grands Projets*, is now one of the liveliest areas of the city, reached easily by the high-speed *métro*, Météor, Line 14. At one end of the gentle Parc de Bercy is Bercy Village/Cour Saint-Emilion, an attractive complex that includes a long walkway of upmarket boutiques and stylish restaurants, culminating in a huge cinema complex. At the other end of the welcoming park, which incorporates ruins and old plane trees into its varied modern landscaping, is the Stade de Bercy, which is the venue for major sporting and musical events. To the sides are commercial areas, both old and modern apartments (many with balconies overlooking the park), artists' studios and some hotels. This has become one of the most energetic areas of town, influenced by the thousands of people who work in the area—walking distance just across the river to the Bibliothèque Nationale François Mitterrand. In its own right, though, the Port de la Rapée (between the Pont Charles de Gaulle and Pont de Bercy) is animated by nightspots, cafés, and even a yacht hotel. All in all, this area has developed a vibrant personality and will continue growing.

Thirteenth Arrondissement (13ᵉ)

Across any of three bridges from Bercy—one being the Simone de Beauvoir footbridge—lies the 13th *arrondissement*, modern or traditional, working class or up-to-the-minute, Parisian or Asian—all depending where you look. The most striking part of the 13th is here just across from Bercy, home of the vast National Library. This area near the river modernises itself almost every day, with ever more residential, commercial, and entertainment possibilities springing up. Yet the large 13ᵉ, situated along the city's southern edge, has for some forty years already been one of the more unusual districts of Paris, known primarily as home to some 30,000 of the city's Asian population. And still, in places, one can see vestiges of small villages and little nooks and crannies of a Paris that once was. This is the 13th, more varied than one would imagine from its history.

It's hard to imagine how this area must have looked centuries ago—an area of sweet pastures and vineyards, the little hamlets of Saint-Marcel and Gentilly and the river Bièvre—all now long gone. First came the butchers, then the tanners of hides and finally the factories for textiles that disposed of their wastes into the Bièvre. Along its banks were workers' housing, cheap shops, squalid nightspots, crime, and disease; the cholera epidemics of the mid-1800s revolved around the open sewer that the Bièvre had become, forcing it to be covered over finally around 1910. Factories continued to rule, but as they slowly departed, so did the workers to the nearby *arrondissements*. It seemed that the 13th was destined to be slums.

But, after the Vietnam War, Asian immigrants came to Paris, seeking cheap rents. By that time some public housing high-rise apartment buildings were replacing slums south of the enormous commercial Place d'Italie in the Olympiades neighbourhood, and now a large, mixed Asian population lives here in an area known as the Triangle de Choisy, starting around the Place de Tolbiac. Between the avenue d'Ivry and avenue de Choisy, a dense international community has sunk its roots, renovating older buildings and enlivening the residential blocks. Here are several large Asian supermarkets frequented by all Parisians, as are the many small groceries and shops and dozens of Asian restaurants, creating an atmosphere unlike any other in Paris.

Yet, even in what seems to be an Asian stronghold, more traditional surprises can be found: the northern broad avenue des Gobelins heading down to Place d'Italie, benefits from the atmosphere and residential popularity of the 5e, its neighbour to the north, and is much sought after. And toward the southwest, by the placid, unassuming Place de l'Abbé Henocque, are little streets of private houses and gardens. Not far is the Cité Floréale, a triangular, flowery nook just off Place de Rungis. More well known, though, and just above, is one of Paris' few remaining old villages—la Butte aux Cailles—an intricate set of hilly cobblestone streets with old-world charm and small town flavour. In fact, low, five-storey houses on leafy streets, small shops and narrow streets still manage to characterise the area. Square Brassaï, high up near the *métro* Corvisart, almost hidden on its northern edge, is frequented by locals, as is the large market on boulevard Auguste-Blanqui. Interesting here, around rue Daviel and Villla Daviel are some art-nouveau buildings and some old-time workers' *villas* somewhat reminiscent of traditional Northern France. And the residents are active in keeping it so, resisting the over-commercialisation that has in other places endangered the traditional Parisian feel.

But if we go back to those bridges coming from Bercy, what may not be traditional at all is at least a glimpse of the Paris of the future. A decades-long futuristic project called Seine-Rive-Gauche has made the once-rather decrepit area bustle with modern offices, galleries and restaurants, a large high-rise residential area, cafés and more, all anchored by the ultra-modern four-building National Library complex. The Université Paris VII, Hôpital Pitié-Salpêtrière and the Gare d'Austerlitz—which also is being refurbished—bring people through the area daily, made easier with the new broad artery Avenue de France and the speedy *métro*, Météor. The strip along the quai Françoois Mauriac, called Port de la Gare, hums day and night, with shopping, bars, concerts, cinema, and more. One installation, the *"Les Docks-Cité-de la Mode et du Design"* houses clubs, exhibits, films, sports, bringing crowds to whatever is going on at that time. This area is certainly one of the noteworthy places to think of—either to live or visit. In general, these planned *quartier*s, across from Bercy and accessible to both the traditional and the Asian, have accomplished the purpose to create an eastern Paris as vibrant and productive as the west.

Montparnasse and Beyond (14ᵉ)

Legendary for the bohemian Montparnasse, the 14th *arrondissement* actually includes so much more that its residents often consider it to be the best-kept secret in Paris. In fact, aside from busy Montparnasse, the hospital complexes that dot the area and the broad avenues that cut the *arrondissement* into a pie, the 14ᵉ has as many residential attractions as any other area in the city.

Montparnasse sits at the northwest corner of the *arrondissement* and encompasses small edges of the 15ᵉ and 6ᵉ. It stretches east to the Observatoire built under Louis XIV and south to the imposing junction at Denfert-Rochereau. But Montparnasse is known not so much for its geography but for its intriguing atmosphere. It was a hangout in the 18th century for students venturing away from the Latin Quarter; later it became famous for its bohemian and intellectual life.

Imagine the intensity of this area less than a century ago, when cheap rents for studios and cheap booze brought poverty-stricken artists to this worker's district from the increasingly expensive Montmartre; world-renowned Amadeo Modigliani, Marc Chagall and Pablo Picasso were a few of these unknown artists who descended upon Paris. Eastern European Jews without a franc to their names also came to escape pogroms and Russian thinkers such as Lenin and Trotsky contemplated revolution during their stays here. In the 1920s, after World War I, came the Americans: writers, artists and their patrons. Paris was a playground for those with American dollars, and unlike in the United

States, the alcohol flowed until all hours in cafés we frequent even now—Le Dôme, La Coupole and La Closerie des Lilas. Unfortunately in 1929, the stock markets crashed, pockets were emptied and the Americans went home. But not, of course, the French. It was about this time that a new breed of intellectuals such as Sartre and Beauvoir congregated at the area around Carrefour Vavin, but when World War II came and the Germans took over the cafés of Montparnasse and closed the nearest *métro* station, the crowd moved up to Saint-Germain.

But legends die hard: the commercial area and cinemas are still always crowded and the cafés and nightspots hum into the wee hours of the morning. The sterile Gare Montparnasse, the Tour Montparnasse, its shopping mall and several concrete apartment blocks do nothing, however, to remind us of what once was. Nonetheless, even here are pockets that are worth noting: Square Gaston Baty, near Edgar Quinet seems a peaceful oasis with terraced cafés and seats for relaxation, and housing opportunities, as well. And the hidden park Jardin Atlantique above the Gare relieves the atmosphere of a station.

The residential secret begins around the expansive Place Denfert-Rochereau. Although the *quartier* has changed and high-rise development has tried to encroach, much of the area remains reminiscent of a Paris that has elsewhere disappeared. Broad streets close to the square, such as rue Froidevaux and boulevard Saint-Jacques, have stately buildings and an open atmosphere. The massive, concrete Place de Catalogne, part residential, part offices, dominates toward the west, but it gives way to the long rue Vercingétorix, whose top portion is now a neighbourhood promenade and park. Renovated studios and apartments with quiet courtyards nestle in some of the short streets (the *impasses*, *cités* and *villas*) and artists' ateliers still dot the entire area. Off the busy avenue du Général Leclerc and just a few steps from the pedestrian market street, rue Daguerre, is the beautiful Villa Adrienne, a residential community overlooking a little park.

The area from Plaisance to Alésia is always energetic, with both commercial and residential buildings on the little streets, some of which will, no doubt, soon be renewed. Rue d'Alésia is known for its discount clothing shops, but it is also the commercial artery in this satisfying part of the *arrondissement*.

But it is the southern area that has it all. Parc Montsouris has beautiful gardens sloping lawns, a terraced restaurant featuring band performances, a puppet theatre for the children and a sizeable lake that is home to graceful aquatic birds. Overlooking this wonder are the apartments on rue Nansouty. Adjacent—and dotting this *quartier* throughout—are exceptional private *villas*. Just across boulevard Jourdan, lying admist another green expanse, is the Cité Universitaire, a cluster of 40 international student residences of eclectic styles dating from the 1920s. This greensward stretches west to the Porte de Vanves, the scene of one of Paris' most traditional weekend flea markets.

Getting around these southern reaches has been made more efficient with the advent of the tramway that so far runs from Porte d la Chapelle to the Pont de Garigliano

Fifteenth Arrondissement (15e)

The largest *arrondissement* with the highest population in Paris, the 15th *arrondissement* is primarily a comfortable middle-class community. Located southwest, it stretches north to the subdued 7e, east to Montparnasse and south to the périphérique. Until recently the province of chemical factories, metallurgies and gasworks, the 15e has few tourist attractions, save perhaps for some offbeat museums and the enchanting futuristic Parc André Citroën. The newly refurbished Centre Beaugrennelle, an ultra-modern shopping mall, is convenient for people from all over the city. Yet, it is the locals who dominate: young Parisian families, middle-level professionals and retired persons, many of whom come for the reasonable rents and the family atmosphere. Prices here are moderate in comparison to other areas on the Left Bank or in the 16^{e}, just across the Seine.

Apartment blocks built in the 1960s and 1970s dominate in a community area along the river called Front de Seine, with an elevated, landscaped walkway connecting the buildings, the

Monoprix supermarket, and across a footbridge to the Centre Beaugrenelle. Here children play in the evenings while their parents chat on benches close by. Just a few streets away, at Place Saint-Charles, modernity gives way to some Belle Epoque buildings and various services catering to a middle-class population. On rue Saint-Charles is one of the area's markets.

Farther down the river, the 14-hectare Parc André Citroën, a beautifully-imagined green space built on the site of a former automobile plant, adds greatly to the revitalisation of the area. Citroën-Cévennes is a residential *quartier* surrounding the revamped rue Balard, with both modern housing and refurbished old apartments. And interest has increased, now that the large, ultramodern international Hôpital Européen Georges Pompidou has imposed itself on the area.

Elsewhere, little communities hold their own. The commercial rue du Commerce, with its shuttered houses, barely looks any different from how it might have been 50 years ago, especially around Place Etienne-Pernet. Here are inexpensive restaurants, neighbourhood shops and the Place du Commerce, a pleasant, leafy square. Past rue Lecourbe, the streets around rue de Vaugirard and rue de la Convention are noted for their comfortable, middle-class ambiance.

Another park surrounded by a residential area is the southeastern Parc Georges-Brassens, built on the site of a former slaughterhouse. With grassy areas, a small lake and a carousel for children, this bucolic park breaks the monotony created by the modern apartment blocks that tower over older buildings. Nearby, however, in Passage de Dantzig is La Ruche, the famous beehive building of artists' studios used by Chagall, Modigliani, Soutine and Léger, among others of Montparnasse fame; studios are still in use today.

Montparnasse, whose northeastern corner abuts on the 14e, is perhaps the 15e at its most interesting. Despite the district's commercial nature and the domination by the Tour Montparnasse, the streets off rue de Vaugirard and rue Pasteur are residential, with proximity to a market, supermarkets and the Maine-Montparnasse shopping complex. As already noted, hidden above the railroad station is the Jardin Atlantique, a landscaped roof garden with fountains, play areas and tennis courts. Close by are the large Hôpital Necker and the famous Institut Pasteur, around which are agreeable little residential nuggets, which benefit from their proximity to the elegant 7^e, with its oases such as Place de Breteuil and the upscale market at avenue de Saxe.

Sixteenth Arrondissement (16^e)

The most aristocratic of Paris' *arrondissement*s, this large area at the western edge of the city was among the last to be incorporated into the city system. Its two main *quartiers*, Auteuil and Passy, were formerly small villages set amidst farmland and a forest stretching west, which was the hunting ground of the French kings. Underground mineral springs turned the area into an aristocratic spa in the 17th century, and it was to this area of rural grace that the nobility retreated to during the Revolution.

Today the 16th *arrondissement* still enjoys a small town atmosphere. Just past the western edge is the Bois de Boulogne—what is left of the royal woods. Some Parisians claim the 16e is boring, for there is little nightlife, and in the summer, many of its residents close their homes and depart, returning only at *la rentrée*. Whether this is a disadvantage is debatable, for the *arrondissement* is also appreciated for its tranquillity, its mid-rise buildings with spacious, costly apartments and its little *villas* and *hameaux*—leafy lanes with a country feel. Indeed, this is one area that is extremely suitable for families with children.

Starting from what was once the hill of Chaillot and is now Place Charles-de-Gaulle, the streets around the spectacular avenue Foch are residential. Avenue Foch itself, the broadest in Paris, has long been home to Parisian wealth. Close by, avenue Victor-Hugo is also chic and expensive, as one would expect from these avenues that radiate out from l'Etoile.

Toward the Porte de la Muette is the Organisation for Economic Cooperation and Development (OECD), its surrounding streets home to many of its diplomats and to old Parisian wealth. Starting at the Place du Trocadéro and cutting across the *arrondissement* toward the Porte, the wide avenue Georges-Mandel continues as avenue Henri-Martin.

Buildings are set back from the double boulevard, whose trees provide shade and cushioning from noise. Somewhat south is the Villa Beauséjour, with some surprising old Russian-style cottages. Families like this area close to the Jardins du Ranelagh and to the Bois de Boulogne.

Past the Trocadéro gardens, Passy takes hold. Here one enters the village: a residential neighbourhood, a church square, several commercial streets, including rue Bois-le-Vent and the main street, rue de Passy, with its high-quality shops and services. The prized residential district lies mainly between avenue Mozart on the north and the long rue Raynouard, although areas around Square Charles-Dickens and rue des Eaux are well worth exploring.

South of Passy, the village and vineyards of Auteuil were among the last areas to be urbanised, and Auteuil remains a small town with a church square. Rue d'Auteuil, the main street, formed part of this picturesque village, along with still enticing streets such as rue Boileau and rue La Fontaine, the extension of Passy's rue Raynouard.

Even in this staid area, there are surprises: the gated community of Villa Montmorency holds 80 private houses in curved, leafy streets in an almost rural setting. Just north, closer to the Jardins du Ranelagh, the buildings in the short Place du Docteur-Blanche are strikingly Art Nouveau. Housing anywhere in this area is expensive and it is a popular area for foreign residents.

Seventeenth Arrondissement (17^e)

Encompassing the old farming areas of Monceau and Ternes on the west, and the workers' villages of Batignolles and Epinettes on the east, the 17th *arrondissement* of today is largely residential, but the area has several 'moods'. Cut neatly in two by railroad tracks heading out from Gare Saint-Lazare, the western area is open and upmarket, while the east is distinctly working-class and crowded.

On its southern and eastern edges and above the stately Parc de Monceau, the 17^e has the feel of its affluent neighbours near l'Etoile. What was once the Plaine de Monceau has been replaced by broad avenues and buildings that were, 100 years ago, the most modern in the city. The avenue de Wagram leads from l'Etoile into the heart of the district, opening up at Place des Ternes with its fresh flower market. Off boulevard de Courcelles and rue de Prony is a residential district only somewhat less aristocratic than the 16e—extremely genteel residential pockets can be found particularly toward l'Etoile.

The area is conveniently near the market streets of rue de Lévis and rue Poncelet, both holding fast to an atmosphere that is disappearing all too quickly. Radiating to its west on streets such as rue Lebon, rue Bayen and rue Guersant, is a solid *quartier* leading to the boulevard Pereire, flanking a grassy esplanade that covers the railroad tracks. Just beyond is Villa des Ternes, leafy and comfortable.

The area northeast of the railroad yards has long been a solid workers' quarter, with only a few solidly residential streets amid others of little distinction. Two parallel streets typify this dichotomy: the working-class rue des Moines, with uninspired five-storey buildings, markets and cafés, contrasting with the nearby Cité des Fleurs, a quiet pedestrian zone of houses with gardens. Yet, the Square des Batignolles with its rolling lawns and little lake is agreeably shared by all, and the city is taking steps to refurbish the entire area, constructing modern apartments, offices, public facilities and a new park.

Anchoring the *arrondissement* to its neighbour Neuilly-sur Seine at the western edge of the city is Porte Maillot, a major transportation hub, but, more important the large Palais des Congrès, which hosts large meetings year-round and houses a large, convenient shopping mall. Residences on the Paris side of the Porte are traditional, but as one heads Into Neuilly, it becomes more upscale, in keeping with the suburban area.

Eighteenth Arrondissement (18e)

Known for the tourists who swarm the *butte* (hill) every day to visit the Basilique du Sacré-Coeur, or for others who hang out at seedy nightspots on the southern edge, Montmartre nonetheless manages to retain some of its well-known character in places and can be an extremely agreeable place to live. Ranging from the comely to shabby, from enclaves of old-time Parisians to those of recent immigrants, the 18th *arrondissement* ascends winding picturesque streets from the boulevard de Clichy and boulevard de Rochechouart, peaks at the Butte Montmartre and flows out to the *périphérique*. It is probably one of the most unpretentious areas of the city, with few historic monuments and little modern development. Some areas are well worth considering and some are definitely not recommended.

An area of fields, vineyards and gypsum mines until the early 20th century, Montmartre became a place of pilgrimage after the decapitation of the Christian bishop, Saint Denis, in ancient times. It was more recently that Montmartre acquired its present reputation when, attracted by the fact that the hilly area laid outside the city's toll walls, and the low rents and cheap nightlife, workers descended here from the countryside during the Industrial Revolution, as did artisans, struggling artists, political protesters and anarchists during the Paris uprisings. Today, however, the southern edge teems with tourists who savour the artificial bohemian atmosphere created by shopkeepers.

Nonetheless, at the western side of Butte Montmartre, between Sacré-Cœur and the Montmartre cemetery, there are some wonderful residential nooks, charming squares reminiscent of Paris past, and winding narrow streets with both older and newer homes, some with gardens. Real estate prices here can be high—though still lower than in more central areas—but the views and atmosphere are quite appealing. Look above the fashionable rue des Abbesses, which intersects rue Lépic, the famous market street; or west, near rue Damrémont. Farther up the hill, rue Caulaincourt is worth a look, and avenue Junot has been nicely restored. Although tourists may wander here, the touristic atmosphere is kept at a distance. The small, green Place Casadesus is frequented by locals and Villa Léandre, one of a few eye-catching alleys of small houses, feels like a quiet country lane, as does the nearby Hameau des Artistes.

Unfortunately, claiming the southeastern edge of the *arrondissement* are Pigalle and Barbès, home to both dubious nightlife and crowded clubs. Some say this area never sleeps. This sometimes unsettling ambiance stretches to rue de la Goutte-d'Or, just off boulevard Barbès, along a poor, cramped workers' *quartier* that is now an area of immigrants. The crowded, bargain department store Tati can be fun, as can the exotic shops and inexpensive markets and restaurants, but this area has a notable crime rate and you may not want to frequent its spots at night. But as just about anywhere else in Paris, cheaper rents are bringing new opportunities for commerce and residence, and this area is already seeing a slight change.

Along with spectacular views, there are some interesting streets and even a vineyard near Sacré-Cœur, but on the back of the slope the rest of the 18e is deeply cut into by railroad yards coming up from the rue du Poteau of the 10e. North of the *butte* is a good market street and there are some oases around Square de Clignancourt. Nonetheless, along its top, the *arrondissement* is fairly charmless, despite the nearby presence of Paris' most famous flea market, jammed every weekend with bargain hunters.

Belleville and Ménilmontant (19e and 20e)

The 19th *arrondissement* is the 1860 addition into the city system, comprising the slaughterhouse town of La Villette and Belleville, then industrial and working-class. Now Belleville— known to be in the 19th *arrondissement*—actually straddles four *arrondissement*s, primarily entwined with its neighbour Ménilmontant which is in the 20th, but also parts of the 10th and 11th as well. Once a slum of radical politics and protest, Belleville was split apart in the final expansion of the *arrondissement*s—an attempt by the government to quell the zone's rebellious spirit. But these areas, along with the former villages of Bagnolet and Charonne, remain inextricably linked and retain an atmosphere of their own. African immigrants, lovers of a bohemian life, and old-time Parisians mix in the cafés and markets, and the many Asian eateries speak to a large community there, as well.

At the northeastern tip, above avenue Jean-Jaurès, replacing an old slaughterhouse village with that name, is the ultra-modern La Villette, a 55-hectare green expanse, science museum and entertainment complex. It begins alongside Canal Saint-Denis and straddles the Canal de l'Ourcq that cuts across the top of the area and ends at the impressive Bassin de la Villette. In the day, families come for the museum, children's programmes, themed gardens, promenades and bicycle rides along the path. In the evening, entertainment takes over and all of Paris comes. As commercial as this all is, it is still a desirable residential district, as old warehouses are being converted into studios and apartments. Moreover, when Baron Haussmann's refurbishing of Paris' central slums sent many lower-class Parisians to Belleville, cottages went up willy-nilly on small, hastily carved roads. These are the spruced-up, charming culs-de-sac, *impasses*, and *villas* of today—a large district that remains mixed in population, atmosphere and price.

The *quartier* is most agreeable from Buttes Chaumont to Place de Rhin-et-Danube, benefitting from its proximity to the beautiful hilly Parc des Buttes Chaumont. How amazing that in forcing the poor to these already overcrowded areas, Baron Haussmann created one of the city's loveliest vantage points! Around the park's perimeter are the broad residential rue Manin and rue Botzaris. Off rue Mouzaïa and rue du Géneral Brunet remain the *villas* of private houses, coveted places to live in, as are some parts of rue de Belleville, still like the high street of a small town. But these and other nooks strewn across the southern part of the *arrondissement* are interspersed with others of dilapidated housing and faceless high-rises designed to replace them, especially around Place des Fêtes, once the village square.

It should be no surprise that this area drew a population looking for work and cheap housing. Immigrants came, some legal, some not: Eastern European Jews came seeking refuge, first from pogroms, then from the Nazis. Then came Greeks, Armenians and Turks, and most recently Asians, Arabs and Africans—again, some with legal papers, others without—bringing a tangible instability and some anger (sometimes explosive) to the area, as the French endlessly debate how to handle the large immigrant influx and its high rate of unemployment. Today this population congregates to the sides of the boulevard de Belleville at the Arab and Asian shops, Muslim and Jewish establishments and the crowded, inexpensive market. Much of this western side where the 20^e meets the 11^e is rundown, but some parts bear the mixed results of urban renewal.

In the 1960s, the 20^e began to experience the same faceless development as parts of the 13^e and 15e, but the outcry of the residents, les Bellevillois, caused at least some areas to be preserved. Thus, this hilly northern part of the district contains apartment blocks, modernised cottages and still some slums. The area immediately above the steep Parc de Belleville is up-and-coming, with new cafés and bars enlivening the area; downhill, it approaches boulevard de Belleville and the sometimes unsettled area described above. The commercial rue de Ménilmontant cuts across the variable area, separating it from the neighbourhoods below.

West of the cemetery Père-Lachaise—the largest garden in Paris—and toward Porte de Bagnolet, lie the old hamlets of Charonne and Bagnolet. In this generally residential area around Place Chanute and Square Séverine are small cottages on hilly, flowery side streets such as rue Paul Strauss. There are also interesting niches off rue Saint-Blaise. Of course, these are all nestled amidst apartment blocks or adjacent to areas that are still waiting to be refurbished. It just depends on where you look.

La Défense and the Western Suburbs

Although the suburbs are beyond the province of this book, some should certainly be considered, for they are popular with the international community. Many foreign residents, especially those with families, commute into the city or to La Défense from the *banlieue* (suburbs), which offer a tranquil lifestyle, spacious gardened homes and proximity to some of the international schools. The suburbs are categorised by those that are near (*la proche banlieue*) and linked by the *métro* to Paris, and those farther out (*les banlieues plus éloignées*), reachable by RER (commuter railway). *La banlieue ouest* (western suburbs) are most in demand, especially by new arrivals to Paris. The standard of living is high and housing is more spacious for property of comparable prices in the city centre. Having a car is essential, however, as not all services or shopping needs can be found in every small town.

Contiguous with Paris, look at elegant Neuilly-sur-Seine and then its neighbour, Levallois-Perret, both at the western edges of the city. Try Boulogne-Billancourt and its neighbour across the Seine, the affluent hill town of Saint-Cloud. Suresnes and Puteaux are also home to many Anglophones, as is Courbevoie, beyond La Defénse.

Just beyond Neuilly rise some 2,000 acres of modern skyscrapers—high-rise residential blocks, France's largest shopping mall and miles of landscaped, connecting walkways. This is La Défense, a multi-use business/residential complex planned in the 1930s, realised in the 1960s and 1970s and topped off in 1989 with the construction of La Grande Arche, a 400-m high arch of two hollow towers, connected at the top and larger than the Cathedral of Notre-Dame.

Some 100,000 people work at La Défense, in the offices of 800 of the world's most important corporations. Thirty thousand people live here, in a pleasant, homogeneous area close to several of the international schools. Housing is agreeable and affordable, built around landscaped squares and elevated walkways that hide the public transportation systems below. The Quatre-Temps shopping centre holds hundreds of shops and restaurants and two large supermarkets. In fact, all conveniences are here, including a variety of cultural attractions, and central Paris is no farther than a *métro* or RER ride away. If La Défense does not have the traditional charms of the city centre, it has real advantages worth considering.

If the south interests you, look at Issy-les Moulineaux— a town of winding streets, its own town square and an atmosphere more casual than some of its neighbours. Just beyond, look too at Meudon, accessible by RER, prized both by commuters into Paris and those who work in the industries that border both sides of the Seine.

Of the outer reaches, Saint-Germain-en-Laye is probably the most well-known and sought after. An affluent country town, it has provided upmarket services to Anglophone residents since the 17th century, when the English James II and his retinue lived in exile here. All conveniences that residents could possibly want are here, which also benefit its less famous neighbour Le Vésinet. The tranquil lifestyle of these areas make them extremely good for Anglophone families—do check them out.

And to the East...

A few of the eastern suburbs are worth looking at, those that have easy access to the centre by *métro*: Montreuil or St-Mandé, for example. These have varied areas, themselves, but generally are noted for their reasonable prices and connection to the city.

Be careful, however, when thinking of the northern or northeastern *banlieu*, which are currently more problematic. Dense housing blocks and industrial compounds characterise these areas, for this is where the many North African immigrants were settled during the various influxes into the Paris region. Overcrowded and monotonous, these northern inner suburbs continue to be in the news for unrest and protests by underemployed youths with few prospects. France has long grappled with the assimilation of these immigrants into society and the job market, but with little success. After the incidents of car burnings of late 2005 and now the horrific terrorist attacks of 2015, the government is trying to make concrete plans toward improving living and economic conditions here. This is much easier said than done, given the resistance to change by the French, even when the citizenry knows it to be crucial. The city's Paris Metropole thought to bring these problematic areas into the city *arrondissement* and benefits system, may well have some effect, if it is actually put into place. Nonetheless, in terms of housing, at present, it's best to stick to the west or south when thinking of a suburban place to live.

At the City's Edges

Two extensive, beloved parks flank the city to the east and west. Both were originally part of a forest that almost surrounded what is now Paris, becoming royal hunting grounds until in the 19th century under Napoleon III, they were developed as parks for the people. Called the "lungs" of Paris, the parks help the city and its resident breathe.

The Bois de Vincennes to the east, at the edge of the 12th *arrondissement* is the larger of the two, at 995 hectares (2,459 acres), giving it an area of about 10 per cent of the city of Paris. The park contains the chateau of French kings, but what draws its visitors are the four beautiful lakes, the Parc Floral and Arboretum—two of the four botanical gardens of Paris—and most recently, the splendidly refurbished and updated zoo with animals in their natural habitats. Young visitors can also see the Ferme George-Ville—a real working farm, enjoy the numerous play areas, and see the Bois des Oiseaux, a bird sanctuary. Horse and bicycle races draw crowds, joggers take to the 32 kilometres of car-free paths, and concerts and other events are also a great draw.

The 'Paris lung' at the western edge of the 16th, the Bois de Boulogne offers in 845 hectares its own enormously varied activities in beautiful natural settings: bridle and cycle paths, waterfalls and lakes, walkways and picnic areas, and two delightful lakes connected by little streams. Just to begin with. The famous Longchamp and Auteuil race tracks are here, as is Roland Garros, the tennis stadium home to the French Open. Paris St-Germain, the football team, plays its home matches here. The extensive Jardin d'Acclimatation appeals to everyone, with its amusement park, menagerie, aviary, charming lake, rock outcroppings, and so much more. Some of the city's interesting restaurants are also here in the Bois de Boulogne, including the Pré Catalan in its lovely pavilion, or the Chalet des Îlles which is in the middle of a lake and reachable by boat. Gardens galore are enchanting—the Serres d'Auteuil greenhouses, the English landscape garden with its watery cascade, and the captivating rose garden of the Bagatelle that in its Orangerie hosts the Chopin Festival each summer.

But now there's something new, something architecturally ultramodern and exciting in the Bois de Boulogne. In 2014, after more than a decade of construction, the Louis Vuitton Foundation opened its exceptional $143 million art museum and cultural center, designed by the renowned Frank Gehry. Next to the Jardin d'Acclimatation, and integrating itself into the lush greenery surrounds, the amazing two-storey glass building is reminiscent of a sailboat, whose many sails are billowed by the wind. The museum itself houses about a dozen galleries, a large auditorium, and multilevel roof terraces that can be used for special events or art exhibits.

MEETING THE PARISIANS

'How can foreigners say they like France, but not the French? It's the French who made the France they like—and keep it that way.'
—Getrude Stein

WHEN YOU FIRST COME TO PARIS, you'll wonder, "What are the Parisians like?" In fact, Parisians are a constant topic of conversation among newcomers, at least until they think (they think!) they have finally understood the essence of the French. But the truth is that the answers—for there are many, and they may not always be consistent—come slowly, or as the French say, *petit à petit*. This is only partly because fathoming the intricacies of any culture takes time. The French are also traditionally private and reserved and do not readily open themselves to people they have just met or accept anything new. Even more important, though, is that the populace of Paris is changing and if it was once easily categorised, this is no longer the case.

The younger generations of Parisians—even those whose roots have long been in this city—live in a world and have attitudes their grandparents could never have imagined. Their Paris is one of plenty, without the scars of privation and hardship due to wars or depression. Their sphere is that of instant news on television and of chatting on the Internet, of universal education, Facebook and Twitter, and affordable international travel. Even without leaving Paris, they can explore the world. And they like it that way—keeping, in their opinion, the best of French refinement and culture while partaking of the international scene. It has moved them to an openness and tolerance even their parents couldn't have foreseen: of gays who openly make up about 5 per cent of the French population and who now have the right to marry and have families of their own, of Parisians of different ethnicities and religions, of newcomers to their city with their own cultural norms, and to the pressing needs and true uncertainties of this millennium that will continually affect their lives.

But they also live in a time when half of the marriages in France end in divorce and where their friends often don't choose the option of marriage at all or choose civil unions called PACS (*Pacte Civil de Solidarité*). Abortion is legal. Real estate prices are high and jobs are scarce. They know that the political and economic realities of the uncertain 21st century influence their futures. Competition is fierce, so they must pay attention and learn. Some of these people are ambitious young professionals who may well, eventually, bring about change to the hierarchical, top-down structure of French society. And others are beginning to start alternative businesses of their own that cater to the needs of the upcoming generations, such as shops that sell cupcakes or vegan burgers, broadening the definition of what it is to be both modern and French. It isn't that they embrace change, it's that change has come to them whether they like it or not.

As for their parents, they perpetuate the stereotype that, while knowing it is necesary, the French don't like change. They worry that foreign cultures—pervasive American commercialism and even the different cultures of their confrères in the European Union—are infiltrating their own. They see their children as being too influenced by external ideas that don't reflect the traditions they revere. There's also too much uncertainty all around. Knowing that globalisation is inevitable, and even understanding that, in many ways, they are benefitting from greater opportunities, they still don't like all this newness one bit. If you talk to these older Parisians—even on a beautiful sunny day on the terrace of a charming café—they'll tell you that everything in their city is going from bad to worse.

And they too wonder who Parisians are these days. As described in Chapter Two, Paris is no longer a city of only 'Parisians'. Some 13 per cent of 'Parisians' are foreigners, i.e., about 300,000 out of 2.3 million, including a large North African influx from the former colonies of France. Others include citizens of EU countries who may now live in any EU country they choose. It's also estimated that some 100,000 English speakers live in the Paris area, some of whom are employees of international corporations or embassies, here for a short term, then moving on and ceding their place to yet more newcomers. Parisians now hear Arabic in the streets and in the *métro*, and English everywhere as well—mostly what the French call 'American', a linguistic distinction Americans don't make.

ANSWERS STILL EXIST

Yet, if Paris is no longer that of Louis XIV and the Marquis de La Fayette, it is clear to foreigners—if not to the French themselves—that cultural legacies do linger on. Paris remains a city of Parisians, a city that is charming as well as efficient, beautiful and welcoming, and this is due to the Parisians. So, one still needs to ask the question: "What are Parisians like?" or more precisely "What can I expect from my new neighbours?" The French continue to embody their history and deeply ingrained traditions. As such, despite the variations in individual experiences that can occur, there are codes for manners and behaviour, clues a newcomer can discern, which will help in you to fit in, whether here for a week or a year. Use the 'The Paris Rules' and you will feel welcome and increasingly see why life here can be so good.

GETTING STARTED

First it should be said that—no matter what—Paris is an extremely agreeable city to live in—graceful, well maintained, efficient, with something interesting going on all the time—and this is the way the French like it.

So just who are they? Basically the French are people who are formal and respectful with others, cordial and polite, direct in their speech, and quite witty and affectionate when they get to know you. Life revolves around their families and friends. They are busy with their work, but they treasure their leisure time, enjoying *la belle vie* or the good life—concerts, cinema, their favourite bistros and cafés. Since they have created these outlets for themselves, they are at your disposition too! Of course, as anywhere else, you'll find shopkeepers you like and restaurants that please you more than others; people you want as friends and others that you don't. With those Parisians who welcome you slowly but surely into their midst, you'll create your own *belle vie* as time goes on, and what will make all this happen is less the Parisians or what they're like, but you and how much effort you make to fit in.

Legendary Rudeness Dismissed

Tourists in the past may have complained so much about the rudeness of Parisians that it has become legendary, but people who come today are surprised to find it just isn't true. In fact, manners, as well as respect, formality and privacy, are extremely important to the French. It's always a mistake to assume in a new country that because the citizens look like you, dress like you and perhaps, even seem to lead the kind of life that you do, they are like you. They're probably not. They're themselves, an amalgam of their particular traditions, as well as political and cultural history. So, bringing your own cultural assumptions and being offended when these are not met is certainly a big mistake.

Take, for example, the welcoming smile. The French had heretofore smiled only when they had a reason to, for example, when meeting a friend. In fact, although this is changing among the modern generations, the French used to be known to have a *mine d'enterrement*—a funereal look. So, if you come from a gregarious culture where people automatically smile when saying hello—even to a waiter in a restaurant or someone sitting down next to you on the bus, you may be taken aback in Paris when your smile is not returned and think it rude, although it is not. But younger generations are more open these days to return the smile.

Yet, as with most legends, this one may have once contained a glimmer of truth. Tourists who came to Paris just some 60 years ago would have dealt with Parisians who grew up during and just after World War II in a climate of

It's common to *faire la bise* when greeting your French friends—but even this follows codes.

hardship and loss and who subsequently faced the Algerian War and student rebellions in their youth. As such, they were often grim and perhaps even suspicious of the droves of cheerful, superficial, high-spending foreigners who were all around. But this generation is thinning out, and the Parisians of today are two generations hence. History has moved on and so have they.

Of course, there are people who are rude anywhere, in any city of the world. It's unavoidable. There are bureaucrats who get tired of answering the same question again and again. There are also Parisians who react negatively to something outside of their own cultural assumptions. And even French who have lived in Paris all their lives have occasional woes of how they were mistreated by someone, sometimes. For newcomers, the stories we tell and retell are those that draw a laugh, most often at ourselves for having gotten it all wrong or at how we were, yet again, misunderstood. It takes some time to get it right. All you can do is be patient and have a sense of humour about it all.

How They Were Brought Up

The real truth is that most Parisians are polite and wouldn't dare be otherwise. It's important to French parents that their child be respectful, considerate and *bien élevé* (well brought up); calling someone *mal élevé* (badly brought up) is an insult. These expectations are passed down through the generations, and although parents these days despair of their children's manners (as parents seem to do everywhere), French children are basically *bien élevé* and grow up to be well-mannered adults. Think of how, when you go into a store, salespeople will say "*Bonjour monsieur*" or "*Bonjour madame*". They also express thanks at the end of a transaction and wish you "*Bonne journée*" (a good day) when you depart. This is, as they say, '*normal*' (perfectly normal and expected).

If you are elderly, someone will give you a seat on the bus. A person who bumps into you will sincerely apologise and ask if you're okay. And, if you have some kind of real problem, there's no one like the French to take it in hand. They're eager to help, to show you the way. If you start by saying

"*Excusez-moi de vous déranger* (sorry to bother you), *mais j'ai un problème* (but I have a problem)," the French will be all ears. You'll certainly get some information, assistance, the use of their mobile phone, or whatever it is you need.

But here's one of the important things to learn: this is where it ends. Most often Good Samaritans

At the start of 2007, smoking was banned in most public places; eating and drinking establishments changed over in 2008. After the total ban was finally in effect, smokers—both old and young—readily adapted to the new conditions. There were few complaints, and those who predicted the demise of the convivial bar must have been pleasantly surprised.

won't give you their names or invite you for a coffee after your *problème* has been solved. You will neither learn about their families or be asked why you are in Paris and what you do. Accepting a younger person's seat on the bus is not an opening to conversation about where you are going that day. Acknowledging an apology for being jostled requires nothing but a nod to say you're fine and perhaps the standard phrase "*Ce n'est pas grave* (it's not serious)". And when you are shopping, expecting the salesperson to volunteer an opinion on how the dress looks on you (once the question of the correct size has been resolved) will leave you disappointed. In short, the French do not intrude on your privacy and they expect you to respect theirs.

How They Grew Up

Blaming Doesn't Help!

You should never accuse a French person of being wrong—especially if there's something you need. With such an emphasis on being correct, the French have difficulty in admitting they are wrong and so they practically never apologise. This generalisation may be going too far, but it has a great deal of truth to it. A bureaucrat may—only under duress—admit to an *erreur* (error), but since errors are innocently made, this means that there is no fault—and no apology will be forthcoming. A *faute* (fault) is something even worse to bring up, for it implies culpability. So, if you are a person who needs to put blame for something gone amiss, you have come to the wrong place!

It's best to take none of this personally for it's just the way the French were taught to be. As children, their upbringing was loving but strict, with expectations for proper behaviour. Their schooling was rigid and competitive. They were taught

The Paris Rules

- Learn French. The French love their language and are pleased when a foreigner makes the effort to speak it. Do the best you can, even if it is not very good at first. If you don't, you will always remain an outsider. Pronunciation is the key, even though your French accent may be more reminiscent of Dracula than of Yves Montand. With just the slightest mistake, you may be looked at as though you were from another planet. For example: *salut* (pronounced 'sa-lue') means 'hello', but *salaud* (pronounced 'sa-loh') is a word not used in polite society.

- Mind your manners. Be respectful and polite. Don't interrupt if a salesperson is busy with another client. Wait for your turn.

- Look good and act in control. Appearances and confidence count. Parisians respond to people who look well put together and who come across as poised, with dignity and spirit.

- Moderate the volume of your voice. Speak softly on your mobile phone, do not shout on the *métro*, and in restaurants be considerate of people sitting close by.

- Be cordial but not familiar. Do not tell everyone your life story, just because they've asked about the weather that day.

- Do not ask Parisians anything personal about themselves, no matter how superficial it seems to you. And never talk about money or volunteer how much something costs, even with friends, unless they have shared something of their own, first.

- Pay attention. Read some of the books mentioned in the Further Reading section and listen carefully to the stories of friends who have already been through the acclimatisation process. Pay attention to each situation for they are not all the same. When you have doubts, just ask a Parisian, who will no doubt be pleased that you are making an effort to understand how Paris works.

- Don't blame a French person for something gone wrong. Convey that you have misunderstood and ask what should be done at this point. It doesn't matter whether you are right or wrong, or even if the other person is evading the truth. What matters is that you get what you need at that point.

- Let nothing faze you. Be firm, but don't get angry. The French, whether they like it or not, will respond to manners. If someone seems unkind, do not take it personally and don't overreact. With cordiality you at least stand a chance of an easy transaction; without it, you do not.

- Read the French newspapers as much as you can and watch the news, so you know what is current in France and in Paris. In other words, be a resident of your city, know what is going on.

- Learn *le système D*. Parisians, too, make train reservations and need help from clerks, and they too get the answer "*non*". The 'D' comes from the word *débrouiller,* meaning to manage or untangle. What it really means is finagling any way you can—within socially acceptable and legal parameters—to get what you want; whether it is a connection through a friend or by using every persuasive charm you have to convince that office clerk to bend a rule (that might not even be a rule at all) just a little. In short, *séduire* or charm someone who is brusque and unhelpful. Play on their sympathy. Rely on their expertise. Be helpless but persistent. Don't take "*non*" for an answer.

- Do not complain about Paris or France, even if Parisians gripe that everything is going from bad to worse. Love Paris every minute and let it be known that you do.

to get things exactly right, to be direct and to the point. They were taught the value of reason and that they should always find the rational solution. Love and respect go hand in hand.

The Superior French?

Another legend that dies hard is that the French think they are 'superior'. (Didn't the word 'chauvinism' come from the French?) Then again, think of how the French look at their lives. They were brought up with an intense cultural pride—a 2,000-year-old history, a continual refinement of values and an adherence to the best traditions will do that for you. They have been taught to be proud of their heritage and language, their literature, art, fashion, wine and cuisine, and even the beauty of their capital. Aren't these things worth being proud of, and isn't this one of the reasons we all love to come to Paris? It isn't that a French person feels superior to any one particular foreigner, it's just that, all things said, the French—no matter of which generation—believe and feel deeply in their souls that it is excellent to be French. And it's rather nice, is it not, to be proud of who you are and where you live?

SOCIALISING WITH THE LOCALS

CHAPTER 4

'I think every wife has a right to insist upon seeing Paris.'
—Sydney Smith

IT STANDS TO REASON that the people most likely to become your first friends are those with whom you already have some personal link: contacts from people back home, parents of other children in the bilingual schools, people you've met at your English-language church or synagogue, or even those you've found through the networking groups mentioned in Chapter 10. Everyone wants to know people from their home countries, and these people may form the core of your social life at the outset, as you share the same language and culture shock is minimised. If these people have lived here a long time, they almost qualify as 'locals', for although they may not be seen as 'Parisians' by the French, they certainly know the ropes and, in addition to including you in their Parisian lives, they can help you along. Their social customs, in fact, may well reflect aspects of both cultures, for newcomers tend to keep their own while also taking on those of the French. They may, for example, invite you into their homes for dinner sooner than the French might, but would still expect you to arrive at least 20 minutes late, which Parisians consider as being on time.

BREAKING DOWN THEIR RESERVE
But you're determined to make some French friends, and rightly so. So how do you meet Parisians? It isn't at all impossible to make French friends. It takes time, patience and effort. It takes being cool and collected, and standing some disappointments. But it's all worth it at the end. If you comport

yourself as someone the French want to know, you'll already have met them halfway, but only halfway, and it is the other half—that famous privacy and reserve—that must be slowly overcome. Some people joke that if you want to make friends quickly in animal-loving Paris, just walk a dog!

Some foreigners have never met their Parisian neighbours; others have become fast friends with the person across the courtyard. Somehow, Paris brings out who you are and responds in kind. If you are someone who is easily irritated by small problems, Paris will no doubt irritate you most of the time, but if you see little problems as challenges, you will approach them with good humour. If you are a person who makes friends easily, you will eventually break down some of the barriers of Parisian reserve, but if you too are reserved in outlook, you will wind up—as is often the case with the Parisians themselves—not knowing the person next door.

Actually, the problem is not meeting Parisians, for you'll also come across them in all the places you normally frequent. Yet, they're busy with their own work and children, and when it comes to socialising, they already have their own friends and families. It's a fact that the French are most comfortable and open with people they already know—extended families and lifelong friends. That leaves you to strike a delicate balance, indicating that you would like to know them better, but allowing them the space to go to the next step at their own pace. Frankly, there's no easy answer on how to move from cordial acquaintances to friends. It depends, as with any relationship, on the individuals.

Nonetheless, there are ways—through inter-cultural groups and networking with people who have already indicated they are open to getting to know new people—and by making sure you let it be known you are interested in making new friends. You might suggest having a coffee sometime or a film that you've both said you've wanted to see. Start slowly, listen for cues and be sensitive to how far, at each point, they are willing to go.

Also, some deep-rooted traditions are being shoved aside, as younger generations are more casual, more flexible, and more international in outlook. Other traditions, however,

Parisian Reserve

Art critic John Russell once commented, "It must seem that in Paris every door is marked 'private', every notice means 'keep out' (even if it doesn't actually say it) and all information is classified." But Russell's is a generalisation, one that may not apply to particular individuals that you meet. And, keep in mind the Bob Dylan song, 'The Times they Are a-Changin'."

remain rock solid. Again, take your cues from your new friends, and even if you know that changes are here and there's no going back, they are slow and not always evident.

A PARISIAN FRIEND

It may take time to make Parisian friends, but once you have made them, they will be loyal for life, going out of their way for you, including you in group dinners at a bistro, in their walks at the Bois de Boulogne or at their evenings at the Opéra Bastille.

If you are from a culture that is immediately welcoming and effusive, but which doesn't translate into deep friendships, you will be pleasantly surprised. Parisians are true friends. But this does not mean that you will be invited into their homes right away, for that takes time. And when you are, it doesn't mean you may then drop in without being invited. It does not mean that you will use the familiar *tu* (you) to address each other. It does not mean that any of the social rules may be broken (even if you do not know what they are until you have broken them). And it does not mean you can be overly intimate, which is worse than not being friendly enough. The Parisians you come to know may enjoy your company and begin to be comfortable with you, but they are after all still French.

So don't stereotype people according to the one or two Parisians who might not respond to your overtures. Most Parisians will look at you as an individual, no matter what they think of the politics of your country. If they see someone who is trying to fit into society, who is genuinely open to understanding Paris and who tries to follow 'The Paris rules' (see pages 70–71), they will see you as an individual. With each person you come to know, you will have to judge *petit à petit* how much to tell and how much to ask. Err on the minimal side. The French are astounded when foreigners— especially the open, gregarious Americans—divulge too early in a budding relationship aspects of their lives that they tell only their oldest friends. Actually, they are just as curious as you are; they just don't show it. It is best to wait for clues and hints from the other party, and gauge each situation to figure out what comes next. If something goes amiss, ask yourself first if there's a code you have unknowingly violated. Yes, there are always more codes to learn; the difference is that with a friend, you have an ally in helping you learn them.

THE ART OF CONVERSATION

It's important to understand that the French love to talk. They love informed, witty conversation on a variety of subjects. They love repartee and banter. One of the worst things they can say about a person is "but he has no conversation". If you have dinner with someone, even in a *restaurant etoilé (*a starred restaurant), the dinner will almost be as much about the conversation as the food.

And even here, there are codes. Don't talk about anything intimate: they don't want to know any details about someone who is ill (not even the name of the illness), about anything dirty, about how pleased (or displeased) you are with your salary. Do not monopolise the conversation and, above all, do not complain or criticise the French—even if your friends are doing so themselves. What with all the uncertainties in the world, everyone has an opinion on politics, but that doesn't mean you should express yours immediately—not about your home country, and especially not about France.

Do talk about things you have in common—films and books or an exhibit you've seen recently; travel; current events (if it is not against the French); an amusing anecdote about something you misjudged. Compliment the food, wine and surroundings. Have a good time. That's what it's all about.

People generally don't split the bill in a restaurant. If you've been invited as a guest, your hosts will pay for the dinner. Be gracious, thank your hosts, and indicate that you'd like to reciprocate the next time. On the other hand, if you're part of a small group that has decided to get together for a drink or have a meal in one of the inexpensive Asian eateries, then expect to split the bill or to indicate that you want to pay your

The French value ideas, conversation and debate—learn the art of conversation and you'll find making friends easier.

share. Follow the lead of other people. Again, though, we have to say that the younger generations of Parisians, while still bringing a traditional air to their relationships, are generally more open, both in their conversation in their curiosity about new people and ideas. Judge for yourself in each situation; let it be known that you're interested in knowing them more, and see where it goes.

IN A PARISIAN HOME

The French have long believed that they are the custodians of
la belle vie—the good life. They also believe that part of this
good life is adhering to accepted standards, what they call
comme il faut, or how things are done. So, if and when you
are invited to into a Parisian's home, there are also codes to
be learned, the sooner the better.

Your hosts will expect you to be on time, although their
concept of this may differ from yours. People generally arrive
between 20 minutes to half an hour after the time called for
the rendezvous. Never arrive even two minutes early or 10
minutes after—you might be interrupting your hostess in the
midst of dressing or doing something in the kitchen.

Expect some physical contact. Colleagues and acquaintances
shake hands when they meet and at the end of the encounter.
When you know people a little better, they may lean with
their face forward, indicating that they have moved from the
handshake to the *bisous*—two kisses, one on each cheek. In
other areas of France, some people do three and even four
kisses, but two is generally the norm in Paris. These are small,
friendly greeting kisses and are often repeated at the end of

the rendezvous. Women also do the *bisous* with each other, as do men who are family members or, sometimes, extremely old friends. Note that even if all the others know each other well and they *se tutoient* i.e.,speak to each other in the more familiar second person singular tense, you shouldn't follow suit until you are invited to—this may take years.

If it's not a casual occasion and you are meeting people for the first time, especially older people or those more senior than you professionally, be formal. When introduced say "*madame*" or "*monsieur*", or even the rather passé "*enchanté* (delighted)" and wait for the people to indicate how they would like to be addressed. Stand up when a woman enters the room for the first time. Be aware that if it is your boss who has invited you to dinner, it is only as a courtesy—he

Entertaining at Home

You may have codes of your own, but it is the French codes you have to learn when entertaining Parisian friends in your home. Some things you'll like; some you may never get used to. Don't fight it.

- People are not usually invited over just for 'drinks'. But lately *le cocktail-dinatoire* (from about 6:30 pm to about 9:00 pm) is gaining in popularity, which is in effect drinks with enough interesting snacks to constitute a meal. Also, the French don't often have a buffet, where dishes are placed on the table and people can help themselves.
- Don't serve too many 'nibbles' before dinner, just champagne or fruit juice and a few nuts. The French save their appetites for dinner.
- Since your guests will straggle in late, don't prepare a dish that needs to be eaten at a certain time or one that will require you to stay in the kitchen cooking at the last minute.
- Young children will not eat with you and your guests unless it's a family dinner or lunch. If teenagers do, they are not to monopolise the conversation.

does not expect to be invited back and to become friends.

Don't bring flowers. Your hostess probably already has fresh flowers, and she wouldn't want to spend time arranging a bouquet that you've brought. If you want to do something with flowers, send an arrangement before or after. If you decide for some reason to bring flowers, do not bring chrysanthemums, which are generally put on graves, or carnations, which supposedly bring bad luck. It's best to ask the florist to send an appropriate bouquet.

Bringing a bottle of wine used to be frowned upon, as it seemed to insinuate that the host's wine cellar was not adequate or, worse, created a confusion if the host had already carefully selected wines for the evening's meal. Now, however, with a casual dinner among friends, people often

- Dress appropriately for the occasion, even if you are doing the cooking. Also make sure that your dishes are 'dressed', with parsley or sauces.
- Use cloth napkins, even for lunch.
- If you are unsure of which wines or cheeses to serve, ask the *caviste* at the wine shop or the *fromager* from the cheese shop for advice. The cheeses should be at room temperature. Take them out of the refrigerator at least an hour before you are to eat them.
- Learn to eat everything with a knife and fork, even fruit. With a fruit course, make sure your guests have the appropriate cutlery. When serving salad, lettuce leaves should be small enough to eat; otherwise you will notice that your guests fold but never cut them.
- Coffee is served after the cheese, fruit and dessert. Offer coffee, decaf or an *infusion* (herbal tea).
- You may clear the table of dishes no longer in use, but don't do the dishes until after your guests leave.

bring a bottle of wine. Your host will most likely put it aside for another time or may decide to include it in the dinner right away, if it is appropriate for the meal.

When your host shows you into the living room, stay there. Don't ask to see the rest of the apartment and don't wander around on your own. Don't go into the kitchen and offer to help the hostess. Just stay where you are put. Don't help yourself to the drinks that might be sitting on the sideboard and don't play the piano, if there is one. Just wait and talk with whomever else is there, or if you're alone pick up a magazine or look at the pictures on the walls or the view out the window.

If there's something you cannot eat, make sure your hostess knows it in advance. Don't use the dinner table to discuss your allergies or dislikes. Eat what is served to you; it's rude to leave things on your plate. Your hostess will ask if you'd like more: in general, you may take more of the main course but not the others. Don't help yourself—even if platters are on the table—unless instructed to do so. Generally, there will be two glasses, one for wine and the other for water. Your host will be generous in pouring, but it is best always to quench your thirst with water and to sip the wine for the taste. The myth of free-drinking French is just that—a myth.

If you have arrived on the *métro*, you may certainly ask to wash your hands before eating dinner; otherwise, avoid using the *toilettes* or leaving the table at all if you can help it. And for heaven's sake, don't announce where you're going; just indicate your question quietly to your host who will show or tell you where to go. Afterwards, sit back down at the table without referring to your absence.

Keep your free hand on the table. This stems from ancient times when people carried swords and daggers. Keeping the free hand on the table showed you meant no harm to the others.

If the dinner runs late, and the host asks whether anyone would like an orange juice or some other non-alcoholic drink, it is time to go. Don't offer to help with the dishes. Just thank your hosts, comment on something that was particularly delicious or enjoyable, then go home.

SETTLING IN

CHAPTER 5

'And each day I will see a little more of Paris,
study it, learn it as I would a book.'
—Henry James

FORMALITIES FOR RESIDENCE

Citizens from European Union (EU) countries do not normally need a passport when entering France from another EU country. However, some type of officially recognised identification such as a national identity card is always required, and passports are the most usually accepted. Also, an accompanying spouse who is not an EU citizen will need a passport to enter the country. Whether or not you need a passport to enter, however, it's important to have with you some sort of official identification.

All non-EU citizens need at least valid passports to enter the country. France also requires that visitors from some other countries have visas, as well. It's best to access the French embassy or consulate nearest you for the exact requirements. Then, with a passport (valid for six months after your departure date) and visa, if necessary, entering France entitles you to stay in France for three months.

Staying More Than Three Months

EU nationals generally have the right to decide where in the EU they want to reside and work. Thus citizens of the 28 member states of the EU do not need a *carte de séjour* (stay permit) to remain in France. This holds true for citizens of the European Economic Area (EEA) and Switzerland as well. Nonetheless, if asked, you will need to provide proof that you have sufficient income to remain in France, such as a bank statement or pension slips, showing that there is enough steady income to continue in the future. It may be helpful to have the *carte de séjour*, since some companies, banks, or other institutions may ask for it. The Europe Direct line gives information on many aspects of the European Union (tel: 00.800.67.89.10.11; http://ec.europa.eu/europedirect).

All non-EU citizens who want to stay in France for more than three consecutive months must obtain a long-stay visa. For questions and information about permits and requirements, check the French Office of Immigration and Integration (OFII) which has Information in English (www.ofii.fr). Another helpful website for expatriates that covers a multitude of issues is at www.justlanded.com.

The first step is to apply for the *visa de long séjour* (long-stay visa), which must be obtained before your departure at the French consulate with jurisdiction over your place of residence. Addresses and information on requirements can be found on their websites (see French Embassies on page 87). The French government requires the application to be made from your own country of citizenship, unless you reside in a different country, and a personal interview required. Processing the visa may take more than two months and some documents must be translated into French by a consulate-approved translator (*traducteur assermenté*). It is rarely possible for a non-EU citizen to enter France as a tourist and then change status.

Some Helpful Websites

- www.france.fr
  Official French website primarily for tourists, but with helpful deeper information, as well. See 'Practical Information'.
- http://paris.fr/english/guide-for-foreign-residents/p8140
  City of Paris. This URL takes you directly to the English-language 'Guide for Foreign Residents'.
- www.prefecture-police-paris.interieur.gouv.fr
  Préfecture de Police. Updates on regulations, changes in the city, etc. Some in English. For personal information, you will need to go in person to the Préfecture.

Documents to Bring

Bring as many of the following documents as possible for the entire family; in fact, bring anything you think might be pertinent. Documents that may need to be translated into French by an approved *traducteur assermenté* are marked with an asterisk. Make photocopies of every document and keep them separate from the originals.

- *Visa de long séjour*
- Proof of domicile, most likely an electricity bill in your name.
- Work permits (as appropriate)
- Passports for the whole family
- Photocopies of the first pages of your passports
- Extra passport photos
- Visa (as required)
- Birth certificate*
- Marriage certificate*
- Divorce certificate*
- Driver's license*

When you go to the Préfecture, take as many documents with you as possible: you will not always be told which documents are required, and if your dossier is not complete, you may have to come back again. You may also need to bring a stamped, self-addressed envelope. Although many of your daily transactions can be done paperless, the Préfecture still relies on paper documents. The Préfecture de Police is at 9 boulevard du Palais, île de la Cité (tel: 01.56.95.26.80).

THE TIMBRE FISCAL

Some official agencies require a revenue stamp rather than cash for their fee, a *timbre fiscal*. Previously, the *timbres fiscaux* could be bought at a tax office or at a *tabac*. Now, however, they can be purchased with a credit card online (http://timbres.impots.gouv.fr). Each transaction has an identification number, which you can then provide to the Préfecture.

- www.service-public.fr
  Link between administration and residents. Lists some of the legalities and obligations of living in France. In French.
- www.diplomatie.gouv.fr/en
  Government website with information for people coming to or investing in France.

French Embassies and Consulates

Citizens of non-EU countries should check the websites of the French embassies in their country or call for information on *visas de long séjour* (www.ambassade-france.com).

Report lost passports at the appropriate *commissariat de police* (police station) and take the report and two passport photos of the exact size specified to your consulate. It is always helpful to have extra photos with you, and this is when having a photocopy of the first pages of your passport will be most helpful.

Always carry your official identity papers with you, as the police have the right to ask anyone to show them. Also, inform the Préfecture of any change in your residence and show evidence of the new address: lease, rent receipt, electricity bill, etc. If your identity papers are lost or stolen, make a *déclaration de perte/ de vol* (report of loss/theft) at your local *commissariat*. Make copies of all your official documents when you receive them.

Carte de Séjour

There are various types of *cartes de séjour*, and each depends on the situation of the applicant. So, check the OFII and the Préfecture de Police websites several months in advance of the expiration of your visa, for getting the residence permit is a lengthy process. You will need the forms and list of requirements (including an in-person interview), which vary according to your type of visa. Don't put this off, for if your visa expires, you may have to return to your own country and start the entire process all over again. Make sure that all instructions and requirements are up to date, and follow all instructions scrupulously.

When dealing with *l'administration* (the bureaucracy),

adhere strictly to the rules. If a form says to bring three black-and-white photos of a certain size, do not diverge from the requirements. Never lose your temper, be sarcastic, or raise your voice, even if you believe you are right about something and the *fonctionnaire* (bureaucrat) is wrong. This won't help you in your quest.

Anglophone Embassies

Foreign embassies are most helpful to their citizens during times of crisis. They replace lost passports and provide information in emergencies, including information on appropriate doctors, dentists or lawyers who speak your language. They do not, however, help people to get out of jail. In emergencies, embassies may act as a liaison between the family at home and the person in France. It's a good idea to carry the telephone number of your embassy in your wallet.

For non-emergencies, embassies renew passports; record births, marriages and deaths; notarise documents and provide advice on matters such as absentee voting and the filing of taxes. Sometimes they offer information on local services, including lists of English-speaking doctors and attorneys, translators and international schools. Some have community liaison offices (of varying responsiveness). Embassies serving the greatest number of residents in Paris provide the most information, but basic services are the same.

Some countries allow their citizens to register their address in Paris, making it easier to replace lost passports, to be contacted in case of emergency, and to receive important alerts. Inquire at your embassy. Most embassies are open for consular affairs in the mornings only; find out when your embassy is open before going, and bring your passport to be allowed in. On the national holidays of both France and of your own country, the embassy will no doubt be closed. Some of the embassies may be on Facebook or have apps of their own. Check their websites.

Note that France, like many other countries, is constantly streamlining and trying to make more effective its immigration, residence, and naturalisation procedures. Thus, make sure to check the appropriate websites often to determine the current requirements that affect your own situation.

- **Australia:** 4 rue Jean-Rey, 75015;
  tel: 01.40.59.33.00; www.france.embassy.gov.au
- **Canada**: 35 avenue Montaigne, 75008;
  tel: 01.44.43.29.00; www.amb-canada.fr.
- **Ireland**: 12 avenue Foch, 75016 (embassy);
  4 rue Rude, 75016 (consulate);
  tel: 01.44.17.67.00; www.embassyofireland.fr
- **New Zealand**: 103 rue de Grenelle 75007;
  tel: 01.45.01.43.43; www.nzembassy.com/france
- **South Africa**: 59 quai d'Orsay, 75007;
  tel: 01.53.59.23.23; www.afriquesud.net
- **United Kingdom**: 35 rue du Faubourg Saint-Honoré, 75008
  (embassy); 18 bis rue d'Anjou, 75008 (consulate);
  tel: 01.44.51.31.00; www.ukinfrance.fco.gov.uk
- **United States**: 2 avenue Gabriel, 75008 (embassy); 75001;
  24-hour tel: 01.43.12.22.22; http://france.usembassy.gov;
  State Department's emergency tel (US): (1-202) 647-5226
  (Say it is an emergency and ask for the duty officer.)

Essential Resources for Anglophones

Even if you're without any French (yet), you can still find what you need in Paris, and in English too. Several print magazines and websites dedicated to Anglophones provide news and services, plus displaying advertisements for housing, products, jobs, various types of agencies, used furniture and appliances.

- www.fusac.fr
- paris.en.craigslist.fr
- www.paris.angloinfo.com
- www.thelocal.fr
- www.paris.expatriatesmagazine.com
- www.connexionfrance.com
- www.expatriates.com

FINDING YOUR PARISIAN NEST
Choosing a Hotel

Even with more than 3,000 hotels in Paris and almost 80,000 rooms, most of the better hotels in Paris are full most of the time. This holds true especially during the popular seasonal events such as the exclusive fashion shows that take place twice a year or the major trade fairs. It is best to make your reservations well in advance. If, however, for some reason you arrive in Paris without a reservation, you can go to the Paris Tourist Office at 25 rue des Pyramides, 75001 (tel: 08.92.68.30.00; multilingual www.parisinfo.com) or one of its branches and they will help find a hotel for you for the night. The main Tourist Office is open every day of the year except on 1 May.

There are hundreds of hotels ranging from sumptuous and exorbitant in price, to the basic and functional. Starting at the top is the recent "palace" rating, which indicates even more luxury than the previously-highest five-star elegantly pampering establishments. Others range from four stars down to the one star, and small boutique hotels are also popular. Dozens of international online hotel guides—including Expedia, Trivago, Priceline, Booking.com and Travelocity—offer a wide display of quality and price. The International hotel chains, such as Hilton, Marriott, Holiday Inn, and Hyatt have their own websites; check especially the Accor Hotels website which covers its Mercure, Sofitel,

Novotel, Libertel, Pullman, and Ibis hotels, all conveniently located around the city (www.accorhotels.com).

- www.parisinfo.com
- www.parishotels.com

Other Options

Bed and breakfasts have long offered a more intimate and less expensive experience than the more impersonal hotels (www.bedandbreakfast.com/paris-france.html). Size, amenities and locations vary, and occasionally in addition to the breakfast included in the price, there is a cocktail hour at the end of the day. Generally these are friendly, welcoming settings at good prices.

A relatively new—and controversial—player is **AirBnb**, (www.airbnb.com) which offers rentals of rooms, apartments, or even houses, by private citizens through the AirBnb company. Started only in 2008, the company, now with some 40 million bookings a year in 190 countries of the world, is gaining popularity. And this is impacting the traditional hotel industry; indeed, not all cities have welcomed AirBnb, for at first it circumvented the taxation system—the occupancy tax—that more traditional lodgings are required to adhere to, but this seems to be being resolved, at least in some places. It's also adversely impacting somewhat the permanent rental markets, as landlords make more money with short-term rentals than with long-term leases. And some of these lodgings, not by private citizens are not legal. But, more than half a million visitors to Paris used AirBnb in 2015, and now there are many thousands of places offered to rent. Of course the habitations vary, but photos are posted and the location specified, so you can see for yourself the options. Also, bookings are done legally through the AirBnb service, so there are at least some safeguards to the transactions. Nonetheless, check with the owner about your requirements and concerns. Allergic to cats? Non-smoking? A private bathroom? Concerned about the neighbourhood at night? Do your own checking to minimise disappointments. Note that the customer now is required to pay a small tax of 83 centimes per night in addition to the normal fees.

Vacation Rentals by Owner follows the same procedures, more or less, with lodgings by private owners offered through a central website, operated by Home Away, a vacation rentals firm with several sites (www.vrbo.com; www.homeaway.com). There are no booking fees, and booking through the service offers a protective fraud guarantee. If payment is made directly to the owner, however, make sure all your questions are answered by the owner, and arrange some protection for your payment.

Short-Term Home Exchange

The least expensive way to stay in Paris for a few weeks or months is home exchange. International home exchange companies list homes available worldwide in brochures and on the Internet. Members pay to list their homes, specifying the dates available, and can search for those in the city of their choice. In your listing, you should describe your home, the surroundings and amenities. You correspond with the people who respond, provide photos of the property, check recommendations of people who have stayed before in that apartment and come to an agreement. Again, ask questions about whether your own priorities will be met.

- **Homelink International** (www.homelink.org)
- **Intervac US** (www.intervac-homeexchange.com)
- **HomeExchange.com** (www.homeexchange.com)

Short-Term Apartments

For stays of more than a week, especially for stays of a month or more, consider *résidences hôtelières* (apartment hotels), which combine the comforts of an apartment with the amenities of a hotel. Suites are of various sizes and include cooking facilities. If regular cleaning services and a concierge are important to you, consider an apartment hotel, although, of course, they are much more expensive than a private apartment. An apartment hotel can be an easy way to spend a month or so, especially while searching for long-term lodgings. The companies below rent short-term, fully equipped apartments of various sizes and prices, as do many others you can find on the Internet. There are dozens of these rental services. Search until you find the right one for you.

Some people think of renting a furnished flat for cash from a private owner. But be aware that laws regulating this kind of rental are starting to be enforced, for the city is concerned that foreigners are buying apartments just to rent them out short-term, that no rental taxes are paid, and that Parisians do not have enough access to affordable housing.

- **Citadines Aparthôtels**: Chain of upmarket apartment hotels (tel: 01.41.05.79.05; www.citadines.com)
- **France Appartements**: Furnished apartments with all services at 97–99 avenue des Champs-Elysées, 75008 (tel: 01.56.89.31.00; www.rentapart.com)
- **Paris Appartements Services:** Short-term apartments at 20 rue Bachaumont, 75002
  (tel: 01.40.28.01.28; www.paris-apts.com)
- **Bridgestreet**: Serviced short-term apartments
  (tel for Europe: + 44 (0) 20 7792 2222; tel for Americas: (800) 278-7338; www.bridgestreet.com)
- **Cattalan Johnson Agency**: Full-service real estate agency (tel: 01.45.74.87.77; www.cattalanjohnson.com)
- **De Circourt Associates**: Full-service agency (tel: 01.43.12.98.00; www.parisrental.com)

Thinking about Apartments

As soon as you know your departure date and have at least a temporary place to stay, start thinking about permanent housing. If your company is sending you to Paris, discuss its relocation procedures. On your own, plan on making contacts well in advance of your departure. Three months in advance is not too early to begin inquiries, to place or look at ads, or to commit yourself with a deposit. If you plan to deal with real estate agencies, you will need time and patience. Call on weekdays, for many agencies are closed on weekends, and in August both landlords and agents may be away on holiday. If you plan to commit to a short-term apartment before you arrive, inquire about all amenities before you sign a contract, and if possible, ask someone you know in Paris to check it out.

It is hard these days to find a decent long-term rental apartment at a decent price. Indeed, for various reasons, including that some owners are not seeking renters, there are fewer apartments on the market. If you see articles discussing 'average' housing prices for rentals, this means, of course, that apartments in the less desirable *quartiers* cost less and those in the trendiest neighbourhoods cost more (if there are apartments to rent in these neighbourhoods at all). Visits to view apartments are sometimes *groupées*, so that everyone interested visits the apartment at the same time and turns in their well-documented *dossier* (application, along with financial and professional references) immediately. If you wait to think it over, you won't get the apartment.

Given the dearth of available rental apartments, landlords are extremely choosy. They ask that applicants for the smaller apartments earn at least four times the rent. Most landlords will ask that at least a year's rent be blocked in the tenant's interest-earning bank account, held against any transgression, such as non-payment of rent. The landlord will no doubt also ask for a *caution*, perhaps a month's rent, which may be used when the tenant leaves, in case there is any damage or remaining bills to be paid.

As for apartments for sale, sales are now increasing once again, and prices in the past year or so have risen by some 14 per cent. Of course, the amenities of each neighbourhood, the resale value of the apartment itself and convenience to the purchaser's lifestyle must all be factored into the overall cost.

Considerations

Do not dismiss a building that seems untended on the outside: many buildings are built around inner courtyards and may be pleasant and quiet on the inside. Many apartments in older buildings have also been modernised. Be sure to open the windows to gauge the amount of noise coming from the street, no matter how high up the apartment. Some relatively quiet streets become extremely noisy between 6:30 pm and 8:30 pm; others may be noisy if there is a late-running bus line or a late-night bar. Thus, do not inspect apartments in August or on weekends, when traffic is light and all of Paris seems calm. However, if the apartment has *double vitrage* (double-glazed) windows, much of the street noise will be filtered out when windows are closed.

Most, but not all, buildings have lifts. Think twice about renting or purchasing an apartment above the third floor of a building without a lift. Although the view may be lovely and the breeze cooling, it can get tedious climbing the stairs day after day, especially when carrying groceries, and the charm will fade quickly. If you wouldn't live in such a building at home, don't do it in Paris.

Many buildings now have a *gardien* who removes the garbage and maintains the building, but is not required to do personal services for the residents. Many live on the premises in a small *loge*, with fixed hours for service. Entry into the buildings is by *digicode* (key panel) or interphone system for secure entry.

When you see an apartment, inspect the appliances, if there are any. Since most kitchens come empty except for the sink—for rentals as well as purchase—some people negotiate the purchase of kitchen appliances and cupboards from the former resident. Otherwise, expect to purchase them for yourself.

Check the electrical wiring and whether all outlets for major appliances are grounded. Inquire about the heating system and check the hot water for temperature and pressure (especially in the shower). Ask whether the heating is *chauffage collectif*, meaning that heating is paid by the building and included in the building charges; or *chauffage individuel*, meaning that the resident pays directly for the heating. In this regard, look carefully at how well the windows close, for Paris is cold in winter and hot in summer. As most buildings have no air conditioning, see if there is more than one exposure, as cross ventilation can at least bring a welcome breeze in summer.

Inspect the facilities in the basement, including your *cave* (storage area in basement). Newer buildings may have underground parking, but the older ones do not and street parking is difficult. If there is no parking, inquire about garage possibilities in the neighbourhood (see also pages 167–168).

In this case, visit the garage to see how cars are parked and to determine hours when the car is retrievable.

Searching On Your Own

Sometimes, good apartments can be found by referrals from friends or in *les petites annonces* (classified ads) placed in newspapers by the owners themselves, who hope to avoid paying the landlord's share of the real estate commission. These ads often say *propriété à louer* (property for rent). Some landlords advertise privately in order to escape signing a lease, to avoid taxes, or perhaps because the apartment is not up to standard. Although the price might seem reasonable, do not accept substandard facilities or fail to be protected by a written contract. Ultimately, there are few bargains.

If an apartment appeals to you, call right away to set up an appointment. Some properties will have open houses, listed as *ce jour,* giving the time of the open house and the address. Bring your passport and *dossier* in case you decide to take the apartment. Because the rare, desirable, reasonably priced apartments go quickly, make a commitment as soon as you can.

If you do not speak French fluently, bring someone with you who does. Sign a document only after you have understood every word.

Understanding the Ads

To decipher advertisements, start with the building itself. Its location in the *quartier* is given as the closest *métro* stop. *Standing* means it is a high-class building, as does *bel immeuble*. Apartments are advertised by *pièce* (room), excluding bathroom and kitchen; by the area in square metres; or by the number of main rooms, as indicated by F1 or F2. An apartment of *deux pièces* has two rooms, plus a kitchen and bathroom. A *studio* is one room and a *studette* may be as small as 18 sq m. A *chambre* may be as small as a *studette*, but without cooking facilities or a shower. *Mezzanine* means there is a loft for a bed. Pay attention to size, for an apartment of 55 sq m, despite the number of rooms, might be too small for your needs. On the other hand, most apartments—except for the old, elegant and extremely expensive—tend to be small, and kitchens and bathrooms especially may not be as large as what you are used to.

Some ads will mention *wc séparé* (separate room for the toilet) plus a *salle de bains* (a room with sink plus bathtub) or *salle de douche* (with a shower).

Unfurnished apartments may have no built-in *placards* (closets) and free-standing *armoires* must then be purchased. *La cuisine* (the kitchen), as mentioned above, may be equipped with only a sink and outlets for you to install your own appliances, unless the ad says *cuisine équipée* or *cuisine aménagée*. A *cuisine américaine* means that the kitchen opens to the living room, perhaps separated only by a bar. An apartment on the *RdeC* (*Rez-de-Chaussée*) is at street level, and an apartment on the *1er étage* means it is one level above. Ads for apartments higher up usually indicate whether or not there is an *ascenseur* (lift). *Cave* indicates a storage area in the basement. *Parking* indicates a garage space and *box* means the garage space has a lockable door.

Agences Immobilières

To look for a long-term apartment, it is best to work with an *agent immobilier* (real estate agent) or relocation service about three months in advance. Agents prefer working on exclusive contracts and smaller agents generally specialise in their own districts—this means you may have to work with several agents in different *arrondissements*. Agents in each *arrondissement* display, in their windows, descriptions of their most desirable listings, usually pinpointed by the closest *métro* stop. All reputable agencies are licensed: their documents show their financial guarantor, insurance company and other references. Also, be aware that agents represent the interests of the landlord, not the tenant.

When contacting an agent, be as clear as you can about your requirements, although these might change as you start viewing what is available. Specifying your budget, location preferences and special needs can help an agent target apartments. Contact an agent several months in advance and follow up by telephone. Ask the agent about financial documents you will need to show in order to be accepted by a landlord. Commissions generally run from 10–15 per cent of a year's rent but are not regulated. Most often the commission is shared by the landlord and the tenant. Ask agents about their commissions and the services included, which sometimes encompasses drawing up the lease and making an inventory of the apartment. There may be a separate charge for drawing up the lease.

Relocation Services

Relocation agencies provide personalised services for the new resident in Paris. Helpful when contacted several months before arrival, their services can be crucial for people who do not have much advance notice of their move, for they can step in quickly with good results. They work first with real estate agencies to find appropriate housing and are experts in negotiating prices. Used to dealing with bureaucratic requirements and formalities, they can help navigate the complicated tangle of work and resident permits, car registration and insurance. They also provide valuable information on schools, household insurance and how to get utilities hooked up. Staff members speak English and are used to dealing with the concerns of newcomers.

Relocation agencies charge a flat fee for all services. They are expensive, but depending on your circumstances and the

Searching on the Internet

If you register with some of these Internet sites below and list your apartment preferences, you will receive an *alerte* when there is an apartment available that matches your criteria. Check the websites daily.

- www.pap.fr
- www.avendrealouer.fr
- www.seloger.com
- www.immostreet.com
- www.lesiteimmobilier.com
- www.explorimmo.com

extent of your needs, well worth the price. They often work with companies that are transferring their employees. See if your company works with a particular relocation service and if they pay all fees. Below are a few current relocation agencies. There are many others, but with any you are considering, be sure to specify your particular requirements in an interview to see if you they can meet your needs.

- 7ᵉ: **A Good Start in France** (8 rue de l'Exposition; tel: 01.45.50.25.30; www.agoodstart.fr)
- 17ᵉ: **Cosmopolitan Services Unlimited** (89 rue de la Boetie; tel: 01.44.90.10.00; www. cosmopolitanservices.com)
- Gennevilliers: **Executive Relocations** (9 rue Thomas Edison, Gennevilliers 92230; tel: 08.21.02.90.90; 01.41.21.70.70; www.executive-relocations.com)

FURNISHED APARTMENTS

Furnished apartments rented by the week or month are more expensive than those leased for a year. Studios and one-bedroom apartments are sought after and thus proportionately more expensive than large ones. There is a great deal of turnover in short-term apartments, so with some effort, reasonably priced, furnished lodgings can be found.

Most people who come to Paris to stay for less than a year rent under short-term contracts. Short-term vacation rentals are not governed by law, but furnished apartments with a rental duration of one year are subject to almost the same laws as unfurnished ones, if the apartment is the primary residence of the tenant. The lease on these apartments (*bail à usage d'habitation en meublé*) can sometimes be negotiated. Real estate agents' commissions are paid by the tenant. Ensure that the landlord has a comprehensive homeowner's policy, even if you are just renting for a year.

Previously, furnished apartments were only required to be equipped with a table, chair and bed. Now however, the lodging must allow the tenant to sleep, eat and live there comfortably in terms of the 'expectations of daily life', so you should inquire specifically about the items you require, such as a desk, a microwave or toaster. Ask the landlord for a detailed inventory (*inventaire détaillé*) and make sure it matches what is actually there. Check and report in writing any irregularities in the apartment, so that you will not be charged for damage upon leaving. Do not hesitate to specify every furniture scratch and stain. When vacating the apartment, the inventory will be checked once again.

UNFURNISHED APARTMENTS

Unfurnished long-term apartments are usually offered in three-year leases (*bail de location* or *bail de trois ans*) if the landlord is a private individual, and for six years if the landlord is a professional or a corporation. Leases are renewed automatically if no notice is issued by the tenant. When giving up the apartment, three months' notice is required (less if the tenant is being transferred abroad), and the letter sent to the landlord must be sent *en recommandée avec accusé de réception* (registered mail with notice of receipt). A tenant, however, may be given notice six months prior to the anniversary date of the lease, and reasons for terminating the lease must be specified: non-payment of rent, impending sale of the apartment, if the owner intends to occupy the apartment, or if it needs to undergo major renovation. A tenant may not be evicted between October and April for any reason.

Rent increases are regulated by law and calculated annually. The landlord will require the caution of up to a year's rent, which stays blocked for the entire length of the lease. The landlord pays interest on the entire sum on deposit. You can pay your rent by cheque or have it deducted from your bank account. Whichever way you decide to pay, request from the landlord a monthly *quittance de loyer* (receipt) for your records.

All residents of a building pay *charges* (miscellaneous expenses), which cover garbage pickup, maintenance of the common areas and lift, landscaping, etc. Housing law states quite clearly which charges may be passed on to the tenant and in which proportion, so if your prospective landlord is an individual and not an established corporation, ask about the charges, what they cover and how they are assessed. These charges, along with the rent, are generally adjusted once a year. Also pay attention to the *taxe d'habitation* (habitation tax) paid by all residents on 1 January. This tax is assessed according to the value of the property, so the more expensive apartments and *arrondissements* have higher taxes.

Before the actual move, the tenant and the landlord conduct the *état des lieux* (inspection of the state of the premises), using a special form that is signed by both tenant and landlord. This procedure is important, for it protects the tenant upon termination of the lease, when the landlord will inspect and charge for any damages. Expect to spend about an hour discussing and noting any damage to the apartment, no matter how minute. Sometimes a *hussier* (bailiff) may be asked to conduct the *état des lieux*; if so, the fee is split between landlord and tenant, since it is a service for both. If you do need to make some repairs or adjustments, get a written *devis* (estimate of charges) from the contractor before starting any work.

PURCHASING AN APARTMENT

Apartments in Paris are generally *en copropriété* (condominiums), in which the resident owns outright the apartment and, jointly with the others in the building, the common areas. The apartment building is almost always managed by an outside *syndic* (a company specialising in building management); the running of the building depends on the *syndic*. The purchaser has the right to know about the financial condition of the condominium association, as well as seeing the bylaws and minutes of previous annual meetings.

If you are considering buying property as a speculative investment, understand that France taxes the worldwide income of its residents. Don't forget too, that property transfer taxes of up to 20 per cent are paid by the seller, and this affects the price of the property—upon buying and resale. In addition, if the resale is under two years, the transaction may be deemed as speculation, with a high capital gains tax. Thus, if you are considering the purchase of a property with the intention of selling it again, explore fully the tax ramifications both in France and your home country.

Upon deciding on a property, the buyer signs a *compromis de vente* (contract) and makes a down payment of about

10 per cent, which commits both buyer and seller, although the buyer has the right to back out within seven days after signing the contract. The *promesse de vente* allows the buyer three months to confirm the purchase and find a loan. Do not sign an *offre d'achat*, which commits the buyer but not the seller, unless it is written with the help of a professional. A secured *offre d'achat* must describe the premises, the amount of the offer and the duration of the validity of the offer (two weeks is the standard). Here too the buyer has the right to back out within seven days. For the buyer, expect closing costs to add about 8.5 per cent to the costs.

All transactions are completed by a *notaire*, a member of the legal profession who deals with real estate and family law. Acting on behalf of both parties (although sometimes each party is represented by a separate *notaire*), the *notaire* researches, prepares and signs all documents. The *notaire* can be crucial to the successful completion of a business transaction. The number of *notaires* in each district is limited and their fees are fixed by law. No matter how well you speak French, choose a bilingual notary. Ask friends who have bought property, at the bank where you are considering taking out a mortgage, or contact the Chambre des Notaires de Paris at 12 avenue Victoria, Paris 75001; (tel: 01.44.82.24.00; www.paris.notaires.fr). Check also a helpful website in English that details real estate sales and purchase (http://notary-paris.co.uk).

Borrowing Money

Many French banks have mortgage plans for foreign buyers, some lending money in whatever currency is required. Mortgages can be at fixed or variable rates and usually run from 15 to 20 years. The amount of downpayment varies.

UCB, a division of BNP Paribas, offers mortgages, with an English-language service (tel: 0800.169.8470; from France: 03.20.18.18.44; www.international-buyers.bnpparibas.com). UK's Barclays also offers home loans and other personal loans in France (tel: 01.55.78.72.27; www.barclays.fr).

Credit Agricole, one of France's major banks, offers Britline, full-service banking, including mortgages, in English (tel: 02.31.55.67.89; www.britline.com).

MOVING YOUR BELONGINGS

Anyone with a legal right to live in France and who has lived outside France during the previous year may transfer used personal belongings—including personal vehicles—without customs charges. EU citizens do not need to go through customs formalities but must have an inventory of the goods. The rest of this section concerns non-EU nationals, who should be aware of the current regulations when they are ready to move. Regulations do change, and if the belongings are for a secondary residence, the requirements are somewhat different. Inquire about all requirements well in advance of shipping, and then adhere to them exactly. Non-EU citizens may import household goods duty free within 12 months of taking up residence in France.

In addition to checking with your French consulate, information in French can be found in Paris from the Centre de Renseignements Douaniers at 84 rue d'Hauteville 75010 (tel: 08.11.20.44.44; www.douane.gouv.fr).

Large international movers such as Allied, Mayflower, United Van Lines and many other large moving companies are experts in transatlantic shipping. Inquire of a mover in your area about its international procedures and affiliates in France and how it can help with bureaucratic requirements for documentation. Some post a list of the required documents on their websites. International carriers can ship and pack almost any item, including automobiles, and will provide free estimates. Some will split shipments between the cheaper sea carriers and the more expensive and faster air carriers. Prices and services vary, so shop around. Ensure that the service on both sides is door-to-door and ask how long it will take for an expected delivery date. Insurance should cover full value of the belongings. It may take as little as two weeks for your shipment to arrive from overseas, or, depending on the ports of exit and entry, it may take up to a month.

To take household possessions out of France, residents must prove that all tax statements have been filed. Some of the international movers post the customs regulations on their websites. Upon clearance, a *quitus fiscal* will be issued, allowing the goods to leave France.

SETTLING INTO YOUR HOME

Once you've found your apartment, you'll want to get settled. This entails, before all else, insuring your home, changing the electricity and gas to your name from that of the previous tenant, and installing the telephone, Internet connections and cable. Each of these actions involves different procedures and must be done immediately, perhaps even before you've actually made the physical move. Then you can start thinking about making the improvements to the apartment that will make living more comfortable—buying the appliances and cabinets for the kitchen, light fixtures for the ceilings (many apartments don't come with them) and even the little things such as the hooks for the backs of doors.

First, Insure Your Home

Even before you move in, inquire of your relocation agency or real estate broker about insurance agencies. This concerns not only home owners but also tenants with a lease, who are required to have property insurance. The most common policy is assurance *multirisques habitation* (multi-risk insurance), covering theft and water and fire damage, as well as third-party liability. Inquire in advance as to your insurer's requirements to ensure that the locks and shutters conform to specifications. Make sure to get a *constat à l'amiable* from your agent, so you can file a claim within the required three days after damage occurs.

Most insurance agencies also handle health insurance and insurance for children in schools. Some well-known insurance companies are AXA, AGF, MACIF and MAAF. Be sure to shop around, compare prices and services and ask among your friends about their experiences with these companies when they have claims to submit. For health insurance supplemental policies, see pages 128–130.

Then, Think Electric

France uses 220 volt, 50-hertz electricity. All current in Western Europe is the same and even most plugs are similar, so people coming from these countries do not need special *adaptateurs*

A Parisian neighbourhood in autumn.

(adaptor plugs). British appliances using 240 volts will not normally need a *transformateur* (transformer), but they will need the continental two-prong plug. Otherwise, if you are thinking of bringing large appliances with you that run on 120 volts, you will no doubt need a transformer as well as the adaptor. Transformers change the voltage, but not the hertz, so both must be appropriate. Some appliances will not function and others such as clock-radios may run too slowly if the hertz are not the same.

Computers, smartphones, tablets and some other electronic devices are meant to be used internationally, generally switching automatically from one current to another. If you have doubts, look at the 'brick' (where the power information is displayed on the cord): if it says 120–240v; 50–60hz, it will switch automatically. Small appliances such as hair dryers also come with dual voltage, often with a small switch to turn to the appropriate setting. If not, adaptors and transformers are available at electronic shops, hardware stores and department stores.

Electricity is expensive in France and people are used to doing more with less. This accounts for the minuterie in the halls of apartment buildings—the button people press for the hall lights to come on, which only stay lit for a few minutes before switching off automatically. Nor do gas stoves waste gas by keeping pilot lights on all the time; instead people usually light the burner or oven each time it is to be used. These may be inconveniences at first for North Americans, but you'll quickly get used to it.

Also, the amount of electricity that comes into your apartment may not allow you to use a clothes washer and dishwasher at the same time. When you contact EDF/GDF (see page 107) for the initial contract, discuss the level of electricity you require and the price for each option.

Note that lamps brought from non-European countries usually need only an adaptor and a French light bulb. Light bulbs historically have been of three types: the French standard circular-bottomed bulb with two prongs that is turned and locked into place, a screw type (*ampoule à vis*), and the older but occasionally still-used bayonet with two

Plugs

- Electric plug: Round with two prongs underneath and a hole centred above, which accepts the ground wire pin (*prise de terre*) that protrudes from the wall outlet. Only a few old, uncovered outlets don't have the pin. All your large appliances should be grounded. Adaptors can be found in hardware stores, at BHV and at Leroy Merlin.
- Telephone plug: Long and narrow, with an extended one-piece insert. Plugs into which the international RJ11 can be inserted can be obtained at Orange shops, FNAC, Darty, electronic shops, and hardware stores.

pins (*ampoule à baïonnette*). The new energy-efficient LED bulbs are increasingly replacing the older incandescent styles, which are slowly being phased out.

EDF/GDF

To inquire about opening your electric and gas account, it would probably be easiest just to go to the EDF/GDF (Electricité de France/Gaz de France) office in your *arrondissement* with a copy of your lease (tel: 01.40.42.22.22; tel in English: 09.69.36.63.83; www.edf.fr). Also bring your chequebook and RIB (*relevé d'identité bancaire*), which is the official identification of your bank account. (For information on the RIB, see page 143).

The *factures* (bills) for electricity and gas are sent every two months. They are based on the previous year's usage; meters are read only a couple of times a year. Thus, if your current usage is less than before, an adjustment will be made on a future bill. You can pay your bill by cheque if you wish; the most common method of paying utility bills is to have the amount deducted directly from your bank account (*prélèvement bancaire*), having provided EDF/GDF with a copy of your RIB. You receive your bills well in advance of the payment date, giving you time to dispute the amount if needed.

France Télécom/Orange

The previous standard France Télécom has now become Orange (www.orange.fr). Although there are other providers of phone services, Orange is still the major provider in France. Along with the newer providers, it offers high-speed Internet and television programming among its options. To meet the growing competition, prices are coming down and services are going up: inquire about all services and costs before subscribing and check out some of the other providers (see page 109).

There is at least one Orange office in each district that handles telephone matters for that area, including bill payment, sales and rental of equipment and subscription to new services. Telephones must be registered in the leaseholder's name. To obtain service, telephones, and telephone books, bring identification and proof of domicile. It's best to go personally, so you can discuss options such as call forwarding, and also the different pricing plans (customer service tel: 1014; English-speaking helpline: 09.69.36.39.00).

Telephone bills are sent bimonthly and also are deducted automatically from your French current account (*compte courant*). An itemised bill (*facture détaillée*) will be sent to you in advance of the date the amount is deducted from your account, giving you time to dispute the bill, if needed. Otherwise, if bills are not paid on time, it is routine for the service to be cut off and a 10 per cent fine levied for reinstatement.

Internet and Cable Television

To hook up to the Internet, no matter who the provider is, you will need either a telephone or a cable connection. For a telephone connection, ask Orange when ordering your telephone service, or with the provider you choose. (See pages 148–149.) For a cable connection, see pages 1051–152 for Internet communication companies. One is Numericable, which is the major cable television company in Paris (tel: 01.77.46.80.80; www.offres.numericable.fr).

Ordering Internet is easier than cancelling a contract. With some providers you have to give notice by registered letter, or there might be a penalty—with exceptions such as moving to a foreign country, being unemployed or under long-term care. You will also have to return the equipment. So, inquire when you order your service everything that might apply to you.

Appliances

Most kitchens come empty except for the sink, so you will have to think about appliances and cabinets. If you are thinking of bringing large appliances from your country, make sure they fit the rooms—kitchens tend to be smaller than what you might be used to. Also, if your appliances are brands not common in Europe, finding parts and service when they break down may be difficult. In general, it may be more economical to purchase appliances in Paris.

Most washing machines in France heat the water internally, using only a cold water tap, so if the washer you import depends on an external hot water tap, it may wash clothes only in cold water. In addition, some apartments are not vented for tumble dryers, but convection dryers are almost as efficient. Many people just don't use dryers at all.

If you have your own washing machine (as well as a dishwasher), you must remember that the water in Paris is extremely 'hard'. This means that minerals (*calcaire*) will build up in the pipes. Products such as Calgonite can prevent this build-up in washing machines and are sold next to detergents. For dishwashers, special salts (*sel*) must be inserted into the machine, as well as a rinsing (*rinçage*) product to avoid streaks on glasses. (A light comes on to inform you when they need to be replenished.)

Major department stores such as BHV (see pages 111; 291) sell appliances, as do the hypermarchés. Occasionally, a shop will be slightly flexible in its prices when several large, expensive items are purchased, or if you are a known customer. Ask about warranties on new products and about *service après-vente/dépannage à domicile* (after sales service/repair), for some shops require 'smaller' items—even something as large as a microwave oven—to be brought back to the store, charging extra for a home call. It is best to get warranties on products and to use licensed repairmen.

Large appliances are delivered and installed. Make sure everything works before the installer leaves; the driver will take back damaged goods. Some stores claim no responsibility for repairs or exchange if damage is discovered after the delivery person has left, although this is slowly changing as France begins to understand the concept of 'customer service'. (In this regard, inspect, too, all delivered furniture before the driver leaves.)

Darty is a major national chain of stores selling appliances and electronics and is known for its excellent *service après-vente*. There are some 15 stores in Paris, including in the Centre Beaugrenelle, so it's best to access its website (www.darty.com).

Cabinets and Equipment

Department stores such as BHV carry all equipment for your apartment, including kitchen and bathroom fittings.

- **IKEA**, the extensive international chain, has six stores in the Paris surrounds, with an enormous selection of home items, including kitchen and bathroom cabinets (www.ikea.com).
- **Habitat** has seven stores in Paris selling furniture and kitchen and bathroom items (www.habitat.net).

For the Bricoleur

Drogueries or hardware stores in every neighbourhood sell home improvement and hardware items, but two centrally located stores offer everything the *bricoleur* (DIY enthusiast) might ever need. Both have warrens of aisles filled with stacks of merchandise and tools, and their staff is generally helpful.

- **BHV** (14 rue du Temple, 75004, the entrance is on rue de Rivoli, across from the Hôtel de Ville; tel: 09.77.40.14.00; www.bhv.fr)
- **Leroy Merlin** (52 rue Rambuteau, 75002; tel: 01.44.54.66.66; www.leroymerlin.fr)

Self-Storage

If your apartment is smaller than you thought it would be and it cannot hold all your household items, consider renting a self-storage locker. Units, clean and dry, come in various sizes. The renter keeps the key and has sole access to the locker. Check to see the hours of access.

- **Une Pièce en Plus/Access Self Stockage**: Offers some 20 self-storage locations. (tel: 0 800 403 405; www.unepieceenplus.com)

A CHILD'S WORLD

Getting your children set for a long stay in Paris should not be difficult. Anything you can find at home for your child can be found here. As in most large cities, disposable diapers, baby bottles and pureed foods are found at supermarkets, and health food shops are now also plentiful. Inoculations required are similar to those in other countries and there are many English-speaking pharmacists and pediatricians. Childhood diseases in Paris are the same as anywhere else, so be prepared for the usual colds and sore throats, especially when children go to school. See pages 125–127 for health-related issues and vaccinations.

French parents expect their children to be well-behaved, and they are. The French view of childhood may not be as relaxed as in other countries, but there are countless opportunities for scheduled activities, structured events and sports. Museums have special educational programmes for children, and puppet theatres and circuses schedule their entertainment for when children are out of school. Activities *hors scolaires* (extra-curricular) are encouraged and often arranged in both public schools and international bilingual schools. Most public libraries have children's books, records and videos; several are devoted entirely to children. Playgrounds and sporting facilities are found in every *arrondissement*. So all told, a child's experience in Paris, although highly structured, should be rewarding and pleasant.

Contacts and Resources

Message (www.messageparis.org) is an English-speaking group for families with young children, as well as expectant and new mothers. Message organises meetings, events, parenthood classes, baby and toddler groups and a working mother's group. Message publishes *The ABCs of Parenting in Paris*, which is an extensive guide to family living in Paris. As Message is a volunteer organisation, contacts change and it's best to access the website to find the latest information.

Paris Mômes (www.parismomes.fr) has an excellent resources site, with boutiques around Paris and an informative magazine that may be subscribed to.

Also interesting for parents of very young children is another English-speaking group called Mums of Paris (www.meetup.com/English-Speaking-Mums-of-Paris), which organizes coffee meetups and events at various venues.

The international organisation La Leche League (www.lalecheleague.org/paris.html) offers information and support about breastfeeding, and the groups with other new mothers.

The *mairie* of your *arrondissement* should also have detailed information about all aspects of schooling in Paris.

Day Care

The French believe in early socialisation for their children. It is widely held that children who have attended day care perform better in their early school years than children who have not, so a high percentage of babies and toddlers are sent to day care.

Some 520 public *crèches* (day-care centres) operate within Paris. *Crèches* are subsidised, with fees based on income and need. *Crèches* are extremely over-enrolled, and many expectant mothers register their child even before birth, so it's better to start looking early. Your *mairie* should have a list of the municipal *crèches* in the *arrondissement* and advice on how to enroll a child.

Children are dropped off at the *crèche* between 8:00 am and 10:00 am and picked up between 4:00 pm and 6:00 pm. A *crèche parentale* is run on the same principle, but parents volunteer in various capacities, so the fees are slightly lower.

An *halte garderie* is flexible in its hours. If there is a place available, a parent may deposit a child for a few hours. The system is designed for mothers who need to schedule appointments or go shopping for a few hours without the child. Children are not registered in advance and a place is not guaranteed on any given day. An *halte garderie privée* is more like a *crèche* in that the child is registered and comes on a regular basis, but the hours are flexible. Unfortunately, as with the *crèches*, there are few spaces available.

French Educational System

The French public school system is demanding and rigorous. For detailed information on the educational system, access the city's website and its 'Guide for Foreign Residents' noted on page 85.

A helpful, comprehensive booklet is *Guide to Education in France*, published by American Women Living in France (AAWE; tel: 01.40.70.11.80; www.aaweparis.org). Cost: €25.

Non-compulsory
- Age 2: *jardins d'enfants* (pre-nursery schools)
- Ages 3-6: *écoles maternelles* (nursery schools).

Compulsory Elementary Education
From the ages 6–16: each student has a *carnet du liaison*, a permanent file with grades and teachers' comments entered year after year.

- *École primaire* (can be coeducational or not). Progresses from preparatory to elementary to intermediate levels. Usually finishes around age 10.
- *Premier cycle* is the *collège* (which should not be confused with the English 'college'). Here, education begins according to each child's aptitude and interests.
- *Deuxième cycle* is the *lycée*, which usually starts around age 15 and lasts until the student graduates at about 18 years of age.
- From ages 15 to 17, preparation for the *baccalauréat* (*bac*). The *bac*, equivalent to and as stringent as the British 'A' levels, is obligatory for university entrance.

Holidays and Days Off
There is a major school break (*les vacances d'été*) of more than two months each summer and there are several shorter but substantial holidays throughout the year: February, November, Christmas and Easter.

Foreign Children in Schools
Selecting a child's school will, of course, be based on many factors besides a school's location or reputation. The age, character and language ability of the child should be considered, as well as the expected length of stay in Paris and perhaps a planned return to a school or university at home. A few parents put their children into French schools immediately. Some parents who are based abroad for the long term prefer private, bilingual schools throughout the child's educational career. Others start their children in the bilingual schools, and after a period of adjustment and language learning, move them into the public or private

French schools. Some people who transfer to several countries over the years prefer international schools, such as Marymount, where the curriculum tends to be standard and grade levels are transferable from country to country.

Foreign children are accepted into French public schools if their French is adequate to progress within the instructional programme. Children in primary schools may enter a conversion programme to learn French (*classe de* CLIN), after which they are placed in the regular system. Schools are crowded and applications should be made in the spring before the fall term; places may not be available, especially in the *maternelle*.

To enroll, bring your child's birth certificate, vaccination certificate (including smallpox, BCG and tetanus), proof of domicile and school records from previous schools. Children must also be insured when they enroll in a school, so if you are asked, show proof of insurance. (See pages 129–130 for insurance companies.) Although public schools are free, there are small charges for textbooks, supplies and meals.

Bilingual Schools

Paris and its suburbs offer more than a dozen international, bilingual or English-language, elementary and high schools.

The international curriculum is stringent, for acceptance into the best European universities is highly competitive. The private schools may be expensive and tuition varies greatly. In general though, costs are pretty much in line with other international schools. Transportation to schools in the suburbs can often be arranged at extra cost, although this may depend on how far into Paris the school buses go. Some important schools are in the suburbs, such as St-Germain-en-Laye.

This list is not exhaustive, so check with your embassy and the AAWE compendium described on page 113.

Bilingual Nursery/Lower Schools and Play Groups

- 7^e: **Montessori Schools:** For children from three to six. (65 quai d'Orsay; for other addresses in Paris, access the website; tel: 01.45.55.13.27; www.Montessori-paris.org).

- 7^e: **Lennen Bilingual School**: An international school that offers bilingual cirriculum for students up to 11 years old, or to fifth grade. It has three locations: 65 quai d'Orsay (tel: 01.47.05.66.55); the kindergarten at 145 rue Saint-Dominique (tel: 01.53.59.90.73); the primary school at 176 rue de Grenelle (tel: 01.44.42.99.00; www.lennenbilingual.com).

- 15^e: **First Steps**: A preschool providing a friendly environment for children from two to five to develop at their own pace. (rue Emile Duclaux; tel: 01.42.19.02.14; www.firststeps.fr).

- 16e: **United Nations Nursery School**: Private school with an international population of students from two to six years old. (40 rue Pierre-Guérin; tel: 01.45.27.20.24; www.unns.net).

- 17e: **La Petite École Bilingue**: For children from preschool to fifth grade, offers education in French/English and French/Russian. (8 place de la Porte de Champerret; tel: 01.43.80.25.34; http://petiteecolebilingue.free.fr).

Bilingual Elementary/High Schools

- 7e: **Collège-Lycée International de Paris Honoré de Balzac**: Public French school that offers free bilingual education, adapted to the needs of international students.

(118 boulevard Bessières; tel: 01.53.11.12.13; http://lyc-balzac.ac-paris.fr).

- 15ᵉ: **École Active Bilingue Jeannine-Manuel**: Peparations for the American SAT, French or International Baccalaureate, with most substantive courses taught in English. Preschool through high school. (70 rue du Théâtre; tel: 01.44.37.00.80; www.eabjm.com).

- 16ᵉ: **Institut de la Tour**: Catholic high school with a section for English speakers. Students prepare for the *bac*. (86 rue de la Tour; Anglophone Section tel: 01.45.04.73.35; www.institutdelatour.com).

- 16ᵉ: **International School of Paris**: From preschool through high school, US and International Baccalaureate programmes. French language instruction. Separate locations for lower, middle and upper schools, all in the 16ᵉ. (6 rue Beethoven; tel: 01.42.24.09.54; www.isparis.edu)

- 17ᵉ: **Ecoole Internationale Bilingue**: Bilingual education from preschool to high school. Five campuses in central Paris, offering curriculum leading to the baccalaureate, the American SAT and British 'A' levels. (117 boulevard Malesherbes; tel: 01.45.63.62.22; www.eab.fr).

- **American School of Paris**: Preschool through high school. American curriculum and the baccalaureate. In operation since 1946, this school has a good mix of nationalities, of which about 60 per cent is American. (41 rue Pasteur, 92210 Saint-Cloud; tel: 01.41.12.82.82; www.asparis.org)

- **British School of Paris**: British curriculum, with an emphasis on French, from preschool through high school; about 70 per cent of the students are British. Students prepare for the 'A' levels. French classes. (Senior school is at 38 quai de l'Ecluse, 78290 Croissy-sur-Seine; Junior school is at 2 rue Hans List, Croissy-sur-Seine; Tel: 01.34.80.45.96; www.britishschool.fr).

- **Lycée International**: Public school, with fee-paying international sections. From preschool through high school; British, American and French curricula are offered. Foreign students take special classes, then a fully bilingual curriculum. (rue du Fer-à-Cheval, BP 230, 78105 St-Germain-en-Laye Cedex; Lycée International tel:

01.39.10.94.11; www.lycee-international.ac-versailles. fr; American Section tel: 01.34.51.74.85; www. americansection.org).

- **Sections Internationales de Sèvres**: French public schools, with fee-paying international sections. Bilingual education with courses in English or German; special courses for non-French speakers. Preparation for the *bac*. (1 parvis Charles de Gaulle, 92310 Sèvres; tel: 01.72.77.70.40; http://sis-sevres.net).
- **Marymount School**: Independent Catholic coed school from preschool through eighth grade, for children of any religion. American curriculum and a French language programme. About 50 per cent native English speakers. (72 boulevard de la Saussaye, 92200 Neuilly-sur-Seine; tel: 01.46.24.10.51; admissions tel: 01.72.77.70.45; www.marymount.fr).

After-School Activities

Most of the international schools arrange some after-school activities. In addition, active English-language scouting and guides troops are open to children of all ages and nationalities. Because troop leaders change, the most reliable information is usually available at your particular embassy and the international schools. For city-sponsored after-school activities, your *mairie* should have information on activities and sports venues in the *arrondissement*, including the *centres des loisirs* that are in each day care and elementary school. And of course, both English-language and French bookshops sell guides of activities for children when they're not in school. Inquire about:

- **ADAC** (*Association pour le Developpement et l'Animation Culturelle*), the public organisation for continuing education, offers a vast variety of courses for children at centres throughout Paris.
- **Ludothèques** (games centres), which offer play-related learning activities, and games and toys to play with and to borrow.
- **Les Centres d'animation** (activity centres) which offer educational, sporting and cultural, activities and outings

There are international schools and curricula in Paris to fit your children's needs; soon enough, they should be as at ease as these French students.

to after-school on Wednesdays, Saturdays and during school vacations.

Parc de la Villette

Once children have discovered the Parc de la Villette, they may not want to go anywhere else (tel: 01.40.03.75.75; www.villette.com). Encompassing about 55 hectares at the northeastern edge of the city, this urban educational park was constructed in 1979 on the site of the city's former slaughterhouse. There are theme gardens and activity parks, a lighted promenade, playgrounds, bicycle paths, pony rides, day-care centres, restaurants, entertainment centres and a spectacular high-tech, interactive museum. Films, concerts, a planetarium and undersea exhibits are all designed for children, from pre-schoolers onwards. For schedules of events, check the website.

The Cité des Sciences et de l'Industrie at 30, avenue Corentin-Cariou, 75019 (tel: 01.40.05.80.00; www.cite-sciences.fr) is the ultra-modern, hands-on science museum. Note that it is closed Mondays, New Year's Day, 1 May and 25 December.

The Géode is an enormous hemispheric screen showing documentaries to viewers seated in the centre (reservations tel: 08.92.68.45.40; www.lageode.fr).

Educational Entertainment

In addition to museum programmes, educational entertainment can be found throughout the city. *Pariscope* and *L'Officiel des Spectacles*, the weekly events magazines, have listings for children's activities, as do the major newspapers. Access the website www.lamuse.net which displays up-to-date details on children's and family activities.

And, of course, museums and more that are sure to delight:

- 3e: **Musée de la Poupée:** Doll museum exhibiting some 500 French dolls. Across the street from the Pompidou Museum, this makes an interesting outing for all members of the family. Closed Mondays. (Impasse Berthaud; tel: 01.42.72.73.11; www.museedelapoupeeparis.com)
- 4e: **Musée de la Magie**: Interactive magic museum, optical

illusions and magic shows. Check the website for hours and special openings. (11 rue Saint-Paul; tel: 01.42.72.13.26; www.museedelamagie.com)

- 5ᵉ: **Musée National d'Histoire Naturelle**: Located in the Jardin des Plantes, with a zoo, hothouses and a playground. Imaginative exhibits on nature and natural history, mineralogy and more. Special exhibits.
(57 rue Cuvier; tel: 01.40.79.56.01; www.mnhn.fr)

- 8ᵉ: **Palais de la Découverte**: Interesting exhibitions and a plantetarium. (avenue Franklin-D-Roosevelt; tel: 01.56.43.20.20; www.palais-decouverte.fr)

- 9ᵉ: **Musée Grevin**: A wax museum with favourite celebrities and some historical scenes, a hall of mirrors and an explanation of how the waxworks are made. (10 boulevard Montmartre; tel: 01.47.70.85.05; www.grevin-paris.com)

- 12ᵉ: **Aquarium Tropical**: Exotic fish and crocodiles. Closed Tuesdays. (293 avenue Daumesnil; tel: 01.53.59.58.60; www.aquarium-portedoree.fr)

- 16ᵉ: **Aquarium de Paris**, Cineaqua: Extensive aquarium near Trocadero. Shows, workshops, animations, and films. Open daily; closed 14 July. (5 avenue Albert de Mun; tel: 01.40.69.23.23; www.cineaqua.com)

Parks, Playgrounds and Zoos

Paris has more than 400 parks and gardens. Both the Bois de Boulogne and Bois de Vincennes have extensive areas designed for children, but almost all the parks have varied amusements for the kids, including playgrounds, go-karts, pony rides or carousels. Most parks are open during daylight hours only. A few of the better-equipped and interesting parks are: Jardin du Luxembourg (with its extensive play areas, tennis courts, marionettes and rental of toy sailboats), Parc des Buttes-Chaumont (with its waterfalls and pony rides), Parc André Citroën, Parc Montsouris (with its sloping lawns and cascading waters), and the Jardin Atlantique hidden above the Gare Montparnasse.

Some 388 aires de jeux (playgrounds) can be found throughout the city; most have large sand pits where the sand is changed frequently enough to be kept clean. Some small squares have carousels. And, throughout the summer there's a popular fun fair in the Jardin des Tuileries, with rides and other attractions.

In Spring, the centuries-old Foire du Trône for two months takes over the Pelouse de Reuilly In the Bois de Vincennes. With rides, a ferris wheel, music, games…and a wonderfully festive atmosphere (www.foiredutrone.fr).

Theatres, Marionnettes and Circuses

Guignols/marionnettes (puppet shows) are among the most popular entertainment for younger children, although the shows may be difficult to understand for non-French speakers. Puppet shows can be found in the larger parks near the play areas. Circuses, which are extremely popular, come and go according to the season; several come just around Christmas, and the famous, international Cirque du Soleil is an annual visitor. Also, check the weekly events guides for current listings:

- www.cirquedhiver.com
- www.cirque-paris.com
- www.alexis-gruss.com
- www.cirquepinder.com
- www.cirque-diana-moreno.com
- www.bartabas.fr

Theme Parks

Theme parks outside Paris are good for weekend excursions, and they are generally easy to reach by car or public transportation. There are a variety of themes to choose from, from the Parc Astérix (named for the beloved comic character) to La Mer de Sable, an American Wild West extravaganza. Disneyland Paris is the most famous, but there are other interesting ones, such as France Miniature, which presents a miniature bas-relief of the historical landmarks and regions of France. For the extensive swimming complex Aquaboulevard, see Chapter 7 (pages 253–316).

- www.parcasterix.fr
- www.merdesable.fr
- www.disneylandparis.com

- www.franceminiature.com
- www.aquaboulevard.com
- www.jardindacclimatation.fr
- www.sealife.fr
- www.thoiry.net

Toys

Hypermarchés and some of the large supermarket chains sell *jouets* (toys) and *jeux* (games) at decent prices, and department stores usually have a good selection of the internationally popular ones tailored to the French market. Shop around, for similar toys can vary in price from store to store. Consider also museum shops, for they often sell interesting, educational materials for children.

For children's clothes, see Chapter 7.

- **FNAC**: The nationwide chain carries electronics, books, videos, computer games and more. There are some ten shops in Paris, Including in the revamped Centre Beaugrenelle in rue Linois, in the 15e. (www.fnac.com)
- **Oxybul**: Eveil et Jeux has five addresses around Paris (www.oxybul.com). Toys, videos and activities are available for children under 12 years of age. Programs for kids.
- 1ᵉʳ: **EOL** (3 rue du Louvre, 75001; tel: 01.43.54.01.43; www.eol-model.fr). A well-stocked store devoted to model-making of all sorts, including figurines, cars, airplanes and boats.
- 12ᵉ: **Apache** (84 rue du Faubourg Saint-Antoine; tel: 01.53.46.60.10). Chain of modern stores, with furniture, toys, some clothing, Internet access and videos. Programs for kids.
- 15ᵉ: **1.2.3.famille** (21 rue Desaix; tel: 01.43.06.06.20; www.123famille.com). An excellent selection of educational toys and games of all sorts for children up to 15 years of age.
- 20ᵉ: **Village Joué Club** (3/5 Boulevard des Italiens; tel: 01.53.45.41.41; www.joueclub.fr). A well-known network of large toy and game stores for children of all ages. The largest in Paris.

Eating Out With Children

Well-behaved children are welcome in just about any eating establishment. If they're bored in the more elegant restaurants of *haute cuisine*, please them with the varied menus at the local bistros and *brasseries*, the inexpensive Asian restaurants that are in every *arrondissement* or the American-style restaurants that offer hamburgers, ribs and fries. Museum cafés, department stores, and cafés in the larger parks, plus most of the tourist venues are child-friendly, as well. Not all restaurants, however, have high chairs (*chaises hautes*) or booster seats.

Many casual restaurants have children's menus, including the citywide chains of Chez Clément, the Buffalo Grill, and the ever-popular Hippopotamus. Try the sandwich chains Pomme de Pain and Toastissimo, Léon de Bruxelles for mussels (to be eaten with the fingers!) and excellent all-you-can-eat *frites*, and La Criée for fish. *Crèpes* are always fun as is the tex-mex chain Indiana. Some restaurants offer crayons to keep children occupied. Le Relais de l'Entrecote, with three locations in Paris, offers steak, lots of fries and salad, and a delicious chocolaty profiterole for dessert, sure to please. The pizza chains offer home delivery for neighbouring areas, and delivery and takeaway are available from some restaurants, ranging from sushi to Indian cuisine. And of course, wherever you go, there's always McDonald's.

- 19ᵉ: **Cafézoïde** (92 bis Quai de la Loire; tel: 01.42.38.26.37). In this restaurant, one might say it is 'parent-friendly', for it is designed precisely for children. On the banks of the Canal l'Ourq and not far from the parc La Villette, this is a varied experience for kids, with activities and games, yoga, music, workshops, and café-style snacks, drinks, and a vegetarian lunch. Open Wednesdays to Sundays, from 10:00 am to 6:00 pm.

TO YOUR GOOD HEALTH!
General Conditions

The medical system in France is consistently listed as one of the best in the world. Linked to its social security system, almost everyone has access to medical care. Patients have a choice between public hospitals and private clinics, and payments are made on a sliding scale: the sicker a person is, the more is covered by the system.

Although the taste of the water in Paris may vary in the different areas, it has been safe to drink since the city spent 12 million francs on water purification systems well more than a century ago. The water has a high mineral content of *calcaire* (calcium and chalk), which is not at all unhealthy, but many Parisians tend to drink bottled water such as Vittel, Volvic or Evian, or slightly fizzy water such as Badoit or any of the inexpensive brands found in groceries. Currently the Brita water filter is popular.

Before You Leave Home

While packing, be sure to include all important medications in your carry-on case, as checked luggage occasionally goes astray. If medication includes syringes or other items that might be questioned, carry with you some proof of their need. To avoid needless questions, make sure that all medicines *sur ordonnance* (by prescription) are in their original, labelled containers. But pay attention to new and changing regulations concerning liquids and creams in your hand baggage: how much you may carry and how they must be packaged.

Bring enough medication to tide you over until you have found a doctor and pharmacy of your own, and until you can determine which medications require prescriptions and which do not. Ask your physician to give you copies of records concerning ongoing treatments and to write new prescriptions using both the trade and generic name of the medication. Bring a copy of your eyeglass prescription and an extra pair of glasses or contact lenses.

For the Children

First, if there is a dire emergency for your child, call SAMU immediately; (tel: 15).

Before leaving your former residence, obtain a copy of your children's vaccination and health records and make sure all inoculations are current. For a child to enter a *crèche* or school, DPT and polio vaccinations are required, as is a tuberculosis vaccination through the BCG combination; vaccinations for *rougeole* (measles), *rubéole* (German measles), *oreillons* (mumps) and Hepatitis B are recommended but optional.

Check with your pediatrician to determine what you should have with you before you find a pediatrician in Paris. If your child has a non-life-threatening health emergency before you are set up with a local doctor, go to a hospital (listed on pages 130–131 by specialty) or call SOS Medecins for a house call (tel: 01.47.07.77.77). Lastly, if you prefer to read a thermometer in Fahrenheit rather than centigrade, you might think about bringing one with you.

Once you are enrolled in the French health plan, your child will be issued a *carnet de santé*, which records all major health information, including vaccinations. The carnet is issued by the *mairie* of your *arrondissement* and is a permanent record of a child's health-related events from birth to age 16.

Health Resources

Finding English-speaking doctors in Paris can begin before departure. The International Association for Medical Assistance to Travellers (IAMAT) a non-profit association, provides a list of approved English-speaking doctors, who have agreed on a pre-set fee (www.iamat.org). Membership for IAMAT is free, but donations are encouraged. IAMAT also has up-to-date information on health conditions worldwide.

Once in Paris, you should be able to find physicians through friends and colleagues, and your embassy should also be able to provide you with a list of English-speaking doctors and dentists.

All people insured under the French system must register with a *médecin traitant* or primary physician. Your *généraliste* (general doctor) is the one who will refer you to *spécialistes* (specialists) as needed in order for the costs to be reimbursed under French insurance. For up-to-date information and health-related news, you can also access the website of the Ministry of Health (www.sante.gouv.fr).

Vaccination Centres

If you will be travelling from France to countries where vaccinations are necessary for typhoid, yellow fever, malaria, etc., you can go to the Centre de Vaccinations Internationales d'Air France, at 38 quai de Jemmapes 75010 (tel: 01.43.17.22.00). It's closed Sunday and holidays. Be prepared to wait. There are others throughout the city, and your own doctor should provide the standard innocuations. You may also access the city's website (www.paris.fr); click on *santé* and you should see a section listing all the vaccination centres in Paris.

Insurance

Administered by the *Caisse Primaire d'Assurance Maladie* (CPAM), the French public health care system is part of the *Sécurité Sociale* (www.ameli.fr). French health care is among the best in the world: doctors are well trained (some make house calls) and procedures are the most modern. The entire working community—employers, employees and the self-employed—contributes to this state-funded insurance plan. Anyone who has a *carte de séjour*—employed or not—is eligible for coverage.

Physicians and private clinics are either *conventionnés*, whereby they abide by the prices set by the *Sécurité Sociale,* or *non-conventionnés*, whereby they set their own prices. In the case of the latter, only some of the costs may be covered if it is determined that the prices for the services performed were not competitive. If a service is *agréé*, it means the services are covered. If it is *non agréé*, the particular treatment is not covered

People choose their own *médecin traitant*, usually a *généraliste*, who authorises visits to *spécialistes* when needed. The patient pays for treatment and medicines and is reimbursed up to only about 70 per cent. Generally, the sicker you are, the more is covered. Laboratory tests are usually covered completely, as are mammograms. *Spécialistes* charge more than *généralistes*, and *honoraires libres* (doctors who set their own fees) are allowed to vary their prices.

When you are enrolled in the French health system, you will be issued a *carte vitale* containing your permanent health plan number and other information. You can check your information at any CPAM office by inserting your card into a machine, usually by the door.

Supplemental Insurance Companies

Remember that French insurance pays only a portion of your medical costs. Private insurance companies sell *mutuelles*—supplemental policies that cover costs otherwise not reimbursed. Shop around, for some *mutuelles* cover more costs than others and ask about dental and eyeglass coverage. Some employers offer *mutuelles* as part of their benefit plan. Students might inquire about health systems as below:

- **La Mutuelle des Etudiants**
  (tel: 08.11.50.56.33; www.lmde.com)
- **La Societé des Etudiants de la Région Parisienne**
  (tel: 01.56.54.36.34; www.smerep.fr)

Coverage for Foreigners

All EU nationals (and some others within Europe) are entitled to receive health services throughout the EU. Obtain the European National Health Insurance Card (which replaces the old E111, and is for one person, not a family). For information, check the websites of the EU (www.europa.eu) or the French health system (www.social-sante.gouv.fr). For long stays, talk with the local French health office about registering in France. Non-hospital expenditures in Paris are reimbursed up to about 75 per cent (with documentation and receipts), so it is important to check on supplemental insurance.

If your company is sending you to Paris, the personnel department should be knowledgeable about health insurance coverage for its employees. Check how you will be covered and the extent of the coverage. If you will be working for a French company, you will have the documents that allow access to the French system. Once in the system, you will have a *numéro d'immatriculation*, an identification number to be used in all health care situations.

Americans (and other nationals) on short stays should ask their insurance carriers about coverage abroad and how to file a claim from abroad. Check about coverage for long-term supplies of medications. Older Americans should be aware that Medicare does not honour claims abroad and should investigate supplemental policies that offer coverage when travelling for limited amounts of time. Canadians are covered by the national health plan only to the amount that similar services are covered at home, so most buy additional insurance. Provincial Ministry of Health Offices and travel agents have information.

INSURANCE FOR FOREIGNERS

Entering the French system may take time, so plan to keep your own insurance until you are registered. (In fact, you can't get your residence papers without proof of insurance.) If you have no insurance, try one of the private international insurance companies that offer policies for people living outside their home countries. They are all costly and their coverage may be helpful the short or long term, depending on your needs. Most offer several different insurance options, and all would be helpful for interim coverage. Check the insurance companies in your own country as well.

Americans might consider the Association of Americans Resident Overseas (AARO), an important organisation in Paris that represents the rights of Americans living overseas (tel: 01.47.20.24.15; www.aaro.org). It is open to anyone and offers several comprehensive health plans for its members. Prices are comparable to other private health plans.

- **World Health Insurance Services Inc**
  (Anthem Arizona, USA tel: (1-877) 679-7900, Outside USA: (001) 623-551-8500; www.worldhealthinsurance.net)
- **BUPA Global**
  (Victory House, Trafalgar Place, Brighton BN14FY, England; tel: (440) 1273 208 181; www.bupaglobal.com)
- **International Medical Group**
  (2960 N. Meridian Street, Indianapolis IN 46208; USA tel: (1-317) 655-4500; www.imglobal.com)

- **Health Care International**
  (95 Cromwell Road, London SW7 4Dl England; tel: (44 (0)
  207 590 8800; www.healthcareinternational.com)
- **Wallach and Company**
  (107 West Federal Street, PO Box 480, Middleburg VA
  20118; US tel: (1-800) 237-6615; (1-540) 687-3166;
  www.wallach.com)

EVACUATION INSURANCE

If your insurance doesn't cover you abroad (such as Medicare in
the United States), you might consider one of the air ambulance
evacuation companies for emergencies. They transport from
the hospital where you currently are to one of your choice in
your home country. Such transport would be extraordinarily
expensive without the insurance. Two are Medjet Assist (www.
medjetassist.com) and MASA Assist (www.masaassist.com),
but there are many others you can find on your search engine.
Prices and services vary, so check several. Carry your insurance
card (and other health-related information) with you.

Hospitals

For life-threatening emergencies, see below. Keep the numbers
handy, just in case. For non-life threatening emergency care,
go to the hospital nearest you. After treatment, you might
be referred or transferred to another hospital that specialises
in the treatment you require. Two major English-speaking
full-service hospitals are headquartered in nearby suburbs
and both are easily reached by public transportation or taxi.

- **American Hospital of Paris**: Full-service private hospital
  with English-speaking personnel, accredited in the United
  States. Also offers dental services. Expensive but accepts
  Blue Cross insurance for inpatient services and provides
  forms for outpatient reimbursement of insurance. Credit
  cards accepted in the emergency ward. *Agréé* but *non-
  conventionné*. (63 boulevard Victor-Hugo, 92202 Neuilly-
  sur-Seine; tel: 01.46.41.25.25; www.american-hospital.org.)
- **Franco-Britannique Hospital (Hertford British)**
  (3 rue Barbès, 92300 Levallois-Perret; and 4, rue Kleber;
  standard tel: 01.47.59.59.59; www.ihfb.org).

> **Emergencies**
>
> In a dire health emergency, call SAMU (tel: 15) or the *pompiers* (fire department) (tel: 18), rather than going on your own to a hospital. The caller's number is automatically registered, and response is swift and effective. Ambulances are routed to the correct hospital by trained personnel. The *pompiers* have the equipment to enter an apartment when the occupant is unable to open the door. The Europe-wide emergency number 112 is also helpful. For other emergency numbers—including 24-hour doctors who make house calls—see the Resource Guide, Chapter 10.

Most public hospitals have *urgences* (emergency rooms). For information on hospitals, see the website of the Assistance Publique: Hôpitaux de Paris (www.aphp.fr). The ones below are centrally located, but make sure you know the hospital nearest you. Generally, your doctor will recommend the most appropriate hospital.

- 4ᵉ: **Hôpital Hôtel Dieu**: Important public hospital, centrally located on Ile-de-la-Cité.
  (1 place du Parvis-Notre-Dame; tel: 01.42.34.82.32).
- 10ᵉ: **Hôpital Fernand Widal**: Poison centre.
  (200 rue du Faubourg-Saint-Denis; tel: 01.40.05.45.45).
- 13ᵉ: **Hôpital de la Pitié-Salpêtrière**: Large, comprehensive hospital complex
  (47 boulevard de l'Hôpital, 75013; tel: 01.42.16.00.00).
- 14ᵉ: **Hôpital Broussais:** Major cardiac centre.
  (96 rue Didot; tel: 10.43.95.95.95).
- 15ᵉ: **Hôpital Européen Georges Pompidou**: The newest and thus most modern of the hospital complexes in Paris. Some English speakers.
  (20 rue Leblanc; tel: 01.56.09.20.00).
- 15ᵉ: **Hôpital Necker**: Children's services and burn centre. Ear, nose and throat services.
  (149 rue de Sèvres; tel: 01.44.49.40.00).
- 17ᵉ: **Hôpital Marmottan**: Drug crisis centre
  (17 rue Armaillé; tel: 01.45.74. 00.04).

Clinics

Private *cliniques* (clinics) often specialise in particular fields. Generally their accommodations are more pleasant and personal than in a public hospital, but their prices are somewhat higher. When you need a particular service, talk to your doctor about the advantages of a hospital or clinic that might be recommended.

Dentistry

Although Paris has excellent dental services with the most modern equipment and trained practitioners, it would be wise to have as much dental work as possible done by your regular dentist before you leave home, giving you adequate time to find another in your new home. If you have ongoing dental problems, bring a set of X-rays with you.

As with doctors, both your friends and your embassy should be able to provide you with recommendations of English-speaking dentists; this should not be hard, for many French dentists have trained in North America or in the United Kingdom. In France, there are no dental hygienists, so it is the dentist who does the routine tasks such as tooth cleaning, giving the dentist a complete understanding of the patient's mouth and dental condition.

Hôpital Hôtel Dieu provides 24-hour emergency *stomatologie* services (dental and mouth care), as does the **Hôpital Pitie-Salpêtrière**. For emergencies you can also contact **SOS Urgences Stomotolagie et Dentaire** at 87 boulevard Port-Royal, 75013 (24-hour tel: 01.43.36.36.00).

The **Centre de Santé Dentaire George Eastman** is a dental institute at 11 rue George Eastman, 75013 (tel: 01.44.97.88.88). It is closed Sundays.

Pregnancy

French maternity care is excellent. In a public hospital, just about all costs are covered under *Sécurité Sociale*. Women in the French health care system must declare their pregnancy and undergo a minimum of four examinations and one *échographie* (ultrasound). A *carnet de maternité* (maternity notebook) will be provided.

Inquire about your obstetrician's hospital or clinic. The services at both public hospitals and private clinics can be equally good, but while clinics may be more comfortable, hospitals may have more extensive equipment and facilities. Except for complicated deliveries, many babies in France are delivered by a *sage-femme* (midwife).

A *doula* supports pregnant women emotionally and physically during pregnancy and also the delivery—with the permission of the doctor. Generally a *doula* provides emotional and educational support during labour and birth, and can help with pain management techniques (www.doulas.info).

Besides the English-speaking hospitals mentioned above, the two hospitals overleaf are well respected for maternity care, especially for high-risk pregnancies. Your doctor will guide you as to the best resources for your pregnancy and may indeed recommend a private hospital, but you should also be aware of Message, the important English-speaking support group for new and expectant mothers.

- 12ᵉ: **Hôpital des Diaconesses**.
  (18 rue du Sergent-Bauchat; tel: 01.44.74.10.10)
- 14ᵉ: **Hôpital Saint-Vincent de Paul**.
  (84 avenue Denfert-Rochereau; tel: 01.58.41.41.41)

Birth and parenting classes for expectant parents are held independently by *sages-femmes* and also at many hospitals. Hôpital Notre-Dame de Bon Secours at 185 rue Raymond Losserand conducts a *sophrologie* programme of relaxation, including Yoga and Lamaze techniques (tel: 01.44.12.32.32). The English-speaking hospitals provide prenatal and childbirth care as well.

All births must be registered within three days at your *mairie*. The hospital provides the forms and information. All births should also be registered immediately at your own embassy.

Pharmacies

Pharmacies display a green neon cross outside; the cross is lit when the shop is open. Pharmacies carry only health products such as prescription and over-the-counter homeopathic remedies, skin preparations, suntan lotions, tooth brushes and healthy cosmetics; beauty and skin products are widely available at department stores and supermarkets, often at better prices.

Pharmacists are highly trained and extremely knowledgeable about medication, of which there are many, since French physicians tend to medicate heavily. Generic equivalents are used and the pharmacist may ask whether you will accept a generic equivalent, which is less expensive and most often equally effective. If you have doubts about a particular product, ask your doctor. Without any prescription though, you can discuss your symptoms (cold, flu, headache, etc.) with the pharmacist, who may recommend non-prescription remedies.

The pharmacy in each neighourhood should display a poster (*placard*) indicating the nearest night and Sunday pharmacy (*pharmacie de garde*). The local *commissariat* will also indicate doctors on call and open pharmacies. Also, you might access the *résogardes* (tel: 3237; www.3237.fr) for a list of the open pharmacies. The pharmacies listed below have English-speaking personnel and several carry English or American products. For 24-hour pharmacies, see Resource Guide in Chapter 10.

- 1er: **Pharmacie Swann**. 6 rue de Castiglione; tel: 01.42.60.72.96. Closed Sundays.
- 6e: **Pharmacie Saint-Germain des Prés**. 45 rue Bonaparte; tel: 01.43.26.52.92. Open daily until midnight; Sundays and holidays until 11:00 pm.
- 8e: **Drugstore Champs-Elysées (Publicis)**. 133 avenue des Champs-Elysées; tel: 01.47.20.39.25. Open until 2:00 am.
- 8e: **Pharmacie Anglaise des Champs-Elysées.**. 62 avenue des Champs-Elysées; tel: 01.43.59.82.30. Open daily until midnight.
- 8e: **Pharmacie Les Champs**. 84 avenue des Champs-Elysées; tel: 01.45.62.02.41. Open 24 hours.
- 9e: **British-American Pharmacy**. 1 rue Auber; tel: 01.42.65.88.29. Open until 8:00 pm; closed Sundays.
- 14e: **Pharmacie des Arts**. 106 boulevard du Montparnasse; tel: 01.43.35.44.88. Open daily until midnight.

Parapharmacies

Parapharmacies, which are generally *libre-service* (self-service) carry cosmetics and non-prescription health care products, including vitamins, homeopathic remedies and skin preparations. Not as tightly regulated as pharmacies, *parapharmacies* are often less expensive and some offer a *carte de fidélité*, giving a discount for frequent purchases.

HIV/AIDS/STD

City-sponsored health centres do free and confidential AIDS testing and several hospitals offer extensive care. Your *mairie* should have information on AIDS care in Paris. Sidaction is an active AIDS organisation (www.sidaction.org).

- **Kiosque Infos SIDA Toxicomanie** (36 rue Geoffroy l'Asnier 75004; tel: 01. 44.78.00.00; www.lekiosque.org). Information about HIV/AIDS, testing and counseling
- **SIDA Information Service** (24-hour hotline tel: 08.00.84.08.00; www.sida-info-service.org)

■ **Act Up Paris** (www.actupparis.org). International activist
association with weekly meetings and notices of events..

Deaths

Deaths must be certified by a physician and reported
to the *mairie* within 24 hours. The certifying doctor will
explain the procedures. Only after such official registration
may a funeral or repatriation take place. Notify your
embassy officially and it will provide assistance with
the paperwork. For information when someone dies, contact
the municipal Urgences Funéraires (tel: 08.00.88.00.88;
www.servicesfuneraires.fr).

BRINGING PETS

Parisians love their dogs. In France, with a population of
about 65 million people, there are some 10 million dogs,
and it is said that in Paris there are more dogs than children.
Well-behaved dogs are welcome in many restaurants and
even on public transportation if they are in baskets or packs.
However, except for service dogs, they are only allowed in
some parks and gardens, and often only in some areas of
the park—and even then, in most cases, they must be on
leash. Landlords may not forbid their tenants to have a pet,
although if the pet causes damage, the tenant is responsible
for the repair. But dogs in apartments must also be well
behaved; if a dog causes too much noise or annoyance
on other aspects, the landlord may cancel the lease. And
Paris is serious about keeping the city clean; dog owners
must pick up the droppings and dispose of them carefully
or engender a fine.

In the Bois de Boulogne and Bois de Vincennes, there
are large open spaces for dogs to run, and the large Parc de
Bercy also has some leash-free areas. Most parks have signs
that indicate if and where dogs are welcome.

To bring a pet into France, get it microchipped well before
your departure date. A rabies vaccination and then a blood
test will be needed after the microchip is implanted, in order
to get the health certificate (Annex IV form for France) from
an accredited veterinarian. Animals under three months that

are not vaccinated will be allowed to enter France only three weeks after its first full anti-rabies vaccination.

An annual blessing of animals takes place in the autumn at the American Cathedral in Paris (www.americancathedral.org) and at the church of Sainte Rita.

MANAGING YOUR MONEY
The Euro

The euro (€) is the national currency of 19 countries of the European Union. (For all information on the European Union, see Chapter 9, and check www.europa.eu). Thus, if you travel in any of the 19 countries here mentioned, you need not worry about exchanging currency or whether you will be left with unused foreign cash when you return to Paris.

Although currency values themselves do not fluctuate within the eurozone, prices do. For example, an Italian car may cost more in Germany than in Italy, so if you want an Italian car you may well decide to go to Italy and drive it back across the open border. Therefore, you still have to shop around for the best deal on high-priced items.

Currency values do fluctuate greatly outside the eurozone. Thus, if you know in advance when you will be travelling outside the eurozone, you still have to pay attention to currency rates and buy when it is advantageous. Rates are published on the Internet and in daily newspapers, and there are conversion apps you can download to your tablet or smartphone; unfortunately, these are bank rates and individual purchasers do not get exactly the same rates.

If you are using a credit or debit card from your home country, be sure to inform them in advance of your travel plans, so they will not suspect fraud on a purchase outside your normal pattern and put a block on your card.

The Need for Cash

If you are arriving in France from a country that does not use the euro (including Great Britain), you will need to have at least enough cash to get into the city from the airport. Try to buy some euros before your departure, for the exchange rate at the airport *bureau de changes* (currency exchange counter) is usually not advantageous. In many airports and train stations however, there are *distributeurs* (automatic cash dispensers), and if these are linked to banks, the exchange rate will be that of the bank.

For those with credit or debit cards, cash is available 24 hours a day at the unbiquitous *distributeurs* (automatic teller machines/cash points). Most have instructions in both French and English. Pictures of the cash networks accepted (Visa, Master Card, Cirrus, Plus, etc.) are displayed, making it easy to know which machines take which cards. Make sure that your Personal Identification Number (PIN) has four numbers only, which is the European standard. Some banks still use six numbers, and usually the first four can be used as your PIN. If you are going to be using your credit card for cash advances, inquire in advance about the interest rate, for it is usually higher than that of normal purchases.

With your card, you may receive cash up to the daily limit that the home bank allows, linked to the exchange rate.

Banks offer the most favourable rates of exchange, but they charge a commission, usually one to two per cent of

WORK HARDER!

the monies changed. Some banks display a sign saying 'no cash', and unfortunately, banks close earlier than *bureaux de change*. And most, though not all, are closed on Saturdays.

If you decide to use a *bureau de change* to exchange currency, it's worth checking out several, for the rates may differ even on the same street; in tourist districts they can be particularly unfavourable. Ask for the rates before proceeding with the transaction, even if they seem to be posted; occasionally they seem advantageous, but they may only be for large transactions. Also, do not be taken in by signs that say 'no commission', for no *bureau de change* may charge a commission—the profit is built into the rate. Occasionally the exchange seems flexible, depending on the person behind the window, but don't ever think you are getting a rate that is better than what the next person in line at the cash point will get.

Most currency exchanges are open Sundays. This includes the city-wide chains of Thomas Cook, ICE, Travelex and Chequepoint.

Traveller's Cheques

Some people still use traveller's checks, but with the advent of *distributeurs*, it is easier and more efficient to just get cash when you need it at a good rate from a bank cash point. There's little point in paying out your cash to a company well in advance of using it; it's best to just get euros when you need them from a *distributeur*.

Traveller's cheques are helpful, though, if you would otherwise make many small withdrawals from the *distributeur*, as banks in your home country and in France may charge a fee each time. So, it's best to withdraw large amounts occasionally or at that point to have traveller's cheques, which your own bank may issue you without charge.

For Lost or Stolen Items

For lost traveller's cheques, most issuers require a police report: go to the *commissariat* in the *arrondissement* in which the loss occurred. The police will issue a *récépissé de déclaration de perte ou de vol* (declaration of theft or loss).

Bring the report and your passport to the issuer of the cheques. For those issuers without an office in Paris, ask at the time of purchase for a toll-free number to call in case of loss. Remember that you must note the numbers of the traveller's cheques, so be sure to keep this record separately from the cheques themselves.

Report lost or stolen credit cards immediately. Often a replacement card with a new number can be issued within 48 hours; be sure to inform any company that is making automatic deductions from your card (such as online services) that the number has changed. Should you be using a French Visa or Master Card, after you have notified the bank, it will inform you of the procedures for informing others.

- American Express (tel: 01.47.77.72.00)
- Visa & Carte Bleue (tel: 08.00.90.11.79)
- MasterCard (tel: (08.00.90.13.87)
- Diner's Club (tel: 08.20.82.01.43)

Sometimes lost articles—even credit cards and traveller's cheques—are turned in to the police. See Resource Guide in Chapter 10 for the address of the city's Lost and Found Departments.

- For lost bank cheques, call 08.92.68.32.08.
- For items lost or stolen on SNCF trains, call 3635 #22.

French Banking

There are many banks to choose from in Paris and these generally offer savings and current accounts, investment opportunities and money market funds. Take your time in choosing. Bring to each bank you are considering a list of questions concerning your particular banking needs. Ask too, if necessary, about the commission charged for processing an international cheque or electronic transfer of funds—these can be high and vary from bank to bank. Ask how long it takes to have access to transferred funds. (If your home bank is affiliated with one in France, transfers of funds from one to the other may be somewhat more efficient, although this isn't always the case.) All banks these days

Look for signs like these to withdraw money from a *distributeur*—this one is of the Caisse d'Epargne, one of the major banks in France.

have Internet access for banking online. Inquire, too, about the conditions for their *carte bleue*, the Visa debit card. If you are considering investing through the bank, ask about their pricing policies. There should be written information on the bank's services.

Convenience of location and opening days and hours might factor into your decision. Banks are generally open from 9:00 am to 5:00 pm, except weekends and holidays. Some banks are open Saturday mornings. If a national holiday falls on a Tuesday or Thursday, banks may *faire le pont* to bridge the long weekend, closing on the previous Monday or following Friday, to give the employees a four-day weekend. Small neighourhood branches may offer more personal service after the staff gets to know you. Otherwise, banking in Paris can be extremely impersonal.

Current accounts may pay interest, and some banks may automatically sweep funds above a certain level into interest-bearing accounts. Interest earned is taxable, so make sure you take into account in which country your taxes will be paid.

Each bank has its own specific guidelines and documentation needed to open a *compte courant* (current account), although there are some general guidelines: when you go to open your account, bring your passport, your *carte de séjour* and proof of your *domicile*, such as your lease or a gas/electric bill in your name. This may not be easy, for without a bank account it's sometimes hard to obtain a lease, and without a lease it's hard to get a bank account. Proof of employment generally suffices, but a letter of reference from a home bank may also be helpful.

Most banks open non-resident accounts. A few will require a hefty initial deposit, especially if there is no direct deposit of a salary cheque.

Opening an account is not immediate. Often you must make an appointment just to see an account representative. Then it takes a few days for the paperwork to be completed and even longer for a chequebook and the *carte bleue* to be issued. Don't assume that anything is provided automatically. Ask for the chequebook (they come in different sizes, so ask to see all available sizes and choose one that suits you best). There is no extra charge for cheques.

Cheques are accepted by most establishments with proof of identity and sometimes with a minimum purchase of €10 or €20. The penalties for returned cheques are so severe that cases of a person writing a cheque with insufficient funds are extremely rare. Some banks will arrange an overdraft limit, but if the bank's procedures for covering a bounced cheque are not followed, the account holder may be blacklisted (*interdit bancaire*). Thus it is important to ask how your bank structures the *dates de valeur*, the amount of time it takes for deposits to be credited, including money orders and bank drafts—withdrawals made on the same date as a deposit may result in an overdraft.

Nowadays most of the banks have English speakers and are accustomed to foreigners. The banks listed under International Banks, however, are known for their international presence.

The RIB

When you open a bank account, you will be given several copies of a RIB (*relevé d'identité bancaire*), which contains the identifying numbers of your bank and account. This is the coupon you will show your landlord, the telephone and electric companies and all the other institutions when you arrange for their payments to be automatically deducted from your account. Your chequebook may also have copies of the RIB at the back.

Carte Bleue

La carte bleue, tthe French Visa card, is actually a debit card. There are no installment payments, no grace periods and no bill sent at the end of the month. Cards are accepted everywhere as payment because they are seen to be safe. Monthly purchases on the card may have a limit, unless prior arrangements have been made.

Carte bleue functions with *distributeurs*, with a PIN that the bank has assigned. *Distributeurs* throughout Paris are electronically linked and bank cards may be used in any of them. There is no charge for using the machines at branches of your own bank, but some banks charge for withdrawals from other banks. Cardholders whose cards have been illegally used by others are generally liable for the amount withdrawn until the date they notify the bank of the problem; the PIN is a secret number and if someone else has used it, the bank considers that it was negligently given out by the cardholder. Make sure no one is looking over your shoulder when you are at the *distributeur*.

La Poste

Post Offices (*bureaux de poste*) are the most widespread banks in France and as they are all connected, they have more branches than any other. In terms of convenience, the local post office may be the most practical place to open a bank account, depending on the types of services you need. La Poste offers all the usual services available at any other bank. They are also *bureaux de change* and many are Western Union agents. However, they are rumoured to be the least flexible and personalised in service. If you are after the convenience, check out several Post Offices in your neighourhood. Some Post Offices have more extensive amenities than others.

International Banks

Some foreign banks have *succursales* (branches) in Paris. They are all full-service banks and adhere to French banking law. In some, in addition to showing proof of your income and your nationality, you need only show that you have a pernament address somewhere, even if it is not in France.

Those listed below provide the same services as French banks, but with added services for foreigners. Their services and websites are in both French and English. Prices for services vary, and they may be more expensive than French banks.

- **Banque Transatlantique**
  (26 avenue Franklin D. Roosevelt, 75372 Paris Cedex 08; tel: 01.56.88.77.77; www.transat.tm.fr)
- **Barclays Bank**
  Barclay's has several branches in Paris. (tel: 01.55.78.72.27; www.barclays.fr).
- **HSBC**: With more than a dozen branches in Paris and with a presence throughout the world, HSBC is one of the more convenient banks. (tel: 0 810 246 810; www.hsbc.fr)

Money from Home

Don't expect cheques or money orders sent from abroad to clear at the bank quickly enough to provide emergency funds; if you have a bank account in France, it would be better to make an interbank electronic transfer. Other faster options exist for receiving funds. In all, the sender pays the fees based on the amount sent; these are fairly expensive, so should be seen only as an emergency measure. *Bureaux de change* are sometimes MoneyGram agents (www.moneygram.com) and La Poste is an agent of Western Union (www.westernunion.com).

How Much Do Things Cost?

Estimating how much it will cost to live in Paris will depend on several factors, including whether your income is in dollars, pounds or euros, etc., that is, how much spending power your income actually has when spending euros. Although you'll surely start by comparing prices in Paris with those at home, it's best to start, early on, by comparing prices in euros from one shop to another. Remember that tax is included in the price quoted and that the tip is already figured into every restaurant bill.

Expensive in many regards, Paris is nonetheless agreeably liveable, as its residents can attest. Most middle-class Parisians have learned how to live satisfactorily, setting their priorities and looking for good value at each turn. They frequent the semi-annual sales, look for promotions, and hound the discount houses. They shop for seasonally plentiful produce at the outdoor markets and eat and entertain well at home—except for meals at their favourite bistros or *brasseries*, at the inexpensive Asian restaurants or, on occasion, in a fine restaurant.

Assume that domestic goods will be cheaper, and imported products more expensive. Fresh produce, cheeses and breads are the least expensive, and some items such as canned goods may be more expensive than what you're used to. Wines range from the drinkable and cheap, good and moderately priced, to the fabulous but astronomical—it just takes a little tasting to figure out what you like and can afford. Goods in tourist areas may cost more than in outlying neighbourhoods. The cinema and theatre cost about the same as in most cosmopolitan capitals, as do sporting and theatrical events.

Gas and electricity bills may be higher than what you're used to, but telephone and Internet plans vary greatly and are getting cheaper, given the increasing competition in the field. Large appliances and electronic equipment that used to be more expensive in Europe than in North America are now generally competitive in price. Imported appliances may still be more expensive, owing to high import duties and taxes. Yet even the prices of these items are quickly becoming more competitive, especially at the hypermarchés.

French Taxes

Residents with income in France are liable for taxes on income from sources worldwide. Non-residents are taxed only on earned income in France (salary and rental income) and non-resident foreigners with vacation homes in France are generally not subject to income taxes. Some countries have multilateral treaties with France by which citizens working abroad are not double-taxed. (For 2015, for example, the American 'exclusion' was $100,800.) You must still file your home tax return on time. Find out the deadline for people living abroad.

The French tax year coincides with the calendar year. Tax filing for salaried employees and independent contractors is due by the end of May. Taxes are based on *le revenu* (earned income) and *capitaux mobiliers* (unearned income).

There are some rebates, exemptions and a standard deduction for married people and those with children. French employers do not withhold any amount for tax. After the tax return (*déclaration de revenus)* is filed, the government calculates the tax due and sends a bill. After the first year in the tax system, the bill may be paid in three instalments or debited monthly from a chequeing account. First-time taxpayers must declare themselves and their taxable income to the appropriate Centre des Impôts.

Taxes at Home

Everyone must determine their tax status at home and in France while living abroad. EU countries have treaties by which there is no double taxation, but everyone should check with their employer or the tax bureau in their home country to determine its current requirements. (Note again the United States exclusion that changes periodically.) EU nationals on secondment are generally not liable for French taxes, but check with your company in advance.

British citizens should request a non-resident ruling as to their tax status. Inquire at HM Revenue and Customs (tel: + 044 1274 204 880k), which also has helpful information on specific tax requirements on its website (www.inlandrevenue.gov.uk).

All Americans must file a federal tax return. Access the IRS website for its information on 'US Citizens and Resident Aliens Abroad' (tel: (1-267) 941-1000; www.irs. gov). Check with the tax department in your home state before departure because state requirements vary widely. Americans should note that in Paris the Internal Revenue Service (IRS) is at the embassy, 2 avenue Gabriel, and is open from 9:00 am to 12:00 noon weekdays (tel: 01.43.12.55.55; email: irs.paris@irs.gov).

Americans should also note the Foreign Accounts Tax Compliance Act (FATCA) requires all foreign banks to disclose to the US IRS the foreign accounts and transactions of United States taxpayers with assets over $10,000. And Americans with more than $10,000 in assets in a foreign country must also report that on their taxes; this also applies to people who are fiduciaries in enterprises or associations.

Sécurité Sociale

Cotisations sociales are paid by companies and all workers, both salaried and self-employed. For salaried employees this generally covers health insurance, disability, retirement pensions and unemployment insurance. Companies withhold a percentage from the employee's paycheck, and the amount is recorded on the pay slip.

Some embassies have booklets that detail the rights of their citizens working abroad. Self-employed people must pay taxes to URSSAF (www.urssaf.fr) and must subscribe to a basic health and pension plan, both of which are expensive. The expected amount is about 40 per cent of your revenue. For information on *la Sécu*, access its website (www.securite-sociale.fr), which also has information in English.

Bilateral agreements also apply to British salaried employees working abroad for their company under 12 months. Employees on secondment will need to provide an E101 form indicating insurance coverage under the UK plan. If employed by a French company, the worker will receive a French Social Security number and be covered by the French system.

Accounting Firms

Your country's embassy should be able to provide a list of English-speaking tax consultants in Paris. International firms are up-to-date on both French and international tax laws and procedures, as well as the treaties between countries. They offer tax preparation advice, help prepare returns, handle audits and offer business-related services. They may, however, be more expensive than French accountants for dealing with strictly domestic matters.

STAYING IN TOUCH

New methods of communication are entering modern life so quickly—even in 'ancient, traditional' France—that any chapter on how best to stay in touch with friends and family abroad will need to be updated by the time it's printed. With smartphones and tablet computers that work in any country, keeping in touch and performing just about any service needed is no longer particularly cumbersome. If France was not previously on the cutting edge of communications, this is no longer the case.

La Téléphonie

Until recently, France Télécom controlled all tele-communications services. Now, however, its privatisation and transformation into the international Orange, as well as new regulations from the EU, have allowed both domestic and international competitors to enter the field. This has forced Orange (www.orange.fr) to adapt, by reducing prices and expanding its calling options, and by providing competitive services in both Internet and television programming.

Moreover, since it is no longer required that customers use Orange for their basic providers, international competitors such as Italia Telecom have entered the French market, also offering packages of services as those mentioned above. (www.aliceadsl.fr). Internet providers are also offering these services at extremely competitive prices, so you should make sure to check out all the options before subscribing to a plan:

- **Free** (www.free.fr)
- **Budget Télécom** (www.budget-telecom.fr)
- **SFR** (www.sfr.fr)

Other Options

There are yet other options for inexpensive calling. Skype (www.skype.com/fr) and Vonage (www.vonage.com), which use the technology called Voice Over Internet Protocol (VoIP) are the most popular.

In effect, you're making phone calls using your computer or—depending on how you configure it—your iPhone, iPod Touch or other smart tablets that access the Internet. As long as you're contacting other users, generally the calls are free, and if not they're extremely inexpensive

Mobile Phones

The French are great users of their *portables*. Some people are even choosing not to have a landline (*téléphone fixe*) at all, using only their cell phones. So, if you have a mobile yourself, expect people to call you on it, even if you are at home sitting next to your landline. Smartphones generally are compatible worldwide. With a simple bi-band cell phone, you'll probably have to buy a new phone. For long or permanent stays, you will no doubt choose a French provider for your home and mobile phones. Before doing so, if you are using a tri-band or quad-band mobile from another country, you'll use the 'roaming' option by selecting among the French providers offered. Most of the newer phones select the French provider automatically, finding the one that has the best reception where you are at that time. Roaming is fairly expensive though, for you are charged both by your provider and by your temporary selection, so it's best used for only a short period. Do your research before you choose a French provider, for each offers its own plans and options.

The boutiques of the three networks below sell their own cell phones, as do Darty and the major electronic chain La Fnac.

- **Bouygues** (www.bouyguestelecom.fr)
- **Orange** (www.orange.fr)
- **SFR** (www.sfr.fr)

Telephone Numbers

Telephone numbers in France have ten digits. Those in the Paris region start with 01 and those in the rest of France with numbers from 02 to 05. A new prefix 09 is not geographically based, and is becoming popular with nationwide commercial establishments. All lines in France can be reached with the ten-digit number, without an additional area code prefix. For international calls, dial 00, then the country and area codes, followed by the telephone number.

All French mobile phone numbers begin with 06 or 07. Keep a record of your phone's serial number (dial: *#06# to obtain it). In case the phone gets stolen—which happens frequently— call your service provider immediately. *Numéros verts* (toll-free numbers) begin with 08.00-08.05 (often shown as 0 800 or 0 805). Higher 800 numbers cost by the minute, and some public service institutions now have four-digit numbers, as well.

North American toll-free numbers (800, 877, etc.) are not toll-free when dialed from abroad. The prefix changes:

- For 800 numbers, dial 880
- For 888 numbers, dial 881
- For 877 numbers, dial 882

Public Phones

There are very few public phones left, and if you do find one, it will take the *télécarte*—a prepaid card to be inserted into the telephone. Credits are deducted according to the length of the call and the number of units remaining on the card appears on the telephone as you speak. *Télécartes* are available at supermarkets and tabacs. Calls to emergency numbers are free from any public telephone.

The French Internet

Currently there are dozens of Internet *fournisseurs d'accès* (providers) in France. New providers are entering the field and prices vary widely, so it is worth checking out the price structures and conveniences of several. If you continue to use your own Internet service provider, you will still need to be able to access it, whether by telephone or cable, so you will need to know the options in France. You will have many options to choose from, including Wi-Fi, broadband ASDL (*haut debit*) and cable, which in Paris is provided by Numericable.

Some charge a monthly fee for unlimited access (*forfait illimité*) and many have a scale of fees, depending on your usage. As mentioned above, some offer calling, and television packages as well, so take into account all the options (including which TV channels are offered) before you decide.

All software and instructions provided will be in French, as will most technical support.

- **Free.fr** (www.free.fr)
- **La Poste** (www.laposte.net)
- **Numericable** (www.numericable.fr)
- **SFR** (www.sfr.fr)
- **Telecom Italia-Alice** (www.aliceadsl.fr)
- **Orange (France Télécom)** (www.orange.fr)

Cybercafés

These days, Internet access (including Wi-Fi) is available almost anywhere, including at hotels, train stations and cafés. In addition to checking your email at cybercafés throughout the city, the city of Paris has installed free WiFi in many of its public spaces—libraries, town halls, and parks. The American Library (see page 184) also offers Internet access to its members; daily membership is available.

The Post Office

La Poste is one of the most important institutions in France It is the country's most wide-ranging bank, handles all post office services and, as mentioned, has its own Internet service.

There are often several post offices in one neighourhood, with yellow fronts and blue lettering. Despite long lines, service is generally helpful and efficient. The yellow post boxes on the street have two slots specifying the mail destination: *Paris et Banlieue* (Paris and Suburbs) or *Province et Etranger* (Provinces and International).

Post offices are open from 8:00 am to 7:00 pm weekdays and until noon Saturdays. For the post office in your district, check the website or phone book. The city's main post office, La Poste Centrale, is open 24 hours daily at 52 rue du Louvre, 75001 (tel: 01.45.28.14.18; www.laposte.fr).

Lettres recommandées (registered letters) are routinely used by the French, as they are legal proof that a person has communicated with another on a certain date. There are two types: *avec accusé de réception*, which has a return receipt, or *recommandée simple*, which does not.

Packages mailed at the post office may weigh up to 30 kg. To determine the weight of a letter or a small parcel, use one of the automatic coin-operated weighing machines that issues the correct postage. There is also a machine that dispenses the appropriate stickers for a package. To avoid flimsy packaging that may be rejected, you can buy sturdy, inexpensive mailing cartons at the post office. To pick up a package or a registered letter, bring identification.

Rush Mail Options

Chronopost International, La Poste's express mail service, guarantees second-day delivery of packages and letters to North America and third-day service to Asia (customer service tel: 09.69.39.13.91; www.chronopost.com). The major international air couriers are also efficient and reliable, although somewhat more expensive.

- **DHL** (59 avenue d'Iéna, 75016; tel: 01.45.01.91.00; www.dhl.fr)
- **Federal Express** (63 boulevard Haussmann, 75008; toll-free tel: 08.20.12.38.00; www.fedex.com/fr)
- **UPS** has outlets throughout Paris, including the Office Depot stores (www.ups.com/fr).

Television

There are six non-cable *chaînes* (channels) in France. With cable, dozens of international and multilingual channels are available, including the English BBC, German ZDF, Italian RAI Uno and the American CNN. France 24 English is a new 24-hour news channel. For information and hook-up, call Numericable (tel: 3990; www.offres.numericable.fr). You can also subscribe to cable at any shop that displays the sign *TV Câble—abonnez-vous ici.*

Weekly television guides are sold at news-stands. Free advertising handouts at sidewalk stands also contain TV listings. Sports and other live events may take precedence over regularly scheduled programming. News and weather reports are frequent throughout the day on most channels.

A single programme is an *émission*; a schedule of émissions is a *programme*.

Imported televisions and DVD/*magnétoscopes* (DVD/videocassette recorders) must operate on PAL/SECAM, the French television broadcast format. Older video players run only on SECAM, making them incompatible with the American system (NTSC), although they are compatible with the European PAL system. Multisystem televisions and VCRs are increasingly available. In order to tape and play the *magnétoscope*, the television set and the recorder must be compatible. There is a *redevance* (yearly tax) on television sets. When a set is purchased, the store notifies the tax authority and the bill comes with the annual bill for the *taxe d'habitation*.

DVD

As with video recorders, DVD players in different world regions run on different operating systems. DVD players bought in North America, for example, can only play DVDs that are labelled either 'Zone 1' or 'All' ('All' means they are playable on any DVD player). European DVDs are Zone 2, and DVDs bought in Europe generally say 'Zone 2' or 'All'. Sometimes a shopkeeper will be willing to enter a code into a DVD player making it multi-region and thus able to play all DVDs. This may, however, void the warranty.

Radio

There are dozens of radio stations that play music or news or chat shows. Some of which stations you get depends on the reception in your area. And, sometimes frequencies change. The BBC is on long wave, Radio 4 at 198 khz medium wave, and BBC World is on at 648 khz AM. It's best to check the weekly events magazines that list the numerous Paris FM stations, as do the television guides. And many radio (and TV) apps can be downloaded to your tablets or smartphone.

English-language Publications

The *International New York Times* is the major English language newspaper published in Paris, available at news-stands and for home delivery. *The Times*, *The Nikkei Financial Weekly*, *The Wall Street Journal Europe*, *USA Today*, *The Financial Times*, *The Observer, The Guardian* and *The Independent* may be found at news-stands, as well as others such as *Vanity Fair* and *Newsweek*. The news-stands in tourist areas have a greater selection. Locally for France, there's *Expatriates Magazine* (expatriatesmagazine.com), and *The Connexion* www.connexionfrance.com).

OUT AND ABOUT
From the Airports to Paris
First of all, you'll have to get into the city. Intercontinental flights most often arrive at Aéroport Charles de Gaulle in the morning. This means that after clearing customs and picking up your luggage, you will be ready to enter Paris during the long morning rush hour. Transit time on the highway can be at least 45 minutes, more if there is an accident or other unforeseen incidents. If someone is meeting you at the airport, they can check the arrival of any flight by checking the carrier's website or by calling the airport information number. To obtain information for both Charles De Gaulle and Orly airports, call 3950 or visit the website (www.aeroportsdeparis.fr).

There are several options to get into Paris from the airport. Your choice will depend on your budget and time constraints, how much luggage you are carrying and the degree of inconvenience you are willing to bear. Taxis, of course, are the most expensive—they charge by the meter, and with surcharges for luggage, prices may run as high as €70 excluding tips. Yet they are the most convenient, dropping individuals off at the door; with some persuasion, the chauffeur might even be willing to help with suitcases—at least as far as the door. Signs in the airport clearly indicate where the taxi stands are to be found. See also section on 'Taxis' on pages 162–163. Here are some other options.

- **Paris Airports Service**
  (tel: 01.55.98.10.80; www.parisairportservice.com).
  Moderately priced minibus service to your door from either airport, or from your door to the airports. Currently, the

price is €28 for one person from Charles de Gaulle, but the price per person is less when there are more people in your party. Reserve in advance via phone or the Internet.

■ **PariShuttle**
(tel: 01.82.28.38.70; www.parishuttle.com).
Same type of service and similar rates as above. Reserve by phone or Internet.

■ **Les Cars Air France**
(tel: 08.92.35.08.20; www.carsairfrance.com).
Buses, with multilingual recorded information, run from both airports into the city every 15 minutes, and between airports every 30 minutes. Depending on the bus, the terminus may be Porte Maillot, place Charles-de-Gaulle, Gare Montparnasse or the Air France city terminal at Invalides. Prices depend on where you get off but currently are under €25 for a round trip. Buy your ticket on board the bus, at any Air France ticket office or at the airport.

■ **RER B**. The inexpensive commuter train goes to the city and suburbs from Terminal 1 or Terminal 2. There are several stops in Paris, including Gare du Nord, Châtelet and Saint-Michel. The RER does not depend on traffic conditions, so it takes about half an hour to get into the city. Currently the price is €9.75 one-way. See 'RER' on page 161.

■ **Roissybus** (tel: 3246). The RATP bus that runs between Charles de Gaulle and Paris. The terminus is by the American Express Office, at the corners of rue Scribe and rue Auber. The trip takes between 45 and 60 minutes. Currently the price is €10.00 one-way.

■ **Orlybus** (tel: 08.92.68.77.14.) The RATP bus that runs between Orly and Paris. The terminus is at the Air France terminal near place Denfert-Rochereau. The trip takes about half an hour. Currently the price is €7.70 one-way.

Finding Your Way

Addresses in Paris are surprisingly easy to find, given that each street has a different name assigned in no particular order. As described earlier, the 20 *arrondissements* are arranged in an outward-moving spiral; the smallest in the oldest, most central sections of town, the largest toward the edge. On streets perpendicular to the Seine, address numbers start at the river and increase as they go; *pairs* (even numbers) are on the right and *impairs* (odd numbers) on the left. Buildings on streets parallel to the river are numbered downstream from east to west. As numbers were assigned according to when particular streets were developed, do not assume that numbers on facing buildings are in the same range. In any case, numbers increase slowly, as different buildings may bear the same number with *bis* or *ter* added to them. Of course, there are exceptions to the numbering system, especially around the Grands Boulevards.

City plans may be obtained at the Paris Tourist Office, bookshops, large department stores and many news-stands. Maps and street atlases come in varying sizes. The best for carrying around is a *Plan de Paris par arrondissement*, one of several pocket-sized books with alphabetical indexes, indications of where a building number can be found, bus and *métro* routes, emergency numbers and more. Some atlases list a street named after a person with the first name first, others list the last name first. There are several apps that can be downloaded to smartphones and tablets.

Walking

Walking puts you in touch with the charm of Paris at every turn. Do not assume that the zebra-striped pedestrian crosswalks are automatic havens from traffic. Although Paris drivers, impatient and aggressive as they may be, do tend to stop for the *piéton* (pedestrian) at the crosswalks, some do not. On the other hand, they may look as though they are about to hit you, but are actually adept at driving under crowded conditions and manoeuvring around pedestrians while maintaining their (sometimes breakneck) speed. And they do stop promptly at red lights, which are often placed directly in front of a crosswalk rather than at the corner. In any case, the best strategy is to pay attention to traffic, cross only at crosswalks and wait for traffic lights (*les feux*) to turn green in your direction. Also, watch out for bicycles, mopeds and scooters, which weave in and out of traffic and zoom around corners. Despite all this, walking is one of the best ways to see Paris, to get around and to get some exercise.

RATP

La Régie Autonome des Transports Parisiens (RATP) is the public transit authority for *l'autobus* (buses), *le métropolitain* (the subway, known as the *métro*) and the Réseau Express Régional (the RER commuter line to the suburbs; tel: 3246; www.ratp.fr).

Maps of the transport system (both for Paris and the suburbs) are available at *métro* stations, on the backs of city maps and in street atlases. Maps of the *métro* and bus system are easy to decipher, and the RATP website is helpful as to general times and locations of stops.

The public transit system is economical, efficient, well maintained and safe. More than five million people use it daily. As in any large city, women travelling alone should be careful late in the evenings; sitting in the first car behind the driver is also recommended. Pickpockets frequent the *métro*, especially in tourist areas, and riders should avoid looking like tourists by not wearing expensive jewellery, intently studying maps or carrying a temptingly thick wallet in the back pocket of trousers.

The Fares

The transit system, formerly divided into zones is now all one zone. Single fare tickets are available, but a carnet of ten tickets costs about a third less per ticket. A ticket is good for one ride of any length on one bus within the city limits and for any number of transfers within the *métro*, so long as you do not exit the gates. Single-ticket transfers on buses may be used on buses in a different direction, and are generally valid for an hour and half. You may not transfer on one ticket from bus to *métro*. Keep your ticket while in the system, for you will have to show it if asked by an inspector. *Métro* tickets and coupons are inserted into a slot and then reclaimed, at which point the entry gate opens. On the bus, tickets must be *validé* (validated) in the *valideur magnétique* behind the driver.

Visitors should inquire about the Paris Visite travel pass, which is issued for one, two, three or five consecutive days, and is valid on all public transportation, including the SNCF trains. The passes, sold by zones, are valid throughout the Île de France, meaning visits to Versailles or to either airport. Buy them at *métro* and train stations.

The Passes

Weekly or monthly passes (*coupons*) are more economical than single-ride tickets. The *carte navigo intégrale* is an electromagnetic card that is valid throughout Île-de-France on all forms of public transport and allows users to get through the turnstiles quickly, for it is swiped along an electronic *valideur*.

You may recharge the weekly pass (*hebdomadaire*) or monthly pass (*mensuel*) at *métro* stations. The *hebdomadaire* starts from Monday to Sunday, no matter which day of the week it was bought. The monthly recharge is good for the duration of a calendar month. To acquire a *carte navigo*, ask for the application form at any *métro* station. In theory, the *carte* is for residents only, but just about everybody who uses public transport has one.

The Métro

Paris has one of the best underground transportation systems in the world. The *métro* is inexpensive, generally clean and efficient. It has 16 lines and 370 well-maintained stations, conveniently located in all parts of the city. It is rare to find oneself more than a five-minute walk from a *métro*.

The *métro* starts running at 5:30 am and the last train leaves around 12:30 am. Rush hours are from 7:30–9:30 am and 5:00–8:00 pm. To calculate journey time, count the number of stops from the beginning to the destination and multiply by 1.5 minutes, adding five minutes for each transfer. Remember, however, that the *métro* runs less frequently in the evenings and on weekends.

Entrances to many *métro* stations are marked with a large 'M' in a yellow circle; some older entrances even have charming grill-work. Each *métro* line is identified by a different number and colour on the subway map, and each *quai* (platform) has well-lit signs indicating the *sortie* (exit), terminus of the train and *correspondance* (interchange point). For example, a white sign indicating 'M6 Nation' is the Number Six line heading toward the last stop of Nation; the opposite direction is labelled 'M6 Charles-de-Gaulle-Etoile'. The *correspondance* signs are orange. *Sortie* signs are blue with white lettering. When there is a choice of escalator or stairs, these are also shown in blue and white.

Large diagrams of the *métro* system are at the entrance to each station and along the *quais*. In each car there is a schematic of the stations and *correspondances* on that line. At the exit of many stations, either just inside or on the street, there is often a map of the *quartier*.

L'Autobus

With some 2,000 city buses and 1,700 *arrêts d'autobus* (bus stops), the bus system is efficient though slower than the *métro*. Riding the bus, however, allows a good view of the city—a not inconsiderable advantage. Fifty-eight lines run within Paris and more go to the suburbs. Many *abri de bus* (bus shelters) have printed information in English, especially those in tourist areas.

Many of the bus schedules are being extended later in the evening, although some still run only from about 6:30 a.m. to 9:30 p.m. *Noctilien* (www.noctilien.fr) is a fleet of 35 night-time buses that run from about 00:30–5:30 am, generally every 10 or 20 minutes. They run within Paris and into the suburbs. Their terminus is Place du Châtelet. Bus service is reduced and some buses do not run at all on Sundays and holidays. There is usually a schedule posted at each *arrêt*.

Buses indicate their direction by displaying the terminus. Bus routes have two digits, and those going to the suburbs have three digits. Each bus route is colour-coded and is displayed on the bus and at the bus stop, which makes it easy to figure out where the bus stops. A diagonal line through the number on a bus indicates partial service. People board in the front and exit from the back, except in double buses where any door may be used. Pushing a red button requests the driver to stop and some doors must be opened by pushing a button.

Until recently there were no intercity buses, encouraging riders to use the trains. Now, however, you can plan bus trips outside the city, as well. The large bus station, Gare Routière Internationale de Paris is situated at the east of Paris at Porte de Bagnolet and can be reached by *métro* line 3, station Gallieni. Check Eurolines that leaves from the Porte de Bagnolet (www.eurolines.com).

RER

The RER is a network of express trains that go to the suburbs in all directions. Stations and routes are specified on *métro* maps, drawn with thicker, different-coloured lines. The RER is faster and quieter than the *métro* and makes fewer stops. RER trains run about every 15 minutes, beginning around 5:30 am and ceasing about midnight. *Métro* tickets are valid on the RER in the Paris area; going farther requires a supplement, unless you have a pass that includes the outer

> For information on the RER B, Orlybus, and Roissybus, access the RATP website (www.ratp.fr).

zones. Lighted signs on each *quai* indicate the destination and each intermediate station for the next train. There are currently four main lines, but several fork off in different directions at some point; therefore, it is important to make sure that the train you are on goes exactly to your destination. Keep your RER ticket, as inserting it into a turnstile is usually necessary to exit the system.

French Railroads (SNCF)

Each of the six Société Nationale des Chemins de Fer Français (SNCF) train stations in Paris serve a different geographical region of France and farther destinations. Train reservations may be made at travel agents and train stations, by telephone or online. Tickets may be picked up at the station at least 90 minutes before departure (toll call info/reservations tel: 3635; www.sncf.com). Transilien is the SNCF train network that services the Ile-de-France.

Some trips are discounted, depending on the passenger's age or how much in advance the reservation is made. Considerably less expensive, discounted tickets are generally non-refundable and non-changeable. Before boarding the train, make sure to validate your ticket (*composter*) in one of the orange machines located at the head of the quais, or risk a fine. The SNCF stations and the directions they serve:

- 8^e: **Gare Saint-Lazare**; 13 rue d'Amsterdam. Northeast.
- 10^e: **Gare de l'Est**; place du 11 Novembre 1918. East.
- 10^e: **Gare du Nord**; 18 rue de Dunkerque. North, including the Eurostar and Thalys.
- 12^e: **Gare de Lyon**; place Louis-Armand. Southeast/South.
- 13^e: **Gare d'Austerlitz**; 7 boulevard de l'Hôpital. Southwest.
- 15^e: **Gare Montparnasse**; 17 boulevard de Vaugirard. West/Southwest. International trains.

The high-speed Eurostar train travels between central Paris (Gare du Nord) and central London (St. Pancras Station) in just over two hours (tel: 08.92.35.35.39; www.eurostar.com).

The Thalys is a high-speed train that travels between Paris (Gare du Nord), Amsterdam, Brussels and Cologne. Reservations are made through SNCF (tel: 3635; 08.99.34.56.05; www.thalys.com).

Taxis

There are some 17,000 taxis in Paris and almost 500 taxi stands, but this does not mean that a taxi is easy to find on a rainy day or at rush hour. The best bet is to wait at taxi stands, which are in every *arrondissement* and have blue and white signs marked 'taxis'. Taxis can be engaged directly from the stand, by telephone, or via the Internet.

Having called for pickup, you will be charged from the time the cab began its trip to pick you up, not from the time you get in. It is thus best to know the location of the nearest taxi stand. A cruising taxi may not pick up a customer within 50m of a stand unless there are no taxis or customers waiting there.

The newer taxies show a green light on the roof when the taxi is available, red when it is occupied. Older cabs may still have three small lights, one of which indicates the type of fare in the cab (day, night or to suburban zones). Each taxi has a *compteur* (meter), the fare is determined by a combination of time and distance. Rates are strictly regulated, raised once annually and consistent throughout the taxi system. There are supplements for each piece of baggage, for holidays, for pickup at the airport and when there are more than three people in a cab—although often drivers refuse (legally) to accept a fourth passenger, being unwilling to have someone ride in the front seat with them (other than their dog). Do not agree to pay for a driver's return trip from the airport and be wary of cut-rate offers. The driver is usually given a 10–15 per cent tip. Some, but not all, accept credit cards; to avoid misunderstandings, inform the driver when you enter the cab if you want to use a card. Below are some major 24-hour radio cabs:

- **Alpha Taxis** (tel: 01.45.85.85.85; www.alphataxis.fr)
- **Taxis Bleus** (tel: 3609; www.taxis-bleus.com)
- **Taxis G7** (tel: 3607; English: 01.41.27.66.9; www.taxisg7.fr)

Taxi drivers undergo several months of training and must be certified to obtain a licence, so they are usually knowledgeable about the city. If you have a complaint, get a receipt with the number of the cab and lodge a complaint with the Service des taxis, Préfecture de Police at 36 rue des Morillons, 75015 (tel: 0821 00 25 25).

Private cabs have entered the scene, offering a fixed price based on the kilometres travelled, and not the time passed. Thus the same journey will cost the same, anytime. For more information, access the website of **LeCab** (tel: 01.76.49.76.49; website www.lecab.fr) or **Chauffeur-Privé** (www.chauffeur-prive.com)

The privately-sponsored and controversial **Uber** taxi service is being protested by the official taxi companies, but at the time of writing continues to operate. UberPOP, however, one of its components, has been judged illegal by France's highest court.

Driving in Paris
Public transportation in Paris is so good that you should not need a car for everyday use. Rush hour traffic is extremely

slow and can be much worse on rainy days. During rush hour, traffic on the *périphérique* slows to a crawl and the major *portes* (entries into Paris from the *périphérique*) and large arteries are generally congested. *Bouchons* (traffic jams) and *embouteillages* (bottlenecks) are daily occurrences. Delivery trucks often block small, narrow streets, stopping traffic until a delivery has been made. Although drivers in Paris generally obey the traffic laws, they are aggressive and impatient. Take public transportation when you can.

Often better than owning a car is the **AutoLib** service provided by the city (www.autolib.eu). About 3,000 electric cars are available for rental for as long as you need one. Check the AutoLib app on your smartphone to find an available car close to you, pick it up at its docking station and later dock it close to where you want to go. There are 500 docking stations (*bornes*) in Paris and more in the suburbs, conveniently located and easy to track on your mobile phone. It's as simple as that. Access the website to find out more about the subscription plans and how it works. It does work, as the 10,000 rentals per day attest.

Driver's Licence

If you drive, always carry a valid driver's licence; visitors staying less than 90 days may use a licence from home. The International Driving Licence is advisable but not required in France (but may be necessary in other countries you visit). It is not available in France but may be obtained from your own automobile association. Students may use their home driver's licence for the duration of their studies. Those with a *carte de séjour* may use their home driver's licence—but not the International Driver's Licence—for one year from the date of issue of the *carte*. The licence must be valid, translated into French and issued before the residence permit.

After residence of one year, a French *permis de conduire* (driver's license) is required of EU residents. Expect the process to take about two months, so apply to the Préfecture before the end of the year. Bring a valid, translated driver's licence, proof of domicile, your *carte de séjour*, two passport-sized photographs and the current fee in the form of a *timbre fiscal*—a prepaid stamp purchased at a *tabac* (usually a café that also sells cigarettes and stamps) or online. The new European standard driving license has (in January 2016) started to appear and will eventually replace the licenses of the individual countries. Your own license should still be valid, though, and you will need to use whatever license you have for insurance and other reasons. Although a French

Métro entrances in Paris are clearly marked.

driver's license is valid for life, this option will gradually over the next decades be phased out. For information on validity in France of your own license, check the website europa.eu/youreurope or call 00 800 67.89.10.11.

Some countries and some states within the US have reciprocal agreements with France to waive the driving test, but all applicants must take the written exam on rules of the road. The exam is in French. To take the driving exam, enrol in a course at a certified driving school; some schools have sections for English speakers. *Code de la Route*, a booklet detailing the rules of the road, is available in most bookshops.

- **Fehrenbach Driving School**
  (53 boulevard Henri-Sellier 92150 Suresnes; tel: 01.45.06.31.17; www.frenchlicense.eu). Classes and materials are in English.

Report a lost driver's licence to the police immediately. They will issue a *récipissé de déclaration de perte ou de vol de pièce d'identité*, an acknowledgment that identity documents have been lost or stolen. Carry this when you drive until you have received a replacement licence.

For traffic violations, France, along with other EU countries, has a system whereby one loses points on the driver's licence for each infraction: the worse the infraction, the more points one loses, and the licence is forfeited when 12 points have been lost. People with foreign licences should understand that, although their licences cannot be taken away, information is computerised and shared. If a licence has become invalid in France, the information will show up on the system of the authorities in other countries. This includes British drivers, for the French system contacts British authorities for points to be subtracted.

For non-injury traffic offences, the police may require an on-the-spot *consignation* (deposit) on the fine. The matter is decided by the Tribunal de Police (traffic court). Police occasionally stop cars to check identity papers, so make sure you are carrying a valid driver's licence, along with the *carte grise* (vehicle registration document) and the *certificat d'assurance* described below.

Parking

With some 1.3 million cars in circulation each day, parking is at a premium. Fortunately, there are parking garages at the major entrances into the city, in the city centre, at most shopping centres and at numerous underground parking garages. Garages and parking meters are marked with a blue sign with a large white 'P' and indicated on city maps. Most ticket machines in the garages accept credit cards. Parking spaces in these garages may be available by the month—helpful if your apartment building does not have parking facilities.

Many city streets have areas marked *payant* (paying). The *horodateurs* (parking meters) operate from 9:00 am to 7:00 pm every day but Sunday; in August some do not require payment. Purchase a ticket from the nearest meter for the length of time you intend to park and place it on the dashboard. The time of expiration should be clearly visible to any meter reader. You can also get a parking ticket that is good all day. Meters accept the *Paris Carte*, a prepaid card that is sold at bar/tobacco (*bar/tabac)* shops.

Residents may apply to the Service Stationnement at 15 boulevard Carnot, 75012 for a *vignette de stationnement résidentiel*, a parking permit that allows reduced-rate parking in their *arrondissement* (tel: 01.44.67.28.28). Access the city's website for more information (www.paris.fr).

Tickets are issued for overtime parking or for parking in an illegal spot. To pay the fine, purchase a *timbre fiscal* from a *tabac* and follow the instructions on the ticket for affixing the stamp. Tickets paid within 30 days are given a *remise* (discount), but you pay more than double if you exceed the three months' deadline. EU citizens should note that unpaid tickets might be forwarded to your home country for payment. If your car is not where you parked it (especially if you have parked near a sign saying *stationnement gênant* (with a picture of a car being towed away), it might have been *remorquée et mise à la fourrière* (towed and impounded). Go to the nearest *commissariat* to determine at which of the six *préfourrières* (car depots) the car is being kept. After 48 hours the car goes to one of four central *fourrières* (car pounds).

Fines for retrieval include towing and storage charges, plus the original parking ticket.

Bringing a Car into France

Cars entering the country by road are not usually recorded by French customs; nonetheless it is important to have the car's registration and insurance papers with you. For shipped cars, the shipping company will be issued a *déclaration d'admission*

Obeying the Laws

Obey all laws, even if it looks as though other drivers are not.

- Wear a seat belt, whether in the front or back seat.
- Seat children under 10 in the back seat; babies must sit in buckled car seats.
- Give priority to cars entering your street from the right, no matter how small the street. If it does not apply at traffic-roundabouts, it will be indicated. The *priorité à droite* is one of the most important driving laws.
- Do not use the *klaxon* (horn) except in emergencies.
- Do not drive or park in the bus lanes or the AXE Rouge express lanes.
- Do not park where it says *parking interdit* or *stationnement interdit*. Although many people double park, park at corners or edge up onto the sidewalk, this is illegal.
- Do not dash through a traffic light just as it is turning red; many traffic lights are placed not at the corner but instead just before a crosswalk, and pedestrians begin to cross immediately upon the change of the light. Do not make U-turns or cross a solid white line. Stay on multi-lane roads, unless passing a car.
- Use high-beam headlights only on unlit roads. Cars behind you that flash their headlights are indicating they will not slow down.
- Obey the speed limits: 130 kph on highways, 110 kph on wet highways, 90 kph on rural roads, 50 kph in the city, 80 kph on the *périphérique*.

at customs, given to the owner when the car is delivered. Cars that have been owned for more than six months (and on which no previous taxes are due) are considered intended for personal use and are generally exempt from customs duties; this does not apply to trucks and utility vehicles. Bring all ownership and tax payment documentation pertaining to the car.

Generally, cars that will remain in the country for less than three months do not have to change their registration. For stays longer than three months, the car should have French *plaques d'immatriculation* (licence plates). You must convert its registration to the French *carte grise* within a year at the Préfecture or *mairie*. Bring your *carte de séjour*, proof of residence and car title.

Automobiles brought into France must conform to countrywide regulations, such as being equipped with a catalytic converter, and will be tested to ensure that they do. Since not all parts for imported cars are available in France, it is advisable to bring a sufficient quantity of small spare parts to avoid frustration.

Purchasing an Automobile

Instead of bringing a car, consider buying a French car on arrival. French cars—Citroen, Renault, and Peugeot are well-known, reasonably priced for their models, and can be repaired easily. When buying a car from a French dealer, you will receive a temporary ownership title; the dealer contacts the Préfecture for the permanent registration, after which you must present the necessary *carte de séjour* and proof of residence. To determine fair prices for particular makes and models, consult the online automobile purchaser's guide l'Argus (www.argusauto.com). Among the websites that discuss car purchases, Just Landed is particularly helpful (www.justlanded.com).

When buying a used car privately, you should obtain from the seller a *certificat de vente* (bill of sale). There should also be a *certificat de non-gage* (indicating that there are no liens or taxes due), the *carte grise* and a *certificat de passage* (indicating the mechanical condition of the car). Within two weeks, you should go to the Préfecture to transfer the title and register for new *plaques d'immatriculation* (licence plates). If you have obtained French licence plates for your car, do not use them until the car insurance reflects those plate numbers.

Automobiles bought in France to be exported within six months are issued a TT (temporary licence plate) by French customs. Legally, you must show proof of domicile, but you do not need to be a resident.

Automobile Insurance

For cars driven into the country, an *assurance-frontière* (temporary insurance policy) is available at the border from French customs. There are policies to cover the period until the automobile leaves France, ranging from eight days to a month; or, in the case of a long stay, until French insurance is arranged.

All automobiles must be insured. The *carte verte/certificat d'assurance* (green insurance card) must be displayed inside the windshield, along with an annually validated *vignette* (tax sticker), which can be bought at *tabacs* in November and which must be in place by December 1. The cost of the *vignette* is based on the age, horsepower and cubic capacity of the car.

Each car must also carry the *carte grise* and a *constat amiable d'accident*, a claim form obtained from the insurance company. In non-injury accidents, the form must be filled out, signed by both parties and sent to the insurance company. A *contrôle technique* (safety certification) must be kept in the car, along with spare headlight bulbs.

Unlimited third-party coverage (*au tiers*) is the minimum automobile insurance required by law, and coverage must be by a French or EU company. *Au tiers limité* includes third-party fire and theft while *tous risques* is comprehensive insurance; there are other more extensive options. Ask your friends or colleagues to recommend an insurance company and compare the services and prices of several companies before you choose. Make sure you read the fine print to find out what the insurance companies don't cover. Do your research carefully, for cancelling an insurance policy is almost as complicated as taking one out. Generally, agents handle home and health insurance, as well as automobile coverage. Policies run for one year and are generally renewed automatically. Ask your own broker for a letter documenting your insurance record. In some cases, a discount is available after one year, which is increased slightly for each year that passes with no claims.

Bicycling

Parisians love their *vélos* (bicycles). Many people ride their bikes as their main mode of transportation, as it's an easy, cheap and even healthy way of getting around. The city is encouraging bicycle riding by creating *pistes* (lanes) that are off-limits to motorised vehicles. Also, the bus lanes and pedestrian streets, all protected from car traffic, are open to cyclists. More lanes are being built, so cyclists have many options for safe riding throughout the city. The *couloirs vélos* (bicycle lanes) are marked by wide, white stripes. They run north and south, east and west, and all around the circular boulevards Maréchal.

It's important to wear a *casque* (helmet) even if not all cyclists do so. Car drivers tend to be aggressive and impatient,

Cycling has always been a convenient way to zip around, whether going to work or doing some shopping.

although occasionally they show courtesy to bikers, probably being bikers themselves. Also, if a car hits a bicycle, the car driver is usually liable. Riding bikes outside the *couloirs* during rush hour can be extremely difficult. Do not ride through a red light: not only is it dangerous, the same fines imposed on automobiles also apply to bikes.

As with the AutoLib electric car programme, **Vélib** offers bicycles to rent with the same procedures and conveniences (www.velib.paris.fr). Some 20,000 bicycles for public use are docked in automatic terminals in all the *arrondissements*. You register and take out a subscription. At the docking station, your credit card is read; the first half hour of use is free, and after that there is a small, escalating fee per 30-minute period (designed to give more riders more chances at bicycles). You may pick up a bike at one station and dock it to any other terminal, where your card is read once again.

People with Physical Disabilities

As of this writing, only some of the public transport system is wheelchair-accessible, but it's getting better: all buses are now wheelchair-accessible and the *métro* has already has many stations with lifts and escalators, and the others are in process of being refitted, station by station. All the stations on the line 14 Météor are wheelchair-accessible. Check the Infomobi or RATP websites (tel: 09.70.81.83.85; www.infomobi.com; www.ratp.fr).

The city continues to improve conditions for the disabled. Almost all sidewalks are sloped at the corners for wheelchair access, and all restaurants opened after 1994 are required to have wheelchair access.

- The **Maison Départmentale des Personnes Handicapées** at 69 rue de la Victoire 75009 provides information relevant to people with physical abilities in Paris (tel: 08.05.08.09.09; www.mdph.fr).
- The **Paris Tourist Office** offers extensive information both in its office and online (http://en.parisinfo.com/practical-paris/visiting-paris-with-a-disability)
- The **website of the city of Paris** also provides information. (www.paris.fr/portail/Solidarites/Portal.lut?page_id = 4947)

Ask at your *mairie* or at City Hall for current information that they may have. Information for people with reduced mobility may be found on the website Jaccede (www.jaccede.com).

A comprehensive, English-language guide is *Access in Paris* by Gordon Crouch and Ben Roberts. The website itself is helpful (www.accessinparis.org).

Although taxi drivers are obliged to take wheelchair passengers, there is no guarantee they will do so. (See pages 162–163 for more options.) Some companies, however, offer services customised for disabled passengers. Taxis for weekends or to the airports should be reserved in advance.

■ **G7 Horizon** (tel: 01.41.27.66.99)

THE CALL OF NATURE

Although they are slowly being phased out, Paris still has its sidewalk *sanisettes* (public toilets), which are easy to use, sanitary and cheap. Look for the oval structures with illuminated *toilettes* signs throughout the city. Museums, the larger hotels, restaurants, cafés, shopping centres and department stores all have public toilet facilities; in a bar or café you will be expected to buy a cup of coffee.

Some *toilettes* have a coin slot that takes €0.20: this usually means they are somewhat clean. Signs on doors may read *Toilettes*; or they may say *Dames/Femmes*, or *Hommes/Messieurs*; or they may only have pictures of a man or a woman.

SAFETY

Central Paris is generally safe. Tourist areas—the Eiffel Tower, Pigalle and Montmartre, around the Pompidou Museum, Sacre-Coeur and Forum Les Halles—see their share of petty thefts, but violence is extremely rare. It always pays to be cautious, however, and to stay on well-travelled streets late in the evenings. Don't carry more credit cards or cash than you need on a particular day, and if you're not going to drive in Paris, there's no need to automatically carry your driver's licence as you would at home. Don't flaunt your valuable jewellery, and men should not keep their wallets in their back pockets, Keep your passport safe and for Americans, carry the passport card instead. Note down all credit card numbers so you can report any loss or theft; don't keep the numbers with the cards or passport.

Also, except for the occasional pickpocket in crowded stations (where, too often, unsuspecting female tourists leave their handbags unguarded, and men their wallets exposed), the *métro* is generally safe, even late at night. Some stations with long corridors without visibility have mirrors at the corners so you can look down the corridors before turning. Each *quai* (platform) has *bornes d'alarme* (alarm boxes). Women who ride the *métro* late at night often sit in the first car directly behind the driver.

Sometimes there are people who prey on your sympathy: the person who claims to have found a gold ring on the sidewalk and wants to sell it to you; the pathetic young woman with a baby who asks if you speak English and then goes into her spiel. Just shake your head and walk on. This is mostly annoying, not dangerous. None of this is to serve as any particular warning. It's all just common sense in a large city where you're not used to manoeuvring the streets and where you might not be at home with the language.

Women should understand that in general, French men are personal and flirty, even in professional situations. This does not necessarily mean they are harassing you sexually. A French man (usually older) who kisses your hand by brushing it lightly or even just bringing it to his lips is being gallant, nothing more. Letting a French man take you to dinner and pay the bill does not necessarily mean a payoff at the end. On the other hand, young French men sometimes think they are acting cool when they openly ogle a pretty woman. If a man persists when told firmly to desist, women might call out loudly to passersby, "*Il m'aggresse*", which means that the man is being too aggressive toward her, or even call the police (tel: 17).

THE STUDENT LIFE
EU Nationals
Citizens of EU countries may study in any other EU country. In France, they must be enrolled in an accredited institution, have health insurance and enough financial wherewithal to

cover their stay in France. EU citizens—including students—also have the right to work in France (see Chapter 9). Upon registering with an institution, the student will receive an identity card that lasts for the period of study and is renewable year by year. Check the Paris website for young people (www.jeunes.gouv.fr).

EU nationals might inquire about the EU's Education Programme, Socrates/Erasmus, which encourages student mobility throughout the community (and in several other countries as well.) Qualifying students at a participating institution may study at another such institution for a year. British students should access the British Council website (www.britishcouncil.org/erasmus).

If you need to learn the language of the country you will study in, explore the Intensive Language Preparation Courses (ILPC), a short period of intense language study that takes place in the host country just before starting the Erasmus period. For more information on the Socrates/Erasmus Programme, access the EU website (http://ec.europa.eu/education/lifelong-learning-programme/doc80_en.htm).

Non-EU Nationals

Non-EU nationals who intend to study for a degree or certificate must apply for the *visa de long séjour mention étudiant* before departing for France. You must already have an *attestation de pré-inscription* (letter of admission) or other forms of acceptance, for example, a *certificat d'inscription* into an accredited institution. Upon arrival in France, you should apply within 30 days for the *carte de séjour temporaire* at the Cité Universitaire International de Paris, Maison International at 17 boulevard Jourdan, 75014. Bring the same documents you used to apply for the initial visa. In addition to your own universities that have study abroad programs, there are companies that specialise in such programs. Look at Study Abroad (www.studyabroad.com). Campus France is the French national agency that focuses on international student services (www.campusfrance.org).

Occasionally the French cultural affairs officer will ask to see academic credentials such as transcripts and diplomas.

If you are coming to France to study at a language school for less than six months, you may be issued a special *visa d'étudiant pour six mois avec plusieurs entrées*, which should waive the regular student permit. Be prepared to show proof of financial means, indicating that you have enough income to maintain yourself while in France. A medical examination and proof of health insurance are also required.

While in France, you will be expected to abide by all French laws. Ignorance of a law will not be accepted as an excuse for having violated it.

Health Insurance

Students must have health insurance. Coverage required is extensive: hospitalisation, outpatient treatment, dental care, medicines and medical evacuation. EU nationals covered by their country's health plans must enclose a French translation of the insurance coverage along with the application. Remember that not all costs of treatment are covered fully under the French health system. For health and insurance information, see pages 128–130 .

Resource Information

For information on the French university system, access the official websites of the Ministère de la Jeunesse, de l'Education et de la Recherche (www.education.gouv.fr). The Ville de Paris also has an informative website (www.etudiantdeparis.fr).

The official Campus France has extensive information on higher education in France, especially helpful for foreign students (www.campusfrance.org.) For Campus France offices in your country, access the website.

Several well-organised official associations offer advice on education, housing, employment, jobs, discounts on services and events, and dealings with the administration.

- **Centre d'Information et de Documentation Jeunesse (CIDJ)**: 101 quai Branly, 75015; tel: 01.44.49.12.00; www.cidj.com
- **Centre Régional des Œuvres Universitaires et Sociales (CROUS):** 39 avenue Georges-Bernanos, 75005; tel: 01.40. 51.36.00; www.crous-paris.fr

■ **Mission interuniversitaire de coordination des échanges franco-américains Paris-Ile de France (MICEFA)**: 26 rue de Faubourg Saint-Jacques, 75014; tel: 01.40.51.76.96; www.micefa.org. (Facilitates the access of American students into French universities and organises academic exchange programmes.)

French University Education

All *lycée* graduates who have passed the stringent baccalauréat (*le bac*) examinations are entitled to admission to a state-run university (*la fac*, short for *faculté*). Universities thus tend to be overcrowded, rigid in their curriculum and impersonal. The Institut Universitaire de Technologie (IUT) is a two-year community college system offering certificates in professional and technical specialties.

Top *lycée* students may choose to apply to a business school or an engineering school, or any other *Grande École*. These schools have limited spaces available, for their graduates ultimately become the French elite—the most powerful politicians and civil servants, and the most influential business professionals in France. Among the most sought-after graduates are those from l'École Nationale d'Administration (ENA), Ecole Polytechnique (X), Institut d'Etudes Politiques (IEP or Sciences Po) and Hautes Etudes Commerciales (HEC).

For business schools, there is a one-year course to prepare for the entrance exam.This course is so stringent that some students repeat the year in order to get a better ranking in the exam and thus to be accepted into a better school. The programme for the engineering schools is similar, except that it is a two-year course. Again, some students repeat the course in order to get into a more prestigious school.

■ **Université de Paris**: a conglomerate of some 17 separate institutions offering degree programmes in particular specialties; each institution has its specialties. The most ancient and illustrious, the Sorbonne, founded in 1253, is now also part of the system and known as Université de Paris IV (tel: 01.40.46.22.11; www.sorbonne.fr).
■ **Collège de France**; a prestigious school founded in 1530. A research and teaching institution whose courses

are open to everyone without advance registration at 11 place Marcelin Berthelot, Paris 75005 (tel: 01.44.27.12.11; 01.44.27.11.09; www.college-de-france.fr).

Degrees

The curriculum at all universities is highly regulated. A stringent core curriculum takes up the first two years, after which the Diplôme d'Etudes Universitaires Générales (DEUG) is awarded, or at a technological university, the Diplôme Universitaire de Technologie (DUT). After a third year the *license* (degree) is awarded. Some business or vocational programmes involve a postgraduate stage (training internship). A *maîtrise* can be added to the license; it requires an added year of study and completion of a dissertation or project and is roughly the equivalent of a Master's Degree. Then the student has a choice between finishing these studies with a more practical diploma called the Diplôme d'Etudes Supérieures Spécialisées (DESS) or continuing toward a doctorat (PhD) by preparing for a diploma called the Diplôme d'Etudes Approfondies (DEA).

Qualifications

Any foreign student applying to a French university for a degree programme must meet the stringent requirements of the rigorous educational system in France. British students, for example, must have their A-levels and American students with the SAT scores are sometimes required to have completed two years of college. Fluent French to the point of being able to read complicated texts is necessary and proficiency tests are given before acceptance into a programme. A few of the Grandes Écoles have small quotas for foreign students, but in general, non-EU students are rarely admitted.

Exam Preparation

Preparatory workshops for college and graduate school qualifying examinations may be taken at the Sight Test Prep/Kaplan Center, 44 rue de Miromesnil, 75008, which offers courses for the GMAT, GRE, TOEFL, SAT, ISAT, etc. (tel: 01.58.18.62.48; www.sight-testprep.com).

English Language Institutions

More realistic options for university study include taking a degree from one of the many fully accredited English-language institutions with degree programs in Paris or taking a year abroad sponsored by a university at home. Some schools have better credentials than others, and some may not suit your particular needs or goals, so explore all possibilities.

- **The American University of Paris (AUP)**: Bachelor of Arts in a variety of fields, such as art history, comparative literature, economics and modern history; Bachelor of Science in applied economics and computers. (102 rue St. Dominique 75007; tel: 01.40.62.07.20; www.aup.edu)

- **American Business School (ABS)**: French school offering an American undergraduate degrees in business administration. Students must have the equivalent of the French bac, British 'A' levels or an American high school diploma. (12 rue Alexandre-Parodi, 75010; tel: 01.80.97.65.50; www.absparis.org).

- **The University of London Institute in Paris**: Programmes in basic and business French, culture, current events, translation. Bachelor of Arts in French studies, leading to a University of London degree. (11 rue de Constantine, 75007; tel: 01.44.11.73.83; www.ulip.london.ac.uk)

- **Parsons Paris**: A branch of the prestigious New School (New York), Parsons offers both credit and non-credit programmes in illustration, fashion design, studio arts, computer graphics, etc., with flexible schedules of day, evening and weekend courses. Bachelor of Fine Arts degree. (45 rue Saint-Roch 75001; tel: 01.76.21.76.40; www.newschool.edu/parsons-paris).

- **Schiller International University**: Graduate, undergraduate and business degrees. The focus is on economics and business, government and public administration. (7–9 rue Yvart, 75015; tel: 01.45.38.56.01; www.paris-schiller.com).

- **Paris American Academy**: Four-week courses in fine arts, interior design, French language & civilisation, creative writing and fashion. Courses begin in January, June, July and September. (277 rue Saint-Jacques, 75005; tel: 01.44.41.99.20; www.parisamericanacademy.fr).

Graduate and MBA Programs

French employers are beginning to look for advanced degrees, such as the Master's in Business Administration (MBA). Corporations are also officially required through the CIF (*Congé Individuel de Formation*) programme to sponsor continuing education (or training) for their employees. Several schools, including those below, offer MBA programmes in English; their curricula vary, so investigate several, including those mentioned above. Most require some years of work experience in addition to a college degree. Those listed below have English-language programmes.

- **INSEAD**: Internationally known French business school, offering a ten-month MBA, as well as doctoral programmes. On the average, students have five years of business experience. (15 boulevard de Constance, 77305 Fontainebleau; tel: 01.60.72.40.00; www.insead.edu).

- **American Graduate School of Business, International Relations, and Diplomacy**: Accredited school for MA and PhD programmes.(101 boulevard Raspail 75007; tel: 01.47.20.00.94; www.ags.edu).

Technology has made research more convenient and portable for students. French undergrad surfing online at a streetside cafe in Paris.

- **International School of Management**: Fully accredited MBA, DBA and PhD programmes in management, plus customised programmes for senior managers. (148 rue de Grenelle, 75007; tel: 01.45.51.09.09; www.ism.edu).
- **Paris Graduate School of Management:** A private, accredited institution offering six different business schools, with majors in business, management, marketing and more—both in French and English. Undergraduate, graduate, and postgraduate programs. (International Office: 17 boulevard Raspail 75007; tel: 01.55.25.69.56; www.business-school-pgsm.com)

Studying French
See Chapter 8.

Cooking Courses
What could be better than learning to cook in this world capital of *haute cuisine*? Short- and long-term cooking classes and demonstrations are both instructive and fun. Some of the language schools offer their own classes, but there are well-known cooking schools that offer both serious long-term programmes for serious chefs and short-term courses for those who just love to cook.

- **Librairie Gourmande** at 92-96 rue Montmartre 75002 specialises in cookbooks (tel: 01.43.54.37.27).
- **Ritz Escoffier School:** Demonstrations and courses of all levels. Also offers pastry courses, wine appreciation, flower arrangement and even cocktail preparations. (Ritz Hotel, 15 Place Vendome (Place Vendome; tel: 01.43.16.30.50; www.ecole-escoffier.ritzparis.com).
- **École Le Cordon Bleu:** Short-term courses and demonstrations are held in English; long-term courses for the serious chef are in French. Other addresses throughout the world and in the Loire Valley, at the Château des Briottières. (8 rue Léon Delhomme, 75015; tel: 01.85.65.15.01; www.cordonbleu.edu)
- **École Lenôtre:** Workshops and demonstrations for the amateur and a professional cooking school for serious

chefs. Also in Cannes. (10 avenue des Champs-Élysées, 75008; tel: 08.11.65.66.56; www. lenotre.com).

Libraries

There are hundreds of *bibliothèques* (libraries) in Paris; there is at least one public library in each *arrondissement*. Some libraries specialise in particular fields, there are even some for children only, such as L'Heure Joyeuse at 6 rue des Prêtres-Saint-Séverin, 75006. To obtain a library card, bring identification and proof of domicile. Some libraries may be open only from Tuesdays to Fridays; check before going. In addition, each University of Paris section has its own library for enrolled students, as does the American University of Paris.

- 4e: **Bibliothèque Publique d'Information:** Extensive multilingual research library, periodicals, a video and music listening room, software library, Internet access. Open daily; hours vary. (Centre George Pompidou, second floor; tel: 01.44.78.12.75; www.bpi.fr).

- 7e: **American Library in Paris:** Europe's largest subscription English-language library with fiction, non-fiction, periodicals, back issues, children's books. Readings, literary programmes, lectures, etc. are also organised. Research facilities available. Tuesdays–Saturdays; 10:00 am–7:00 pm. Sundays: 1:00 pm-7:00 pm. (10 rue du Général-Camou; tel: 01.53.59.12.60; www.americanlibraryinparis.org).

- 13e: **Bibliothèque Nationale de France, François Mitterand:** Twelve million volumes (many in English), reading facilities. An exhibition centre, auditorium, conference room and restaurants also found on the premises. (11 quai François-Mauriac; tel: 01.53.79.59.59; www.bnf.fr)

A complete list of public libraries—'Bibliothèques de la Ville de Paris'—should be available at your *mairie*.

STUDENT HOUSING

If you are enrolled in a school for the fall semester starting in October, start your housing search in the summer. Do not come to Paris at the end of September and expect to find decent quarters when other students are also looking. If you are under 18, you may need a *garant* (guarantor), most often a parent, to guarantee financial responsibility and to sign the lease for an apartment. Inquire about housing at the resource organisations mentioned above, at the institution with which you will be affiliated and, perhaps, at the Paris Tourist Office, which can sometimes be helpful. The bulletin boards at the American Church and the American Cathedral often have notices of people looking for roommates or for sublets. See Resource Guide in Chapter 10 for addresses.

The Ville de Paris sponsors a major international housing campus, Cité Universitaire, at the southern edge of the city at 19 boulevard Jourdan, 75014 (tel: 01.44.16.64.00; www.ciup.fr). Forty buildings of different national styles are spread across sprawling grounds that include housing for registered foreign students, as well as sports and cultural facilities. Countries have their own buildings and students usually stay in the hostel that corresponds with their nationality.

The Accueil Familial des Jeunes Etrangers at 23 rue du Cherche-Midi, 75006 is an *au pair* agency that also helps young adults find rooms in a family home in exchange for work, or paying rooms (tel: 01.42.22.50.34). See also pages 344–345 for information on *au pairs*.

Temporary Housing

Young people may stay inexpensively (and temporarily) at the *auberges de jeunesse* (youth hostels). The maximum stay is generally six nights. Hostels generally are crowded, so book in advance. Membership cards for Hostelling International can be purchased before departure at travel agencies that cater to budget travel, as well as at hostels themselves. Hostels generally have no facilities for ensuring the safety of valuables, so if you are bringing extensive baggage or a computer, staying in an inexpensive hotel might be better than in a hostel.

Fédération Unie des Auberges de Jeunesse (FUAJ) at 27 rue Pajol, 75018; (tel: 01.44.89.87.27; www.fuaj.org), runs several hostels in the city centre. You can reserve and pay in advance at any hostel that is a member of Hosteling International (www.hihostels.com).

STUDENTS AND RATP

If you will be using the public transportation system regularly for school, investigate Imagine R, the RATP yearly pass for students that allows unlimited use of public transportation for a steeply discounted price (www.imagine-r.com).

THE WORLD CAPITAL
OF FOOD

CHAPTER 6

'Eating in France is a ritual that
can reach religious proportions.'
—David Applefield

FRENCH CUISINE

Parisians love their restaurants. They love to eat in this capital of gastronomy, and when they're not eating, they're talking about where they have recently eaten or where to eat next. One of the greatest pleasures, for instance, is partaking with close friends of a memorable meal to celebrate whatever is the event of the moment. Savoring the tastes of the food and wine, enjoying each other, and creating new memories, centers itself in the restaurants of Paris.

Exploring restaurants, each with its own approach to flavours and textures, will give you the unparalleled opportunity to participate in what is considered one of the world's great art forms. With more than 13,000 eating establishments, ranging from the newly trendy food trucks and casual cafés to world-renowned restaurants, dining within your taste and price range is possible. Of course, the more refined the restaurant, the higher the price: a full meal in a restaurant with Michelin 'stars' may cost more than €400 per person, and even an average three-course dinner in a small bistro can cost about €40, including a carafe of the *vin de la maison* (house wine).

While Paris itself is not known for a particular cuisine, the city has, luckily, taken to its heart the finest traditional, regional cuisines of France, while also embracing the innovative and adventurous inspirations of the modern, international world. Although there is little that is truly cheap here, prices are more reasonable in neighbourhood *bistros* and *brasseries* and in the Asian and North African eateries where the food, although not as beautifully presented, can be tasty. New young chefs (many of whom trained with the masters) are breaking the traditional bounds and drawing crowds with inventive combinations and lower prices for their stylish creations; their rents in the outer *arrondissement*s can be cheaper than in the centre, meaning their prices may also be more reasonable, at least while they're on the way up.

Nouvelle cuisine, an adaptation of traditional cooking that uses lighter foods, combinations of the freshest ingredients and small portions did not catch on in Paris, although people are nonetheless eating lighter foods and smaller portions. This is partly because the portions served were usually already smaller than in restaurants elsewhere, especially In North America. 'Doggy bags' didn't exist in France until very recently; only now with the determination of the government to cut down on food waste, are restaurants required to provide their customers with the means to take home uneaten portions of their meals. (And grocers must now by law donate their still-good but out-of-date foods rather than throwing them away.)

Cuisine de terroir, which is currently popular, offers dishes in slightly larger portions and combines regional ingredients with more traditional recipes. 'Slow food' offers leisurely meals that respect both the ecology and culinary traditions of the region and has its *passionnés* (fans) in Paris.

The restaurants of the regions of France may advertise *cuisine de province/cuisine régionale*. These vary in quality and price, but it is possible to get a wide understanding French cuisine without leaving Paris: for example, the sausage and sauerkraut dishes of Alsace, tomato- and olive oil-based dishes of Provence, pork dishes from Lyon, cheese dishes from Savoy or the creamy specialties of Normandy. *Cuisine bonne femme* means home-cooked food, and a dish labelled '*fait maison*' means that it is totally prepared in-house. In fact, regulations now declare that only with total in-house preparation may a restaurant—or even just a dish—be declared *fait maison*. This is reassuring to Parisians who want to know they are getting what they are paying for.

Restaurants of all levels are also catering to the simpler tastes and budgets of a younger generation that is not willing to spend €100 on one meal, a younger set that tends to frequent the more casual bistros, wine bars, tearooms, the burger joints, sushi bars, and the inexpensive Asian restaurants. Fish restaurants and bistros are also increasingly attractive to people concerned about health and fitness. (Fish is freshest on Fridays and some fish restaurants are closed Mondays.) And 'bio' and vegan restaurants are burgeoning, as well.

Happily, international restaurants abound. Vietnam, that once belonged to France, has an enormous presence with numerous eateries to choose among (especially in the 13th *arrondissement*, where hundreds of small eateries represent Asia well) and there are examples from almost every continent and country to choose among.

Do not underestimate the offerings at museums, airports, or train stations. At the top of the Centre Georges Pompidou, for example, the sophisticated restaurant Georges overlooks Paris, and the restaurant in the Musée d'Orsay offers traditional dishes in an ornate old-world setting. Also, inside the Musée des Arts Décoratifs, the Saut du Loup has views over the Tuileries Gardens. The train station, Gare de Lyon, itself houses the highly-rated Le Train Bleu, which is exceptionally beautiful, and the airport Charles de Gaulle now offers an assortment of stylish, meals and snacks from the city's known establishments. On the roof of the Théâtre des Champs Elysées, also is Maison Blanche, a graceful surprise. Food courts offer choices at the stylish Carrousel du Louvre shopping complex, adjacent to the Louvre, and the ultramodern Centre Beaugrenelle in the 15th *arrondissement* has an entire floor for its food court. These are just a few examples.

All in all, what this means is that with some pleasant exploration you are sure to find what pleases you, and you'll eat very well, at a price that suits your needs.

THE AGREEABLE SEARCH

Reading about restaurants and their ratings can be a lifetime hobby here. Bookstores carry an array of guides devoted to dining in Paris, and dozens of websites claim to suggest the 'best' eateries of all categories and levels. (Guides themselves are online). The most prestigious, the *Guide Michelin*, annually awards up to three stars to the best restaurants; when a three-star restaurant loses a star, the scandal makes news all over the world. News of restaurants also appear in the daily newspapers and Parisians keep track of the opening or closing of restaurants and when a famous chef leaves one establishment for another or opens his own.

All tourist guides recommend restaurants, rating them according to their readership—some concentrate on inexpensive establishments catering to a budget traveller, while others may feature upmarket restaurants. Along with *Michelin*, *Gault-Millau* and the reader-rated *Zagat* guides are the most famous. But there are dozens of others, such as the well-respected *Gayot* and *Cheap Eats in Paris,* that describes moderately-priced locations throughout the city.

The Internet, of course, abounds with suggestions for the best restaurants in particular categories or even *arrondissement*. Check such websites as the extensive and varied Paris by Mouth (www.parisbymouth.com), Trip Advisor (www.tripadvisor.com) and Yelp (www.yelp.com) for customer reviews. The Tourist Office occasionally publishes a booklet of recommendations all around the city and also has ideas on its website (www.parisinfo.com). Your own friends and colleagues will, of course, recommend their favourites, and over time, in general, the 'best' restaurant for you will be the one where you are most comfortable and well fed, no matter which levels you have explored.

Do not be hidebound. Experiment with dishes you have never heard of and foods not popular in your own country. Try the French regional dishes, and take the *métro* to the 13th *arrondissement* and explore the little Asian eateries until you find the ones you like the best. No matter the orientation, France knows what to do with food. Even in restaurants of *haute cuisine*, expect to find beautifully prepared dishes made from inexpensive meats such as tripe, brains or kidneys—all considered delicacies by the French. After trying them, you might see why.

And yes, no matter the above, it is still possible to get a bad meal in Paris, as it is anywhere. It may be the day off of the regular chef and the replacement isn't up to the standard you're used to. Or perhaps the restaurant was just not to your taste or standards. For instance, locals rarely frequent the large establishments along the Grands Boulevards, for they generally cater to tourists, and although the food can be good, the service tends to be impersonal and prices high. (If a placard menu is printed in three or four languages with pictures of different flags, you can be sure it caters to tourists.

How to Choose Where to Eat

It used to be that a category of eating establishment meant something. A restaurant was of a higher refinement than a bistro, and a bistro was more complete than a café. But categories these days are blurring, and what you might consider an upmarket restaurant with high prices, might bill itself as a bistro. Even guidebooks differ in their particular categorisations.

What an eating establishment is called matters less, of course, than the specialties of each, the quality of ingredients and their preparation, the service and the price. Good establishments of any category will be sought out, so except in fine restaurants, do not expect to find a quiet corner for a private conversation. This said, thinking about categories can still be helpful.

The Restaurant

France has some 600 Michelin-starred restaurants of which seventy are in Paris, with nine receiving the ultimate accolade of three stars. Starred establishments run from the merely outstanding and opulent to the world-famous and exorbitant, but in all, the ambience, presentation of the food, and the exquisitely attentive service are part of the value of the experience. In these, the prices match the setting. But for special occasions, they truly are special.

As you will see, some of the temples of *haute cuisine* feature the name of the chef, for true gourmets follow the progress of *les maîtres de la gastronomie*—such Alain Ducasse, Guy

Savoy, Alain Senderens, Yannick Alléno, or Joël Robuchon. It's exciting when a master chef opens a 'baby bistro' that offers the same quality with simpler presentations and more moderate prices. These occurrences make the news, and rightly so: Parisians follow their master chefs the way they do their restaurants.

But think of the hundreds of other restaurants that may not be starred by Michelin, but which may be outstanding in their way, serving what may be called *cuisine bourgeoise*. In smaller restaurants the patron may personally supervise all dishes that come from the kitchen and make recommendations on wine, whereas others may have dedicated *serveurs* at each table, plus a *sommelier* to discuss the wine. In any, service will be efficient but not rushed, and a full meal may take two or three pleasant hours. Pay attention, too, to those up-and-coming young chefs who have trained with the masters and who are coming into the light. Bringing their own understandings of modern French cuisine to an appreciative clientele in what are sometimes called 'gastrobistros', these are the next great chefs to follow.

The Bistro

A bistro, on the other hand, once conjured up the image of hearty, home-cooked food in a casual, welcoming setting. Now, however, these friendly neighbourhood eateries still dot the neighbourhoods, but bistros range all the way to the extremely sophisticated and chic (*haut* bistro or neo-bistro) crossing the line to what was once the province only of restaurants. Here is where labels truly matter less. Some say that 'bistro' (alternatively spelt as 'bistrot') is a Russian word meaning 'hurry' and was introduced into France by Russian soldiers in 1815. Others claim it comes from the word *bistrouille*, which in certain northern regions is a mixture of coffee and *eau de vie*. Whichever is true, you may eat more quickly than in a restaurant, but you probably won't be rushed to leave. The menu in casual bistros is often written on a blackboard and is changed daily according to what is in season, supplementing traditional dishes such as *bœuf bourguignon* (beef stewed in red wine) and *blanquette de veau* (creamy veal stew). Meals run from the modern and trendy, traditional and hearty, to old favourites imaginatively executed with the chef's own twist. Decent house wines are offered by the carafe, but more impressive wines can also be found. What's best is to find a place where after a while you can become a regular, eating well and feeling at home.

Cafés And Bars

The café is an all-purpose eating establishment: you may linger over a breakfast croissant and coffee, dash in for lunch, stop for a cup of tea and a snack in the afternoon, or enjoy a drink and a meal in the evening. (In fact, unlike a bistro, you can just have a drink any time of day.) Ranging from the famous and expensive, to those catering to regulars from the *quartier*, the basic café does not generally bother much about decor. Outdoor tables are sought after in summer, and are busy late into the night. Most importantly, cafés are often the community gathering places for friends, such as the Bar Ourcq, with its relaxed summer seating along the canal. Each neighbourhood café has its own personality

Know Your Beverages

- *Café*: strong black coffee. Also *expresso*, *un express* or *un café noir*
- *Café serré*: double strength expresso
- *Noisette*: expresso with a dash of milk
- *Café allongé*: coffee with hot water to dilute it
- *Café filtre*: black coffee, less strong
- *Café au lait*: coffee with milk
- *Café crème*: coffee with steamed cream or milk
- *Décaféiné* or *un déca*: decaffeinated coffee
- *Thé nature*: plain tea
- *Thé citron*: tea with lemon
- *Thé au lait*: tea with milk
- *Infusion*: herbal tea
- *Chocolat chaud*: hot chocolate

and loyal *habitués* (regulars), and can be a lot of fun. Many remain true to their name, but others—depending on the clientele—are excellent, and gone is the day when you'd pass them by if you wanted a good meal at a low price. Café Pouchkine, for example, with three elegant locales for teas, divine pastries, and full repasts with some specially created Russian dishes, brings the concept of a café to new heights (www.cafe-pouchkine.fr).

Most neighbourhood cafés close around 11:00 pm; those in touristy areas stay open later. If a table at a café has a placemat and a table setting at mealtimes, it is reserved for those who come to eat; find a bare table if you just want to have a cup of coffee. For a quick coffee or a mineral water, stand at the *comptoir* (counter), where the prices are cheaper.

A bar has more to do with atmosphere than with alcohol, and some daytime cafés are popular bars by night, serving drinks and simple meals or snacks until the wee hours. People go to their favourite bars at all times of the day: for a quick jolt of coffee in the mornings, for a simple lunch, for an aperitif before the theatre or drink after, or just to relax with a fruit juice in the afternoons. The 'happy hour' has become popular in early evening. Some bars have pleasant terraces, others are known for their music, and some are just popular as hangouts. Although there are hip bars throughout the city, it is a local bar in your neighbourhood that will lure you in—and keep you coming back.

As for fruit juices, if you order an orange juice, you will most likely get something in a can; order, instead, an *orange pressée* or a *citron pressé* (lemonade) for a freshly squeezed drink served with a carafe of water to adjust the strength as you like.

Brasserie

The word "*brasserie*" in French means brewery, and, happily, Paris has joined the ranks of the artisanal hand-crafted beers served in lively pubs, accompanied by appropriate meals. *Brasseries* began serving beer in the 17th century, and soon started offering hearty Alsatian sausages and *choucroute* (sauerkraut), plus Alsatian Riesling and Gewürztraminer wines. Nowadays, however, *brasseries* have evolved into casual restaurants that stay open all day, serving simple meals and fresh fish, usually nicely presented and reasonably priced. Bright, lively and bustling, it is highly recommended to reserve in advance for the more popular ones. Pay attention to the decor: some look like traditional beer houses while others have an inviting Belle Epoque decor or Art Deco wood panelling and sparkling glass and mirrors. Others, such as the Brasserie Barbès with its four floors, rooftop patio, and dancing, go way beyond. The word *brasserie* itself has also become chic, with the one-star eating heaven 114 Faubourg in the Hotel Bristol calling itself a *brasserie*. (It's all in the comparison: the Bristol's Epicure restaurant currently has three stars!) For real beer pubs and several craft beers on tap, though, see Beers on pages 227–228.

Business Hours

Restaurants and bistros open around noon and are busiest between 1:00 pm and 2:30 pm. They close after lunch and reopen for dinner. Lunch is a popular meal to eat out and restaurants are fill quickly. When considering an elegant restaurant, think about first trying it at lunch, when the portions served are smaller and less expensive than at dinner, but overall of the same quality. Dinner service starts around 7:30 pm and restaurants begin to fill up around 8:30 pm, taking their last order about 11:00 pm. *Brasseries* and cafés serve food all day, as do the *salons de thé*. Most restaurants close one day a week, and until recently it was hard to find a restaurant open on Sunday, except for kosher and Asian establishments.

Some establishments close on weekends and around holidays, and even those of *haute cuisine*, do close for a *fermeture annuelle* (annual holiday) sometime in July or August. If they stay open, they may keep an irregular schedule, closing on the weekends or for lunch on Monday. Check their website for opening hours, especially in summer.

LA CARTE

First, note that in a restaurant, you will be brought *la carte*, which is the menu. *Le menu* does not refer to the 'menu' as we understand it in English, that is, the list of food items available, but instead it refers to a set meal of two or three courses, specially selected for that day. Ordering *à la carte*, that is, from the standard *carte* is the most expensive way to dine, so it's best to check out the day's menu. Restaurants of all calibres offer their menu (also called the *formule* or *prix fixe*). The price is determined according to the number of courses ordered and of course, by the level of the restaurant. The set menu generally is offered at lunch (*midi*); and may include a glass of the house wine. In the evening, some of the finer restaurants may have a *menu dégustation*, meaning a sampler plate highlighting different specialties of the chef.

A *plat du jour* (daily special) may be written on a paper inserted into the *carte*. In bistros, the daily *carte* may be a chalkboard brought to your table to view. Aside from the lower price, another benefit of the *plat du jour* is that you'll be eating food that is at the height of its season. In autumn, for instance, game dishes such as boar, hare, pheasant and venison appear, as well as wild mushrooms—*chanterelles*, *cèpes* and *girolles*. (Omelettes with wild mushrooms are popular for lunch, and rightly so.) Spring and summer see *navarin d'agneau* (spring lamb stew), *morilles* (morels), asparagus, melons and other seasonal produce.

Your *serveur/serveuse* (waiter/waitress) is the best source for questions concerning the meal. The waiter profession is a respected one in France, and waiters, knowledgeable about ingredients and methods of preparation, take pride in what they serve. Waiters generally wear a similar uniform of black trousers, white shirt and often, a black bow tie. In better restaurants, they may wear dinner jackets, while in cafés and *brasseries* they may wear a black, pocketed vest. Waiters are cordial, but they do not presume—as they tend to do in America—to be your friends; you should not presume so either. Treat them pleasantly and with respect.

Do not hesitate to discuss with the *serveur* the ingredients in a dish you would like to order, to specify politely what you can and cannot eat, and to ask advice. The waiter will agreeably go back to the kitchen to discuss with the chef,

How Do You Like Your Food?

When ordering, understand that the French generally like their food cooked minimally.

- *bleu* is hardly warm.
- *saignant* is browned on the exterior and warm on the inside.
- *à point* is medium.
- *bien cuit* is well done—although perhaps not well done enough for foreigners.

Specify in advance if you insist on having your meat well done. Veal may be *rosé* (pink) and poultry may also remain pink toward the bone. Also, if you like fish but hate the bones, ask to have it *préparé*, and your *serveur* will debone it for you.

but if he says that your request "cannot be done", it could mean intransigence on his part; more likely than not, it means that the success of the dish requires a special method of preparation that cannot be altered. In such a case, order a different dish.

For a full meal, start with an *entrée* (appetiser), then have the *plat* (main course). *Salade* (salad), heretofore served after the *plat*, is now usually served as an *entrée*. After the *plat*, a variety of cheeses may be offered; select a few of different textures. Then comes dessert and after that, *café*. If this all sounds like too much food, don't be concerned about ordering less. It is no longer frowned upon to order two courses instead of a three-course meal, and it is acceptable to share an appetiser or dessert, or to skip the cheese or dessert altogether. Some people have started to order two appetizers, and the waiters' frowns are becoming less frequent. The French drink coffee after dessert, not with it, and except for breakfast, they do not drink *café crème* with meals, just one small and potent *café*. Yet times are changing, even in Paris—tell the waiter your preference politely and with a smile, and flexibility may be in store.

MAKING RESERVATIONS

Dinner reservations at the top 'starred' restaurants can be made a month in advance. For the currently fashionable restaurants, call weeks ahead; for a restaurant in the neighbourhood, perhaps the same day or a day or two before the dinner. Lunch reservations are somewhat easier to obtain. *Maîtres d'hôtel* may ask for the number of *couverts* (table settings) rather than how the number of people. Some ask that confirmation be made on the day, and if they do not know you, may ask for your telephone number. And don't forget that in making reservations, one usually uses the 24-hour clock: thus if you want to dine at 9:00 pm, ask for a reservation at 21 *heures*.

Cancel a reservation if you cannot make it, and do not arrive late, thinking mistakenly that you will just have to wait—seating is generally prompt, the *maître d'hôtel* having gauged when the previous party will vacate the table, and many of the best restaurants have one seating only. In the best restaurants men usually wear jackets. Although dining out is more casual than heretofore, it is still best to dress appropriately for the establishment; it heightens the sense of occasion.

A large number of restaurants have their own website, from which you can reserve your table, and there are online services such as La Fourchette (www.lafourchette.com); The Fork (www.thefork.com/city/paris/415144) or Book a Table (www.bookatable.co.uk/paris-restaurants).But it's still best just to call, especially if you have special requests or a large party. Websites can have English options and have English speakers for the phone.

YOUR OWN DECISION

First, decide what you want for a particular meal. Do you want a formal meal in a restaurant or something light and fast? Do you value a warm welcome and friendly, casual service? Do you want to sample the dishes of an innovative chef? Do you want to celebrate a great occasion and take part in a gastronomic experience that you will always remember? Or on a particular day, do you just want your meat cooked to a crisp and some coffee with the main course (no matter how barbaric it seems to your waiter)? In the case of the latter, you should stick with restaurants that cater to an international clientele. In any case, respect each restaurant for what it is.

A two-star restaurant may not whip up a hamburger for your kids (although priding themselves on service, they may well do so). Value for the money is always the key.

If you have dietary restrictions, you will no doubt find helpful information on the web: e.g., for *cacher* (kosher) restaurants, check out www.123cacher.com or www.kosherinfrance.com. And for *halal*, try www.paris-halal.com. Vegetarian and vegan restaurants (known as "bio") are also present on the web. (See pages 234–235.)

Some places advertise *à volonté*, meaning that for a particular dish, you may eat as much as you want for the price listed. And the newest establishments are listed as 'accessible'; more information is available on ww.parisinfo. com under its 'practical Paris' section.

All restaurants display their menus, from which you can ascertain the type of cuisine, the specialties and the price range. When passing an inviting restaurant, step in and ask for a business card to take note of the location and telephone number, and look in at mealtimes to see whether a place seems filled with locals—people who already know what is good or bad, what is 'in' or 'out'.

The Terrace

One thing just about all Parisians want is to eat outside. From two rickety chairs at a small table outside a bar/tabac to the most elegant gardened terrace with a three-star meal, Parisians find them all. When the first ray of the sun appears in the spring, outdoor eating becomes a must. Cafés open their large windows that had been closed all winter, sun shades are opened once more, and menus take on a summery feel. You'll find the cafés in your own neighbourhood that suit, but hundreds of others outdoor opportunities around town await.

Dozens of hotels offer the finest of outdoor dining or even just a snack. To name just a few, think of the roofs of the Warwick (8e) or Raphael (16e), the terraces of the Royal Monceau (16)e and Les Jardins du Marais (11e), or the courtyards of the Mandarin Oriental (1er) and Fouquet's Barrière (8e).

And the museums, as well, from the Louvre with its famous neighbor Café Marly to the Musee Rodin with its elegant gardens, or nearby the Musee du Quai Branly (both in the 7e). And, as mentioned above, the popular Georges at the top of the Pompidou, has a view, as well as an extensive menu. Certainly, you'll find the cafés in your own neighbourhood that suit you best, but hundreds of others outdoor opportunities around town await.

Smoking

Remember that smoking is banned in all public places. If you must smoke, find a place with a terrace or other outside tables. Even so, be sure to ask your non-smoking neighbours If your smoking bothers them. Most often they say it's fine with them, but it's polite to ask first. Electronic cigarettes have become popular instead, and the e-clope boutiques sell e-cigarettes.

Dispose of your cigarettes properly. Paris is cracking down: if you just throw your cigarette butt on the ground, you may be fined 68 euros.

The parks small and large offer the opportunity to munch on a sandwich you bought at a nearby bakery, either with a picnic on the grass or on a bench, but in some you can purchase snacks or more in their kiosks: on the edge of the Park Montsouris (14^e), for example, is the charming garden of the restaurant Pavillion Montsouris, and the Luxembourg Gardens houses some kiosks for snacks, with chairs for sitting and watching the passing scene. Both the Bois de Boulogne and the Bois de Vincennes are destinations for fine eating in the leafy surrounds, while never leaving Paris.

The Bill and the Tip

L'addition (the bill) will not be brought to you automatically, for it would seem rude to presume you are finished if you are not. Signal the waiter by saying "*monsieur*" or "*s'il-vous-plaît*" never "*garçon*" even though that is what you may have been taught in elementary French class. If the waiter is nearby, say "*l'addition, s'il-vous-plait*", or make the universal hand signal that will be recognised right away. Most restaurants accept credit cards, although a few don't, especially some of the small Asian eateries in the 13th. If this is important to you, check before going. If using a credit card, do not include a *pourboire* (tip), which is already included in *l'addition*—this is indicated on the menu by *service compris*.

Although the service is always included one way or the other (even in a café), the customer should leave a small amount on the table: perhaps five per cent in moderately-priced restaurants and more in refined restaurants. Be sure to check the bill for accuracy.

BUT WHERE?

The oldest commercial centre of Paris, the establishments in the inner *arrondissements* on the Right Bank catered to the business trades and to diplomats currying favor with the kings. This is no longer completely true, although most of the city's Michelin-starred establishments are still here (Lassere, Pierre Gagnaire, Pavillion Ledoyen, Taillevent, and Alain Ducasse at the Plaza Athenée, among others). Yet farther afield, a short *métro* ride now can take you to formerly run-down areas but that are now are increasingly fashionable. The Marais in the 4th is probably the most easily accessible, and walking on rue des Rosiers shows its kosher and other Middle Eastern eateries open on Sunday. But think too of Oberkampf in the 11th, which—by continuing the dynamic Bastille area with its myriad popular cafes—has a lively spirit quite late. Close by, the expanse around the Place de la République is also coming up quickly now that the extensive renovation is complete. More is sure to come. And you can find an *avant garde* vitality on the banks of the Canal St-Martin which border on several eastern *arrondissements*, and which seem to have new exotic opportunities to explore every week. Up in the 18th, new eateries in Montmartre are making their mark, humming until closing time. And adjacent to the east in the 19th, while you might not call bustling Belleville 'fashionable', it certainly is worth exploring for its halal, kosher, and Asian establishments on just about every street. At the opposite extreme, the 12th *arrondissement* is a marvel of rehabilitation, with the Cour St-Emilion and the enchanting parc de Bercy bordering the Palais Omnisports stadium.

The Left Bank, long noted in the 5th *arrondissement* for its intellectual and artistic life, can still boast small, almost inexpensive store-front restaurants and cafes in the Latin Quarter. But the Left Bank too has its enterprises of *haute cuisine* (La Tour d'Argent, Arpège, Guy Savoy, the centuries-old Laperouse, le Violon d'Ingres, and of course the Jules Verne up on the Eiffel Tower) along with hundreds of others at all levels that give these southern *arrondissements* their neighborhood feel. Think of La Motte Piquet in the 15th, for example, where just by the *métro* stop there are almost a dozen restaurants and cafes with terraces that draw locals, as does the area near *métro* St-Charles, near the Centre Beaugrenelle—or over by Convention. Montparnasse is legendary for its nightlife and eateries, and still doesn't disappoint—neighboring the smaller cafes are the stylish la Couple and Le Dome, and the Japanese star Toyo. To its south in the 14th, the offshoots of Alesia are popular with a different crowd, as is the 13th to the east, with its very distinct faces. Since the construction of the Bibliotheque Nationale, a new neighbourhood has arisen around the avenue de France. No longer drab, it now sparkles with its own set of smart cafés, whereas around avenue de Choisy the hundreds of Asian eateries dominate. But that's not all: the modern and the international here are grounded near the busy place d'Italie by the ancient and nostalgic Butte Aux Cailles village, with its cobblestone streets, small bistros and bars, reasonable prices, and old-world appeal.

Herewith just a few representative examples; in your own *arrondissement* you'll find your favorites among all the categories, including the international offerings that add vitality to every quarter. For a few of these, see "An International Sampling" on page 213.

The Right Bank:

- 1er: **Les Cartes Postales** (7 rue Gomboust; tel: 01.42.61.23.40). The streets just off the modern glass enclosure of the Place du Marché St-Honoré sport animated cafés—with both indoor and outdoor seating—that are popular especially with office workers at lunch. But there are others, such as les Cartes Postales, with its imaginative 'new French' cuisine, that resonates into the evenings as well. In this attractive setting, it's also possible to sample multiple smaller plates, many with a slight Asian touch. Intimate ambience and friendly service. Closed Sundays.

- 1er: **L'Escargot Montorgueil** (38 rue Montorgueil; tel: 01.42.36.83.51). Just above the Les Halles area that itself is undergoing a much-needed upgrade, and in the famous market street that crosses into the 2e, this fine two-centuries-old restaurant has been listed as a heritage site. Here are some the best snails in Paris, frogs' legs, and also an admirable *canard à l'orange* —but there are tasty gastronomic dishes of all sorts. Try the lunch menu at €17.50. Open daily till late.

- 2e: **Frenchie** (5 rue Nil; tel: 01.40.39.96.19). Between Les Halles and the Rex, Frenchie is both restaurant and wine bar. Popular for its chef who brings international sensibilities to his dishes, it's best to reserve well in advance. Closed weekends. Luckily, Frenchie To Go is just to the side at 9, rue du Nil, with deli-style dishes to take out, pastries, coffee, etc. Open daily.

- 4e: **Benoit** (20, rue St-Martin; tel: 01.58.00.22.05). Old style décor in this bistro first opened in 1912, but most modern now as part of the master chef Alain Ducasse's group of restaurants. Not far from the Hôtel de Ville, Benoit offers French classics and some 300 wines. Open daily.

- 4e. **Le Tastevin** (46, rue Saint-Louis en l'île; tel: 01.43.54.17.31). Among several good restaurants on the Île St-Louis, Tastevin's classic menu has long been recommended by locals as well as tourists, especially for its lamb and beef dishes using only selected producers. Excellent fish and seafood as well. Closed Mondays and Tuesdays. For a casual experience—again, among others here—there's the **Brasserie de l'Isle Saint-Louis** at 55, quai de Bourbon, conveniently located on the very tip of the island and across from the cathedral, with an outdoor terrace to take in the sights. Since 1953 it has offered homemade classic *brasserie* cooking (tel: 01.43.54.02.59). Closed Wednesdays and doesn't take reservations.

- 8e: **Flora Danica** and **Restaurant Copenhague** (142 avenue des Champs-Elysées; tel: 01.44.13.86.26). Appreciated by locals but too often missed by tourists strolling the boulevard, the Maison du Danemark discretely maintains two not-inexpensive but captivating restaurants, plus a take-out boutique. If you love fish, especially salmon, this is the place to go for salmon of all sorts—smoked, marinated, poached and roasted—and other equally sophisticated dishes. Although there are dozens of touristy places on the Champs-Elysées, these and the **Drugstore Steakhouse** at the Drugstore Publicis at No. 133 stand out (tel: 01.44.43.77.64). Especially esteemed at the Drugstore here is **L'Atelier de Joël Robuchon** (tel: 01.47.23.75.75), one of France's master chefs. The terrace at Drugstore's *brasserie* is always crowded and fun, yet the service can on occasion be hurried.

- 8ᵉ: **Rue Marbeuf** has two particular restaurants enjoyed by anyone who comes across them. **La Fermette Marbeuf** at 5 rue Marbeuf is an *art nouveau* beauty near the American Cathedral serving toothsome *brasserie* food (tel: 01.53.23.08.00). Closed Sundays, but open to midnight other days. Just down the street at No. 12 is **Chez André**, that since 1936 has also provided a traditional French *brasserie* menu (tel: 01.47.20.59.57). Open daily until late. Both have moderate prices and usually friendly service.

- 8ᵉ: **Lazare** (Parvis de la Gare Saint-Lazare; tel: 01.44.90.80.80). Somewhat distant from the glamour of the Champs-Elysées but convenient for friends from the chic western suburbs to meet—is Lazare, just by the upgraded train station Gare Saint-Lazare. And here we see that gone are the days when the station neighbourhoods were to be avoided at all costs. At Lazare, chef Eric Frechon supervises traditional dishes gone modern, with weekly specials, a daily menu at €19, and an extensive wine list. Open daily from breakfast until midnight.

- 9ᵉ: **l'Opéra Restaurant** (Palais Garnier, place Jaques Rouché; tel: 01.42.68.86.80). Nestled to the side of the mighty opera building, the terrace here is packed once the spring sun appears. The offerings are upscale, but there is also a daily menu and snacks and smaller late meals—all perfectly located for after the opera or a long day of shopping at the two nearby department stores Printemps and Galeries Lafayette. Close by and just off the major boulevard des Capucines (that soon turns into the Boulevard des Italiens), there are quite a few more informal opportunities.

- 9ᵉ: **Le J'Go** (4 rue Drouot; tel: 01.40.22.09.09. A play on the word *gigot* (roasted leg of lamb), this excellent restaurant just off boulevard Haussmann specialises in lamb dishes from Quercy, and other dishes from this region in southwest France. Order chops for the individual diner or roasts for the entire group. Closed Sundays.

- 10ᵉ: **Hutch House of Hot Dogs** (63, rue du Faubourg Saint-Denis; tel: 06.88.85.03.92). This small lively eatery typifies the out-of-the box endeavours in this part of Paris. Hot dogs, burgers, bagels, even a fish burger, plus its own artisanal pale ale. Another location is nearby at 3, rue Saint Marthe (tel: 01.42.47.07.36). Too crowded? Hop on over to **PNY** (Paris New York) at 50, rue du Faubourg Saint-Denis, which also has fine hamburgers, fries, and even a portobello mushroom burger for the vegetarians. For other addresses, check its website (www.pny-hamburgers.fr). And for a different set of options here, is the Passage Brady, noted for its Indian shops and regional curries.

- 10ᵉ: **Brasserie Terminus Nord** (23 rue Dunkerque; tel: 01.42.85.05.15). Across from the Gare du Nord with its Eurostar and Thalys international trains, it's well worth a visit while you wait. Typically appointed with its large mirrors and wooden bar, serving traditional yet updated food by friendly, helpful staff.

- 11ᵉ: **Le Chateaubriand** (129 avenue Parmentier; tel: 01.43.57.45.95). Rated one of the top 50 restaurants in the world, the lovely €70 tasting menu here near the avenue de la Republique is one of the best examples of why this area is now so fashionable. Innovative dishes assembled from the best ingredients of the moment. Reservations open three weeks in advance. Closed Sundays and Mondays. For a change of pace, try **Ober-Salé** at 17, rue Oberkampf (tel: 01.43.38.46.68). Innovative twists on traditional dishes in this small locale, bringing crowds in the evening, but more available at midday. Open Tuesdays to Fridays lunch and dinner, and Saturday evenings.

- 12ᵉ: **Le Train Bleu** (located in the Gare de Lyon; tel: 01.43.43.09.06. It may be in a train station, but you'll wish the train would never come. A beautiful Belle Epoque dining room, with frescoes on the ceilings, murals on the walls and classic French cuisine. Certainly not cheap, but a worthwhile Paris experience, to be sure, whether you're catching a train or not.

- 12ᵉ **Chai 33** in the Cour Saint-Emilion in Bercy Village is one of a number of fun restaurants in this entertainment destination bordering the beautiful park that originally was an entrepot for wine (tel: 01.53.44.01.01). Stroll in the park, browse the shops, go to the multiplex cinema, and have a meal and a glass of wine from the wide-ranging cellar of Chai 33. There are others in the charming cobblestone lane, and with the swift Meteor (Line 14) *métro*, the Park de Bercy and the Cour-Saint-Emilion, although seemingly distant from the city center, they really aren't.

- 16ᵉ. **le Petit Rétro** (5, rue Mesnil; tel: 01.44.05.06.05). Near the place Victor Hugo with its circle of cafés, le Petit Rétro boasts an original and fetching century-old decor with ceramic Art Nouveau motifs. Its modernised *haute bistro* menu draws the professional Right Bank crowd for lunch, and a classy clientele in the evenings. The prices are bistro-reasonable. Closed Sundays. Yet the long and narrow 16th *arrondissement* has different faces: trendy and expensive, residential and relaxed. Near to the Etoile and out the avenue de la Grande Armée all the way to the hub at the Place de la Porte Maillot, the establishments tend to be a bit more upscale.

- 16ᵉ: **Hiramatsu** (52 rue de Longchamp; tel: 01.56.81.08.80). Near the place du Trocadero with its own set of well-attended cafés, there are has some outstanding possibilities. One of the most noteworthy is the one-star Hiramatsu with its refined and imaginative French cuisine with a delicate Japanese attitude. With only 36 covers, this is an expensive but exceptional experience. Closed weekends and all of August.

- 17ᵉ: **l'Huitrier** (16 rue Saussier-Leroy; tel: 01.40.54.83.44). Some of the best oysters in Paris, outstanding fish dishes and good value for money in this neighbourhood gem. Hidden in a narrow street around the corner from the vibrant market street at rue Poncelet. Best to reserve, for with its regulars, it isn't really hidden anymore. Open Sundays.

■ 18ᵉ: **Jeanne B** (61 rue Lepic; tel: 01.42.51.17.53). Near rue Lepic and rue des Abesses in Montmartre, it's hard to choose among the establishments around the market street. The latest opening from the owners of a group of restaurants in the 11th near the trendy Bastille-Republique-Oberkampf nexus— Jeanne B has a modern setting with a menu of contemporary interpretations—terrines, spit-roasted chicken, lamb, savory tarts, and more—to eat in or take out. Open daily. In the same market street is **Antoine de Montmartre**, at 102 ter, rue Lepic (tel: 01.53.09.23.93). Again, a chef with other restaurants is joining the popularity of the area with a modern open kitchen concept that allows diners to watch the chefs as they work their magic. Meals may be ordered in small or large portions, and the variety is well-planned and intriguing. Closed Mondays.

- 18^e: **Wepler** (14 place de Clichy; tel: 01.45.22.53.24). Right on the busy place de Clichy stands this old favourite, specializing in oysters and other seafood. Bustling, crowded, not at all quiet, it's a lot of fun with plenty of good food and a buoyant atmosphere. Open daily until midnight.
- 19e: **Au Boeuf Couronné** (188 avenue Jean Jaurès; tel: 01.42.39.44.44). Across from the new Philharmonie, this steakhouse in an old-time bistro setting offers itself as 'the temple of meat in Paris'. Appealing for dinner before or after the concert. Open daily.
- 20e: **Le Baratin** (3 rue Jouye-Rouve; tel: 01.43.48.39.70). A respite from the Asian and African eateries in Belleville, this small bistro/wine bar near the *métro* Pyrenees offers what might be seen as home-style cooking, but the chef adds her own contemporary Latin twist that keeps aficionados from all around the city coming back. The wine selection includes some unusual organic wines. Closed Sundays and Mondays.

The Left Bank

- 5e: **l'Agrume** (rue des Fosses-St-Marcel; tel: 01.43.31.86.48). Slightly out of the way of the atmospheric Latin Quarter, and a few streets south of the Grande Mosquée, this Michelin-rated bistro attracts folks who come back again and again, raving about it, watching the chef at work, and paying under €50 for the brilliant fixed-price menu. Small but sweet, the service is good and it's entertaining as well as delicious. Open Wednesdays–Saturdays. But so many fine little eateries in the 5th make for culinary explorations galore.
- 5e: **Brasserie Balzar** (49 rue des Ecoles; tel: 01.43.54.13.67). Brasserie Balzar has been a fixture of the Latin Quarter close by the Sorbonne and the Collège de France since 1890. Perhaps still a meeting place for students and intellectuals, the Balzar is nonetheless a destination for people who want a true *brasserie* experience, and perhaps the sighting of a celebrity or two.
- 6e: **Le Relais de l'Entrecôte** (20 rue Saint-Benoit; tel: 01.45.49.16.00). At this fun steak bistro just off boulevard

St-Germain, there's no choice except for dessert. You tell the waiter how you like your meat prepared, and the salad, steak and *frites* (fries)—all good—will come. Beware; they don't take reservations and there's always a line. For other addresses, check the website (www.relaisentrecote.fr).

- 6ᵉ: **Le Voltaire** (27 quai Voltaire; tel: 01.42.61.17.49). A walk along the *quai* brings you to this refined and elegant café both intimate and welcoming, it serves toothsome dishes that are always perfectly prepared and presented. Make sure to reserve well in advance. Open Tuesdays to Saturdays.

- 6ᵉ: **Un Dimanche à Paris** (4-6-8 cour du Commerce Saint-André; tel: 01.56.81.18.18). Tucked into a charming old cobblestone passage off St-Germain at Odéon, this combination chocolate shop, tea room and lovely restaurant with a tower from the 13th century focuses on the sensibility of chocolate. Gourmet dishes all with a hint of chocolate. Choose your dessert in the shop. Open Tuesdays dinner to Sundays lunch.

- 6ᵉ: **Bouillon Racine** (3 rue Racine; tel: 01.73.20.21.12). Come for the decor, stay for the food. A stunningly beautiful Art Nouveau traditional restaurant just off boulevard St-Michel and near the Musée Cluny, the Bouillon Racine serves as a tea room in the afternoon, and later a well-populated happy hour. On some nights it can get crowded and hectic around 9:00 pm, so without reservations, be prepared to wait or go earlier.

- 6ᵉ: **Le Mâchon d'Henri** (8 rue Guisarde; tel: 01.43.29.08.70). In the flashy St-Germain, there still remains at least one typical old-time bistro: tiny, and friendly, crowded with locals—lots of them regulars—just extremely enjoyable, offering good, hearty Lyon-inspired food. Its chalkboard menu changes with the seasons.

- 6ᵉ: **Huîtrerie Regis** (3 rue de Montfaucon; tel: (01.44.41.10.07). This minute storefront between the *métro* Mabillon and the covered *marché*, serves only the freshest oysters and prawns (*crevettes*) with their usual accompaniments. Closed Mondays.

- 7ᵉ: **L'Atelier du Joël Robuchon** (6, rue de Montalembert; tel: 01.42.22.56.56). Originally a long counter—but now with tables as well—diners are welcomed to sample the superb creations of this Michelin-starred master chef, who has restaurants all over the world. Some recently say this might be the best French restaurant in Paris, so be prepared to pay handsomely for the experience. (See also page 216.)

- 7ᵉ: **Le Petit Lutétia** (107 rue de Sèvres; tel: 01.45.48.33.53). Passing by Le Bon Marché on a chic neighbourhood street of shops and cafes, this well-known old bistro/*brasserie* has been bought by the widespread Costes Group and undergone a recent facelift. Hoping other changes will be few, for now the locals can still appreciate the classic *confit de canard* plus the more modern offerings of the chalkboard specials, the hearty portions, and the comfortable atmosphere.

- 7ᵉ: Heading toward the Eiffel Tower, rue St-Dominique may seem owned by the famous chef Christian Constant. First he opened **Le Violon d'Ingres** at 135 rue St. Dominique (tel:01.45.55.15.05). It may be an elegant one-star restaurant, yet it still conveys an intimate neighbourhood feel. At No. 131 the **Fables de la Fontain**e there are perfectly-selected seafood, and also at No. 135 **Les Cocottes**, serving little pots of the freshest ingredients—and happily, without needing reservations. The tempting **Café Constant** just down the street at No. 139 has traditional *brasserie* food, from breakfast through dinner, and is a favourite any time of the day (tel: 01.47.53.73.34).

- 7ᵉ: **Petrossian le 144** (144 rue de l'Université; tel: 01.44.11.32.32). Still in this outer part of the 7th, specialties in this recently modernised restaurant are its selections of imported caviars and mouth-watering fish dishes, presented in a beautiful and refined setting, with tasting menu of caviar, and a well-priced lunch menu at €35. Open Tuesdays–Saturdays. The Petrossian boutique—its 'Temple of Caviar' (and other delectables) is at 18 boulevard de la Tour-Maubourg (tel: 01.44.11.32.22). Open Monday–Saturdays. Other Petrossian outlets are in the Drugstore Publicis on the Champs-Elysées and in the Lafayette Gourmet on boulevard Haussmann.

■ 7e: **Au Petit Sud-Oues**t (46 avenue de la Bourdonnais; tel: 01.45.55.59.59). And now just a few streets from the Eiffel Tower, this smart Southwestern French restaurant tucked behind its specialty take-out counter is a hidden treasure. Reserve well in advance to marvel at the scrumptious *foie gras*, *confit*, *cassoulet* and other truly luscious duck dishes. Closed Sundays.

■ 13e: **Tempero** (5, rue Clisson; tel: 09.54.17.48.88). Seemingly out-of-the-way to some, but close to both the National Library and the major hospital Pitié-Salpêtrière is this high-quality modern bistro that fuses with some international-cuisine overtones—both from Brazil like the chef and a bit of Asia as well. A small place with a small menu, but each entrée and main course are carefully selected and executed. Open for lunch daily, and for dinner Thursdays and Fridays. Closed weekends.

■ 14e: **Le Zeyer** (62 rue d'Alesia; tel: 01.45.40.43.88). Holding its own even after a century here on the busy place d'Alesia, the brasserie Le Zeyer may be all things to all people: a café, restaurant, bar. Specialising in seafood and with a reasonable €37 menu, it's central to the attractions of the southern 14th: the catacombs, the clothing stores of rue d'Alesia, and not too far from the RER-B station near Denfert-Rochereau.

■ 14e: **Pavillon Montsouris** (20 rue Gazan; tel: 01.43.13.29.00). The Parc Monsouris at the southern border of the 14th is one of the pearls of Paris. With its lake and cascade, its abundant foliage and flowers, and its wide lawns, it's reminiscent of an English garden. On its eastern edge, the terrace of the enchanting Pavillion Montsouris has been welcoming its visitors since 1889 and is listed as one the historic monuments of France. Opening right onto the park, it's a good way to spend an afternoon, especially if you take its €51 three-course menu—ensuring that you have enough time to enjoy the surroundings as well as the cuisine.

■ 15e: **Café du Commerce** (51 rue du Commerce; tel: 01.45.75.03.27). The 15th is the largest *arrondissement* in

Kosher, halal, and other specialty cuisines are plentiful in Paris. This kosher pizza place is at 11 rue des Rosiers in the Marais.

Paris, with its own distinct neighborhoods, each with its own dining character. The Café du Commerce typifies the 15ᵉ: attractive but not flashy, this classic two-story *brasserie* is reliable, and locals come to this area around metro Emile Zola for the consistently hearty—yet modernised—menu. Not too hungry? Come for a snack or a beer, or try the lunch menu at under €20—a bargain. There are many such in the 15ᵉ. Closer to the Eiffel Tower is **Casse-Noix**, at 56, rue de la Federation (tel: 01.45.66.09.01). The menu shows the seasonal specialties interpreted by chef Pierre-Olivier Lenormand, and there's a worthwhile tasting menu for parties of eight or more. The three-course menu at €33 is also attractive. Closed weekends.

An International Sampling

France having been a major colonial nation, Paris abounds with North African and Asian restaurants. Although Asian restaurants and *traiteurs* are found in most all *arrondissements*, the 13ᵉ is known as having good, inexpensive Chinese and Vietnamese restaurants, as is Belleville in the 19ᵉ, also popular for its North African storefronts. Moderately priced Indian and Pakistani establishments abound in and around the Passage Brady in the 10ᵉ, with Japanese restaurants around rue Sainte-Anne in the 2ᵉ (see Sushi on pages 216–217). 'American food' is currently popular, but this seems mostly to extend to bagels and hamburgers. Some, of course, are more "American" than others.

- (American): 4ᵉ & 5ᵉ: **Breakfast in America** at 17 rue des Ecoles 75005 near metro Cardinal LeMoine (tel: 01.43.54.50.28 and at 4, rue Mahler 75004, near metro St-Paul (tel: 01.42.72.40.21). Real American breakfasts such a blueberry pancakes and authentic bagels, served all day, and a Sunday brunch. The burgers here are well-known, plus sandwiches and wraps, chicken and veggie burgers. Open daily until 11:00 pm.

- (American) 2ᵉ, 3ᵉ, 10ᵉ & 20ᵉ. **Blend** (44, rue d'Argout; tel: 01.40.26.84.57). Hamburgers and more hamburgers, but intriguing combinations with the finest ingredients and toppings, plus crispy fries and good prices. Three other addresses, all popular and busy, but usually the wait isn't too long. For other addresses, check the website (www.blendhamburger.com).

- (Chinese) 5ᵉ: **Mirama** (17 rue Saint-Jacques; tel: 01.43.54.71.77). At this popular Chinese restaurant, lines spill out of the door for its special dumpling and noodle soups, as well as the roast duck and pork. Open daily.

- (Chinese) 13ᵉ: **Délices de Shandong** (88 boulevard de l'Hôpital; tel: 01.45.87.23.37). A small storefront like so many others in the 13th, this one is well-known among China experts for its specialties of the Shandong province in northeast China, south of Beijing. Seafood is excellent, and in many dishes, grains are more prevalent than rice, which is more plentiful in the south. Closed Wednesdays; takes reservations.

- (Italian) 12ᵉ: **Sardegna a Tavola** (1 rue de Cotte; tel: 01.44.75.03.28). Authentic Sardinian dishes in an attractive Italian-style setting near Place d'Aligre. Always crowded, reserve ahead. Closed Sundays.

- (Japanese) 6ᵉ: **Toyo** (17, rue Jules-Chaplain; tel: 01.43.54.28.03). Just off boulevard Montparnasse, Toyo shows off the inventive recipes of the Japanese chef Toyomitsu Nakayama. Moderately priced for the quality of the offerings. Closed Sundays and Monday lunch, and much of August.

- (Japanese) 18^e: **Guilo Guilo** (8, rue Garreau; tel: 01.42.54.23.92). Japanese fusion food here is the key, and diners enjoy the set menus while seated at a surrounding bar where they can see the food being prepared. Innovative fresh recipes, far from the ubiquitous sushi bars in concept. Make sure to reserve. Closed Sundays and Mondays.

- (Korean) 2^e: **Guibine** (44, rue Ste-Anne; tel: 01.40.20.45.83). In a street known for its Japanese restaurants, Guibine stands out for its Koerean food—barbeque, bibimbap, and excellently spiced fish dishes. Closed Mondays.

- (Lebanese) 16^e: **Noura** (27, avenue Marceau; tel: 01.47.23.02.20). Authentic Middle Eastern specialties such as hummus, tabouleh, marinated meat dishes and good Lebanese desserts. Other addresses, including the Centre de Beaugrenelle. Open till late.

- (Mexican) 5^e: **Anahuacalli** (30 rue des Bernardins; tel: 01.43.26.10.20). More Latin restaurants are cropping up in Paris, and this cosy Mexican upscale restaurants remains a favorite, with quality ingredients and friendly service. Reserve in advance.

- (Middle Eastern) 4e: **Chez Marianne** (2 rue des Hospitalières Saint-Gervais; tel: 01.42.72.18.86). Create your own plate of delicacies from a list of Middle Eastern and Central European specialties such as hummus, falafel, *foie de voillaie haché* (chopped chicken liver), etc. An extremely popular and casual venue.

- (North African) 10e: **Zerda Café**: 15, rue Rene Boulanger (tel: 01.42.00.25.15). Rated among the best couscous restaurants in Paris, this Algerian café with the Berber touch of the chef has a charming décor and some tables outside. Sure to be even more visited now that the renewed atmosphere of the renovated Place de la Republique is creeping into the surrounding neighbourhoods.

- (Pan-Asian) 13e: **Tricotin** (15 avenue de Choisy; tel: 01.45.84.74.44). Crowded, noisy, cheap, fast and good (as are dozens of other in this noted Asian area of Paris). Pick and choose from Chinese and Vietnamese dishes, a wide choice available for soups and appetisers.

- (Thai) 7^e: **Thiou** (49 quai d'Orsay; tel: 01.40.62.96.50). Upscale authentic Thai representations of traditional dishes such as Phad Thai and black cod. Closed Sundays.
- (Thai) 15^e: **Sawadee** (53, avenue Emile Zola; tel: 01.45.77.68.90). Adding spice to this rather staid part of the 15th, Sawadee has long offered authentic Thai cuisine in an ambiance as typically Thai as the food. Closed Sundays.
- (Thai) 20^e: **Royal Bangkok** (4 rue du Cher; tel: 01.46.36.46.24). Perhaps off the beaten track, but authentic Thai specialties at reasonable prices.
- (Vietnamese) 5^e: **Kim Lien** (33 place Maubert; tel: 01.43.54.68.13). It's hard to choose among the good, inexpensive Vietnamese establishments in Paris, but this one has a wide selection of well-prepared dishes, just off boulevard Saint-Germain and across from a popular market.
- (Vietnamese) 13^e: **Pho Banh Cuon 14** (129 avenue de Choisy; tel: 01.45.83.61.15). As the name suggests this eatery in the Asian area of Paris sports lines out the door for its special Tonkin rice noodle soup. Options for its additions—different meats, vegetables and herbs, make a full meal. Often rated among the best in the city.

Sushi

And of course, now there's sushi in all around Paris, fresh and mouth-watering, and usually not expensive. Around rue Ste-Anne straddling the 1st and 2nd *arrondissement*s, good Japanese eateries are plentiful. Adding to the appealing opportunities, Joël Robuchon has opened **Sushi Shop**, a small chain for take-out and delivery of sushi, as elegant and appealing as you'd expect from a master chef (tel: 0826 826 628; www.sushishop.fr).

- 1er: **Kinugawa** (9 rue du Mont Thabor; tel. 01.42.60.65.07). Expensive but first-class sushi in an upmarket setting. Generally crowded, so reserve in advance. Closed Sundays.
- 6^e: **Tsukizi** (2bis rue des Ciseaux; tel: 01.43.54.65.19). A tiny sushi bar in a short, narrow street. A few tables,

a small counter, but excellent sushi. Reserve in advance. Closed Sundays.

- 11ᵉ: **Sukiyaki** (12 rue de la Roquette; tel: 01.49.23.04.98). Fine sushi and other Japanese selections in a popular local restaurant just off Place de la Bastille.
- 16ᵉ: **Matsuri** (2–4 rue de Passy; tel: 01.42.24.96.85; www.matsuri.fr.) Good sushi on a conveyor belt allows you to have a fast lunch and choose only the dishes you wish as they move by. Reasonable prices. Other addresses, home delivery also available.

Restauration Rapide

For quick meals, it is easy to find a *casse-croûte*, sometimes called *le snack*. The daily markets in the various neighbourhoods sell *quiches* or ready-made still-hot dishes. Supermarkets offer pre-made sandwiches, bakeries make theirs fresh, as do the *traiteurs* that can be found in all neighbourhoods.

It is also easy to stop briefly at a café for a *croque-monsieur* (grilled ham and cheese sandwich) or a *croque-madame* (the same sandwich but with a fried egg on top). Some places offer items *sur le pouce* for people on the run. The Italian *panino* (sandwich), made on fresh, warm bread, has become popular. **Toastissimo** is a small chain selling good *panini*, as is **Pomme de Pain**. **Lina's** makes sandwiches to order on the bread of your choice. And some places advertise that their bread comes from Kayser or Poilane.

Chinese food for take-out in little storefronts all seems to be the same, perhaps coming from some central kitchen somewhere, but it's inexpensive and filling. And they sell pre-made sushi, as well; but for a gourmet sushi experience, look for **Sushi Shop** (see Sushi above). The food truck has also taken Paris by storm. When the first one "Le Camion Qui Fume" was a success, others such as "Cantine California" and "Camion Gourmet" began to follow. Now there are others, offering burgers and tacos to somewhat gourmet offerings that can be eaten with the fingers, for the most part, without cutlery—previously not something the French much cared for. A summer treat is Igloo, that offers frozen yogurt with a choice of toppings. A few trucks move from place to place, others are stationary.

Back to bagels, again, **Ari's** has several interesting shops on the right bank, serving bagels, and also a freshly-made 'soup of the moment', vegetarian options, smoothies and boxed "*formule*" lunches in which you select the breads, drinks and desserts for yourself. Check its website (www.arisbagels.com.) Also check the national chain **Bagelstein**, with more than 15 shops just in Paris, which offers its own type of bagel sandwiches, muffins and more, with stated combinations or those you create (www.bagelsteincom).

And don't forget the food halls at Au Bon Marché and Galeries Lafayette, or the food courts at the Carousel du Louvre or Centre Beaugrenelle. These particularly show that take-out food and quick service in Paris can still be of the quality insisted on by the French.

- 4ᵉ: **L'As du Falafel** (34 rue des Rosiers; tel: 01.48.87.63.60). This crowded kosher eatery serves among the best falafel and *schwarma* (sandwich of shaved meat) in town. Order from the takeaway window or eat at tables jammed together. Closed Friday afternoons and Saturdays.
- 6ᵉ: **Cosí** (54 rue de Seine; tel: 01.46.33.35.36). The best sandwiches! You choose from a wide choice of fillings to stuff into bread steaming hot from the wood-fired oven. Friendly welcome. English spoken. Open daily.
- 9ᵉ: **Big Fernand** (55 rue du Faubourg Poissonnière; tel: 01.73.70.51.52). Promised to be swiftly prepared, eat your delicious hamburgers (or chicken burgers) here, get them to go, or have them delivered rapidly to your home or office. Other addresses (www.bigfernand.com).
- 18ᵉ: **Bob's Bake Shop** (12, esplanade Nathalie Sarraute; tel: 09.84.46.25.26). Great sandwiches on delicious bagels, tartines, vegan protein shakes and cold-pressed juices.

Crêpes

Crêpes are the traditional French fast food, and deserve their own mention. *Crêpes*, originally from Brittany, are extremely thin pancakes (made from wheat or buckwheat) and can be sweet or savoury, depending on the fillings you choose.

They take about a minute to cook, so they are fast, cheap, and filling. Tiny storefronts all around the city, offer *crêpes*, but there are also true Bretonne *crêperies*, where you can sit down and enjoy the inventive fillings in either the wheat or usually gluten-free buckwheat versions (*la galette*), perhaps with a salad and a bottle of cider or beer. Several cluster around rue du Montparnasse and rue Odessa, with lines out the door. Below just a few of the most well-known, with first-rate *crêpes*, friendly service and some decor.

- 3ᵉ: **Breizh Café** (109 rue Vielle du Temple; tel: 01.42.72.13.77). Galettes galore in the Marais, and artisan beers to choose from. Rated one of the best. Closed Mondays and Tuesdays, and a few weeks in August.
- 5ᵉ: **Le Pot O'Lait** (41 rue Censier; tel: 09.83.26.76.80). Gluten- and peanut-free galettes, crêpes, and fresh salads to go with, and a clean, modern ambience.
- 6ᵉ: **La Crêperie des Canettes** (10, rue des Canettes; tel: 01.43.26.27.65). Long established in the well-trod Saint-Germain, its galettes and *crêpes* are highly respected, and its offering of pancakes with maple syrup can be comforting.
- 11ᵉ: **La Crêperie Bretonne Fleurie** (67, rue de Charonne; tel: 01.43.55.62.29). Quaint almost cozy décor in an off-the-tourist-track location, past the Bastille.
- 14ᵉ: **Crêperie de Josselin** (67, rue du Montparnasse; tel: 0 1.43.20.93.50). One of the most popular of the rue du Montparnasse *crêperies*, it's small, but worth the wait in line. Closed Mondays.
- 14ᵉ: **Des Crêpes et des Cailles** (13, rue de la Butte aux Cailles; tel: 01.45.81.68.69) Here is the ambience of old Paris, and although small, with quality offerings and ciders, and amicable service.
- 15ᵉ: **TY Breiz** (52, boulevard du Vaugirard; tel: 01.43.20.83.72). Since 1970, offering an international clientele *crêpes* and salads, plus Berthillon ice cream. Closed Sundays and Mondays.

"Bio" And Vegetarian

Given the French reliance on meats, cream sauces and butter, it used to be difficult to find vegetarian, much less vegan options in Paris. This is no longer true; restaurants now offer vegetarian options, and "bio" (biological/organic) and vegetarian restaurants are increasingly sprouting up—even some gluten-free. Some of these are not entirely vegetarian, offering a few fish or meat dishes for those who want them. For example, the small chain of Le Paradis de Fruits (with ten eateries in Paris) appeals to both meat eaters and vegetarians who appreciate the vegetable curry, salads, tofu dishes, and more. And Café Pinson—juice bar and café—also has several addresses serving gourmet organic vegetarian fare. Vegetarian fare is standard at Asian and Indian restaurants, and meatless dishes are common among the Italian and *cacher* (kosher) restaurants as well. Note that currently GMO (genetically-modified foods) are illegal in France (www.gmo-free-regions.org).

Visit the website of the Association Végétarienne de France (vegetarisme.fr), and for just one among dozens of Internet sites, here is one that is wide-ranging: (www.happycow.net/europe/france/paris/).

- 2e: **Bio Burger** (46, passage Choiseul; (el: 01.49.26.93.90). Organic meats make the outstanding hamburgers here in one of Paris' famous passages. Vegetarian/tofu burgers as well. Also in the 9th *arrondissement* at 10, rue de la Victoire (tel: 09.81.81.88.33). Open through lunch; closed Sundays.
- 3e: **Bob's Kitchen** (74, rue des Gravilliers; tel: 09.52.55.11.66) A small but well-known cantine off rue Réaumur with good prices on veggie soups, smoothies, salads and main courses and more. Open daily. See also Bob's Bake Shop above and others of Bob's Food (www.bobsjuicebar.com).
- 3e: **Le Potager du Marais** (24, rue Rambuteau; tel: 01.57.40.98.57). Picturesque vegan restaurant with an eclectic menu of French cuisine, including nicely-made desserts. Small and well-populated, it's best to make reservations. Probably more pricey than one would expect in a vegetarian locale. Closed Mondays and Tuesdays.
- 4^e **CRU** (7, rue Charlemagne; tel: 01.40.27.81.84). Not entirely vegetarian, but just about everything here is raw: carpaccio, tartares, fruits and vegetables. The courtyard

is lovely, and the concept works. Closed Sunday evenings and Mondays.

- 5^e: **Le Grenier de Notre Dame** (18, rue de la Bucherie; tel: 01.43.29.98.29). This was the first vegetarian/macrobiotic restaurant in Paris and still going strong. Wines are available, as are fresh fruit or vegetable cocktails, and the three-course menu works well at €12.50. Open daily.
- 7e: **Arpège** (84, rue de Varenne; tel: 01.47.05.09.06). This Michelin-starred restaurant is truly *haute cuisine* with imaginative vegetarian dishes by the starred chef Alain Passard. Extensive tasting menus, with gourmet prices to match. Closed weekends.
- 10e: **Krishna Bhavan** (24, rue Cail; tel: 01.42.05.78.43). Indian soups and curries, *crêpes*, exotic sauces (some with dairy), and all vegetarian. Open daily.

Salons de Thé

Parisians drink tea but until recently, not usually other than at breakfast. Now, though, tea is making its mark; tea rooms are sprouting up, hotels offer high teas, and you can rest your feet in the café of a museum or department store with a much nicer selection of teas than before. If you order tea in a bar, you will get a tea bag or something already sweetened. But Parisians are coming to delight in the *salons de thé* (tea salons), which in addition to tea, serve coffees and light meals, often in a tranquil ambience. Tea rooms tend to stay open all day, closing around 7:30–8:00 pm salons. Many of the local establishments sell teas to take home, including *tisanes/infusions*.

Perhaps the most elegant is the small chain **Mariage Frères**, with salons and shops in three locations (www. mariagefreres.com). Come for lunch, order from the long list of well-described teas and savour the delicious scones and pastries. The teas and accessories are on sale in the adjoining shops, as well.

- 1er: **Angélina** (226 rue de Rivoli; tel: 01.42.60.82.00). The most famous in Paris. Teas, light meals and an unforgettable *chocolat chaud*, a wintertime favourite of Parisians, and year-round with tourists.

Remnants of a visit to a Paris café.

- 1er: **Jean-Paul Hévin** (231 rue Saint-Honoré; tel: 01.55.35.35.96). Yes, a teahouse, but also with what could be what some people claim is 'the world's best *chocolatier*' with unbelievably enchanting pastries, teas, several different, equally wonderful types of chocolat chaud, plus light lunches and snacks. Closed Sundays.
- 5e: **La Mosquée** (39 rue Geoffroy Saint-Hillaire; tel: 01.45.35.97.33). Located in the Grande Mosque.
- 8e: **Café Kousmichoff** (71, avenue des Champs-Elysées; tel: 01.45.63.08.08) Above the tea shop is a refined tea room, offering a tempting selection of their Kusmi teas.
- 8e: **Ladurée** (16 rue Royale; tel: 01.42.60.21.79). Fashionable, always crowded and famous for its macaroons. Full meals are possible as well. The salon at 75 avenue des Champs-Elysées stays open until 1:00 am (tel: 01.40.75.08.75). Also at 34 rue Jacob (tel: 01.44.07.64.87).
- 16e: **Cape and Cape** (19, rue Vineuse; tel: 01.45.24.77.70. Specialising in the newly-popular rooibos healthful tea, this location has a small boutique, but the Cape and Cape rooibos teas can be found in other tea shops and salons. Access the website for locations (www.capeandcape.com).

Ice Cream

La glace (ice cream) has traditionally been consumed in summer, but with international gelato shops opening throughout Paris (Amorino, Gelati d'Alberto), it is becoming popular year round. The best Parisian *glaciers* (ice cream makers and parlours) prepare their creations using fresh ingredients. What makes French ice cream so good is that the flavours taste so real. Moreover, with smaller portions and less butterfat than the imported ice creams, a dish or cone of French *glace* is not overwhelming. The famous *chocolatier* chain **La Maison de Chocolat** not only has chocolates and rich desserts but rich ice creams and sorbets both in cones and in boxes to take home. And the long-established Raimo has several locations (and a tea salon) using only natural and seasonal ingredients in their ice creams (www.raimo.fr). Of course, supermarkets and the frozen food chain Picard (see page 238) carry ice creams and dessert confections, but the handmade are always worth seeking out. Häagen-Dazs is available at supermarkets, but also has more than a dozen outlets throughout Paris.

- 4ᵉ: **Berthillon** (31 rue St-Louis-en-l'Ile; tel: 01.43.54.31.61) Open Wednesdays to Sundays.
- 6ᵉ: **Gelateria Grom** (81, rue de Seine; tel: 01.40.46.92.60)
- 6ᵉ: **Ben and Jerry's** (1 rue du Four; tel: 01.43.25.10.63)
- 7ᵉ: **Martine Lambert** (39 rue Cler; tel: 01.45.51.25.30)

Fruit of the Vine

Wine has been produced on French soil since the time of the Romans 2,000 years ago. Currently, about a quarter of the world's annual wine production originates from France, amounting to about two billion gallons, culled from some three million planted acres. Despite the seemingly large selection in wine shops around the world, most French wines are not exported, so living in Paris affords the best opportunity to taste and learn about wine.

The French, obviously, love wine and so are knowledgeable about their country's wine-growing regions and offerings. They generally understand which wines go best with which type of meal, enhancing both the appreciation of the meal and the wine. This can be easily—and pleasantly—learned by tasting wines at any of the city's many wine bars, taking every opportunity to explore the *cartes des vins* (wine lists) in Paris restaurants and by asking advice from a knowledgeable sommelier. You might also explore the Musée du Vin at rue des Eaux/5 square Charles Dickens, 75016, and try its restaurant and wine tastings (tel: 01.45.25.70.89; www.museeduvinparis.com).

It is not necessary to order an entire bottle of wine. Although the French have a reputation for great alcohol consumption, most people consume alcoholic beverages, primarily wine, only at mealtimes, sipping for the taste but drinking water to quench the thirst—this brings out the flavour of the wine and lessens the effect of the alcohol. Even some of the better wines are now available in half-bottles, and restaurants serve some wines by the glass. In neighbourhood restaurants, the house wine is generally a decent *vin de table* and comes in several sizes: *un carafe* is a litre, *un demi* is half a litre and *un quart* is a quarter of a litre. *Un pichet* (a pitcher) can be had for a *demi* and a *quart*. Regional restaurants offer a selection of wines that compliment their cuisine. Order, too, some water: un *carafe d'eau*, which is tap water and provided free, or mineral water, either sparkling (*gazeuse*) or still (*plate*).

Drinking hard liquor such as whisky before dinner is thought to deaden the taste buds. Instead, try an *apéritif*, such as vermouth, *pastis*, *kir* (white wine with a drop of blackcurrant liquor or *crème de cassis*) or *kir royal*, made with champagne. After dinner, a *digestif* would be a subtle *cognac*, the fuller *armagnac*, *calvados* or any fruity *eau de vie* such as *poire William* (pear).

Learn about French regional wines by frequenting the city's ubiquitous *bars à vin* (wine bars). Each has its particular emphasis on both wines and food. Open for lunch and early evening meals, wine bars are similar to cafés, but the food choices tend to be more simple: light foods and salads, plus *charcuterie* (cold cuts), olives, and the like. Wine bars can be wood-panelled and staid, or modern and noisy. Wine bars are popular as much for their sociability as their fare, and people linger after work or late in the evening. Prices are determined by the wines sampled, and these range from the ordinary to first-class.

Actually, as with restaurants, the distinctions between a wine shop (*cave*) and a wine bar are blurring, as some wine bars sell their offerings by the bottle (or case), while many *cavistes* also have tastings and sometimes the little bites of snacks that traditionally go with them. For example, Nicolas, the extensive city-wide chain of wine shops, has some with wine bars. Other wine shops have tastings (see pages 250–252 for *caves*).

- **L'Ecluse**, with its six locations in Paris, is a popular restaurant/wine bar, where you can actually order some of the most prestigious wines by the glass to accompany your meal (www.lecluse-restaurant-paris.com)
- 1er: **Juvéniles** (47 rue de Richelieu; tel: 01.42.97.46.49). A casual wine bar and restaurant where English is spoken. A large selection of French and imported wines, by the glass as well as the bottle. Choose from hearty fare or smaller plates with a modern twist on the traditional. A fun place with helpful service. Closed Sundays and Mondays.
- 1er: **La Taverne Henri IV** (13 place du Pont-Neuf; tel: 01.43.54.27.90). On the Île-de-la-Cité, this old wine bar has been remodelled and updated. A good selection of wines, and the platters of cheeses and charcuterie are carefully selected. Closed weekends.

- 6ᵉ: **Chez Nous** (10 rue Dauphine; tel: 01.43.26.42.69). Only some 20 seats at this small, friendly wine bar off boulevard St-Germain, catering both to tourists and knowledgeable locals. The bar snacks are exceptionally good—with smoked fishes gravlax, and bio selections added to the fare—and the owners clearly are knowledgeable about their wines.
- 11ᵉ: **Le 11ème Domaine** (14, rue des Trois Bornes; (tel: 01.47.00.38.32). In the trendy Oberkampf area, this small, friendly wine bar suits both regulars and tourists. Cheeses and *charcuterie* accompany wines suggested by the helpful staff. Closed Mondays.
- 12ᵉ: **Le Baron Rouge** (1 rue Théophile Roussel; tel: 01.43.43.14.32). A lively wine bar adjacent to the buzzing Marché Aligre, the street is Closed Sundays and transformed into an oyster party. Bundle up in winter and be prepared to stand outside and eat dozens of oysters (or cold cuts) shoulder to shoulder with the crowd, downing your meal with glasses of crisp white wine.

Wine shops where one can find the myriad regional wines of France.

Pubs

Beer has taken on a new image in Paris, with artisan hand-crafted beers becoming very much appreciated, especially by a younger crowd. *Bière à la pression* is draft beer and comes in three sizes: the most common *demi* (8 oz), *sérieux* (16 oz) or *formidable* (about a litre). France produces a few standard bottled beers, Kronenbourg being the best known, for until now, Belgian bottled beers such as Stella Artois and Leffe were more popular. Asian restaurants have their own selections such as Sapporo, Asahi, or Singha. If you order a *bière*, you would have asked for a bottled beer. For draft beer, order *un demi* or whatever size you want. For events, the Paris beer week takes place each spring (laparisbeeerweek.com).

Parisian beer houses generally sell their brews in an entirely Gallic ambience. Currently, however, it is the pub— Irish, Australian, British and Scottish —that has hit the city hard, and more are springing up. They stay open late, host special events for their country's holidays, show sporting events on large television screens, arrange dart competitions and offer just about anything to be found in a traditional pub, including the food. Belgian beers, especially the Trappist and Abbey beers, are popular in the craft beer pubs, either on tap or in bottles. Funky Maps Paris (www.funkymaps.com) has current information on the pub scene, including scheduled pub crawls.

- **The Frog** is a popular chain of English pubs with locations all around the city, serving fresh-brewed ales from imported British ingredients, and other draft beers: (www.frogpubs.com.) the Frog in the Cour St-Emilion and near the British Library in avenue de France, add greatly to the ambience of the areas.

- A chain of Australian pubs, **Café Oz**, offers Australian (and New Zealand) hospitality, with great beers, food, Sunday brunch, and of course, football and rugby on the TV screens, Some live concerts, and music by DJs opens up the dance floor, as well (www.cafe-oz.com).

- 5ᵉ: **Académie de la Bière** (88 bis boulevard de Port Royal; tel: 01.43.54.66.65). A dozen beers on tap, Belgian beers, and year-round patios to enjoy them.

- 6ᵉ: **The Highlander** (8 rue de Nevers; tel: 07.61.74.47.89). Two floors of activities with a Scottish flavour—televised sports matches, weekly events.
- 6ᵉ: **The Moose** (16 rue des Quatre Vents; tel: 01.46.33.77.00). Canadian sports bar and grill; good burgers, a large selection of beers, and some Australian wines.
- 6ᵉ: **O'Neil** (20 rue des Canettes; tel: 01.46.33.36.66). Brew pub that is frequented by locals and tourists alike, in the heart of St-Germain. Good food, as well.
- 6ᵉ: **Little Temple Bar** (12, rue Princesse; tel: 01.43.26.79.95). Near Mabillon, a fun bar with a definite Irish feeling—long wooden tables, darts, board games, and of course, live streaming of sports matches. Irish beers and whiskeys, including some nights for dancing.
- 11ᵉ: **La Fine Mousse** (6, avenue Jean Aicard; tel: 09.80.45.94.64). Off rue Oberkampf and near Ménilmontant, a French pub with a large selection of artisan beers, some 20 beers on tap, and good food.
- 14ᵉ: **Falstaff** (42, rue Montparnasse; tel: 01.43.35.38.29). A dozen taps, a hundred bottles, lots of Belgian beer.
- 18ᵉ: **Le Super Coin** (3, rue Baudelique; tel: 09.50.07.04.90). Only a few beers on tap, but an amazing list of French craft beers from small producers all around the country. The beer menu describes the beers, and the staff also obliges. As of this writing, there's no food service, but it's okay to bring your own.

Student Restaurants

Resto U (*restaurant universitaire*) is a chain of low-priced restaurants for registered students, operated by Centre Régional des Oeuvres Universitaires et Scolaires (CROUS). Some are cafeterias and others are *brasseries-grilles*. The food is plentiful and nourishing. Students with a valid student card may buy tickets at any Resto U during lunch and dinner hours. Tickets may be bought individually or more cheaply in a *carnet* of 10. For a list of the restaurants, contact CROUS at 39 avenue Georges-Bernanos, 75005 (tel: 01.40.51.62.00; www.crous-paris.fr).

EATING IN
Knowing How

Knowing how and when to shop for food is the key to eating well at home in Paris, whether you intend to cook or not. Wide-ranging options include buying fresh ingredients and starting from scratch, or buying the artistically prepared, ready-to-cook meats from the butcher and adding already cleaned potatoes and vegetables. You can also buy entire, freshly cooked meals from a *traiteur* that advertises *vente à emporter* (takeaway), or even high-quality frozen meals. For times when even these easy options are not appealing, you can order a meal by telephone for *livraison à domicile* (home delivery), from Japanese sushi to Italian pizza and Indian curries.

The quality of fresh ingredients in Paris is extremely high, as food for sale is regulated by law. Butter, cheese, poultry and vegetables must conform to the standards set for the region from which they come, and the label *appellation d'origine contrôlée* monitors the quality of both food products and alcoholic beverages. Thus, food at outdoor markets, neighbourhood *traiteurs* and supermarkets, all conveniently located in every *quartier*, are of a certain standard. *Agents de conservation* (preservatives) are rare, so food will taste better and be fresher but may spoil quickly. Check the *date de péremption* (expiration date) on packaged foods, indicated by '*vente jusqu'à*' or '*consommer avant*' followed by the expiration date. (North Americans should remember that the date is written in the order of day, month and year.) If you have bought an expired product, take your receipt and the product back to the shop immediately, and it should be exchanged in most cases.

Groceries are open from about 8:00 am until 7:30 pm, although neighbourhood shops may take a lunch break, and others may stay open later, depending on the neighbourhood. Supermarkets stay open all day, some until 10:00 pm. *traiteurs* and bakeries are open on Sunday mornings to supply the traditional Sunday lunch, as are outdoor markets. Small specialty shops may close on Monday, but supermarkets are

Where to Get What

- *Alimentation générale*: grocery
- *Boucherie*: butcher's; *boucherie chevaline*: horse-meat butcher
- *Boulangerie*: bakery; *pâtisserie*: pastry store
- *Brûlerie/torrefaction*: coffees and teas
- *Charcuterie*: delicatessen meats
- *Confiserie–chocolatier*: candy, handmade chocolates
- *Épicerie*: small grocery
- *Fromagerie*: cheese store
- *Poissonnerie*: fish market
- *Rôtisserie*: spit-roasted meat and chicken
- *Traiteur*: prepared foods for takeaway
- *Triperie*: tripe and innards
- *Volailler*: poultry shop

open all day, six days a week, year-round. In the summer, small shops will post signs announcing their *fermeture annuelle* (annual closure) for the entire month of July or August. And some outdoor markets have a reduced number of stalls and some groceries close altogether until *la rentrée* in September.

Europe is on the metric system (see Resource Guide in Chapter 10 for a conversion guide). Thus, people used to ounces and pounds will have to convert to grams and kilograms when looking at a food package. (1,000 milligrams = 1 gram and 1,000 grams = 1 kilo = 2.2 pounds.) With fresh produce, however, it is common to ask for *une livre* (a pound).

The Markets

Most of Paris food supply comes from the largest fresh produce market in the world, Rungis, which is about seven miles (11 km) south of the city centre. It is an amazing display for the freshest of produce, meats, dairy products, and flowers. Some of the tour operators can take you on an early-morning multi-lingual tour of Rungis. Check their websites.

The shopping at the *marché* (food market) is one of the

most pleasant aspects of French life. Vendors sell fish, meat and the freshest vegetables, and quality is generally high. Most also sell candies and some offer clothes and gadgets. The markets listed directly below are *couverts* (covered) and permanent. They open every day but Monday, closing for lunch, opening again around 4:00 pm, and closing around 7:00 pm. Covered markets usually have only food items and flowers, although some now have other stalls, and even cafés. Not all markets are equal in their range of merchandise, quality or price. These market buildings can be quite charming, depending on their age and upkeep.

Remember that it is usually the *commerçant* (vendor) who selects the produce, and vendors do not take kindly to customers pawing through the merchandise, although it is permitted at some stalls. After meeting your order, the vendor may ask, "*avec ceci?*" ("what else would you like?") If you need nothing more, say "*ça sera tout, merci.*" ("That's all, thanks.").

Note that the old covered market at 33, rue Secrétan (la Halle Secrétan) in the 19th has been completely refurbished internally and now also houses shops, a charming market and more, while keeping its traditional ambience.

- 3ᵉ: **Marché des Enfants-Rouges**; rue de Bretagne
- 3ᵉ: **Marché du Temple**; rue Perrée
- 6ᵉ: **Saint-Germain**; rue Mabillon
- 8ᵉ: **Marché Europe**; rue Corvetto
- 8ᵉ: **Marché de Castellane**; between rue Tronchet and rue de l'Arcade
- 10ᵉ: **Marché Saint-Quentin**; boulevard de Magenta
- 12ᵉ: The inexpensive, international **Marché Beauvau**; Place d'Aligre
- 16ᵉ: **Marché Saint-Didier**; rue Mesnil
- 16ᵉ: **Marché de Passy**; rue Bois-le-Vent

Some 65 open-air markets (*marché volant*) float around the *arrondissement*s, appearing on certain days in one location and moving elsewhere on others. Markets are generally open from 8:00 am–1:00 pm; Larger areas have more than one, open on different days or a different selection of vendors. Each market has its own personality, and some have an international flavour to match their surroundings. Information about markets can be found on many sites on the Internet. For the ultimate in market experiences, visit Le Potager du Roi, the charming vegetable garden of Louis XIV at Versailles (www.potager-du-roi.fr). Still a working garden, run by the National Horticultural School, the market shop sells freshly picked produce.

Market Streets

A *rue commerçante* is a pedestrian street lined with food shops and often has a lively air. Like the covered markets, most are open on Sunday mornings and closed Mondays. In small shops that are not *libre-service* (self-service), you may be asked to pay at the *caisse* (cashier) after ordering your food, then to bring the receipt back to the counter to receive the packages.

- 2e: Rue Montorgueil: pedestrians only. Charming old street of shops and cafés.
- 5e: Rue Mouffetard: Paris' most famous.
- 7e: Rue Cler at avenue de la Motte-Picquet: high-quality, two-street-long *rue commerçante*.
- 14e: Rue Daguerre: in a residential neighbourhood near Denfert-Rochereau.
- 17e: Rue de Lévis: pedestrians only, an old-time village atmosphere prevails.
- 17e: Rue Poncelet: beginning at avenue des Ternes, an upmarket market street.
- 18e: Rue Lepic: a famous market street at the foot of Montmartre.

Supermarkets

Supermarket chains ensure convenient one-stop shopping in just about every *quartier*; they are all *libre-service*. They range from the reliable and well-stocked Monoprix, to the mid-level Franprix and G-20, down to the unadorned Leader Price—one of the original cheap supermarket chains with their occasionally sparse stock. Monoprix also has a chain of small Monop shops to pick up things at the last minute.

Shops lining market streets present beautifully-arranged seasonal produce.

Most supermarkets within the city close on Sunday; some are open on Sunday mornings, depending on the neighbourhood.

People with cars can head for the *banlieue* where gigantic hyper*marchés* offer a wide selection and low prices; they also carry electronics and household items. These include Auchan, Casino, Intermarché and Carrefour, which has some small outlets in the city. Small shopping baskets can be found by the entrance to each supermarket. Wheeled *caddies* (carts) may be linked together by a lock, requiring the insertion of a one euro deposit, which is returned when the cart is reinserted into the rack. Small plastic bags are now officially being phased out; some may still be bought—at a price, but most people bring their own reusable bags. The charge for home delivery depends on the amount spent.

Many supermarkets now have self-service checkouts, which are fast and efficient; when there's a problem, there's usually a staff member nearby to help. Do bring your own carrier bag.

Food Halls
In addition to the supermarkets, food halls (usually in department stores) offer upmarket, international and more

costly selections. Both food halls below have a dazzling display of products of the highest quality, lovely prepared foods for takeaway and an impressive international selection. The British emporium Marks & Spencer has five outlets in the city, its high-quality food halls offering quality ready-made foods, bakery items, and much more, including clothing (www.marksandspencer.fr).

- 7ᵉ: **La Grande Épicerie de Paris** (38 rue de Sèvres; tel: 01.44.39.81.00).
- 9ᵉ: **Galeries Lafayette Gourmet** (35 boulevard Haussmann; tel: 01.40.23.52.67).

Shopping "Bio"

For eating natural foods, the true term is "*biologique*," but most people just say "bio" (pronouced bee-oh. Although the floating weekly markets have organic "bio" foods, there are only a few that are 100 per cent organic. As with the regular markets, these offer fresh meats, fish, cheeses, and produce, and some prepared foods as well. Most are open from 9:00 am to about 3:00 pm.

- 6ᵉ: The **Marché Biologique Raspail** on Sundays starts at rue de Rennes, and is one of the most extensive and popular.
- 14ᵉ: The **Marché Biologique Brancusi**, just south of the Gare Montparnasse at rue de l'Ouest, Is small, focusing on produce, cheeses, and some seafood items.
- 17ᵉ: **Marche Biologique des Batignolles** on Saturdays along the boulevard des Batignolles, has some of the same vendors as at Raspail, and yet is less crowded.

There are also now dozens of "bio" food shops selling natural foods and cosmetics, also with gluten-free products and natural wines. Look for the sign AB (Agriculture Biologique). There are also a few well-known chains, and there are dozens of smaller organic shops and coops in just about every *arrondissement*: Bio Culture is an online ordering service for natural foods (www.panier-bio-paris.fr).

- Chain: **Naturalia** (www.naturalia.fr).
- Chain: **Bio c' Bon** (www.bio-c-bon.eu/fr).

- Chain: **La Vie Claire** (www.lavieclaire.com)
- Chain: **Biocoop** (www.biocoop.fr)
- Chain: **Les Nouveaux Robinson** (www.lesnouveauxrobinson.coop)
- 5e: **Dietetique Mouffetard** (96, rue Mouffetard; tel: 01.43.36.59.34)
- 14e: **Dietetic Shop** (11, rue Delambre; tel: 01.43.35.39.75)
- 14e: **Elan Nature Paris** (107 bis avenue du Général Leclerc; tel: 01.45.42.35.00)
- 15e: **Biocoop Grenelle** (44, boulevard de Grenelle; tel: 01.45.77.70.14)
- 19e: **Canal Bio** (46 bis quai de la Loire; tel: 01.42.06.44.44)

Ordering Groceries Online

You can order groceries online for home delivery from supermarkets, as well as from Picard, the frozen food specialist described on page 238, and Telemarket, that offers a one-stop grocery ordering service from quite a few supermarket chains (www.telemarket.fr). See also the section on 'Eating Out at Home' starting from page 238.

- **Auchan** (www.auchandirect.fr)
- **Carrefour** (www.ooshop.com)
- **Picard** (www.picard.fr)
- **Monoprix** (www.monoprix.fr)
- **Houra** (www.houra.fr)
- **Simply** (www.simplymarket.fr)

Groceries for Homesick Anglophones

Don't Americans need an Oreo once in a while and don't the English pine for Hobnobs? The shops below specialise in items from Anglophone countries. Make sure the products have not expired, although packaged goods can last well longer than the date indicated. Supermarkets and food halls also carry international packaged goods, but sometimes deliveries are delayed, so buy more of an item you particularly like when you chance upon it. And don't forget the Marks and Spencer food halls mentioned above. Some Internet sites offer a good selection as well: My Little America (www.mylittleamerica.com) and My American

Market (www.myamericanmarket.com). For British goods, the British Corner Shop (www.britishcornershop.co.uk).

- 4^e: **Forence Kahn** (24, rue des Ecouffes; tel: 01.48.87.92.85). It may not be American, but it's a great American-style deli, with authentic bagels, smoked fish, delectable cheesecake, and more. Eat in or on the terrace, or take out. Closed Mondays and Tuesdays.

- 4e: **Thanksgiving** (20 rue Saint-Paul; tel: 01.42.77.68.29). American grocery and restaurant with some homemade foods for takeaway, fresh seasonal ingredients. Open Sundays, closed Mondays.

- 7e: **The Real McCoy** (194 rue de Grenelle; tel: 01.45.56. 98.82). A small American grocery. McCoy Café around the corner at 49 avenue Bosquet also has some products. Open daily.

- 10e: **Epicerie Anglaise** (5 cité Wauxhall; tel: 01.42.00.36.20). Irish, English and Scottish products at reasonable prices, from smoked salmon to whisky, haggis, bacon and cheeses. Closed Sundays and Mondays.

International Offerings

International shops tend to cluster around *rue commerçantes*— the entire area of Belleville, for example, is international in flavour. Asian, African, Middle Eastern and Japanese food shops are also found in the 2e, around rue Sainte-Anne, while the 13e is a focal point for the varied Asian community. Indian groceries can be found in the Passage Brady in the 10e and a smaller selection of Indian packaged goods at the Grande Epicerie of Le Bon Marché. Supermarkets carry some lines of international foods such as Old El Paso, Häagen Dazs and Ben and Jerry's ice cream, but the food halls have the most extensive selections. In addition to the anglophone sites above check the websites of other countries that deliver of their products abroad, such as Spain, for example (www. spanishtaste.fr; tel: (0034) 91 831 11 19).

Paris also offers kosher groceries, *traiteurs*, butchers and bakeries. Look for the kosher chain Hypercacher, around rue des Rosiers in the Marais, and in the market street rue Cadet in the 9th *arrondissement*. The same is true of halal restaurants and food stores, which are more found in the northeastern *quartiers*, especially around Belleville.

- 2^e: **Kioko** (46 rue des Petits-Champs; tel: 01.42.61.33.65). Two-level Japanese supermarket, selling everything you could want, including freshly-made sushi. Open Tuesdays to Saturday.s

- 4e: **Izraël** (30 rue François-Miron; tel: 01.42.72.66.23). A wonderful bazaar-like hodgepodge, including spices teas, olives, dried fruits and more from around the world, and fixings that you never thought you would find in Paris.

- 13e: **Tang Frères** (46–48 avenue d'Ivry; tel: 01.45.70.80.00). Large Asian supermarket. Open Sundays, closed Mondays. Has other addresses.

- 13e: **Paris Store** (44 avenue d'Ivry; tel: 01.44.06.88.18). Another Asian supermarket, next to Tang, this outlet of the Paris Store chain has some different items and attitudes than Tang, and has its devotées.

Traiteurs

Almost every neighbourhood has small *traiteurs* offering *plats à emporter* (prepared dishes for takeaway). *Charcuteries*, particularly known for their variety of smoked and salted pork products, also have prepared dishes; the two categories overlap slightly. As one would expect, the selection is mouth-watering, from stewed rabbit and guinea fowl *fricassée*, to roasted chicken and veal or beef loin, with potatoes, rice, vegetables such as cooked artichokes, salads on the side, and desserts rounding off the meal. Dishes change according to the season. Monoprix has a serviceable takeaway department and the *traiteurs* at the food halls are exceptional. The Asian *traiteurs* are the least expensive, but are uniform in their offerings.

Some elegant *traiteur* chains, such as those below, are known for their artistic and flavourful creations, with prices to match. They have addresses throughout the Paris region, so it's best to check the Internet or the phone book for the ones nearest you.

- **Fauchon** (www.fauchon.fr)
- **Dalloyau** (www.dalloyau.fr)

- **Hédiard** (www.hediard.fr)
- **La Comtesse du Barry** (www.comtessedubarry.fr)

EATING OUT AT HOME

Just about any type of cooked meal can be delivered à domicile (to the home). Generally, if a business' name starts with 'Allô...' (hello), it probably offers home delivery of products or services.

- **www.alloresto.fr** is a website that represents dozens of restaurants throughout Paris, organised by specialty and location. There are establishments of all grades, prices and ethnic specialties. Order directly on the Internet for delivery to your home or office. You pay according to what the restaurant accepts—cheque, cash or *tickets restaurant* (vouchers given to employees by their companies that are the equivalent of cash and can be used as payment at some restaurants).
- **Matsuri** has some ten Japanese restaurants in Paris, plus sushi that can be picked up or delivered. Order by phone or online (tel: 08.00.94.11.11; www.matsuri.fr).
- **Sushi Shop**, the elegant take-out sushi chain of Joël Robuchon, also does deliveries. (tel: 08.26.82.68.26; www.sushishop.fr).

Frozen Food

People who work late cannot always get to the stores in time to buy the appropriate ingredients for a meal. Thus, frozen food (*les surgelés*) is handy. In addition to prepared dishes ready to cook or just to reheat, frozen ingredients such as herbs, *crème fraîche* and sauces, fish fillets, meats, cleaned vegetables and desserts are available. Supermarkets all have frozen food sections, and the quality and selections vary.

- The high-quality chain **Picard** stocks only frozen food, and which has some 50 outlets in Paris. A monthly catalogue details special offers.
  (info tel: 08.01.13.12.11; www.picard.fr)

BAKERIES

A *pâtisserie* specialises in desserts and often sells breads; a *boulangerie* sells bread and simple desserts as well. The distinctions overlap—indeed, you will see *Boulangerie-Pâtisserie* with good cakes found in bakeries; nonetheless, the *pâtisserie* has more refined and beautifully decorated offerings. Neighbourhood bakers also sell freshly-made sandwiches and quiches.

Bread is always fresh in Paris, and people have their favourite breads and bakeries. This is important, for each year the *Grand Prix de la Baguette* is awarded to the *baguette* considered that year as the best. By law, *boulangeries* must choose their flour, and knead and bake the bread on their premises; otherwise they may not call themselves *boulangeries*. Bakeries—*boulangeries* or otherwise—may carry a sign that says '*tradition française*' or '*pain maison*' meaning that the *baguettes*, the staple for most French, are

Bread, Glorious Bread!

- *Baguette*: a long, thin loaf made from flour, water, yeast and salt. *Demi-baguette*: half a *baguette*. *Ficelle*: a thin and crispy *baguette*
- *Bâtard*: similar to a *baguette* but thicker
- *Brioche*: sweet, buttery roll or bread made with eggs
- *Croissant*: crescent-shaped pastry rolls, eaten at breakfast: '*nature*' is without butter, '*au beurre*' is with butter
- *Pain au chocolat*: flaky chocolate-filled pastry, also eaten at breakfast
- *Pain*: a bread loaf
- *Petit pain*: a roll
- *Pain de campagne*: country-style bread, comes in various shapes
- *Miche*: a large country bread
- *Pain au levain*: sourdough
- *Pain de mie*: sandwich bread, which can be bought *tranché* (sliced).

baked on the premises. Most bakeries sell *pain à l'ancienne*, which is generally made with unbleached flour and non-chemical leaven. A current favourite is the *boule*, a round dark-coloured country-style bread with a crunchy crust.

The weight and price of *baguettes* are government-regulated; those of specialty breads are not. (Some bakeries get around this by sprinkling the bread with flour and calling it a *baguette campagnarde*.) Not all breads are equal and certainly not all *boulangeries*. With more than 1,000 in Paris, just shop around for those that suit your taste.

For breakfast, *baguettes* are sliced lengthwise and buttered and/or spread with jam (*tartine*). At lunch, the bread is used for sandwiches, and at dinner it is torn off in chunks. This is all done immediately before eating, as *baguettes*, made with no fat, tend to dry out quickly. Bread is baked early in the morning, late in the afternoon and on Sunday mornings, so it's easy to buy bread just before you want to eat it. Everyone else is doing the same, so on Sunday mornings, for example, expect to wait in line at the most popular shops. Supermarkets carry both fresh and packaged breads. Note also that *baguettes* are generally not wrapped but are, instead, handed to the customer with a small paper square to hold while transporting home.

Pâtisseries specialise in nicely decorated *gâteaux* (cakes) and *tartes* (fruit pies or tarts). Some are particularly known for their elegant creations and there is some overlap with chocolate shops, such as the elegant multi-store Lenôtre and Dalloyau.

Each *quartier* has its *boulangerie*s and *pâtisseries*, and although the norm is to close in August, at least one bakery in each neighbourhood stays open. Supermarkets and some *traiteurs* also offer well-made desserts, but of these the food halls have the most imaginative (and expensive) creations. Small bakeries generally close for lunch and reopen until 8 pm. The internationally-known **Maison Kayser,** with more than a dozen bakeries within Paris is extremely popular (www.maison-kayser.com). And the celebrated **Poilâne** has

Indulging Your Sweet Tooth

- *Baba au rhum*: *brioche* dough baked in small molds and soaked in rum
- *Charlotte russe*: ladyfingers (oval pieces of dry sponge cake) placed around whipped cream
- *Dacquoise*: meringue of nuts, sugar and shaved chocolate, layered with whipped cream
- *Éclair*: small, rectangular *choux* pastry filled with flavoured cream and topped with icing
- *Financier*: almond cake
- *Madeleine*: small almond tea-cake with characteristic scallop markings
- *Merveille*: hot sugared doughnut
- *Millefeuille*: literally 'thousand layers', layers of puff pastry filled with cream and dusted with sugar
- *Palmier*: sugared, crisp cookies shaped like palm leaves
- *Sablé*: shortbread, variously flavoured with chocolate or almond, sometimes with jam in between layers
- *Savarin*: molded cake of baba dough, sprinkled with rum and filled with cream

two shops (8 rue du Cherche-Midi; tel: 01.45.48.42.59; and 49 boulevard de Grenelle; tel: 01.45.79.11.49; www.poilane. com). Products may also be ordered online.

Le Grenier à Pain, which won the *Grand Prix de la Baguette* a few years ago, has several locations in Paris (www. legrenierapain.com). And for his outlets in Paris, check the website of **Gontran Cherrier**, a young and upcoming artisan baker, and try his truly innovative combinations. One address is 22 rue Caulaincourt in the 18th *arrondissement* (tel: 01.46.06.82.66; www.gontrancherrierboulanger.com).

Some neighbourhood bakeries such as the Rose Bakery at 46 rue des Martyrs in the 9th *arrondissement* are also cafés, offering delicate dishes, and opportunities to sit for a while with a cup of coffee and a fresh pastry (tel: 01.42.82.12.80). Its vegetarian restaurant is at 30 rue Debelleyme in the 3rd *arrondissement* (tel: 01.49.96.54.01); closed Mondays.

- 2e: **Stohrer** (51, rue Montorgueil; tel: 01.42.33.38.20). Founded in 1730, one of the city's best *traiteurs* and bakeries, Try the Baba au Rhum, and its wonderful creamed cake called *puit d'amour* (well of love).

- 4e: **Sacha Finkelsztain** (27, rue des Rosiers; tel: 01.42.72.78.91). In the historically-Jewish Marais, this wonderful bakery offers rye breads, blini, strudels, poppy seed cakes, cheesecakes, and so much more.

- 6e: **Gérard Mulot** (76, rue de Seine; tel: 01.43.26.85.77). Outstanding *pâtissier*, *chocolatier* and *traiteur* at the Marché St-Germain.

- 5e: **Patisserie Ciel** (3, rue Monge; tel: 01.43.29.40.78). Enticing variations of beautifully-created angel food cakes (or chiffon cake) in a small tea room that offers aromatic Japanese teas. Eat lunch and taste the pastries, or buy a cake to take out (three sizes to choose from), settled into its origami box—or order to be delivered. Open daily.

- 6e: **MasMoudi** (106, boulevard Saint-Germain; tel: 01.56.81.00.55). A Tunisian *patisserie* near boulevard St-Michel, with honey-based baklava, samsa, stuffed dates, and other delectables with nougat and pistachios. Gift boxes and specials for Ramadan. Another address is at 64, boulevard Sébastapol (tel: 01.83.94.86.73). At St

Germain, closed Sundays; at Sébastapol, open Tuesdays to Fridays. Order for delivery (tel: 06.24.77.79.67).

- 14ᵉ: **Dominique Saibron** (77, avenue du Général Leclerc; tel: 01.43.36.01.07). Breads—including an organic version leavened with honey and spices—desserts, and a café, in this artisan bakery at the bottom of the 14th.

- 15ᵉ: **Max Poilâne** (87, rue Brancion; tel: 01.48.28. 45.90). Sourdough and other specialty breads, plus easy dessserts. Order online (www.max-poilane.fr).

- 17ᵉ: **We are Tiramisù** (10, rue de Bayen; tel: 09.84.21.01.31). A shop that specialises in—and takes to new levels—the famous Italian dessert. Different flavors and sizes, other mouth-watering desserts, using all-natural ingredients. Closed Mondays.

FISH

Parisians have high expectations for their fish. Thus, a broad selection of *poisson* (fish) and *fruits de mer* (seafood) is readily available, some of which, such as shrimp, may be precooked. Fish is sold fresh at supermarkets and at the *poissonnerie* (fish market) daily, except on Mondays, and at outdoor markets and the *rues commerçants*. The food halls also have exceptionally good fish every day.

The *poissonnier* (fishmonger) will price a whole fish by its weight and clean it too. Fish also comes in fillets or *darnes* (steaks), priced by weight by the piece. Almost all *poissonneries* make fish soups. In supermarkets, soups and fish preparations are found in refrigerators near the fish counters. Inspect the packing and expiration dates on the packages. On the other hand, most fish is frozen on the boat directly after having been caught, so you can also buy excellent frozen fish preparations at reputable places like Picard.

Smoked fish and caviar are highly prized, with offerings at all levels of quality and price. The food halls mentioned above have the most choice. Comptoir du Saumon and Caviar Latian have several addresses. Those below have excellent selections of caviar, smoked fish and snails.

- 7ᵉ: **Pétrossian** (18 boulevard de la Tour-Maubourg; tel: 01.44.11.32.22).

- 8ᵉ: **Caviar Kaspia** (17 place de la Madeleine; tel: 01.42.65.66.21)
- 8ᵉ: **La Maison du Caviar** (21 rue Quentin-Bauchart; tel: 01.47.23.53.43)
- 15ᵉ: **La Maison de l'Escargot** (79 rue Fondary; tel: 01.45. 75.31.09).
- 15ᵉ: **Paris Caviar** (130 rue Lecourbe; tel: 01.55.76.69.20).

MEATS AND MORE

Meats in France are high-quality. French lamb is world-famous, and beef, pork and veal are all available at the *boucherie* (butcher). Cuts may be unfamiliar to you, but if you describe to the *boucher* (butcher) what you want, he can provide it.

That few hormones are used in raising cattle means that the meat may not be particularly tender and will require longer cooking time or thinner cuts. Meat is also not aged very long, so its texture may be different from what you are used to. Chopped or minced meat is usually ground to order and should be cooked and eaten the day of purchase. In fact, butchers generally cut meats to order, rather than pre-package them, and some are known for specialty cuts and artistic creations.

Although butchers are usually closed Mondays, the supermarkets have fresh meat every day, either packaged or freshly cut. Food halls have the most outstanding cuts and can cut to order. Butchers are found in the outdoor markets and in the *rues commerçantes* as well.

Some meat shops are more specialised. Flavourful, lean horsemeat, much less popular than heretofore, is still sold at the *boucherie chevaline* and at some *marchés*. *Marchands de volaille* or *volaillers* specialise in poultry. *Rotisseries* sell hot, cooked poultry and at some other meats, such as pork ribs or rabbit, cooked on the *tournebroche* (*rôtisserie*), and some will roast turkeys for holidays. Most shops make a distinction, both in quality and price, between the *poulet fermier* (free-range chicken) and the traditional chicken. More sought after are establishments that specialise in *fois gras*—both elegant and pricey.

Ham and fresh pork products can be bought at both the

boucherie and *charcuterie*, although the latter is traditionally known for its pork products and has a wider range of sausages and pâtés, as well as a larger selection of prepared takeaway foods and salads. Both supermarkets and *charcuteries* stock *jambons de pays* (hams) from different regions of France, the most famous being the *jambon de Bayonne* (ham from Bayonne). The kosher *charcuteries* sell the same types of products, but made with beef or turkey.

- 7ᵉ: **Au Petit Sud-Ouest** (46 avenue de la Bourdonnais; tel: 01.45.55.59.59). Small shop carrying regional specialty products, with an elegant restaurant behind. Sells *foie gras, canard confit, cassoulet*, wines and tinned products.

- 8ᵉ: **Boucheries Nivernaises St-Honoré** (99, rue du Faubourg St-Honoré; tel: 01.43.59.11.02). One of the prestigious butchers in Paris, providing hand-cut specialties to restaurants as well as to individuals. Excellent and artistic cuts of beef, lamb, pork. Closed Mondays.

- 8ᵉ: **Granterroirs** (30 rue de Miromesnil; tel: 01.47.42.18.18). Both a restaurant and an upscale epicerie, with regional specialties, terrines, velvety *foie gras*, truffles, cheeses and jams. From the rustic tables, diners can view the products lining the walls. Another location in the suburb Levallois; In Paris, open weekdays; in Levallois, also open Saturdays.

- 14ᵉ: **Boucherie Hugo Desnoyer** (45, rue Boulard; tel: 01.45.40.76.67) another location with restaurant is at 28, rue du Docteur-Blanche 75016 (tel: 01.46.47.83.00). One of the top suppliers to restaurants in Paris, the quality of his products carries over into his retail shops. Luckily, you can sample his cooked fare on the spot, and won't be disappointed. Both locations close Sundays and Mondays.

FROMAGERIES

Cheese is an important part of French cuisine and a conversation point at any table. Cheese is grouped into families according to their production, texture, flavour and nutritive value. They can be made from the milk of a *vache* (cow), *brebis* (sheep) or *chèvre* (goat), each with its own flavour; aged or not; made from whole or skim milk; pasteurised or non-pasteurised (*lait cru*); hard, semi-soft,

Fromage de chèvre or goat cheese—just one of the hundreds of varieties of cheese available from the *fromageries* of Paris.

soft, or one of the various stages in between. They may be white, creamy yellow, orange or brown, and come in large wheels or small disks that are sliced, cut or whole, some with edible moulds and rinds, and even seasonal. This vast variety of cheeses means, in fact, that most have not been exported. Newcomers from countries in which cheeses are pasteurised may not have tasted the most flavourful of the French cheeses, and a very pleasant education is in store.

For same-day eating, ask for soft and semi-soft cheeses that are *bien fait* (perfectly ripe); for consuming later, they should be *pas trop fait* (not quite ripe).

Cheese is served between the *plat principal* and the dessert, and it should be served at room temperature. Some people do not refrigerate their cheeses, keeping them instead in a special layered cheese container and eating them soon after purchase. If you refrigerate, keep each cheese wrapped separately, so as not to mix flavours. Some cheeses keep longer than others, and uncut cheeses continue to age.

At dinner, serve cheeses of different textures and flavours. A *plateau de fromage* (cheese platter) generally offers at least one mild and one strong cheese, a blue and a perhaps some soft, semi-soft and hard. Begin with the mildest and move on to the strong.

All supermarkets carry packaged, pasteurised cheeses, as well as some of the unpasteurised. But the best—the most interesting and delicious— may be found at the *marchés*, the artisanal *fromageries* and the crémeries (that also sell butter, eggs and milk). *Fromageries* all carry their own selections, can advise on what is seasonally the best, and suggest the perfect cheeses for any event. Every *quartier* has its own cheese shops, each carrying the well-known cheeses, but also a slightly different and unusual selection for which they are noted by their regulars. Many of these shops finish the aging (*affinage*) of the cheeses on their premises.

Charles de Gaulle famously said: "How can you be expected to govern a country that has 246 kinds of cheese?" When he asked his rhetorical question some 50 years ago, there were at least 250 kinds of cheese. Now there are more than 400, ranging from the ancient Roquefort (said to have been a favourite of Charlemagne), to Boursin, an invention of the 20th century.

One of the best *fromagers*, Androuët, has seven shops in Paris (www.androuet.com) or order through houra (see above). And the extremely well-respected Laurent Dubois has three outlets (www.fromageslaurentdubois.fr).

- 7e: **Barthélémy** (51 rue de Grenelle; tel: 01.42.22.82.24)
- 7e; **Crémerie Quartrehomme** (62 rue de Sèvres; tel: 01.47.34.33.45)
- 12e: **Fromagerie Lefèbre: Fromageries de Paris** (229 rue de Charenton; tel: 01.46.28.10.21)
- 14e; **Boursault** (71 avenue du Général Leclerc; tel: 01.43.27.93.30)
- 16e: **Fromager Lillo** (35 rue des Belles Feuilles; tel: 01.47.27.69.08)
- 17e: **Alléosse** (13 rue Poncelet; tel: 01.46.22.50.45)

TEA AND COFFEE

Teas and coffees, once just staples of the Parisian day, have suddenly become super-chic. Supermarkets and internationally-minded food halls sell more brands of packaged teas and coffees than heretofore and fresh coffee beans from around the world. Beans are also sold at *brûleries/torréfactions*, many of which are known for particular selections. Some even work with customers to determine their preferred blends and keep the recipe on file. *Torréfactions* generally also offer a selection of fresh teas. Le Comptoir Richard has for more than half a century been selling superior coffees, teas, herbal teas, and powders for hot chocolate (www.comptoirsrichard.fr).

- 1er: **Cafés et Thés Verlet** (256 rue Saint-Honoré; tel: 01.42.60.67.39)
- 2e: **Brûlerie San José** (30 rue Petits-Champs; tel: 01.42.96.69.09)
- 4e: **La Caféothèque** (52, rue de l'Hôtel-de-Ville tel: 01.53.01.83.84)
- 5e: **Brûlerie Maubert** (3 rue Monge; tel: 01.46.33.38.77)

Tea lovers should also buy their teas at the tea salons: **Mariage Frères**, as mentioned on page 221 is the most outstanding (www.mariagefreres.fr) Look also for the addresses for **Le Palais des Thés** (www.palaisdesthes.com). For inexpensive Asian teas, try **Tang Frères**.

- 5e: **La Maison des Trois Thés** (1 rue Saint-Médard; tel: 01.43.36.93.84). Closed Mondays.
- 8e: **Les Thés d'Emilie** (76 boulevard Haussmann; tel: 01.43.87.39.84) Twinings teas.
- 13e: **L'Empire des Thés** (101 avenue d'Ivry; tel: 01.45.85.66.33. Open Sundays.
- 15e: **Merry Monk** (87 rue de la Convention; tel: (01.45.75.88.41). Specialising in teas, with packaged products such as, marmalades, biscuits, and coffees. Teas and tastings, and also rooibos tea.

CHOCOLATES

Chocolat is not just appreciated in Paris, it's almost a cult. People talk about chocolate in almost the same way they talk about wine, from the *chocolat chaud* found in tearooms and the determined creations of famed *chocolatiers*, to the simple *tablettes* (bars) sold at supermarkets. Chocolates in France are so delicious because they contain a high percentage of cocoa—sometimes more than 70 per cent—and the higher the quantity of cocoa, the richer the confection; even chocolate bars in supermarkets display the percentage of cocoa in each bar. Look for chocolate in the form of fish just before April Fool's Day ('April Fool' is *'poisson d'avril'*, and poisson means *'fish'*), hearts before Valentine's Day, bunnies and chickens before Easter, and even chocolate mushrooms in autumn. To see chocolates being made and to buy many of his different chocolate bars, visit the chocolate factory of the master chef Alain Ducasse, at 40, rue de la Roquette, near the Bastille (tel: 01.48.05.82.86). It's open to visitors Tuesdays to Saturdays.

For Belgian chocolates, try the famous *chocolatier* Pierre Marcolini who has several shops with his hand-made confections, as do the more commercial Godiva, Jeff de Bruges, Daskalidès and De Neuville. For a dazzling chocolate experience try Jean-Paul Hévin, mentioned on page 222.

- **Maison du Chocolat** (www.lamaisonduchocolate.com). Luscious chocolate desserts and frozen treats.
- **Comptoir Le Chocolate Alain Ducasse** (26, rue St-Benoit; tel: 01.45.48.87.89). International chocolates with fruits or spices, pralines.
- **Henri Le Roux** (1, rue de Bourbon le Chateau; tel: 01.82.28.49.80). Relax with one of its Asian teas, choose three chocolates and relax.

Chocolatier nonpareil

There's little to say about the two boutique chocolatiers below, because even superlatives aren't good enough. Once you try their extraordinary confections, you may never go anywhere else. Be prepared to pay handsomely for perfection.

- Patrick Roger; 108 boulevard Saint-Germain, 75006; tel: 01.43.29.38.42.
- Pierre Hermé; 72 rue Bonaparte, 75006; tel: 01.43.54.47.77.

- **Lenôtre** (www.lenotre.com). Remarkable and candies and other items.
- **Debauve & Gallais** (30 rue des Saints-Peres; tel: 01.45.48.54.67). One of the city's oldest and most venerated.

WINE

When choosing a wine, it helps to describe the meal to be served with the proprietor of the *cave* (wine shop). Be clear as to the desired price range of the wine, in order to be shown the most appropriate wine. Discuss too, the temperature at which the wine should be served. White wines are served chilled, as are some red wines. Note that the shape of the bottle varies according to the type of wine and the region. The percentage of alcohol varies as well and must be indicated on the label.

In general, French wines (and other Old World, European wines) are classified by the *terroir*—the interplay of the soil and climate upon the vines. Thus, what are indicated on the label is generally the type of wine and the area of the château. Only recently has the type of grape appeared on the label, as the wines of the New World do.

In addition to neighbourhood *caves* with personalised service, there are reliable chains with wines of all categories and prices. Nicolas, a franchise operation with more than 200 shops in Paris, has at least one shop in each *arrondissement*. The advice of the *caviste* (wine merchant) is only as good as the owner of each franchise, but most are fairly knowledgeable. Repaire de Bacchus, another franchise, has more than 20 shops throughout the city. Many shops will deliver wines depending on how much is bought.

Supermarkets also have fairly extensive selections of domestic and some foreign wines, and during the *Foire aux vins* (Wine Fair) in October, the supermarkets offer an even broader selection and knowledgeable sales personnel. Some, such as Carrefour, bottle wines under their own label. Galeries Lafayette Gourmet Food Hall and Le Bon Marché also propose their special collections, plus occasional promotional sales and opportunities for tasting. *Traiteurs*, such as Fauchon and Hédiard, are often helpful in their advice. Check the weekly events guides for wine festivals. Refer to the websites of the *caves*, and the Wine Bar section on pages 225–227.

- **BiBoViNo** with its three Paris shops, offers a new concept in wine sales: the excellent high-quality wines in boxes, (the 'bag-in-box'). For people who doubt the quality of the wines—even those reduced in sulfites—they may be tasted before purchase (www.bibovino.fr)

- 2e and 13e: **Legrand Filles & Fils** (1 rue de la Banque; tel: 01.42. 60.07.12). Lovely shop in the Galerie Vivienne, with well-priced *vins de pays*, vintage wines, *eaux de vie* and other brandies. Wine bar, books, accessories and some food products.

- 6e: **La Dernière Goutte** (6 rue de Bourbon-le-Château; tel: 01.43.29.11.62). The American proprietor is extremely knowledgeable about his estate-bottled wines. Wine tastings Saturdays, open Sundays.

- 6e: **La Cave du Senat** (16, rue de Vaugirard; tel: 01.73.74.10.40) A table with options for tasting, in this shop that fine wines from both small and large producers. Across from the Luxembourg Gardens.

- 7e: **Ryst-Dupeyron** (79 rue du Bac; tel: 01.45.48.80.93). Known for its lovely armagnacs, aged calvados, and wines from Bordeaux. Catalogue available.

- 8e: **Les Caves de Taillevent** (228, rue du Faubourg Saint-Honoré; tel: 01.45.61.14.09). A vast assortment of wines, plus regular Saturday morning wine tastings.

- 8e: **Les Caves Augé** (116 boulevard Haussmann; tel: 01.45.22.16.09). Prestigious shop with mature wines and some reasonably priced younger ones.

- 11e: **Au Nouveau Nez** (104 rue St-Maur; tel: 01.43.55.02.30).

Sip some wine in this small sparse locale or take home some bottles of their natural wines. Also at 52 rue de Bagnolet in the 20th *arrondissement* (tel: 01.43.56.94.55).

- 14ᵉ **Les Caves des Papilles** (35 rue Daguerre; tel: 01.43.20.05.74). More than a decade in the famous market street, this *cave* specialises in natural, organic wines, with tastings and events.

CHAMPAGNE

Although vines have been growing in the northern Champagne region of France since Roman times, the second fermentation that produces the famous bubbly that people revere didn't come into being until the 17th century. And lucky for connoisseurs, its refinement and prestige have increasingly grown. Today, only wines grown in that one region and produced by the *méthode champenoise* may legally be called champagne. All others are generally called sparkling wines.

There are many producers of champagne, and with extremely pleasant exploration, you'll find your favourite, for flavours are very different. Just a few of the top labels (in no particular order) are Dom Perignon, Bollinger, Moët & Chandon, Philipponnat, Krug, Cristal, and, of course, the internationally known Veuve Clliquot.

Work with your *caviste*, pay attention to the tastings when they're announced, and you might even take a weekend up in Reims or Epernay and visit the tasting rooms of the *grandes marques*. Learn which champagnes you like and then you'll appreciate the words of the great English economist John Maynard Keynes: "The only regret in life is that I did not drink more champagne."

ENJOYING PARIS

CHAPTER 7

'When I dream of an afterlife in heaven,
the action always takes place at the Paris Ritz.'
—Ernest Hemingway

PARIS, ANY TIME OF THE DAY

There's always something to do in Paris, any time of the day or night. From cultural (and not-so-cultural) opportunities to shopping, from sports to educational courses in just about anything you might want to know, Paris does not disappoint. It's a city of some 60 museums; a place where classical music is as important as popular music, where 300 films are shown each week in a variety of languages and where discos start to swing at 1:00 am. Two hundred and fifty theatres show anything from Shakespeare's plays to the naughtiest revues in late-night cabarets. In fact, cultural activities of all sorts are important to the French and are allocated about one per cent of the country's annual budget—more than what most other nations spend. The *mairie* also subsidises cultural festivals throughout the year, some offered free of charge.

People who do not speak French should have few problems finding where and when everything is. The city of Paris has an extremely detailed website (www.paris.fr), as does the Paris Tourist Office (www.parisinfo.com). The *mairie* (town hall) of your own *arrondissement* will have information on all aspects of the district, from shopping to sports, and just about anything you could want. It's up to you to figure out what suits you best.

FINDING OUT WHAT'S NEW

Parisians eagerly await the publication of the weekly events guides. Available each Wednesday morning at news-stands, both *Pariscope* (€0.70) and *L'Officiel des Spectacles* (€0.70) provide detailed descriptions of the week's activities, from sporting events, special exhibitions at museums and art galleries, theatre, concerts and films, to recommended restaurants, bars and discos. *Figaroscope* is the events listing of the daily newspaper, *Le Figaro* (www.evene.lefigaro.fr), and young people especially often access the LeMag on the Nova Planet website (www.novaplanet.com/novamag). There are several others including the internationally-known *Time Out* (www.timeout.com/paris).

PARIS ITSELF

Start by getting to know the city and its surroundings. There are many multilingual guided tours available, whether through a guide or a recording. For opportunities offered by RATP, access the RATP website (www.ratp.com). In English, click on Visit Paris. You may buy various passes that allow getting on and off the buses at any of the stops. This is also true of Big Bus Paris (tel: 01.53.95.39.53; www.bigbustours.com/paris).

- **Open Tour** (tel: 01.42.66.56.56; www.paris.opentour.com/en). Hop on and off this multi-lingual, guided two-decker sightseeing bus. Four routes and 50 stops, it offers one and two day passes.
- **Paris Walks** (tel: 01.48.09.21.40; www.paris-walks.com). Guided walks in English for various parts of the city. Daily two-hour tours (rain or shine) may include a walk through Hemingway's Paris, Île-de-la-Cité, Montmartre, the Latin Quarter, the Marais and more. Reservations not required for most tours.
- **Fat Tire Tours** (tel: 01.82.88.80.96; www.fattirebiketoursparis.com). Bicycle tours in English around Paris, starting at the Eiffel Tower. Motorised Segways are available for those who want less strenuous outings. There's also a Paris Night Bike Tour that has a boat cruise on the Seine. Reserve in advance.
- **Not a Tourist Destination Tours**; (tel: 01.71.50.97.97; www.notatouristdestination.com). Multilingual guided tours off the regular routes. Food tours (pastry shops, cheese and wine shops, etc.), fashion tours for both men and women,

tours for kids and teenagers, and an evening-out tour that will help you discover the most fashionable bars and clubs in Paris. Groups are small and tours can be customised to your needs.

- **Paris City Vision** (tel: 01.44.55.61.00; www.pariscityvision. com). Coach or minibus tours of the city, plus tours to Disneyland Paris, Versailles, Giverny, Mont Saint-Michel and other parts of France.
- **Paris Story** (11 bis rue Scribe, 75009; tel: 01.42.66.62.06; www.paris-story.com). A multi-media tour of the 2,000-year history of Paris.

MONUMENTS AND MORE

As you're out and about. you'll see monuments that are history lessons in themselves. There are some 37 national monuments and museums, and knowing something about them as you go on your way, will allow you to better appreciate the city's beauty and pride. The Paris Tourist Office's website (www.parisinfo.com; click on *"visiter"*)

has extensive information, and the official website for information on monuments (www.monuments-nationaux.fr). Climbing to the top of the Eiffel Tower or touring the Cathédral de Notre Dame are always popular, but think of these other activities as well:

- **Batobus** (08.25.05.01.01; www.batobus.com). Run by the Port Autonome of Paris, the Batobus is in effect a tour of the city by boat. Running on a daily regular schedule, it makes eight stops, including at the Eiffel Tower, Louvre and Notre Dame. Prices vary, depending on how far you want to go, whether you want a one- or two-day pass or whether you are an adult or child. With the passes, you can get on and off at will to visit museums or monuments near to the stops.

- **Canauxrama** (tel: 01.42.39.15.00; www.canauxrama.com). Cruises on the canals of Paris, the Seine and the Marne. Enjoy learning about Paris through its rivers and canals and going through the locks—an experience not to be missed.

- **Les Catacombs** (1 avenue du Colonel Henri Rol-Tanguy 75014; tel: 01.43.22.47.63; www.catacombes.paris.fr). In 1785, the cemeteries in overcrowded Paris were becoming a health problem, so many remains were dug up and transported into a former quarry. See six million bones and skulls lined up along a path of about 1.5 km, all noted according to the cemetery from whence they came. Both macabre and fascinating.

- **La Tour Montparnasse** (tel: 01.45.38.52.56; www.tourmontparnasse56.com). The 56th floor of the Montparnasse Tower offers an exceptional 360-degree view of Paris, with interactive terminals, historical photos, a media presentation and explanations of the viewpoint from where you are. Open every day until late at night.

- **Père-Lachaise Cemetery** (16 rue du Repos, 75020). The 'Westminster Abbey of Paris' where thousands of famous people who lived in Paris have been entombed. Parisians go to what may be the most visited cemetery in the world for a Sunday afternoon stroll, walking along the landscaped aisles and stopping at the graves of the famous or loved.

They also admire the interesting sculptures and pay homage at the memorials to the deported of World War II or to the heroes of the Paris Commune who were lined up and shot at the Mur des Fédérés. Get a map from a stand outside the cemetery and find the tombs of famous people such as Edith Piaf, Gertrude Stein, Oscar Wilde, the famous 12th-century lovers Abélard and Heloïse, and even Jim Morrison of The Doors, who died in Paris in 1971.

- **Les Égouts de Paris** (Pont de l'Alma, across from 93 quai d'Orsay, 75007 (tel: 01.53.68.27.81; www.egouts.tenebres. eu/visite.php). Open Monday–Thursday, Saturday–Sunday, from 11:00 am–5:00 pm, closes at 4:00 pm in winter. Many people take a guided tour of the sewer and water management system of Paris. Smells can be... peculiar... and sometimes in the rainy season, flooding causes closure of the area. Nonetheless, it's an interesting experience.

THE GREATEST ART

Paris, of course, has some of the most well-known museums in the world. They range from 'the greats' such as Le Louvre to the educational such as the Musée du Vin (Museum of Wine), down to the truly offbeat such as the Musée d'Eventail (Museum of Fans). Check the city and Tourist Office websites, and those of the individual museums that interest you. Wikipedia also has a list of museums in Paris.

Many of the city's museums only charge entry for their special exhibits; their permanent collections are free, for example, at the Musée du Petit Palais, Musée Carnavelet, Musée Cernuschi and Musée Cognacq-Jay. In addition, the national museums generally have reduced rates for people over 60 years old and under 18, and all are free (for the permanent collections) on the first Sunday of each month. If you are in Paris for just a short visit (or if you have friends coming to Paris for a visit), there are three museum passes to consider: two, four or six consecutive days or five consecutive days; there are others. Passes are sold at museums, monuments, *métro* stations and the Paris Tourist

Actually, if you spent 30 seconds in front of each piece of art at the Louvre, 24 hours a day, it would take you more than seven months to view it all.

Office. City museums are usually closed Mondays, and national museums close Tuesdays. Museums usually open at 10:00 am, closing around 6:00 pm, and some have a late opening one night a week.

Do not think that once you've seen the Louvre, the Musée d'Orsay and the Pompidou, you've seen everything worth seeing. There are dozens of other spectacular art museums, as well as science museums, and not to overlook the newest Musée du Quai Branly, which specialises in the arts and civilisations of Africa, Oceania and the Americas. As we mentioned earlier, there are also the Musée de la Poupée (Doll Museum), Musée de la Magie (Museum of Magic), plus there's the marvelous Musée Gourmand du Chocolat (www.museeduchoclat.fr). And in the 10th there's even a small private museum, the Musée d Eventail, showing fancy fans and fan-making. So, given that it could take several months or more just to begin to grasp the Louvre, there's certainly enough in Paris to edify you for quite some time.

Not only that, there are special temporary exhibits in most of the museums, and you can find them listed in the weekly events guides. And over time museums upgrade their own collections, such as the Louvre working for almost a decade to revamp its Islamic Art installation, at what might seem an unimaginable cost of more than 80 million euros.

TICKET PURCHASE

Billets (tickets) to events are sold online and at the box office several weeks in advance, and for some events long before that. Box offices themselves are generally open for ticket purchase from 11:00 am to 7:00 pm. Most accept telephone reservations although lines are often busy, and credit cards are accepted. Pick up tickets at least an hour before the performance, and be prepared to stand in line when purchasing tickets and picking them up at the venue before the event.

Major events, however, sell out quickly, especially those with big-name performers, so buy tickets as early as possible. You can also access the websites of agencies that handle cultural, entertainment and sporting events, but of course for the convenience you pay their commission in addition to the price. The Fnac stores have ticket agencies: you can also order by telephone or online (tel: 08.92.68.36.22; www.fnacspectacles.com or in English: www.fnactickets.com).

As in any major city, tickets to cultural events are expensive. Yet, season tickets are sometimes available at preferential prices, and there are inexpensive performing arts and film festivals, as well as free year-round church concerts and city-sponsored festivals. Some theatres sell reduced-price tickets just before a performance, but to have access to a wide choice of half-price tickets on the day of a performance, it's worth checking the Kiosques at 15 place de la Madeleine, Place Raoul Dautry at the Tour Montparnasse, or at Place des Ternes. If you do get tickets from the Kiosque, make sure the tickets do not say *sans visibilité*, meaning that at least a part of the stage will not be visible from your seats. On the other hand, some people accept such tickets and take a chance on moving to a better seat if someone doesn't show up or leaves at the *entr'acte* (intermission).

If you have no ticket at all, try standing at the entrance before the event is to begin with a sign saying '*CHERCHE UNE PLACE*' ('ticket wanted')—people sometimes sell their extra tickets.

Students and young people under 26 may also visit one of the Kiosques Paris Jeunes for reduced prices to events, and check the website www.etudiantdeparis.fr.
- **Kiosque le Marais**: 14 rue François Miron 75004
- **Kiosque Goutte d'Or**: 1 rue Fleury 75018
- **Kiosque Champ-de-Mars**: 101 quai Branly, 75015

THEATRE

Parisians have been flocking to the theatre since the 17th century, when the Comédie Française was founded under Louis XIV (www.comedie-francaise.fr). Performances ranged from classic tragedies and political satire, to slapstick and farce. Some productions were so risqué that Louis XIV finally censored what could or could not be performed. But Parisians loved all the offerings, and when they didn't, they let their displeasure be known with catcalls, whistles and generally rowdy behavior, becoming part of the spectacle themselves.

Although audiences are better behaved these days, Paris is still a city that appreciates live performances and has more theatres than any other city in the world. No matter what you wish to watch, you'll probably find it, from international classics in elegant and historical surroundings to offbeat performances in funky, non-mainstream storefronts. Extremely innovative is Le Centquatre-Paris, which is a large hangar-like multi-use space at 5, rue Curial in the 19th *arrondissement* (www.104.fr). In a distinctly collaborative approach, here are theatre, dance, cinema, music, residencies for emerging artists—plus shops, a kids' place, several modern cafés, and much more.

The Comédie Française (www.comedie-francaise.fr) performs at three venues: the Salle Richelieu, the Théâtre du Vieux Colombier, and the Studio-Théâtre Galerie du Carrousel du Louvre Look for an enormous repertoire ranging from the classics of Molière, Racine and Corneille to works by playwrights such as William Shakespeare, Samuel Beckett and Anton Chekhov. These are performed in French of course, although there are performances in the original language from time to time. For current and upcoming productions at some 60 theatres in all parts of the city, access these websites (www.canaltheatre.com or www.theatreinparis.com) for productions with English subtitles.

- **La Cartoucherie** (www.cartoucherie.fr) in the beautiful Bois de Vincennes at the eastern edge of Paris is a complex of eight theatres, staging an imaginative range of international works, both classics and avant-garde.
- **L'Odéon, Théâtre de l'Europe** at place de l'Odéon, 75006 (tel: 01.44.85.40.40; www.theatre-odeon.eu). After a 30-million-euro renovation, this venerable theatre—one of six subsidised national theatres in France—glows with beauty. Its mission is to 'bring to life the artistic heritage of Europe', and it does so by staging international productions, often in their original languages.
- **Le Bouffes du Nord**: 37 boulevard de la Chappelle, behind the Gare du Nord 75010 (tel: 01.46.07.34.50; www.bouffesdunord.com) was 'rediscovered' in 1974, after

having been abandoned decades before. Now renovated (although its rather dilapidated look has been deliberately maintained), it is the base of famous director Peter Brook, whose experimental productions—often in English—are consistently sold out.

English-language theatre troupes are sparse but do turn up from time to time. There is also Word for Word, an experimental theatre group from San Francisco, which performs each spring at the American Library in Paris (www.americanlibraryinparis.org).

CINEMA

Since the Lumière brothers presented the first 'moving pictures' in 1895, the French have regarded cinema as an art form like any other, and it receives much the same attention. Hundreds of films are shown each week in theatres across the city, either in French (*version française—vf*) or in the original language (*version originale—vo*) with French subtitles.

The selection is outstanding: *films nouveaux* (recently released films) and *exclusivités* (films on general release)

are plentiful, film festivals showcasing certain directors or types of films are popular, and *reprises* (older films brought back) are often screened.

New films open on Wednesday. Check the weekly events which list the week's films by subject and by theatre in each *arrondissement*. The listings state the time of the *séance* (projection), which usually starts off with advertisements and trailers, and how many minutes later the film itself starts. Allô Ciné has a useful website (www.allocine.fr).

Arrive early for the newest films and be prepared to queue for tickets and to enter. Doors usually open about 10 minutes before the *séance*. Most theatres now have vending machines or snack counters in the lobbies; and some now have cafés of their own.

The Salles

Gaumont, UGC, and Mk2 are major first-run, citywide cinema chains with multiplexes. Generally each chain shows a particular set of films at all its theatres but at slightly different times, making it convenient to see any film. Some have a late-night show on weekends, and they all indicate which films are in vo. The Champs-Elysées has several cinemas on both sides of the avenue. Some of the newer multiplexes, such as in the Cour Saint-Emilion or the MK2 Bibliothèque offer modernity to the highest degree. Yet, art films are also shown across the city, with the greatest concentration of salles in the 5th and 6th. Action is a small chain that specialises in the screening of old films, and look also for cinemas such as L'Arlequin, Saint-André-des-Arts, and Quartier Latin.

Some museums such as the Louvre and the Centre Pompidou screen films, and especially interesting theatres are the Studio 28 in Montmartre, the international Cinéma des Cinéastes at Clichy, the Balzac in the Latin Quarter, the remodelled old Louxor with its upstairs terraced restaurant, the enormous Grand Rex, and the Pagode in the 7th *arrondissement*. Max Linder Panorama, one of the especially attractive cinemas, has a curved panoramic screen, and La Géode at La Villette is a stunning IMAX venue.

Cinema Prices

Although prices may seem high for the cinema, they are generally in line with cinemas in other capital cities. The major cinemas still offer *cartes privilège* (discount cards) and theatres at the Forum des Images (forumdesimages.fr) have discount programmes. Some of the major cinema chains have done away with senior discounts, but others have reduced prices for the first showing of the day, which is usually just before noon. There are also cut-price film festivals, and in summer, La Villette hosts the free Cinéma en Plein Air outdoors in the park. Rent a chair or bring a blanket and a picnic dinner. Forum des Images also organises a similar Cinema au Clair de Lune, screening films around a chosen theme outdoors at selected spots in the city. These free outdoor screenings always attract a large crowd.

CLASSICAL MUSIC

Music of all kinds, music at all hours, music everywhere—that's Paris. Look for seasonal offerings of classical music, performances by visiting artistes and church concerts, etc. In addition to the weekly events guides and the city's websites, one interesting website is www.classictic.com, that lists many concerts all around Europe.

Classical music is publicly supported at national and local levels, and Paris boasts symphony orchestras, chamber groups and church ensembles. There are also performances by international guest orchestras, chamber groups and visiting soloists on tour, as well as regular concert performances by museums and churches. The newest addition to the classical firmament is the outstanding Philharmonie de Paris in the Parc de la Villette, a cultural institution of large and small concert halls, exhibition and rehearsal spaces, plus restaurants and bars (www.philharmoniedeparis.fr). It is also home to the contemporary music group, Ensemble InterContemporain. (www.ensembleinter.com). Nearby, in avenue Jean-Jaurès is the Conservatoire National Supérieur de Musique et de Danse de Paris (www.conservatoiredeparis.fr).

The main concert season is from October to June. Get tickets early, for concerts sell out quickly, especially those with famous conductors or soloists. Subscriptions to concert series are available, and subscribers have first choice for seats. Some *salles de concerts* (concert halls) offer student discounts just before performances.

Classical festivals are held throughout the year—pleasantly outdoors in summer. See the listing of annual festivals at the end of the chapter. Those in the nearby suburbs and accessible by public transportation are listed in the weekly events guides. Look too for religion-oriented music at holiday times, such as the Festival d'Art Sacré, and church music around Christmas and Easter.

Radio-France organises the most concerts in Paris and is the administrator of the Orchestre National de France (that generally performs at the Théâtre des Champst-Elysées) and the Orchestre Philharmonique (tel: 01.42.30.15.16; www.radiofrance.fr). Listen to Radio France podcasts currently available as apps for Android and Kindle Fire. Radio France also has apps available on the ITunes Store.

Free Concerts

Paris has a long tradition of free concerts. In May and June, classical and jazz concerts are held at the Parc Floral of the Bois de Vincennes, and free concerts are held in public gardens throughout the summer. No admission is charged to attend performances by students at the École Normale de Musique and the Institut National des Jeunes Aveugles or rehearsals at the Maison de Radio-France.

Along with their paid concert season, many churches offer free concerts of sacred music throughout the year (especially Eglise Saint-Roch on rue Saint-Honoré), although generally not in August. In winter, it's wise to bundle up, for some of the oldest churches can be cold.

The Opera

The Paris Opera is one of the pillars of the Parisian musical scene, attracting international stars to its major season, which runs from September to mid-July. The Opéra Bastille at Place de la Bastille, 75012, opened in 1989, is one of François Mitterrand's Grands Projets and is the largest opera house in the world (tel: 08.92.89.90.90; www.opera-de-paris.fr). The Bastille offers opera performances in the Grande Salle, and other concerts and performing art festivals in the smaller Amphithéâtre and Studio. It generally stages 16 operas per season with a varied repertoire.

When the Opéra Bastille was built, it was originally intended that the beautiful Opéra Garnier at Place de la Opéra be used only for ballet and other dance concerts. Now, however, it also hosts opera, putting on smaller works and special programmes. Schedules and reservations can be obtained through the numbers and website above.

The best seats are, of course, expensive. Reserve online or at the box office, if you go personally, it is best to go on the first day that tickets are available and wait in line. Although the box office opens at 11:00 am, some people arrive by 7:00 am for tickets to the most popular performances.

DANCE

The Ballet de l'Opéra National de Paris (the world's oldest ballet company) performs primarily at the Opéra Garnier, integrating some contemporary works into its classical repertoire; use the same sites to get information as you would for operas. The Bastille also hosts international productions.

You can catch contemporary dance performances at two venues: The Théâtre de la Ville at 2 place du Châtelet, 75001 (tel: 01.42.74.22.77) and the Theatre des Abbesses at 31 rue des Abbesses (tel: 01.48.87.54.42; overall website www.theatredelaville-paris.com). There are also regularly scheduled ballet performances at the Palais des Congrès at Porte Maillot and the Théâtre des Champs-Elysées at 15 avenue Montaigne, 75008 (tel: 01.49.52.50.50; www.theatrechampselysees.fr)..

For Vegas-style cabaret dance spectaculars, perennially popular are the Moulin Rouge (www.moulinrouge.fr), the Folies Bergére (www.foliesbergere.com), the Lido (www.lido.fr) and The Crazy Horse (www.lecrazyhorseparis.com).

Currently, however, it is the offbeat theatres that are staging the most interesting performances. Look for Asian and Middle Eastern dance troupes at the Centre Mandapa at 6 rue Wurtz, 75013 (tel: 01.45.89.99.00) and contemporary dance at L'Etoile du Nord, 16, rue Georgette-Agutte, 75018 (tel: 01.42.26.47.47). Check *Pariscope* for other venues.

AND THE MODERN

From blues, jazz and the hottest rock to the most mellow *chansons* (songs); in music bars, discotheques and enormous stadiums, there is not an evening in Paris when something is not going on. If you have patience, your favourite group will eventually come to Paris, for they all do at one time or another.

The major stadium for big musical events is the Palais Omnisports de Paris-Bercy. Another large venue is Zénith at 211 avenue Jean-Jaurès, 75019 at La Villette (www.le-zenith. com). And the Olympia at 28 boulevard des Capucines is an old-time music hall that still attracts the crowds for both retro and modern sounds (www.olympiahall.com). In fact, different styles overlap throughout Paris, especially for Latin and African music, which can now be found just about everywhere.

Au Lapin Argile, a famous cabaret in Montmartre. Nearby is the world-renowned Moulin Rouge. In addition to traditional revues, Paris also boasts the trendiest clubs and bars, making for a bustling nightlife.

Fortunately, resources are plentiful to learn what's current. And since venues change and concerts get sold out quickly, check the Internet sites daily, and reserve as soon as you can. And listen to Radio Nova (101.5FM; www.novaplanet.com), and the jazz station TSF (89.9FM). As usual, the city and tourist office websites can be helpful, and there are several others, including www.parisbouge.com

- **New Morning** (7–9 rue des Petites-Ecuries, 75010; tel: 01.45.23.51.41; www.newmorning.com. Ever popular, hosts jazz, salsa, world music, blues and just about anything interesting that is passing through Paris. There's dancing, drinking, and a hip crowd.

- **Bataclan** (50 boulevard Voltaire, 75011; tel: 01.43.14.00.30; www.bataclan.fr). As of this writing, the lovely old theatre is planning its remodeling and reopening after the terrorist attack of November 2015. Check its website for further news, and when reopened, its schedule of popular international rock and dance concerts.

- **L'International** (5-7, rue Moret, 75011; tel: 01.49.29.76.45; www.linternational.fr). No entry fee for this varied bar and concert venue. Its detailed website lists the upcoming concerts.

- **Nouveau Casino** (109, rue Oberkampf, 75011; tel: 01.43.57.57.40). Concerts ("underground") with touring groups, a dance club, electronic music, parties, adjacent to the long-popular bar/pub Café Charbon (tel: 01.43.57.55.13), in a neighbourhood that goes on well into the early hours.

AND ALL THAT JAZZ

Parisians have loved jazz since World War I, when American black soldiers first introduced it to the city. The Banlieues Bleues jazz festival held here in spring draws internationally known jazz performers.

- **Le Caveau de la Huchette** (5 rue de la Huchette, 75005; tel: 01.43.26.65.05). Most famous for traditional jazz.

- **Duc des Lombards** (42 rue des Lombards; 75001; tel: 01.42.33.22.88). This is one of the coolest jazz spots in the city.

- **Les Disquaires** (4,-6, rue des Taillandiers 75011; tel: 01.40.21.94.60). A bar with a dance floor, serving up a melange of jazz and soul, and even the Brazilian samba, but jazz rules the roost.
- **Le Caveau des Oubliettes** (52, rue Galande: tel: 01.46.34.23.09). A crowded well-known jazz club in the Latin Quarter, with an intimate underground setting for concerts and jam sessions.
- **Sunset Sunside** (60 rue des Lombards, 75001; tel: 01.40.26.46.60). A perennial favourite, this double venue hosts both electric and acoustic big-name groups and soloists.

OKAY, LET'S GO!

But the question remains: what to do on a Saturday night on the town? With hundreds of nightspots in twenty *arrondissements*, it's hard to choose. Of course, the central areas around the Place Vendome are still stylish and fashionable—and expensive. But just beyond, the Marais is a mix of hip gays and lesbians, plus a vibrant Jewish community, with nightspots and eateries to which much of Paris comes. But the changing life of the Right Bank starts at the Bastille area, now so popular among the younger crowd with its cafes, music venues, and bars that it can get overcrowded, but still fun and bustling until the early hours. The holds true—and perhaps more so just above at Oberkampf, not long ago run-down and seedy. Cool and trendy, Oberkampf and its outlying neighbours Gambetta and Menilmontant have brought a new nightlife to this northeastern part of the city, as have the banks of the Canal Saint-Martin, always on the move. To the northwest, Montmartre, especially around rue des Abbesses, is smart, and tourists especially congregate around Pigalle, with its X-rated adult shows, and the Moulin Rouge.

Yet the Left Bank still invites. While the 7th is still quiet and staid, with some fine dining possibilities, it certainly doesn't call for late night entertainment. But Saint-Germain hums at all hours at its famous cafes, and jazz spots and more nightlife—especially jazz clubs—can be found all around the Place Saint-Michel. The Latin Quarter in the 5th with its universities still has an inexpensive student atmosphere; its eateries, bars, and pubs are casual and relaxed.

DANCING 'TIL DAWN

In Paris, the truly *branché* (plugged in) crowd changes its preferences seemingly with the wind, but whichever the wind, it does not start blowing until late. *Boites* (discotheques) are popular, but not before midnight, and dancing can last until dawn. Many clubs impose a cover charge, often including the first drink (*consommation*). If not, the first drink can be expensive. Occasionally entrance fees are waived and some clubs distribute free-entry coupons around town. On summer nights, though, look for free dancing (and sometimes classes) on various *quais*, for tango and salsa..

- 1er: **Le Chacha Club** (47 rue Berger, near Les Halles; tel: 01.40.13.12.12). As much a concept as a bar, Le Chacha has several rooms and several themes: A trendy restaurant, wine bar with a small but serviceable dance floor and a good Dj, a terrace for those rare fine evenings, and interesting visiting artists and events—all contributing one of the most *branché locales* in this part of the city. Open 9:00 pm–6:00 am, Wednesdays through Saturdays.
- 6e: **Cubana Café** (45-47, rue Vavin; (tel: 01.40.46.80.81). Havana in Paris. Tapas, good drinks including a great mojito. Latin music starts around 11:00 pm.
- 11e: **Le Balajo** (9m rue de Lappe; tel: 01.47.00.07.87). A classic since 1936 for dancing, especially for Cuban salsa on Thursday nights, and rock and roll on Wednesdays. Classes, animations. Closed Sundays.
- 11^{e}: **Favela Chic** (18, rue du Faubourg du Temple; tel: 01.40.21.38.14). Always loud with a variety of electronic and Latin music, Favela has been an institution for people who thrive on all things Brazilian. Closed Sundays and Mondays.
- 14^{e}: **La Pachanga** (8, rue Vandamme; tel: 01.56.80.11.40). Salsa, bachata and kizomba, classes in Cuban salsa, at this venue near Montparnasse. Open until 5:00 am on weekends.

THE GAY AND LESBIAN SCENE

Although most establishments in Paris have been at least gay-friendly, since the legalisation of same-sex marriage life for gays has been more normal, yet the areas that are still the most tightly knit are the Marais and around the Beauborg. Paris is a fairly open and tolerant city, and homophobic incidents are rare. Nonetheless, as with anyone walking about in the wee hours in neighbourhoods that like to party, it's best to stay on well-lit streets.

To find the most up-to-date information on the gay scene in Paris, access www.gayparis.com. The online magazine Tetu (www.tetu.com) keeps tabs on Paris happenings, as does the website of radio station Fréquence Gay at MHz 98.2 which carries information on resources. For social and activist groups and networking, see the Resource Guide in Chapter 10. New venues are opening up and the popularity often changes, but here are a few of the currently well-known:

■ Men's club: **Le Club 18** (18 rue de Beaujolais 75001; tel: 01.42.97.52.13). Small and timeless, with music and dancing midnight till dawn. Open weekends and public holidays' eves.

- Men's bar: **Duplex Bar** (25 rue Michel-le-Comte, 75003; tel: 01.42.72.80.86). One of Paris' oldest gay bars, still going strong. Eclectic music, good drinks. Open daily from 8.00 pm–2.00 am.

- Men's bar: **Quetzal** (10 rue de la Verrerie, 75004; tel: 01.48.87.99.07). Completely redone and modernised, this bar has a dancing area and terrace. Live DJs on weekends. Open daily from 5:00 pm–5:00 am.

- Men's café: **Open Café** (17 rue des Archives, 75004; tel: 01.42.72.26.18). Great summer terrace at this trendy and popular café that draws a crowd, especially early evenings. Open daily from 10.00 am–2.00 am.

- Men's bar: **Raidd Bar** (22, rue du Temple 75003; tel: 01.53.01.00.00). Known for its 'showers and go-go boys', Raidd is much more than that. Theme nights, such as Brazilian on Wednesdays, and an enhanced shower show on Thursdays. Always crowded, go early to see the shows.

- Mixed bar: L**a Mutinerie** (176–178 rue Saint-Martin, 75003. Feminist, festive, cultural, political, and an encompassing welcome to the LGBT community at this friendly-café/bar. Concerts, debates, films, spectacles, DJs. Formerly the Unity Bar.

- Women's bar: **La Champmeslé** (4 rue Chabanais, 75002; tel: 01.42.96.85.20). There are very few lesbian bars in Paris, and the atmosphere keeps changing. This, however, is one of the original, now a classic. International beers on tap, good cocktails, plus readings, cabaret shows, art exhibitions and charity nights. Open from 3:00 pm; closed Sundays.

DAY TRIPS THROUGHOUT THE PARIS AREA

Some of the most celebrated historical French sites are within the Paris region and can usually be reached in less than an hour by the national SNCF trains or the commuter RER trains—both inexpensive. However, if you're interested in guided tours in English, try a tour bus company that offers comfortable coach rides not only to spectacular sites near Paris, but also those farther afield: south to 'chateau country' (the Loire Valley), up to the 'champagne country' near Reims, and even as far north as Mont Saint-Michel and the walled city of Saint-Malo in Brittany. Most Paris hotels display brochures of these tour companies; otherwise, contact one of these:

- **Link Paris Tours** (tel:1-866-996-9727; www.linkparis.com)
- **Paris City Vision** (2 rue des Pyramides, 75001; tel: 01.44.55.61.00 www.pariscityvision.com)
- **Paris Trip** (Cité de Pusy 75017; tel: 01.56.79.05.23; www.paris-trip.com)

Basilique Royale de Saint-Denis

Although this imposing basilica is in the northern Parisian suburb of Saint-Denis, it isn't exactly an 'out-of-town' trip, for it's easily reached by *métro* line 13. Construction of the basilica began in 1122 and many of the kings of France are entombed here, from Dagobert in the 7th century to Louis XVI and Marie-Antoinette, both guillotined in 1793 during the French Revolution. Sometimes called the 'Westminster Abbey of France', this masterpiece of Gothic architecture was built on the spot where Saint Denis is said to have been buried in the 3rd century. Legend goes that the patron saint of France walked to this spot carrying his own head after having been decapitated by the Romans.

La Défense

Just a few minutes west from central Paris and lying on the RER Line A, La Défense is a 750-hectare major business complex in France, headquarters to the country's most important corporations (www.ladefense.fr). Completed in the 1970s, more than 100,000 people work in some 100 modern skyscrapers and more than 30,000 people live in residential high-rise buildings that are linked by landscaped gardens and walkways dotted with sculptures and a large pool with musical water displays. There's a small train that gives a tour of the area. Don't miss the Quatre-Temps shopping mall, one of the largest in France. Take the glass elevator to the 35th floor of La Grande Arche for a spectacular view of Paris.

Château de Versailles

Approximately 20 km southwest of Paris, about half an hour away by RER Line C, the Chateau de Versailles is the most spectacular and famous palace in France, if not the world. It was built by Louis XVI who had engaged the same architects and landscapers used by the unfortunate Fouqet for his Château Vaux-le-Vicomte. With some 700 ornately decorated and furnished rooms that hold 6,000 paintings and 2,000 sculptures, plus some 800 hectares of gardens, fountains, and woods, it's best to put aside an entire day for Versailles. (Check its website below for the schedule of fountain displays during summer.) Adjacent is the Petit Trianon, a palace designed for Mme de Pompadour in 1768 and later given to Marie Antoinette by Louis XVI. Not far is the Potager du Roi, the 'kitchen garden' of Louis XIV, now run by the National Horticultural School. The Grande Écurie (Big Stable) houses a museum of coaches (www.chateauversailles.fr). For detailed information on all attractions in the town of Versailles, contact the Office de Tourisme de Versailles at 2bis avenue de Paris, Versailles (tel: 01.39.24.88.88; www.versailles-tourisme.com).

Château de Chantilly

Less than a half an hour from Paris by train from the Gare du Nord or 45 minutes by RER Line D, lies the entire domain of Chantilly, a bequest to the Institut de France. The palace is called Musée Condé after the former owners—princes who were cousins to the French kings. The cream-coloured Renaissance palace, rebuilt after it was destroyed during the French revolution, is surrounded by a lake and houses an extensive collection of paintings and books. The exquisite Grand Stables, now a horse museum, are worth a visit in themselves. Nearby is the Hippodrome racetrack that sponsors the annual Prix de Diane Hermès, one of the most fashionable equestrian events of the Parisian season. The 15,000-acre forest is popular for hiking and cycling (www.domainedechantilly.com).

Château de Fontainebleau

A 45-minutes train ride from Gare de Lyon to Fontainebleau-Avon and a short bus ride will take you to this exceptional 16th-century Renaissance palace built by François I and expanded by later kings, even Napoleon, who bid farewell from its courtyard as he went into exile. The palace is sumptuously decorated and adorned with tapestries, paintings and frescoes. Once the hunting grounds for French kings, the Fontainebleau forest that surrounds the town is now a popular weekend outing for Parisians (www.musee-chateau-fontainebleau.fr).

Cathedral of Chartres

About 95 km southwest from Paris and accessible by train from Gare Montparnasse, the charming town of Chartres is famous for the stained glass windows of its cathedral, built between 1145 and1220. One of the greatest French Gothic cathedrals, Notre Dame de Chartres is noted for its magnificent 'Chartres blue'-and-red windows. Stroll through the preserved medieval streets of the town to the 13th-century Église Saint-Pierre, which also has stained glass, visit the museum and see some particularly fine old houses as you walk down to the banks of the river Eure. In the summer months, there is a local tourist train that makes a round of the town (www.discover-chartres.com).

Château de Vaux-le-Vicomte

Only 25 minutes from Gare de Lyon to Melun by train or by the RER Line D2, this exquisite 17th-century country chateau (www.vaux-le-vicomte.com) was built by Nicolas Fouquet, Finance Minister to Louis XIV. To celebrate the completion of the magnificent chateau, the unfortunate minister invited His Majesty to a lavish *fête* that included a display of Chinese fireworks, bejewelled elephants, a musical composed by Lully and a play written by Molière. Consumed by jealousy and anger at the extravagance of his Finance Minister, the king had Fouquet arrested for embezzlement and sentenced to life imprisonment. He then proceeded to hire Fouquet's architect and landscaper to build his Château de Versailles! Check for opening times and special events.

Giverny

It's easiest to use one of the tour bus companies mentioned above to tour the charming home and gardens of Impressionist painter Claude Monet (www.fondation-monet.com), located some 76 km northwest of Paris. Take time, too, to visit the Musée d'Art Américain, which holds a collection of works of American Impressionists, many of whom studied or resided in France. If you take the train, it's about an hour from Gare Saint-Lazare to Vernon, where a bus then takes you to Giverny. Monet's lovely garden and pond with its Japanese bridge have been immortalised in his paintings, especially in his paintings of water lilies.

Auvers-sur-Oise

Some 30 km to the northwest of Paris, Auvers-sur-Oise (www. auvers-sur-oise.com) was the final home of Dutch painter Vincent Van Gogh. Take the train from Gare du Nord to Cergy-Pontoise, then the local train in the direction of Creil.

After visiting the Auberge Ravoux where Van Gogh lived and died, a stroll through the town will provide a well-documented tour of the buildings that have become so familiar through Van Gogh's paintings, including the Église Notre Dame. There are several museums and the atelier of the painter Daubigny, and you can also walk up the hill to the cemetery where Van Gogh and his brother Theo were buried. Linger over lunch at the elegant Hostellerie du Nord before heading back to Paris.

Brussels, Belgium

It takes slighly over an hour to reach downtown Brussels from Gare du Nord by the Thalys train. Make your reservations through SNCF (www.visitbrussels.be; www.sncf.fr). Imagine lunching on moules frites (mussels and French fries) with a refreshing Belgian beer in a restaurant on the beautiful Grand Place, then browsing for a few hours at the Royal Museum of Art, before taking the train back to Paris. All in all, an easy and lovely afternoon well spent. There's much more to see in Belgium, however, especially including the charming towns of Ghent and Bruges (www.visitbelgium.com).

Disneyland Resort Paris

The European Disney theme park can be reached in less than an hour by RER Line A, or directly by bus from Charles de Gaulle airport. The Disney Village offers hotels, restaurants and shops for those who want to stay more than one day to visit the Disneyland Park and its five differently-themed attractions. Golf Disneyland has three 9-hole courses (which may be combined into 18-holes) and is open year-round. There is also the Walt Disney Studios, which exhibits films and animation productions. Add water activities, tennis courts and year-round entertainment, and Disneyland isn't just for the kids (www.disneylandparis.com).

SPORTS AND FITNESS

The French, although passionate sport spectators, were not much known for being extremely *sportifs* (sporty) themselves. This has changed considerably however, as younger people are becoming fitness-conscious. They are smoking and drinking less while exercising more. *Gymnases* are opening all across Paris, jogging is popular, rollerblades are seen on the streets and in the *métro*, and some main city streets have bicycle paths. Paris offers an extensive system of public sports facilities, including tennis courts, swimming pools, gyms and running tracks, all increasingly crowded. The daily sports newspaper *L'Equipe* has information on all current sporting events, as do the weekly events guides.

Access the city's website for individual sport and fitness opportunities (www.paris.fr) and your own *mairie* should know about your own *arrondissement*. For a list of all the sports federations, access the city's website (www.en.parisinfo.com) and see "Sports Federations". And the Fédération Sportive Gaie et Liesbienne Ile-de-France is an umbrella association fostering amateur sports for gays and lesbians (www.fsgl.org). Paris FItness is an overall website that details myriad fitness opportunities (www.parisfitness.com).

Spectator Sports

The main indoor public arena is the Palais Omnisports Paris-Bercy at 8 boulevard de Bercy, 75012. It holds football, tennis and volleyball matches; ice-skating competitions; equestrian events and rock concerts. The Parc des Princes, located at the southern tip of the Bois de Boulogne, at 24 rue Commandant-Guilbaud, 75016, is a 50,000-seat stadium where football (soccer to Americans) and rugby games are played, and for tennis, the French Open is at Roland Garros. Then, there is the 80,000-seat Grande Stade de France, constructed in the late 1990s just beyond the northern edge of the city in Saint-Denis, where the finals of the World Cup matches in 1998 were held. In addition to sports matches, it currently hosts large musical events. The stadium is easily reached by RER and *métro*.

Like most Europeans, the French are avid football fans. The football season runs from the end of July to the following April. The Paris team is Paris Saint-Germain (www.psg.fr) that plays at Parc des Princes. Season tickets are available and single tickets may be purchased online, at the stadium or at ticket agencies. Buy tickets well in advance, for the important matches sell out early.

Horse races are also popular. The Hippodrome d'Auteuil and Hippodrome de Longchamp are in the Bois de Boulogne, and each has its particular racing season and events. The Hippodrome de Vincennes in the Bois de Vincennes is known for its trotting meets. Bets may be made at the track or off-track through the Pari Mutuel Urbain (PMU) at many tabacs (www.pmu.fr). For information, see Paris Turf, a racing magazine (www.paris-turf.com).

The Two Largest Parks

As described in Chapter 2, the two largest parks with the most sporting opportunities are located to the western and eastern edges of Paris; both the Bois de Boulogne and the Bois de Vincennes have extensive possibilities.

In the Bois de Boulogne just at the edge of the 16^e, there are running tracks or just paths for a walk, a workout course, 28 km of bridle paths, artificial lakes with rowboat rentals and bicycle rentals to use on 15 km of cycle routes. as well tennis swimming pools, tennis courts, and even badminton. The Parc de Bagatelle has an old castle and lovely rose gardens. The Jardin d'Acclimatation has a children's playground and amusement park, zoo, donkey rides and puppet shows. And there's actually a campground for tenters and RVs.

The Bois de Vincennes stretches east from the 12^e. Larger, more wooded, less built up and often more tranquil than the Bois de Boulogne, 32 kilometres of car-free jogging and rollerblading paths and walking paths, and cycling tracks, bridle paths, rowboat rentals on several of the four lakes, baseball and football fields, and a large tennis facility are just some of the park's attractions. The Parc Floral has play areas for kids, a working farm to visit, a mini-golf course, and ping pong tables. Sporting or not, don't miss the completely renovated, stunning zoo, and the amazing bird sanctuary.

BECOMING FITNESS CONSCIOUS
Running

Parisians do not often practise *le footing* (jogging) around city streets, for traffic and pollution can be unpleasant, but people do jog along the *quais* with their broad sidewalks and lovely views. Weekends, *le jogging du dimanche* sees runners head for the Bois de Boulogne or to the Bois de Vincennes. In the city centre, people run in the Tuileries, the Champ-de-Mars, Parc Monceau, Parc des Buttes-Chaumont, in the Parc de Montsouris, along the banks of the Canal Saint-Martin, the Jardin du Luxembourg and even the staircase up to Sacré-Coeur.

Some 24 of the city's *centres sportifs* (sports centres) have running tracks; eight are indoors. Buy a subscription ticket, which allows entrance to the track, showers and locker rooms. Tracks are closed to the public when schools or the organised running clubs have reserved them.

Several marathons are well-organised. The Paris Versailles (www.parisversailles.com) is a 10-km run held in the autumn. The Paris marathon (www.schneiderelectricparismarathon. com/us) takes place in April and can see up to some 30,000 runners. It's best to reserve early for both.

Bicycling

Bicycling is a popular sport and there are clubs and special events for cyclists. If you don't have a bike of your own, you can rent one, although buying one second-hand is not expensive. For detailed information on cycling, contact the Fédération Française de Cyclisme 1 rue Laurent Fignon78180 Montigny le Bretonneux (tél : 08.11.04.05.55; www.ffc.fr). Of course, the Velib program (see page 173) is the most efficient system to use bikes for the short term and for excursions.

- 11e: **Paris à Vélo, C'est Sympa** (22 rue Alphonse Baudin; tel: 01.48.87.60.01; www.parisvelosympa.com). New and used bikes, and guided tours.
- 11e: **Bicloune** (7 rue Froment; tel: 01.48.05.47.75; www. bicloune.fr). New and used bikes, replacement parts.

Some of the SNCF trains have bike racks and many do not charge extra for transporting bikes. Bicycles are also available for rent at some SNCF train stations in the countryside.

Les Centres D'Animation

In the municipal sports system, some 51 *centres d'animation* train adults and children in a wide variety of activities. Among the cultural activities offered are lessons in music, dance, language and the performing arts. There are also dozens of sports courses, including martial arts, tennis, fencing, golf, basketball and other ball games, water sports and even pétanque (a traditional game using metal balls). A small enrollment fee is charged. Inquire at your neighbourhood sports facility and ask at the *mairie* of your *arrondissement* for local information (www.paris.fr/pratique).

Aquaboulevard

One of the most extensive sports complexes in the Paris area is Aquaboulevard de Paris, at 4–6 rue Louis-Armand, 75015 (tel: 01.53.78.15.75; www.aquaboulevard.fr). It is part of the Forest Hill chain of sports and tennis clubs, and seems to have everything. It has both indoor and outdoor facilities, including 11 tennis courts, six squash courts, practice and miniature golf, gym and aerobics programmes and a huge swimming complex with a tropical lagoon. There are shops and restaurants as well. A day-long family destination.

Gyms

More than 100 *gymnases* exist throughout the city, with different facilities and programmes. Both public and private gyms are crowded, and they all vary in amenities and services, so look around before joining. Private clubs are opening (and closing) at a rapid rate in each neighbourhood. Inquire at your local *mairie* about the pools and gyms In your *arrondissement*. See Paris Fitness for information on private gyms (www.parisfitness.com).

- **Les Cercles de la Forme** (www.cerclesdelaforme.com. Fifen centres around Paris offering a full range of fitness courses, dance classes and cardio training.
- **CMG Sports Club** (www.cmgsportsclub.com). A chain of 22 full-service gyms throughout the city, some with swimming pools.

Tennis

There are some 43 public tennis centres in Paris with more than 170 courts, and they are always crowded. To reserve your courts, you will need have the Paris Tennis card, which you can get in any of the tennis centres; bring identification, and you will be given your access code or have it sent to you by SMS or email (www.tennis.paris.fr). Charges are by the hour and are reasonable. It costs more to play in the evening when the courts are lit.

You can also join tennis clubs, which themselves have arrangements with courts around the city. The French Open (known in France as Roland-Garros) begins in the last week of May. The Paris Open takes place at Bercy in November. Tickets may be difficult to obtain except for early rounds.

Swimming Pools

There are more than 30 municipal swimming pools sprinkled around Paris. They are well maintained, and many are quite attractive. Swimming is one of the most accessible sports and pools are crowded year-round. This means that most pools are heavily chlorinated, so to keep bathing suits from falling apart too quickly, you should rinse them out thoroughly after each use. Men must wear trunks, not boxer bathing suits, and in theory women must wear a one-piece suit, although this rule is sometimes broken. A swimming cap is required for both sexes.

During the school year, students have priority and pools are closed to the public, except for a few hours early in the morning, during lunchtime and in the evenings. Inquire at your pool for its schedule, especially during vacations when public access is increased. In the public pools, check how your clothes and valuables will be kept, because some facilities are more secure than others.

You may buy a single-day entry, but a 10-visit card or a three-month pass are more economical and allow access to any public pool. Inexpensive, this is one of the true bargains of Paris. Also, for a treat, visit one of the particularly interesting pools, such as the Piscine Joséphine Baker, which floats in the Seine off Quai François Mauriac. The pool can accommodate some 500 swimmers and has a retractable glass roof over its man-made 'beach'. Although most pools have some striking feature, also among the interesting are the art deco Piscine Pointoise Quartier Latin, the Piscine Keller that cleanses its water with ozone filtering, not chlorine, and the Piscine Butte-aux Cailles with its warm sulphurous water. Explore as many as you can, especially those that have retractable roofs or in general are open in summer. (And see Aquaboulevard above.)

Rollerblading and Skating

Rollers (rollerblades) are enormously popular. Pari Roller (www.pari-roller.com) organises a Friday night *randonnée*

Even policemen sport rollerblades for the Friday evening events, enjoying themselves while protecting the crowd.

(outing) that sees thousands of bladers cruising the streets of Paris. The staff guides bladers along the routes and police, also on rollerblades, patrol traffic, protecting the participants. Routes change and starting points are announced in advance. The *randonnée* starts around 10.00 pm at the Montparnasse tower and usually follows a three-hour course. Although it moves quickly, the route is long and the event generally lasts until the wee hours of the morning.

The Sunday afternoon *randonnée* is a family-oriented and beginners event, run by Rollers et Coquillages, starting near place de la Bastille (www.rollers-coquillages.org). You can also access the website of the Roller Squad Institute (www.rsi.asso.fr).

For ice skating, try the place de l'Hôtel de Ville, which is flooded and frozen in winter, making a pleasant rink.

Golf

Golf is increasingly popular in France, but it is expensive. To play golf regularly or to obtain a handicap, you should have a permit, which may be issued on a daily, trimester or annual basis. Inquire at the Fédération Française de Golf at 68 rue Anatole-France, 92309 Levallois-Perret (tel: 01.41.49.77.00; www.ffgolf.org). Ask also for information about golf tournaments in the Paris area.

There are no full-sized *parcours* (golf courses) in Paris itself, but there are almost 100 throughout Île-de-France. Don't miss Golf Disneyland, described above (tel: 01.60.30.60.53; www.disneylandparis.com). Some of the private clubs, such as the exclusive Golf de Saint-Cloud, have waiting lists of several years, and most require recommendations. Fortunately, some are open to non-members certain days of the week. In general, you must bring the membership card to your own club and proof of your handicap.

Oriental Arts

Some 18 of the municipal sports centres offer yoga, and almost all of them some kind of martial arts training, including aikido, jiu-jitsu, judo, karate or taekwondo. The Fédération Française d'Hatha-Yoga at 7, rue de Plaisance 75014 offers information on yoga in Paris. (tel: 01.45.44.02.59; www.ff-hatha-yoga.com). The Fédération Karaté et Disciplines Associés is at Porte d'Orléans, 39 rue Barbès 92120 Montrouge (tel: 01.41.17.44.40; www.ffkama.fr).

Boules

Fun to watch or play is the classic French *pétanque* (commonly called *boules*), in which metal balls are thrown toward a small spherical target. It can be played wherever there is a level surface and is played in town squares all over France, with onlookers commenting on every throw. To play, you need a set of *boules* (balls), which are available at most sporting goods stores. In Paris there are a dozen *boulodromes* (bowling pitches), including the Luxembourg Gardens, the Arènes de Lutèce and the Bois de Vincennes.

Sports Clothes and Equipment

Active wear can be found in department stores and at some of the discount shops. The upmarket international chains Fila and Lacoste have shops in the city, as do the sports footwear chains Foot Locker and Adidas; sizes are consistent in these stores.

- **Au Vieux Campeur** (48 rue des Ecoles 76005; tel: 01.53.10.48.48; www.auvieuxcampeur.fr). Chain of specialised stores offering high-quality camping, climbing and diving equipment, hammocks, sleeping bags, travel books, accessories, etc.
- **Courir** (www.courir.com). Chain of sports shoe stores selling internationally known brands at very good prices. Also at Aquaboulevard.
- **Decathlon** (www.decathlon.fr). Several stores selling sporting clothes and equipment, including for bicyling. Good prices and service.
- **Go Sport** (www.go-sport.com). Chain of sporting equipment stores. Extensive selection of clothes at reasonable prices.

SHOPPING
Haute Couture

Paris is, of course, the capital of *haute couture*. *Haute couture* may affect only a few men and women who can afford thousands of euros for a handmade suit or dress; the fashion industry nonetheless occupies a prominent position in Paris and the world. Paris has always been known for its couturiers—Dior, Chanel, Givenchy, Hermès, Lanvin and Saint Laurent among so many others—and is now also feeling the presence of international designers such as the German Jill Sander, the Italian Giorgio Armani, the Japanese Issey Miyake and the Americans Ralph Lauren and Calvin Klein plus many of the younger designers on their way up.

The famous Parisian *haute couture* fashion shows take place in February and July, but unless you are a celebrity, a fashion editor at a prominent magazine or newspaper, or a particularly heavy spender, do not expect to be invited. Just one outfit, intricately hand stitched, perhaps festooned with glittering ornaments and cut drastically up the middle or down the side, can cost more than most of us spend on our annual budget for clothes! And beautiful as the creations are, they have little to do with the experience of shopping in Paris.

Many of the couturiers have, however, *prêt-à-porter* (ready-to-wear) salons, selling clothes and accessories under their *griffe* (designer label). Their *prêt-à-porter* may not be hand-stitched, but are of a high quality and expensive too. Many are housed in what is known as the 'Golden Triangle' near the Rond-point (roundabout) des Champs-Elysées, in streets such as avenue Montaigne or rue François 1er and rue du Faubourg Saint-Honoré. If you are really interested in exploring a couturier's line of *prêt-à-porter*, do not let the sometimes frigid attitudes of the salespeople intimidate you or dissuade you from looking around.

Top designers who are not couturiers are called *créateurs*. Their *prêt-à-porter*, also of the highest quality, can be quite costly, but somewhat below the range of the couturiers.

Haute couture aside, clothes in general tend to be expensive in France, although prices remain relative to their quality. Tax on clothes (included in the price) may also be higher than you're used to. Until recently there were few outlets for imported inexpensive labels, thus Parisians traditionally purchased fewer items but of high quality, especially classic items that would not quickly go out of style. This is why style has always been more important than fashion and why Parisian women so often seem so carefully put together, with a scarf tossed over the shoulders of a classic white blouse or a pin at the collar of a tailored dress.

Today, however, the revitalisation of Paris, the inclination of tourists to spend money on clothes and the new welcome extended to foreign businesses mean increased imports at all levels of quality and price. The presence of international chains such as Gap, Marks & Spencer, Zara, Levi's and C&A, is offering new options for inexpensive yet durable clothing, especially for young people. Shopping in Paris is becoming much like shopping in any other city, but you can still find areas of Parisian character if you try.

Where to Shop

This section does not pretend to be exhaustive in terms of clothing stores—there are so many individual boutiques that it would take a telephone book to list them all. There are dozens of websites, and all guides have sections on shopping; and there are even several dedicated just to shopping in Paris. However, while these guides include a range of shops—both in category and price—and they often offer some unique, offbeat ideas, they are often geared toward the tourist who has discretionary funds to spend in a limited amount of time.

Most of the inner *arrondissements* have their own shopping areas, in keeping with the character and economic level of the neighbourhood. Besides the fashionable streets noted above, Place des Victoires on the Right Bank is a designer nucleus, as is the area around Place des Vosges. At the top of the 16th is avenue Victor-Hugo, leading down toward the aristocratic rue de Passy, both known for their upmarket flavour.

On the Left Bank, shops on boulevard Saint-Germain and along rue de Rennes are increasingly fashionable. Some international top designers have opened their own boutiques to the dismay of the longtime residents who hoped to keep the village atmosphere of the area intact—they haven't succeeded. Nearby but slightly out of the tourist scene, streets around place Saint-Sulpice, rue de Grenelle and rue de Sèvres are lined with boutiques of all categories and prices, from established and upcoming designers down to the most basic shops—they just take exploring to find.

Of course, inexpensive shops can be found throughout the city. The department store Tati (see page 293) always has interesting merchandise if you can ferret it out, and the streets around place de la République and the huge Paris garment district at Sentier and Place du Caire are good places to look for bargains. Rue d'Alesia in the 14th has historically provided clothes at a discount, but this does not always mean they're cheap. For shops that are deemed good value for money, including discount shops, see the compendium *Paris Pas Cher* (www.guideparispascher.com).

When to Shop

Although Parisians may be interested in the *nouveautés* (new collections), many wait for the *biannual soldes* (sales) to buy clothes, when all shops, including the most fashionable, offer reduced prices. During the *soldes*, the line around the block at designer boutiques can be daunting, as clever shoppers may have inspected the merchandise in the stores prior to the opening sale date. About half of all consumer purchases are made during the January and June sales. Sales are regulated by the government: they are allowed only after Christmas and in a six-week summer period, and merchandise must have been in the store for at least 30 days, to ensure that inferior merchandise is not brought in solely for a sale. Toward the end of the sales, some stores will advertise *deuxième démarque* or *dernière démarque*, indicating further markdowns in price. Many shops also have *promotions* throughout the year, when items on the sales floor are marked for clearance or special items are brought in for a particular promotion.

Shops are generally open from 10:00 am–7:00 pm. Some of the smaller shops might close for a few hours at lunchtime. Department stores are open all day and generally stay open slightly later one evening a week.

A new law has allowed shops in some designated tourist zones to open on Sundays. These include, for example, the areas around the Champs Elysées, the Marais, the Centre Beaugrenelle, St-Germain des Prés, St-Emilion, and les Halles. Otherwise, with only a few exceptions, shops are Closed Sundays, except around Christmas. August can also make for difficult shopping, as many of the individual shops close for the month. The department stores, fortunately, are open all day, six days a week, all year round.

The Customer

If you come from a society where the customer is always right, then you'll be surprised in Paris that this is not the case. Sometimes, it even seems like the salesperson is doing you a favour by just waiting on you, and you may have to wait for her to finish her conversation with another salesperson to be even noticed. Just wait where you can be easily seen, make eye contact when you can and don't show any impatience. Inspect all items before you purchase them. In many stores you will not be able to return or exchange items once they are purchased.

Size Conversions

Basically, you have to try on clothes and shoes until you see what size fits and not simply rely on the size shown on the label. Some companies use several factories to make their clothes, which means that different dresses or suits of the same designer may not actually fit the same, despite showing the same size. And, of course, different designers have different sizing policies. In general, an American woman should add 30 to her dress size to find the comparable size. Thus a size 12 woman would look for a 42. British women should add 28. For men, a size 'small' shirt translates to about a 37–38 and a 'medium' is about 40. For a chart, see the Chapter 10.

Sizing policies may begin to change as the French woman herself is changing. With better nutrition and exercise, the French woman's waist is said to be 10 cm wider than the average post-World War II size, and manufacturers may well be forced to modify the cut of their creations, so women won't have to buy larger sizes.

Department and "Concept" Stores

As in any large city, the department stores in Paris vary in their approach to the merchandising and pricing of their goods. The most prestigious department stores such as Galeries Lafayette and Printemps are called *grands magasins*, each with its own personality and branding. Although they may cater to tourists and be staffed with English speakers, they basically sell what appeals to the French. To cater to the endless flow of tourists, the *grands magasins* provide services such as currency exchange, ticket and travel agencies, as well as tourist information. The *grands magasins* also have weekly fashion shows and offer discounts to tourists.

In some department stores, as in some food shops, it is common to select the merchandise, get the bill from the salesperson, take it to the *caisse* to pay, and only then take the validated receipt back to the salesperson to pick up your order. In some, it is possible to get one overall bill (*carnet d'achats*) and to pay for all selections at one time.

Department stores participate in the biannual sales, but since there are periodic promotions on clearance merchandise, the sales prices are sometimes not much lower.

Recently the "concept" store has arrived in Paris. Not a full department store, it takes a theme and develops a "concept" that embraces what a particular type of customer might want--whether it's just for men or just for lifestyle, or perhaps just the unusual: a few examples below.

- 1ᵉʳ: **Colette** (213, rue Saint-Honoré; tel: 01.55.35.33.90; www.colette.fr). A modern-decor concept store that caters to trendy lifestyles with euros to spend, with hip clothes and accessories, hair and cosmetic products, books and media, and knickknacks of all sorts. Food, pastries, and an extensive water bar.

- 3ᵉ: **Merci** (111, boulevard Beaumarchais; tel: 01.42.77.00.33; www.merci-merci.com). A concept and destination store on three levels in an old factory, that says it is both like and not like others, donating its profits to an educational endowment fund. The best and most interesting of home products, clothing, books and a book café, and a café where you can watch a film while you eat. The canteen has healthy food, as well.

- 3ᵉ: **WAIT** (9, rue Notre Dame de Nazareth; tel: 09.82.52.84.34; www.wait-paris.com). WAIT Is a concept store for men, from A-Z, with fashion designs, sunglasses, surfing and skateboard gear—just about everything a man could want.

- 4ᵉ: **BHV (Bazar de l'Hôtel de Ville)** (40 rue de Rivoli; tel: 09.77.40.14.00; www.bhv.fr) Huge department store carrying everything at fair prices, and especially known for its wide variety of home-improvement items.

- 7ᵉ: Le **Bon Marché** (24 rue de Sèvres; tel: 01.44.39.80.00; www.lebonmarche.com). A *grand magasin*, the city's oldest and still one of the best. Elegant merchandise, beautifully presented, for the family and for the home, plus in its second building, one of the city's finest food halls.

- 9ᵉ and 14ᵉ: **Galeries Lafayette** (40 boulevard Haussmann; tel: 01.42.82.34.58; www.galerieslafayette.com). A *grand magasin* comprising several large buildings offering just about everything—designer wear, exquisite lingerie, hairdressers, a gourmet food emporium, household items, etc. Other services such as currency exchange, a ticket agency and a shoemaker are available too. There is a much smaller branch at Centre Commercial Maine Montparnasse.

Look up from the tempting wares while shopping at Printemps to admire the beautiful glass dome above. The decor changes according to the seasons and festivities, but it's never less than exquisite, especially at Christmas time.

- 9ᵉ, 13ᵉ and 20ᵉ: **Printemps** (64, boulevard Haussmann; tel: 01.42.82.50.00; www.departmentstoreparis.printemps. com). Another *grand magasin* with services to rival that of Galeries Lafayette, located just next door. Men should check out **Printemps de l'Homme**, a separate six-floor emporium dedicated to them. Try the *brasserie* located under a beautiful Art Nouveau dome. Open until 10:00 pm on Thursdays. Also at Centre Commercial Italie 2 (tel: 01.40.78.17.17) and 21 cours de Vincennes (tel: 01.43.71.12.41).

- 16ᵉ: **Franck & Fils** (80 rue de Passy; tel: 01.44.14.38.00; www.francketfils.fr). A venerable shop that long catered to elegant Parisian women, it now has added Franck Homme to its repertoire. Part of the Bon Marché group, the café offers meals, afternoon teas, and more in the spirit of the Grande Epicerie.

- 18ᵉ: **Tati** (4 boulevard Rochechouart; tel: 08 92.68.08.60; www.tati.fr). Sprawling shops with merchandise at low prices. Has other addresses. **Tati Or** sells jewelry at reasonable prices.

- **Monoprix** (www.monoprix.fr). Chain of basic merchandise stores and supermarkets, with branches in most *arrondissements*. Good prices, many products under the store's own label. Hours vary according to the location.

Shopping Centres

Many of the *centres commerciaux* (shopping malls) have entrances/exits linked to the *métro*, making shopping convenient in inclement weather. An easy *métro* ride to La Défense leads directly into Les Quatre Temps, the largest shopping complex in France, with hundreds of clothing and shoe shops, household stores, restaurants, services and the *hypermarché* Auchan (www.les4temps.com). Open Sundays.

Lying outside the city, but easily reached by car and public transportation, La Vallée Outlet Shopping Village is a complex of some 100 upmarket and designer stores selling clothing, shoes, leather goods and housewares at discount prices (www.lavalleevillage.com). You can catch a shuttle bus from the RER station Val d'Europe at Marne-la-Vallée, or take the train to the station Marne-la-Vallée-Chessy-Parc Disneyland.

- 1er: **Carrousel du Louvre**, 99 rue de Rivoli. A mall attached to the Louvre. Two underground levels filled with an assortment of upmarket shops. Open Sundays.
- 1er: **Forum des Halles,**101 Porte Berger. Enormous mall, with hundreds of shops of all sorts and levels, including a large FNAC and a multiplex theatre. A years-long renovation keeps it open but sometimes inconvenient.
- 13e: **Bercy Village, Cour Saint-Emilion**. At the end of the beautiful parc de Bercy, this isn't exactly a shopping center, but it does have a charming lane of shops and restaurants that culminates In the large, modern multiplex cinema. An outing for the day, if you include the park, which is a destination in itself.
- 14e: **Maine Montparnasse**. Near the Tour Montparnasse, at place du 18 juin 1940. Large mall that includes Galeries Lafayette and C&A.
- 15e: **Centre Beaugrenelle**, on rue Linois, near Front de Seine. After years of remodeling, this formerly shabby multi-level shopping mall shines in its glory. Ultra-modern, ultra-fun, there are dozens of shops, a whole floor for food courts, a Marks & Spencer department store and food hall, and a multiplex cinema.
- 16e: **Plaza Passy**, 53 rue de Passy. A small, popular, modern mall with international shops and a supermarket in the heart of the fashionable Passy district.
- 17e: **Boutiques du Palais des Congrès**, Porte Maillot. Upmarket fashion shops, food shops, tea rooms, etc.

Discount/Second-Hand Clothes

Paris swarms with discount clothing shops, which are extremely popular with Parisians. There are several types: some shops sell new but out-of-season designer clothes, while others, known as *dégriffé*, sell clothes with the labels taken out or mutilated. The *dépôts-vente* (consignment shops) sell slightly used clothes of fashionable ladies who may have worn them only once. Look too for shops that advertise *vêtements d'occasion* (second-hand clothes) or have the word '*troc*' in their names (this could mean that clothes may be exchanged for others after inspection by the shops). *Fripe* means the shop specialises in retro clothes, while *solderies* refers to shops where there is a permanent sale.

Some designers maintain discount shops for their out-of-season designs. If the word '*stock*' is in the name, it means the shop sells new clothes from a designer or factory. (Designers often contribute overstock to the crowded biannual *braderies*, or jumble sales at the Porte de Versailles.) See *Paris Pas Cher.*

- 1er: **Didier Ludot** (24 galerie Montpensier at Palais Royal; tel: 01.42.96.06.56). *Haute couture* and accessories. Prices may not be inexpensive, but they are certainly significantly lower than the original prices.
- 4e: **Plus Que Parfait** (23, rue des Blanc Manteaux; tel: 01.42.71.09.05). Upscale men's consignment shop in the Marais.
- 6e: **Le Mouton à Cinq Pattes (Homme)** (138 boulevard Saint-Germain; tel: 01.43.26.49.25). Vintage clothes and previous season's stock. A popular shop, so you have to buy what you fancy right away or it will be gone. Women's shop at 8, rue Saint-Placide (tel: 01.45.48.88.26).
- 9e: **Le Jupon Rouge** (12, rue Mayran; tel: 01.48.78.54.54). Seemingly an interesting mix of elegant consignment shop, vintage clothes, flea market, furniture and accessories. Always worth a serious browse.
- 14e: **Madame** de (65, rue Daguerre; tel: 01.77.10.59.46). Saying it sells contemporary and retro clothes, an eclectic collection in a *depot vente* on the famous market street.
- 16e: **Reciproque** (95–123 rue de la Pompe; tel: 01.47.04.30.28). Specialised upmarket discount stores in one street. Open Tuesdays–Saturdays.

Catalogue Shopping

Catalogue shopping itself has been popular for some time, and companies such as La Redoute (www.laredoute.fr), and 3Suisses (www.3suissses.fr), now also sell their merchandise on their websites. Prices are generally fair, returns are accepted (with the appropriate paperwork), and occasionally there are special sales. International shopping websites generally will ship to France. Duty on merchandise imported from outside the EU can be high, so check to see whether the company has an online service within the EU, where shipping between countries does not entail duty fees. Anything from food to electronics may be ordered and received quickly and at reasonable prices.

Children's Clothes

Style often extends from adults to children, in Paris, and kids can be dressed very well. Stores range from the elegant to the basic; it just depends what you want. Whatever it is, though, you'll be sure to find it. All department stores carry a variety of children's clothes; some *dépôts-ventes* sell children's clothes, and even some of the basic supermarkets like Monoprix will carry children's Items.

Du Pareil au Même, **Jacadi** and **Natalys** are French chains for children's clothing, and **Le Petit Bateau**, with several stores, sells colourful, comfortable and reasonably priced items. The international chains Benetton, Baby Gap and Gap Kids also have shops throughout the city. See *Paris Pas Cher* for well-priced children's clothes.

For traditionally French elegant clothes, the stylish **Bonpoint** Is at 15 rue Royale (tel: 01.47.42.52.63; www.bonpoint.com). For the more fashionable, try **Tartine et Chocolat** at 24 rue de la Paix (tel: 01.47.42.10.68; www.tartine-et-chocolat.fr). Both have several branches.

For one-stop shopping, try **Bonton** at 82 rue de Grenelle, 75007 (tel: 01.44.39.09.20; www.bonton.fr). Kids' furniture, toys, books, clothing and accessories. Closed Sundays.

- 6e: **Chercheminippes** (various addresses in rue du Cherche Midi 75006; www.chercheminippes.com). Good discounts on children's clothes; women's and men's clothing and decorations, in different shops in the same street.
- 13e: **Troc Lutin** (6 rue des Cinq-Diamants; tel: 01.45.81.44.57. *Dépôt-vente* for designer clothes for kids up to 14 years old, plus a sports and games section.
- 15e: **Bambini Troc** (45 rue de l'Abbé Groult; tel: 01.42.50.77.93). *Dépôt-vente* for children and expectant mothers, plus other items for children.

For children's shoes, try the chain **Petits Petons** with four shops in Paris; **Six Pieds Trois Pouces**, which sells shoes under its own label at three outlets; as well as some international brands such as Reebok.

Shoes

Shops such as Charles Jourdan, Christian Christian Louboutin, Walter Steiger or Stéphane Kélian offer meticulous workmanship in styles both fashionable and classic—with prices to match. Department stores gather many brands and prices under one roof, and discount shoe stores that sell end-of-the-line models and overstock can make purchasing fashionable shoes much more affordable. This holds true for children's shoes as well.

Look for shoe shops clustered in rue du Dragon and rue du Cherche-Midi. Rue Meslay, near Place de la République, has several discount shoe stores, as does boulevard Magenta. For shoes at particularly good prices, including discount shops, see *Paris Pas Cher*.

Shoe sizes are in centimetres. Shoes are basically sold in one width (medium), but each brand has its own sizing standards, so you have to check out different brands until you find the one whose sizes best fit your feet. In general, an American woman's size 6–7.5 would correspond to sizes 37–39 and a British woman's size 6–7.5 would be sizes 38–40. A man's shoe size 9 would be about a size 42 for both American and British men. The brands below have several outlets in Paris.

- **La Halle Aux Chaussures**: Inexpensive self-service shoe stores with shoes for the entire family, plus accessories.
- **Arche**: Classic but trendy and expensive women's shoe shops, selling colourful, modern, and very comfortable shoes.
- **Mephisto**: Popular French chain selling comfortable, supportive shoes. Not cheap, but much cheaper than buying them in North America

Cordonneries (shoe repair shops) can be found in any *arrondissement* and BHV has a repair service. Some *métro* stations also have shoe repair and polishing booths—look for signs near the WC that indicate '*cireur*'. The Talons Minute shops offer fast repair service.

Products and Services

No matter what you need (or want), it can no doubt be found somewhere within the city's confines. The brand names might not be the same and the exact item might have some minor differences, but globalisation—a source of worry to the French—means that many imported items are found here, from food brands to computers, clothing and cosmetics to children's games. Prices for these items, once quite high, are now fairly reasonable, owing to worldwide competition and the Internet. For appliances, utilities and home repair resources, see Chapter 5.

Unfortunately, the French idea of 'customer service' still revolves around the old Latin saying: "*caveat emptor* (let the buyer beware"). First of all, always count your change; mistakes can be made, and cashiers can be harried. As a foreigner, you have to be somewhat more careful about the rare dishonest person taking advantage of someone unfamiliar with the currency. Look at any order form carefully before you sign it. Ask all your questions in advance (including about their returns policy), for afterwards if something isn't to your liking, you may not be able to exchange it.

But this is beginning to change, at least in the larger stores. If you need to exchange damaged merchandise (which for some reason, you could not have noticed before purchase), make sure you have all your receipts and the original packaging before you set off. When negotiating with the salesperson, be extremely polite, don't indicate that the shop did anything wrong, and don't raise your voice; if anything will work, it's *politesse* (politeness). Also, if you, as you begin exploring your new neighbourhood, let it be known to shopkeepers that you have just moved to the *quartier*

Darty

The one major shop that prides itself on its *service après-vente* (after-sales service) is Darty, the nationwide chain of appliance, electronics and household stores (see Chapter 5), where repair service is rapid and efficient. www.darty.com

and are not a tourist, they'll understand that you are asking for good service.

Some shops offer a *carte de fidelité*, meaning that after you spend a certain amount, you are entitled to a discount on your next purchase. A *carte d'adhérent* means that as a cardholder you are entitled to discounts and rewards for shopping. Some bookshops and cleaners offer these rewards.

BOOKSHOPS

Parisians love to read, so there are *librairies* (bookshops) in every neighbourhood, and all department stores carry books. Some, especially those in the tourist areas, carry English-language books. There are also several well-stocked shops devoted to English-language books. You can expect to pay about 20 per cent more for a new book than you might at home. Shops that buy, sell and trade used books are cheaper. Shops generally place special orders if the books are on the inventory. For online purchases, there's always Amazon and Apple's iBooks.

You may also borrow books from the American Library (see page 184), which houses some 120,000 titles in English, current periodicals and DVD/videocassettes. The library also organises author evenings and other events. Membership rates are reasonable. Check out, too, the *bouquinistes*—the small open-air stalls that line the *quais* on both sides of the Seine from the Musée d'Orsay to Pont de Sully, selling old books of all sorts. On weekends, it's fun to browse at the Marché aux Livres (book market) at Square George-Brassens, 75015 for bargains. The Salon du Livre (Paris Book Fair) that takes place in late spring is open to the public.

- 1er: **Galignani** (224 rue de Rivoli ; tel: 01.42.60.76.07). Books in English and French; specialises in art books.
- 1er: **W.H. Smith** (248 rue de Rivoli; tel: 01.44.77.88.99). British book chain; open Sundays, 1:00–7:30 pm. Readings and meet-the-author events.
- 4e: **I love my Blender** (36 rue du Temple; tel: 01.42.77.50.32). Named so because it blends French and English books in its stock. A small shop with an interesting collection. Open daily.

The famous Shakespeare and Company bookshop in the Latin Quarter, revered hangout of book lovers and well-known—and would-be—writers.

- 4ᵉ: **Let Mots à la Bouche** (6, rue Sainte-Croix de la Bretonnerie: tel: 01.42.878.88.30). This multi-lingual shop in the heart of the Marais has books in French, some in English, DVDs and more. More than a bookstore, it's also a focal point for the LGBT community. Open daily.
- 5ᵉ: **Abbey Bookshop** (29 rue de la Parcheminerie; tel: 01.46. 33.16.24). The 'Canadian' bookshop. Special events, book signings, friendly Canadian management.
- 5ᵉ: **Shakespeare & Company** (37 rue de la Bûcherie; tel: 01.43. 25.40.93). Famous shop packed with new and used books.
- 6ᵉ: **Berkeley Books of Paris** (8 rue du Casimir Delavigne; tel: 01.46. 34.85.73). Second-hand books.
- 6ᵉ: **San Francisco Book Co** (17 rue Monsieur-le-Prince; tel: 01.43.29.15.70). Second-hand books.
- 11ᵉ: **Attica** (15 rue Boussingault; tel: 01.55.28.80.14). Books in many languages, international DVD, etc.

COMPUTERS

Although *ordinateurs* (computers), *imprimantes* (printers) and associated *informatique* (IT) products have traditionally been expensive, prices are now more competitive—at least in the new megastores and the *hypermarchés* in the nearby surburbs and along the *périphérique*. Prices vary somewhat from store to store, so it pays to shop around. For online shops with diverse stock, check these websites (www.rueducommerce.com; www.discount.com). Be sure to compare brands and prices.

Several chains sell small electronic goods, computers, *logiciels* (software) and associated items. Fnac carries everything hi-tech, including computers, software and accessories. Software is, of course, in French; if you need software in other languages, bring your own. Think also of the keyboard, for the French *clavier* (keyboard) does not at present use the Qwerty format; you can change the language of your system, but the actual keyboard remains the same. Note too that the American chain Office Depot has several locations in Paris, for office equipment of all sorts.

If you bring your own computer to France, bring proof of purchase with the serial numbers of the computer (or printer) just in case customs officers ask you to prove that the equipment is yours and not for resale. This is happening much less frequently now that almost everyone has a computer, and often only if someone is bringing numerous electronics with them in all at once.

- **La Fnac** (www.fnac.com). Chain with an extensive offering of CDs, cassettes, videos, computers, peripherals, software and books. The Fnac in the Centre Beaugrenelle on rue Linois (75015) is especially well-stocked.

Apple has two shops in central Paris: in the Carrousel du Louvre at 99 rue du Rivoli (tel: 01.43.16.78.00) and near the Opéra Garnier at 12, rue Halévy (tel: 01.44.83.42.00). If you need help from one of the "geniuses," reserve in advance, otherwise you'll wait several hours. Find a store on its website (www.apple.com/fr/retail/).

Technical Support
Power outages are rare, but to suppress the occasional power surges, buy a *parasurtenseur* (surge protector) at computer shops and hardware stores.

- **Micro King** (33 rue Dautancourt, 75017; tel: 01.53.06.65.10; www.micro-king.com. On-site emergency repairs, Internet and network installations, upgrades and repairs.
- **Sourys** (tel: 01.40.82.90.92; mobile: 06.25.05.64.70; www.sourys.com). On-site emergency computer repairs for Mac and PC, networks, Internet, ASDL, tablets, smartphones. Training in hardware and software usage and excellent, clear advice.

COSMETICS/PERFUMES

Department stores sell international brands of perfumes and cosmetics, and some carry their own brand names. Hypo-allergenic beauty products can be found in pharmacies, and parapharmacies have an even wider selection. Fashion houses such as Chanel and Dior develop their own perfumes, and a few *parfumeries*, for example, the well-known Annick Goutal, create their own fragrances. A great selection of cosmetic brands can be found at Sephora that has several shops in Paris (www.sephora.fr).

For cosmetics, product name, colours and numbers differ from country to country, so a shade you bought at home may not exist in Paris, or it may exist under a different name. If possible, bring along your old product for comparison. Inexpensive chains and supermarkets such as Monoprix also carry internationally known products.

FLOWERS/PLANTS

Fleuristes (florists) are found in every district and many are open Sunday mornings. Selections vary according to the season. When purchasing flowers, you will be asked if they are '*pour offrir*' (to offer as a gift): if so, the flowers will be trimmed and wrapped. Most florists deliver; those that advertise 'Interflora' can send flowers abroad (toll-free tel: 08.25.20.20.20; www.interflora.fr). Aquarelle and Monceau Fleurs are chains of well-priced shops, as is Au Nom de la Rose, which does lovely arrangements with roses. Food markets sell inexpensive flowers. These markets are dedicated to flowers:

- 4e: **Île-de-la-Cité**. Closed Sundays, when a bird market takes over.

- 8e: **Place de la Madeleine**. Open Tuesdays–Sundays.
- 17e: **Place des Ternes**. Closed Mondays.

Truffaut at 85 quai de la Gare, 75013 is an excellent, well-priced supermarket for plants and flowers (tel: 01.53.60.84.50; www.truffaut.com). It carries plants of all types and sizes, and offers landscaping services for your garden or balcony. Open Sundays, it offers home delivery.

HOME FURNISHINGS

In addition to the furniture stores listed below, the major department stores carry large selections of home furnishings, all in keeping with the overall style and quality of that particular store. With all shops, however, ask about the delivery policy—some charge extra for delivery.

For home improvement items, the basement of **BHV** is a haven for the *bricoleur*. It is a warren of aisles and byways, filled with stacks of merchandise large and small—just about anything you need for home improvement and repair (www.bhv.fr). This is also true of the **Leroy Merlin** nearby, at 52 rue Rambuteau (tel: 01.44.54.66.66; website: www. leroymerlin.fr). To find specific addresses and opening hours of chain stores, access their websites.

If you need to buy a new mattress, check out the department stores, or access **Matelsom**, which sells mattresses by phone or online (tel: 08.92.69.16.91; www. matelsom.com). Specify what you are looking for and they will deliver within 48 hours. Note that bed sizes (and thus, linens) are slightly different from those in North America.

- **Marché Saint-Pierre** at 2 rue Charles Nodier, 75018 is a discount warehouse for fabrics, linens, curtains and other such items (tel: 01.46.06.92.25; www.marchesaintpierre. com). Closed Sundays, and Mondays in August. There are other similar shops in the area.
- **Habitat** (www.habitat.fr). International chain with inexpensive furniture, household items and tableware.
- **Ikea** (www.ikea.fr). International chain selling inexpensive home furnishings, with several stores in the Paris region. Most conveniently, it is just off the highway to the airport.

- **Maison de Famille** (www.maisondelafamille.fr).With four outlets in Paris, Maison de la Famille offers everything for the home in attractive multi-level shops.
- **Pier Import** (www.pierimport.fr). Chain carrying colourful, inexpensive housewares and furniture.
- **Compagnie Française de l'Orient et de la Chine** (www.cfoc.fr). Small, upmarket chain for Oriental furniture, table linens, fabrics, clothing, etc.
- 7^e: **Reveblanc** (155 rue de Grenelle; tel: 01.47.05.93.13; www.reveblancgroup.com). Linens outlet shop, with brand-name, high quality merchandise. Bilingual staff.
- 7^e: **Roche-Bobois** (193–197 boulevard Saint-Germain; tel: 01.45.48.46.21; www.roche-bobois.com). Several upmarket shops offering modern, stylish furniture, including Galeries Lafayette.
- 7^e: **The Conran Shop** (117 rue du Bac; tel: 01.42.84.10.01; www.conran.com). Well-known British firm selling modern furniture and kitchen accessories.
- 9^e: **Lafayette Maison** (www.galerieslafayette.com). Across from the main Galeries Lafayette stores on boulevard Haussmann, a multi-storied 10,000 sq m annex devoted to everything you could need for the home.

Used Furniture

Used furniture is available from a variety of sources, including the *marchés aux puces* (flea markets) listed below. You'll find well-maintained antiques, just as you'll see furniture that is simply well-used—you'll have to scout. The shops below are popular with a quick turnover of merchandise.

- 14e: **La Salle des Ventes du Particulier** (116 rue d'Alésia; tel: 01.45.42.42.42).
- 19e: **Dépôt Flandre** (63 quai de la Seine; tel: 08.99.34.12.44).

Antiques

Stores specialising in antiques cluster in various parts of the city. Several of these 'villages' are open on Sundays and closed early in the week. There are also periodic antique markets, usually in spring and summer, mentioned in the weekly events guides.

- 1er: **Le Louvre des Antiquaires** at 2 place du Palais Royal.
- 4e: L**e Village Saint-Paul** at the intersections of rue Saint-Paul and rue Charles V. Closed Sundays.
- 7e: **Carré Rive Gauche** along rue des Saints-Pères and rue du Bac.
- 15e: **Le Village Suisse** at avenue de la Motte-Piquet at avenue de Suffren.

Kitchen and Dining Equipment

Department stores sell kitchen and dining equipment, and small kitchen appliances are sold in *drogueries* (general stories) and some *quincailleries* (hardware stores). Shops on rue de Paradis specialise in tableware. Geneviève Lethu is a well-known chain of upmarket tableware shops with a range of styles and prices (www.genevievelethu.com).

- 1er: **Dehillerin** (18–20 rue Coquillière; tel: 01.42.36.53.13). Famous two-level, kitchen equipment emporium.
- 1er: **Mora** (13 rue Montmartre; tel: 01.45.08.19.24). Kitchen supplies, utensils, dishes, paperware. In business for more than 150 years.
- 2e: **A. Simon** (48 & 52 rue Montmartre; tel: 01.42.33.71.65). Long-established supplier of kitchen equipment, dishes, glasses, utensils, pitchers and other gadgets.
- 6^e: **Culinarion** (99 rue de Rennes; tel: 01.45.48.94.76). Practical kitchenware shop.
- 15^e: **Kitchen Bazaar** (11 avenue du Maine; tel: 01.42.22.91.17). Modern implements; other addresses.

Outdoor Markets

The outdoor street markets described in Chapter 6 usually carry non-food kitchen items, clothes, umbrellas, some cosmetics and sometimes even furniture. For an interesting artisans' market, try:

- **Marché Parisien de la Création.** In Montparnasse, at the entrance to the Edgar Quinet Métro (Line 6), some 120 artisans display their creations in this art and design market. Open Sundays, 10:00 am–7:00 pm.

Flea Markets

The city's flea markets are a wonder to behold. If you need something that you haven't found elsewhere, you might just find it at one of the extensive flea markets. Merchandise changes, and sometime something cheap is a rare find, and other times it's just something cheap. That's what makes the flea market experience fun—and challenging. In addition to furniture, antiques, housewares and bric-a-brac, some also carry inexpensive clothes. The markets are not open every day; so be sure to check.

- 12e: **Marché aux Puces d'Aligre**, Place d'Aligre. Good flea market selling mostly household odds and ends, but there are also good discounted clothing shops. Open Tuesdays–Sundays.

- 14e: **Les Puces de Vanves**, avenue Georges Lafenestre, at Porte de Vanves and Porte Didot. Furniture, odds and ends, paintings, etc. sold in the mornings; used clothes in the afternoons. Open on weekends, 7:00 am–7:30 pm.

- 18^e: **Les Puces Saint-Ouen/ Clignancourt**, between Porte de Saint-Ouen and Porte de Clignancourt. Huge flea market, divided into several mini-markets. The most famous of all the flea markets, selling antiques, clothes, shoes, books, records, etc. Open Saturdays, Sundays and Mondays. Restaurants that serve all day ensure a leisurely browse of the market.

- 20^e: **Les Puces de Montreuil**, avenue de la Porte-de-Montreuil. Appliances, old furniture, used clothing, crockery. Open Saturdays, Sundays and Mondays, 7:00 am–6:00 pm.

HAIR AND BEAUTY SERVICES

When it comes to hairdressers or barbers, it's always best—no matter where you live—to ask your friends for recommendations. You can start off by shopping around. Look into the windows of *coiffeurs* and see which are busy and what kind of clientele they serve. Hair salon chains offer reliable services, as do the hotels and department stores, often charging less than the small neighbourhood *coiffeurs*—a source of increasing consternation among the independent operators. Although a *shampooing et brushing* (wash and blow-dry) or a *coupe* (cut) at the chains may cost less, the quality varies according to the stylist—as is the case anywhere—and turnover of stylists tends to be higher than in neighbourhood salons. Salons have their prices posted in the windows.

If you use an off-brand hair dye, bring a few bottles with you until you find a comparable colour, but international brands such as L'Oreal, Wella, Redken and others are in salons here. Tips are not included in the price, and everyone who attends to you—shampoo person, hair stylist, cloakroom attendant—gets a tip based on the level of service. Most shops close on Mondays. Get recommendations from your friends, or see *Paris Par Cher.* The chains listed below are well known and reliable—depending, of course, on the expertise of each *coiffeur*—and they have shops throughout Paris. Many *coiffeurs* serve both men and women.

- Jacques Dessange
- Jean-Claude Biguine
- Jean Louis David
- Maniatis
- Saint-Algue

Paris is also known for salons where hairdressers undergo *formation* or training, and these offer low-cost cuts to customers willing to take a chance on a (well-supervised) student's ability. *Salons de perfectionnement* give established stylists the opportunity to update their techniques. These salons are often open on Mondays, when regular salons are closed. Some salons perform both hair and beauty services (*coiffure & esthétique*), but most are separate. An *institut de beauté* (beauty treatments) performs manicures, pedicures, waxing, facials, massages and makeup applications, and sells its products. Some *parapharmacie* also offer *soins de beauté* (beauty treatments).

LAUNDRY AND DRY CLEANING

Fortunately, *laveries automatiques* (self-service laundromats) are found in every area, for unfurnished apartments are often not equipped with *lave-linges/machines à laver* (washers) or *séche-linge/séchoirs* (dryers), and apartment buildings do not have laundry rooms. Some furnished apartments come with washers but no dryers. Washers in the laundromats take one *jeton* (token) per load. Bring your own soap, bleach and softener to avoid paying for them at laundromat rates. The *super-essorage/essoreuse* (spinner machine) removes moisture, saving money on dryers. Some laundromats also have facilities for inexpensive, self-service dry cleaning.

Teintureries offer high-quality dry cleaning at high prices but are worth it for your most elegant outfits, since the quality of cleaners can vary considerably Most cleaners (*nettoyage à sec/ pressing*) are also *blanchisseries* (laundries) for washing and pressing items. Cleaning and laundry are expensive because much of the finishing work is done by hand, not machines. Less costly options are either not to press your washed clothes, or to have clothes cleaned but not ironed. Some dry cleaners ask for payment in advance, and most accept cheques and cash only. The cleaners listed below are especially known for their work on fragile items:

- 7ᵉ: **Pressing de la Bourdonnais** (29 avenue de la Bourdonnais; tel: 01.45.51.86.91). The 'American Dry Cleaner in Paris'. Environmentally friendly.
- 8ᵉ: **Parfait Elève de Pouyanne** (57 boulevard Haussmann; (tel: 01.42.65.34.23). Elegant and refined, since 1903. Also at 31, rue de Longchamp 75116 (tel: 01.47.27.11.62).

OPTICAL SERVICES

Eyeglasses and contact lenses are expensive, and most chains of *opticiens* (opticians) are no less expensive than the independent shops. Alain Afflelou, Lissac Frères and La Générale d'Optique are chains with reasonably priced products.

When coming to France, bring an extra pair of glasses with you and an up-to-date prescription. SOS Optique is a home repair service for eyeglasses (tel: 01.48.07.22.00). If you have an eye emergency and cannot get to the Hôpital Hôtel Dieu or Hôpital des Quinze-Vingts, call SOS Oeil for a house call (tel: 01.40.92.93.94). The Fondation Ophtalmologique Adolphe de Rothschild at 25 rue Manin, 75019 is a major eye clinic (tel: 01.48.03.65.65; www.fo-rothschild.fr).

ANNUAL FESTIVALS AND HOLIDAYS

Parisians love their holidays and events. There's something going on somewhere in Paris almost every day of the year, be it a military parade, a display of antiques, a poetry weekend, a neighbourhood fair, an outdoor concert, a film festival, a sporting event, or a public wine tasting. The city regularly sponsors periods of reduced-price theatre or cinema tickets and, in summer, seemingly endless free outdoor events. If a national holiday (*jour férié*) falls on a Tuesday or Thursday, they are likely to '*faire le pont*' (make a bridge) to the long weekend by by closing shop on the Monday before the holiday or the Friday and Saturday after. This is common practice for most offices and some businesses, even banks.

In addition to the national holidays (listed in bold below), there are dozens of cultural festivals. Many of the regulars are listed below, but others crop up and dates change; it's best to keep yourself informed. Check the website of the Paris Tourist Office at 25 rue des Pyramides 75001 (www.parisinfo.com) or the city of Paris itself (www.paris.fr). Also consult the weekly events magazines *Time Out*, *Pariscope* or *l'Officiel des Spectacles*.

January
- **1 Jan**: **Jour de l'An (New Year's Day)**—A national holiday. Basically a day for family visits and leisurely meals at home, sometimes with the exchange of gifts.
- 6 Jan: Epiphanie—La Fête des Rois. A traditional pastry—*la galette des rois*—is baked with a little figurine (*la fève*) inside. *Galettes* are eaten at home and at friends' homes. The person who gets the slice with *la fève* is the 'king' or 'queen' for the day.

February
- Early Feb: Chinese New Year. Festivals and parades, especially in Chinatown in the 13ᵉ.
- Mid-Feb: Paris Face Cachée: Happenings and events in unusual venues, sometimes not open to the public.
- Late Feb: Foire à la Ferraille de Paris. Amusing fair in Bois de Vincennes with antiques and knick-knacks.

- Feb-March: Some of the Six Nations Rugby matches are held at the Stade de France.

March

- Early March: Salon International de l'Agriculture. World's largest agriculture exposition at Parc des Expositions, Porte de Versailles. Food and wine from the provinces, prize-winning livestock, farm equipment, etc.
- Mid-March: Printemps du Cinéma. Three days of films at reduced prices during this popular annual event.
- Late March: Banlieues Bleues. Suburban jazz festival with world-renowned musicians.
- March/April: Foire du Trône. Amusement park on the Reuilly lawn at Porte Dorée, at the edge of the Bois de Vincennes.
- March/April: Festival du Film de Paris. Previews of international films, held at various theatres around the city. Often attended by directors and actors.
- March/April: Paris Festival of Sacred Art. Easter concerts at churches around Paris. Also in November.

April

- 1 Apr: April Fool's Day. Pastries and chocolates in the shape of fish, as 'April's Fool' translates to '*poisson d'avril*', '*poisson*' meaning 'fish'.
- Pâques: Easter Sunday
- **Lundi de Pâques (Easter Monday)**—a national holiday
- Early to mid-April: Paris Marathon
- Late April: Salon du Livre. Book fair at Porte de Versailles
- Late April to May: La Foire Internationale de Paris. fair at the Parc des Expositions with everything from furniture to food, gardening equipment and wine-tasting.
- Late April/Early May: La Mairie de Paris Vous Invite au Théâtre. Two theatre tickets for the price of one.

May

- **1 May: Fête du Travail (Labour Day)**—a national holiday. A parade near the Bastille; people give each other sprigs of *muguets* (lily of the valley) for happiness and good luck.

This is the one day of the year when the Tourist Office is closed.

- **8 May: Victoire 1945 (V-E Day)**—a national holiday. Celebrates the World War II victory in Europe in 1945 with a parade on the Champs-Elysées.
- Mid-May: Les Cinq Jours de l'Objet Extraordinaire. Many antique shops on the Left Bank hold open houses.
- Mid-May: La Nuit des Musées: Europe-wide culture extravaganza, when museums stay open with cultural events and entertainment and special exhibits.
- **Sixth Thursday after Easter: Ascension (Ascension Day)**—a national holiday.
- **Second Monday after Ascension Day: Pentecôte (Pentecost)**—a national holiday. Pilgrimages to Sacré-Coeur.
- Late May: French Open Tennis Championships. Two-week tennis tournament, one of the four annual 'Grand Slams', held at Stade Roland Garros in the Bois de Boulogne.
- Late May: Festival de Paris. Dance, theatre and music at various locations.
- Mid-May to July: Festival de Jazz de Paris. Jazz concerts throughout the city.
- Last Sunday: Fête des Mères. The same commercial hype for Mother's Day as anywhere else.

June

- All month: Foire Saint-Germain. Held at place Saint-Sulpice, this varied fair features poetry readings, music, lectures and more. One of the most popular of the year.
- All month: Festival de Saint-Denis. Several weeks of classical music at Saint-Denis, a suburb to the north.
- Early June, odd numbered years only: Salon International de l'Aéronautique et de l'Espace. Paris Air Show with displays of aircraft and air shows, held at the Parc des Expositions du Bourget, which is at the Le Bourget airport.
- Mid-June: Prix du Président de la République. Horse race at the Hippodrome de Vincennes.
- Mid-June, on a Sunday some weeks after Mother's Day: Fête des Pères (Father's Day).

A crowd eagerly awaits a concert during the Fête de la Musique, held annually on 21 June, the longest day of the year.

- Mid-June: Grand Steeplechase de Paris. Annual steeplechase at the Auteuil racetrack in the Bois de Boulogne.
- Mid-June to mid-July: Festival Chopin à Paris. An annual Chopin festival held in the Orangerie de Bagatelle of the Bois de Boulogne.
- 21 June: Fête de la Musique. A vibrant welcome of summer with music played in all parks and many squares and street corners. The Champ de Mars, the esplanade leading to the Eiffel Tower, sometimes welcomes half a million music lovers until the wee hours of the morning, with major programmes and performers.
- Late June: Grand Prix de Paris. Horse race at Longchamp racecourse, in the Bois de Boulogne.
- Mid-Late June: Marche des Fiertés. Lesbian, Gay, Bi and Trans Pride March. Held near the Bastille, this is one of the happening events of the year, with floats and wild costumes, and nightlife events.

July

- July/August: Le Cinéma en Plein Air. Free films on a big screen in the park at La Villette. They start when it gets dark, which can be quite late. Bring a blanket or deck chair for the grass and make yourself comfortable.
- 13 July: Bastille Day's Eve. Festivities to open Bastille day, including Les Bals des Pompiers—balls organised by the Fire Department in various districts. They take place in the streets, attracting numbers who dance for hours.
- **14 July: Le 14 Juillet**—a national holiday. Impressive military parade on the Champs-Elysées and fireworks after sunset (that is, quite late) at the Trocadéro. Get to the Champ de Mars early—half a million people come to picnic and enjoy the evening.
- Mid-July/Mid-August: Paris, Quartier d'Eté. Music and dance festival in various venues.
- Mid-July/Mid-August: Paris Plage. For several years, the city of Paris has been importing sand and creating a 3-km beach along the Seine. Chairs, cafés, showers, fountains, palm trees and three million visitors—sunbathers or strollers—enliven the *quais* in summer.

- July/August: Musique en l'Île. Concerts in the Eglise Saint-Louis, on the Île Saint-Louis.
- Mid-July/Mid-September: Festival Estival de Paris. Classical music in churches and museums.
- Late July: Arrivée du Tour de France Cycliste. The end of the Tour de France on the Champs-Elysées.

August
- **15 Aug: Assumption Day**—a national holiday

September
- Mid-Sept: Opera season opens.
- Mid-Sept: Jazz at La Villette. One of the best jazz festivals, featuring international groups.
- Mid-Sept: Fête de l'Humanité. Workers' festival at La Courneuve, a northern suburb. Sponsored by *L'Humanité*, the independent (formerly Communist) newspaper. Stands of international communist parties offer crafts and foods of their countries, plus music and a lively atmosphere.
- Mid-Sept: Journées du Patrimoine. Long lines form one weekend each year when the major buildings and palaces of France are opened to the public. In Paris, this includes the Palais de l'Elysée (the President's official residence), the Matignon (the Prime Minister's official residence), the Palais du Luxembourg (the Senate) and hundreds of other buildings.
- Mid-Sept to December: Festival d'Automne. Major performing arts festival.
- End of September: Fête de la Gastronomie: a festival of French cuisine, with thousands of events around France to promote French gastronomy. Check the events guides for Paris venues.

October
- First Sunday: Prix de l'Arc de Triomphe. Horse race at Longchamp.
- Mid-Oct: Foire Internationale d'Art Contemporain (FIAC). International fair of contemporary art.

- Nuit Blanche: One night of culture from dusk to dawn, with theatre, music and arts of all sorts in a celebratory atmosphere all around the city.

November

- **1 Nov: Toussaint (All Saints Day)**—a national holiday. Parisians visit the graves of their loved ones in advance of Jour des Morts (All Souls Day), placing chrysanthemums on their graves. On this one day, the oldest cemetery in Paris, the Cimetière du Calvaire, which dates from the 13th century, is open to visitors. Toussaint follows Halloween, which has caught on in Paris.
- 2 Nov: Jour des Morts (All Souls' Day).
- 1–7 Nov: Paris Open. Tennis championships at the Palais Omnisports de Paris-Bercy.
- Early Nov: Salon d'Automne. Art salon in the Grand Palais.
- **11 Nov: Armistice 1918**—a national holiday. Veterans Day, celebrating the World War I Armistice.
- Mid-Nov: Trophée Lalique de Patinage Artistique. Figure skating competition at the Palais Omnisports de Paris-Bercy.
- Mid-Nov: Paris Festival of Sacred Art. Concerts in churches around the city.
- Third Thursday: Arrival of the Beaujolais Nouveau. Always a great source of conversation among wine lovers and critics.
- Late Nov: Salon du Chocolat. Great chocolate fair and market at the Carrousel du Louvre, 99 rue de Rivoli, 75001. More than 100 European chocolate-makers display and offer their products, and give demonstrations of chocolate recipes.
- Late Nov: Cheries-Cheris: Festival du Cinéma Gay et Lesbien de Paris. Week-long gay and lesbian film festival. Check the events guides and the Resource Guide in Chapter 10. Check also Ciné Pride (www.festivalcinepride.com)

December

- All Month: Christmas in Paris. Animated *crèche* (nativity scene) outside the Hôtel de Ville. Main shopping streets are illuminated and store windows in the department stores are beautifully decorated. Stores are generally allowed to remain open on Sundays in December.

- Early Dec: Salon Nautique International. International boat show at the Porte de Versailles.
- 24 Dec: Réveillon (Christmas Eve). Feast at midnight, with traditional offerings such as oysters, *foie gras*, truffles, *marrons glacés* (glazed sweet chestnuts) and, of course, the *bûche de Noël* (log cake). Midnight mass at city churches.
- **25 Dec: Noël (Christmas)**—a national holiday. Turkey with chestnuts is a specialty.
- 31 Dec: Midnight festivities on New Year's Eve.

PARLEZ-VOUS FRANÇAIS?

CHAPTER 8

'In Paris they simply stared when I spoke to them in French; I never did succeed in making those idiots understand their own language... '
—Mark Twain

THINKING ABOUT FRENCH

The French are convinced that theirs is the most beautiful language in the world. This is not new—almost 400 years ago in 1635, under the reign of Louis XIII, Chief Minister Cardinal Richelieu founded L'Académie Française expressly to watch over the French language and ensure its purity. It was also meant to unify a country that was still divided by dialects, from the north to the south. Today, the Academy is still going strong, its primary mission being to set the rules and standards on usage, vocabulary and spelling. It continues to update and publish the definitive dictionary of the French language, first issued in 1694; oversees works on grammar, logic and other such subjects; and it administers several prestigious literary prizes.

Although the Academy has ruled that words—even those associated with newly evolving technological developments—should be French and not imported from English (or other languages), this rule is not always abided by in common usage. For example, many people use 'franglais' (français-anglais) terms, such as '*uploader*', '*le chewing gum*' and '*le software*' (instead of the approved French term, '*logiciel*')—a corruption of the language, the French pronunciation notwithstanding. English words such as 'weekend' and 'snack' have also made their way into daily usage, producing '*le weekend*' and '*le snack*'. And a bus driver who drives too quickly is routinely called '*un cowboy*'.

L'Académie Française

To be elected as one of the '40 immortals' of the French Academy is one of the highest honours a person can receive. Among the approximately 300 former Academy members are Jacques-Yves Cousteau, Voltaire, Victor Hugo, Alexandre Dumas (the son), Honoré de Balzac, François-René de Chateaubriand, Eugène Ionesco, Alexis de Tocqueville and, surprisingly, the French-born American writer Julien Green who lived in Paris and wrote in French. Green was the first non-French national to be elected. It was not until 1980 that a woman, novelist Marguerite Yourcenar, was elected.

HISTORY OF FRENCH

The first written example of early French—not the version we know today—dates as far back as 862. French is one of the Romance languages, along with Italian, Spanish, Portuguese and Romanian. What binds these languages is their common origin in the spoken language of the ancient Roman Empire. Using this base, these languages evolved according to the ethnicity of the peoples of the conquered territories, as well as the legacy of the conquerors who forced the Romans out.

In Gaul (present-day France), the native Celts spoke Gaulish when the Romans arrived in about 52 BC, but not for long, as Latin became the language of the upper classes— the rulers, teachers and even merchants who traversed the Empire. Fortunately for the beautiful (and some say, extremely romantic) French language as we know it today, the Romans were supplanted by Germanic Franks, such that by the 5th century, the Latin language spoken in France had incorporated some Germanic words, in addition to Celtic ones. The lasting presence of the Franks and their great rulers (including Charlemagne, King of the Franks and the Lombards, and first Holy Roman Emperor) was instrumental in allowing the language to develop admidst wars and migration. This distinguished French from the other emerging Romanic languages.

This 'Old French' lasted for about 400 years, during which the dialect spoken in Paris became pre-eminent, as the power—cultural, as well as political—of the city grew. 'Middle French' lasted only a few hundred years, but it was important, for it was when separate French languages began to be fused into one, and when the Francien dialect of the Paris region supplanted the others, allowing the French language—and ultimately France—to become unified.

By the 16th century, François I was using French instead of Latin for official documents throughout the entire realm, taking it beyond a spoken language. By the time of the French Revolution, the language was pretty well-standardised across the realm. And it is this French, which has not stopped evolving, that is the basis of the French we speak (or try to) today.

LANGUAGE SCHOOLS

Learning French should be among your first priorities upon taking up residence in Paris. There are many language schools for foreigners and each one has its own methods and varieties. Depending on the course and the school, students at some of these schools qualify to apply for a student visa. Some also have programmes for *au pairs*, who must be registered in a recognised language course. The programmes of the schools below are officially accredited, but there are many others—check with the consulate in your home country, which may have brochures of language schools in Paris; the Paris Tourist Office website which generally has detailed ads for such schools; and Europa Pages (www.europa-pages.com/france). Pick a school that suits your needs and budget, and one that is convenient enough for you to attend and not slack off.

You will learn enough at any of these schools to get around and to read directions, instructions, advertisements and listings for cultural events, but improving is up to you. But, think too about a school that also concentrates on the culture; just learning the language without understanding its nuances in various situations may not be helpful in all the situations you encounter.

- 5ᵉ: **Cours de Civilisation et Langue Française de la Sorbonne** (214 boulevard Raspail; tel: 01.44.10.77.00; www.ccfs-sorbonne.fr/index.php). Serious language and culture courses at the Sorbonne; high school diploma required.

- 6ᵉ: **Alliance Française** (101 boulevard Raspail; tel: 01.42.84.90.00; www. alliancefr.org). Worldwide network of language schools. General, business and customised language programmes, as well as courses in French culture, literature, etc.
- 6ᵉ: **Institut Catholique de Paris** (21 rue d'Assas; tel: 01.44.39.52.00; www.icp.fr). Two semesters each year of courses in the language and culture of France for all levels and needs—basic and professional. Summer course in July consists of 20 hours of lessons weekly, with excursions.
- 8ᵉ: **Institut de Langue Française** (6 rue Daubigny; tel: 01.45.63.24.00; www.ilf-paris.fr). Short- and long-term programmes, and some specialised courses, with one for children. Evening classes available.

GETTING STARTED...
SOME PRONUNCIATION HINTS

Even before you enroll in a school, you'll be hearing French and trying out those words you already know. (See the Glossary in Chapter 10.) Listen carefully and see what you can decipher when other people speak to you, although it won't always be easy, for accents and intonations vary. It's also hard sometimes for a newcomer to know the rules of pronunciation, and when you ask three French speakers to clarify something in grammar or pronunciation, they might all have different answers! But that's what happens with languages, for they are almost living entities that change with the times and under external influences, especially with younger generations imposing their own cultural norms. Thus it's best just to know the current rules and to obey them as well as you can—and to laugh at yourself when you make a terrible mistake and vow not to make the same mistake again.

It's important to understand that each syllable in a French word is stressed fairly equally, with just a slight emphasis on the last syllable (by lengthening its duration just a tiny bit). For example, whereas the word 'lí-brary' in English stresses the first syllable, the French word '*li-brai-rie*' stresses each syllable equally with a slight emphasis on the last syllable. There is little variation in this, even for words imported from other languages. The city of Montevideo, which in Spanish has the emphasis on the penultimate syllable, is pronounced 'Mon-te-vi-de-o' in French.

It's hard to discern the differences in pronunciation with some words, although there are nuances that you will learn

It Just Takes Practice

- É/é (*accent aigu*): the letter 'e' is pronounced as in the English word 'say'.
- È/è (*accent grave*): the letter 'e' is pronounced as in 'desk'.
- Ç/ç (*cédille*): the letter 'c' is pronounced with a 's' sound, as in 'see', and not a 'k' sound as in 'key'.
- ¨ (*le tréma*) over a vowel: the vowel is pronounced separately from the one directly before. Thus, the word '*laïc*' is pronounced 'lah-eek'.
- The letter 'r' is not at all produced from the front of the mouth as we do when speaking English, but from the back of the throat, near the uvula. If you try to pronounce the 'r' by lowering your tongue in front and raising it in back, you might feel like you are beginning to gargle, but the French will better understand what you are saying.
- The letter 'n'. If the letter 'n' comes after a vowel, it is not pronounced in itself. Instead, the preceding vowel is nasalised. Also, if there is an 'n' after a 'g', as in the word '*agneau* (lamb)', the combination is pronounced 'nya'.
- EU/Œ: This two-vowel combination has little reference in English. Words such as *peu*, *jeux* and *Sacré-Coeur* are pronounced like the English interjection 'er', but without the 'r' at the end. Form your mouth as though you were going to blow a bubble, then say 'er' by slightly puckering your lips.

eventually. For instance, *hôtel* and *autel* (altar) are pronounced almost identically, as are *faim* (hunger) and *fin* (end). There's no embarrassment in asking someone (politely) to repeat something —the French are pleased when a foreigner makes an effort to learn their language.

French uses the Roman alphabet, and many letters are pronounced in the same way as in English. But letters are often pronounced according to their position in a word, and some are silent, such as the 's' or the 'x' when they appear at the end of words. The letter 'e' at the end of a word is not pronounced, unless it is accented. In fact, if a verb (for example, in the third person plural form) ends in 'ent', none of those letters are pronounced. So, '*ils doivent*' (they must) is pronounced 'eel doive'.

Also, the French do not usually pronounce the last consonant of any word, but this too can vary. If a word following one ending in a consonant begins with a vowel, that final consonant is pronounced, elided into the next word. So, if someone tells you that they slept *dix heures* (10 hours), what you will hear is 'deeser'. It can be complicated, for when someone tells you they have used *huit oeufs* (eight eggs) in their omelette, you will hear 'weeter', for not only has the last consonant of the word '*huit*' been elided into the following vowel, the final 's' in the word '*oeufs*' is unpronounced, as is the final consonant that precedes it. Do not give up hope, soon you'll get the hang of it too!

In terms of names, for the most part they follow the same rules. So although people—especially foreigners—might have their own ways of pronouncing their names, the French generally pronounce them in a French way. Thus, the name of the Italian poet Dante is pronounced 'Dahnt' and the ladies' dress shop Weill is pronounced 'Vey'. Sometimes the pronunciation of names is unclear even to Parisians: for example, the street name rue Desaix is pronounced by some as 'desay' and others as 'desex'.

Don't give up. Do your best and listen to how the French pronounce words and your pronunciation will improve. If French kids can learn all this, so can you.

'... Paris advances alone towards its destiny;
where the people lead no government can follow.'
—Maguerite Duras

THE EUROPEAN UNION

In the late 1950s, France became one of the six founding members of the European Economic Community (along with Belgium, Germany, Italy, Luxembourg and the Netherlands). Since then another 22 countries have joined—most recently some countries from the sphere of the former Soviet Union—bringing to 28 the total number of member states in what is now called the European Union (EU). These communities—that total about 500 million people—have pooled their economic resources to create a forceful single market throughout which services, goods and capital can move freely. The *de facto* headquarters of the EU is in Brussels, Belgium, but there are EU entities in many other countries (www.europa.eu).

There are no longer any trade barriers among member countries, and their citizens may live in any EU country they wish. The goal is to balance the national interests of each country with those of the overall community, allowing diversity while creating a community-wide identity. Thus, in addition to economic benefits, a unity is developing among countries that had heretofore been impossible. (This also means that war between member states is no longer likely.).

At the official level, governments are working towards this intricate balance. In general, the populace of France understands and accepts the benefits of the union; nonetheless people are increasingly concerned about the dilution of their national identity and about the number of foreigners allowed to live in their country. They worry about the disappearance of the culture and traditions of which they are so proud, and there are no easy answers to these concerns. So, if you are going to settle in France and perhaps open a business, it is important to understand the ethos of your own community but remember that France—along with all the other 27 countries—adheres to all regulations of the EU.

THE FRENCH ECONOMY

There are several official websites to help understand the economic, population, and consumer statistics of France:

- **The National Institute of Statistics and Economic Studies** (www.insee.fr)
- **The Organisation for Economic Cooperation and Development** (www.oecd.org/france)
- **World Bank Group: Doing Business** (www.doingbusiness.org/data/exploreeconomies/france)

PARIS BUSINESS SCENE

Although the official governmental policy is to decentralise the French economy, the Greater Paris area remains dominant in the economic scene. With a population hovering around 12 million, Île-de-France (Paris and its surrounds) accounts for 70 per cent of all company headquarters in France, 30 per cent of research and development and 25 per cent of the labour force. It accounts for some 5 per cent of the entire European Union's gross domestic product, and is the most important in France. Some 500 of the largest international corporations are located here, and overall, there are more than a half-million enterprises of one sort or another. About 8,000 foreign companies of all financial levels currently operate in the Paris area. The ultramodern business skyscrapers of La Défense, built to ensure that central Paris' age-old charm remains untouched, houses the headquarters of major French corporations and many multinational giants (www.parisladefense.com). Paris alone has some 250,000 enterprises, and is a centre for trade throughout Europe.

Not only is Paris the country's business, political and administrative centre, it is also the centre of attraction for the more than 70 million tourists who visit France each year, making it the most visited country in the world. The city welcomes some 16 million visitors each year, and the entire region double that. In the region, most of the 150,000 hotel rooms are often completely occupied. Almost 20 per cent of the salaried workers in Paris work in tourism-related sectors.

In addition, embassies are headquartered in the French capital, as are other international organisations such as UNESCO (United Nations Educational, Social and Cultural Organisation; www.unesco.org) and OECD (Organisation for Economic Cooperation and Development; www.oecd.org). These create hundreds of diplomatic and supporting staff positions, with periodic rotation of personnel. Hundreds of non-governmental organisations (NGOs) accredited to UNESCO also bring professionals from all over the world to the Paris area. These, plus all the commercial businesses, have brought a significant expatriate community to Paris and its suburbs. As a result, many shops and services have sprung up to meet the needs of this vital community.

FRENCH BUSINESS INFORMATION

Fortunately, there is a wealth of government-generated information concerning the starting up of businesses in France. The most efficient way to begin is to access the many relevant websites and links—some are governmental, designed for the French, but the information is accessible to all. An English version is often available, indicated by an icon of a British flag. (See also the section below for assistance specific to Anglophones.) If you do a search on the Internet on 'doing business in France', you will find a long list of resource links to aid you in your research. Be aware of when the information was posted, for regulations change, and the consolidation of agencies is also taking place.

- **Agence France Entrepreneur** (tel: 01.42.18.58.58; www. apce.com). Offers official information on setting up a company in France, including information on options for company structure, taxation laws, etc.

- **Bpifrance** (tel: 01.53.89.78.78; www.bpifrance.fr). Provides assistance and advice on financial support to innovative companies with strong marketing prospects during the start up and development processes.
- **CCIP** (Chambre du Commerce et d'Industrie de Paris); 27, avenue Friedland 75008 (tel: 08.20.01.21.12; www.cci-paris-idf.fr). Public agency that regulates and facilitates business. CCIP represents 400,000 companies, which account for 20 per cent of all French economic activity. It also provides helpful information on setting up businesses in France, and on training and orientation. Check its extensive website for all its activities and news.
- **Invest in France** (m.invest-in-france.org) is the official site for investing in France, has branches worldwide and posts a booklet with helpful information.
- **Business France** (http://sayouitofrance-innovation.com). Mainly an aid to exporting French products and fostering international investment in France, it can bring together French business people and their foreign counterparts.
- **US Commercial Service** (www.buyusa.gov). Offers good information to American companies on exporting to France (and other countries.)

GREAT BRITAIN

Great Britain is the third largest export market after the United States and Germany. More than 1,800 UK companies have subsidiaries in France, and the prevailing opinion is that anything sold in the UK is likely to sell here. The British governmental department, UK Trade & Investment, offers information on doing business worldwide (www.gov.uk).

- **The British Embassy** (35, rue du Faubourg Saint-Honoré; tel: 01.44.51.31.00; www.gov.uk/government/world/france).
- **French Chamber of Great Britain** (Lincoln House, 300 High Holborn, London WC1V 7JH; tel: (44-0) 207.092.66.00; www.ccfgb.co.uk). Provides assistance for British investment in France, and is the representative body for Franco-British activities.

La Grande Arche—the ultra-modern sculpture and symbol of La Defense, just to the west of Paris. About 100,000 people work here in the French headquarters of some 800 of the world's most important corporations.

United States

The United States and Foreign Commercial Service (US &FCS) is located at the American Embassy at 2 avenue Gabriel, 75008; (tel: 01.43.12.70.83; www.export.gov/france). The US&FCS helps American companies to enter the French market on issues relating to sales, licensing agreements, joint and direct investment, etc. The service also works with French firms that want to represent American manufacturers, use American products or set up joint ventures. The Commercial Service can brief Americans on French economic conditions and specific markets.

Australia

Australian Business in Europe (ABIE), the government entity that promotes Australian international trade, is located at the Australian Embassy: 4 rue Jean-Rey 75723 Cedex 15; (tel: 01.40.59.33.00; www.abie.com.au; www.austrade.gov.au).

Canada

The Canadian Embassy at 35 avenue Montaigne, Paris 75008, has a Trade and Investment Department; (tel: 01.44.43.29.00; www.tradecommissioner.gc.ca/fr).

CHAMBERS OF COMMERCE

Chambers of commerce facilitate bilateral business by publishing current information, setting up meetings and seminars, and issuing directories of companies present in France.

- 7^e: **Chambre de Commerce France-Canada**
  (5, rue Constantine; tel: 01.43.59.32.38;
  www.ccfc-france-canada.com).
- 8^e: **American Chamber of Commerce**
  (77, rue de Miromesnil; tel: 01.56.43.45.67;
  www.amchamfrance.org).
- 8^e: **Chambre de Commerce et d'Industrie Franco-Britannique** (10, rue de la Bourse; tel: 08.25.595.702;
  www.francobritishchambers.com).

LEGAL FORMS OF ENTERPRISE

Business options for the would-be entrepreneur include setting up a new and independent business; purchasing and taking over an existing business; and leasing a business in which the owner retains the title but the lessee operates the business, assuming all risk. Before creating any enterprise, it is important to understand how much of your own assets will be at risk in each structure. A knowledgeable attorney should suggest the simplest structure possible and take care of all bureaucratic requirements. For information in French, check the website of Auto-Entrepreneurs whichh includes an URSSAF booklet "Le Régime Auto-entrepreneur" (www.lautoentrepreneur.fr).

- *Entreprises Individuelles:* the simplest form—one person, whose assets are at risk, receives the profit or loss. No minimum capital investment required. Sole proprietorships, independent business people and sole traders.
- *Société en Nom Collectif (SNC):* rarely found, it is a private corporation of at least two partners, jointly and severally liable without limitation for losses.
- *Société à Responsabilité Limitée (SARL):* private limited company with a minimum capital of just €1 and liability limited to investment. For medium-sized businesses requiring little financing, this is the simplest type of limited-liability company, with a minimum of two shareholders and a maximum of 50. Headquarters may be in a private home for a maximum of five years.
- *Societé Unipersonnelle à Responsabilité Limitée (EURL):* like a SARL, but with sole proprietor as a limited-liability company. Liability is limited to investment in company.
- *Societé Anonyme (SA)*: corporate structure for large companies traded on the stock exchange involving at least seven shareholders and a set minimum for capital Investment. Strict auditing standards are required.

A *succursale* is a branch office of any company that is registered in France: it must keep its own accounting books (except for the balance sheet), issue its own invoices and receipts, and pay taxes. A *filiale* (subsidiary) is a separate entity of a company operating under French statutes, with new partners and new capital stock. Both must be registered at the Tribunal de Commerce. A *bureau de représentation* is a small office that represents a company headquartered elsewhere.

ATTORNEYS AND EXPERT HELP

Many bilingual law firms in Paris specialise in *droit des affaires* (business law). All attorneys must pass the French bar exam to practise law under their own name. Because fees can be high, be clear as to your financial limits; on the other hand, be wary of any cut-rate offers. Some attorneys will sign a *convention d'honoraires* with their clients to set out the fee structure.

Make sure the lawyer you are considering is an expert in precisely the area you need—many are knowledgeable about employment legislation, which is important if your business requires hiring personnel. The American and British embassies publish lists of Anglophone attorneys in the Paris district but make no recommendations.

A *notaire* may be helpful in rights concerning patents, copyrights and royalties, while an *expert-comptable* should help set up the financial reporting system to reflect the official French (and EU) method of accounting. The filling out of employee payslips, complicated in its legal intricacies, is often contracted to an *expert-comptable* rather than done in-house. A *comptable* (accountant) generally works in a company and does the financial record keeping on a daily basis. International consulting firms, although probably somewhat more expensive than local French firms, are expert in new business transactions and also serve as *experts-comptables*.

For professional help in English to understand the legal intricacies of business in Paris and its administrative requirements, you might contact Jean Taquet, a *juriste* who specialises in civil and commercial law for expatriates (tel: 01.40.38.16.11; mobile: 06.16.81.48.07; www.jeantaquet.com).

THE LABOUR POOL

Foreign-controlled firms currently account for 22 per cent of the French workforce, so it would be wise to take into account the rigid labour laws and the costs of hiring employees when considering any new venture. Social benefits such as health insurance, unemployment insurance and retirement benefits are costly for both the employer and the employee.

Note also that French employees are entitled to five weeks of holiday per annum, or two-and-a-half days per month worked. Currently, the standard work week is 35 hours. As French businesses are cutting down on labour-intensive procedures to rely more on technology, labour-intensive investments are especially encouraged.

Women make up just under half of the working population—subsidised childcare and tax breaks for home childcare workers help to boost this figure. Since the mid-1980s, men and women are by law equal in the workplace, yet women are still paid about one-third less than their male counterparts, and few women hold top positions.

Union membership has declined over the past decade and now accounts for about eight per cent of the workforce. Although strikes and protests may seem frequent, they too have declined by more than half in the past two decades.

The high level of unemployment has in recent years led to anger and civil unrest. Yet, official efforts to reform the current system in which it is difficult to fire employees from their protected positions and to hire new people, has also contributed to the problem. Everyone knows that the system must change, but nobody wants it to affect them.

BUSINESS ATMOSPHERE
French management remains traditional in its approach to business, which means that new ideas are slow to take hold. Hierarchical structures persist, and usually it is the top manager or director who ultimately makes the business decision, no matter with whom the initial meetings were held. Decisions are arrived at slowly, as all ramifications are considered and the French reluctance toward change has to be overcome, if at all.

Yet, younger people on their way up the corporate structure—especially those who hold advanced degrees—have a more international outlook, and it is they who will eventually change the face of French business procedures. Some are already expressing frustration with today's 'top-down' decision-making, although they understand that changes will come only as generations of leaders change or when France

Do's and Don'ts in Business Situations

- Do make an effort to understand how the French culture and way of life differ from your own. Read as much as you can before you make your business contacts.
- Do make an effort to speak French, at whatever level you can. Without fluency in French, you will be at a disadvantage next to your EU colleagues and competitors. If your French is not adequate, apologise nicely.
- Do learn how the French do business, for it may be very different from the business customs of your home country. Hierarchical structures persist, and the French are formal, legalistic and extremely courteous in their business dealings.
- Do your homework. Find out all particulars about the companies you wish to deal with and write or call the appropriate contacts before arriving in Paris to set up meetings; confirm these meetings one day ahead.
- Do write all initial letters in French, unless you have ascertained in advance that English is acceptable. You can always have someone translate letters for you. Also, acknowledge all letters promptly and follow up a meeting with a letter, whether mailed, faxed or emailed, as appropriate.
- Do ensure that presentation materials are in French.
- Do arrive on time for a business meeting. Remember that France uses the 24-hour clock. Thus, a business meeting scheduled for 1500h is at 3:00 pm.
- Do be formal in initial greetings (by letter, telephone or a face-to-face meeting); it is recommended to

begins to slip in international markets. But make no mistake: while they may be more casual and open in their approach, and more are willing to take on wider challenges, they are no less determined in achieving their business goals. The general rules—the 'Do's and Don'ts' listed below will still apply.

use the appropriate titles when addressing business partners.

- Do shake hands at the beginning of a meeting and just before leaving.

- Do make sure that you have a business card ready to exchange at meetings and social events. It should contain your name and title, business affiliation, fixed telephone line and mobile numbers, fax number, email address and website of your company. *Papeteries* (stationery stores) make stylish cards, but these may take some time to be ready.

- Don't mistake a seemingly cold formality for lack of interest. Similarly, heated discussions and even negative comments about ideas and proposals may indicate a high interest in the project.

- Don't automatically assume that the French still like long business lunches. Long business lunches are less popular than in the past, owing to time constraints and the tendency to eat and drink less during business hours. Nonetheless, lunch is still seen as a pleasant method to cement a business relationship, but not to close a deal.

- Do not expect to have finalised orders or agreements after a first meeting, which is generally seen as an opportunity to size up the company or product.

- Lastly, take into account that in August nothing will get done, for there is no one around to do it. (This also means that if your business depends on a year-round cash flow, you should understand that Parisians disappear in August and sometime around Christmas and Easter.)

Also, some younger entrepreneurs are thinking outside the box and starting their own small businesses—food trucks or cupcake companies, for example, or "concept stores" whose themes focus on one type of customer—that don't depend on the established systems, and the populace is responding well to new ideas and approaches to business.

NETWORKING
Given the rigid structures and formal approach of the French business environment, it is important to cultivate all opportunities for personal contact. The Anglophone community in Paris is active in networking for people of similar interests. See Resource Guide in Chapter 10 for a list of helpful networking possibilities.

OFFFICE SPACE
Offices may be rented or purchased as a leasehold. If you purchase office space, be sure to select an appropriate *notaire*. Whether buying or renting, use a commercial, rather than residential, estate agent. Standard business leases are for

nine years unless prior agreement is reached for another time frame. The lease will be renewed automatically for the same duration unless the tenant informs the landlord (or vice versa) six months before the lease expires. EU nationals, Canadians and Americans are afforded the same lease protections as French citizens.

The British firm Jones **Lang Lasalle** at 40-42 rue la Boetie 75008 specialises in real estate and corporate services (tel: 01.40.55.15.15; www.jll.fr).

Agents may also be found through the **Fédération Nationale de l'immobilier** at 129 rue du Faubourg Saint-Honoré, 75008 (tel: 01.44.20.77.00; www.experts-fnaim.org).

Temporary Offices

Fully equipped offices may be rented by the day, week or month. Most offer secretarial and translation services, message-taking, mail delivery, copiers and other office services; some are accessible six days a week. The following websites offer more information:

- **Multiburo** (www.multiburo.com)
- **NCI** (www.groupenci.com)

THE JOB HUNT

Foreigners hoping to work in Paris should take into consideration that salaried jobs are hard to find. The persistently high unemployment rate of over 10 per cent has resulted in the tightening of regulations for hiring non-EU citizens. Also, the government policy of the decentralisation of French industries over the past few decades has reduced jobs in the Paris area by about 200,000 positions.

Fluent French is almost always a requirement; without it, job possibilities are minimal. For non-EU citizens, with the exception of certain cases as noted below, the appropriate working papers must be obtained before a position may be offered. Non-French companies may send personnel abroad for overseas assignments, but generally, overseas operations hire locally. Libraries in your home country should have resource materials on international companies and recruitment fairs for overseas positions. It is not a good idea to come to France as a tourist, hoping to find employment and obtain residence status. On the other hand, a 2006 law is making it easier to get certain jobs in specific regions of France. Before making any choices, inquire at the appropriate organisations, and see whether you fit any of the criteria.

In addition, as violent events have exploded off and on since 2005, partly owing to the discontent in the immigrant communities and their high rate of unemployment (up to 25 per cent among the youth in the Paris suburbs) the entire populace has become alarmed. After the terrorist attacks of 2015, the government has thought of proposing new plans to bring the suburbs into the *arrondissement* system, and in this way creating new opportunities for individuals and their communities. Thus, employment issues will no doubt remain in the forefront of governmental attention, but it is hard to know when (or if) the reforms and changes will be forthcoming and what the populace—accustomed to protectionist policies for their own jobs—will accept. It's always good to remember that the French understand that change is necessary, but not it if affects them.

The Chambre du Commerce et d'Industrie (CCIP) maintains a website for enterprises to list their positions open (www.bourse-emploi-paris.fr).

WORK FOR EU NATIONALS
If jobs are available, most EU nationals with a valid identity card or passport may work in France without obtaining a permit. (There are still restrictions for Croatian nationals; check the EU website for more current information (www.europa.eu). EU citizens may apply for most jobs, except those in the civil service or some high security positions in the private sector that require French nationality. Generally, employment rights and conditions, including benefits, salary, training, working conditions and *Sécurité Sociale*, are the same for EU nationals as for French citizens.

In their job search, EU nationals should acquaint themselves with the services of EURES (European Employment Services), a joint programme of the European Commission and the public employment agencies of the EU countries and Switzerland (http://ec.europa.eu/eures/home.jsp?lang = en). EURES offers information, advice and job placement opportunities for EU citizens who wish to work somewhere in the EU.

EU nationals and anyone who has a resident permit in France may also register with and directly use the services of Agence Nationale pour l'Emploi (ANPE), the French public employment services, whose website has a special section for young job seekers between the ages of 18 and 26 (www.pole-emploi-fr).

British citizens should consult the job centre website (www.gov.uk). Also contact the Franco-British Chamber of Commerce in Paris, which maintains a job file (www.francobritishchamber.com).

WORK PERMITS FOR NON-EU CITIZENS

Non-EU citizens even with an appropriate *carte de sejour* will find it difficult to obtain a position just by looking. When applying for a position, do so only in the field of your education and experience; French employers do not often hire people with the intention of training them. If you are transferred to France by a non-French company, you must have the *autorisation provisoire de travail* (temporary work permit), which is valid for the duration of the mission (no more than one year) and should have the same length of validity as the *carte de séjour*. This permit is renewable. Your company should fulfil most of the bureaucratic requirements and provide information and advice for settling in. Sometimes a French corporation may hire a foreign executive or highly qualified technician; these corporations have all the information on visas and work permits. The Office Français de l'Immigration et de Integration (OFII) has helpful information (www.ofii.fr), as does Direccte Ile-de-France (www.Idf.direccte.gouv.fr).

France has, for some years, discouraged the hiring of non-EU nationals, as the level of unemployment for its own citizens is too high. Thus, it has the right to veto the request for a foreign employee if the monthly gross salary offered is less than their current requirements, and if there are unemployed French in the specific field. And since there is unemployment in just about any sector and for any position, the request may well be automatically denied, unless the employer can demonstrate the unique qualifications of the candidate. On the other hand, there are some positions—such as teaching at universities—that are not covered by this regulation.

CONTRACTS

Contracts are of the two types described below. Make sure that all pertinent items are specified in the contract, including job description, salary, vacation and retirement benefits. Most contracts also mention the *convention collective*, which details employee rights.

- *Contrat à durée indéterminée* (CDI): a contract without a term limit, although there is generally a *période d'essai* before the contract binds either party. This protects the employee.
- *Contrat à durée determinée* (CDD): a contract for a fixed term, generally from three to six months, with a maximum duration of one year. These contracts may be renewed once.

Travailleurs indépendants are self-employed professionals such as lawyers, CPAs or architects, who have obtained a licence to practise. Those engaged in project-oriented professions such as consultants, editors or translators also fall within this category. The *carte de séjour* required for *travailleurs indépendants* is easier to obtain, since neither URSSAF (the body overseeing the Social Security system) nor the Préfecture has the right to veto a request. Indeed, URSSAF simply verifies the legality of the request based on the activity proposed, although there are strict guidelines defining which jobs may be taken on by the self-employed and how they must be performed in order to qualify; the applicant must prove the soundness of the project to the Préfecture.

An *employé salarié* receives a monthly salary, from which *Sécurité Sociale* costs are deducted. Salaries are either stated as *salaire brut* (gross salary, before deductions) or *salaire net* (net salary, after deductions). The pay is often automatically deposited into the employee's bank account, which is efficient because all cheques are *chèques barrés* (indicated by a bar across the check) and they must be deposited by the payee, not cashed. The employee receives a *fiche de paie* (pay slip) recording income and deductions.

An independent worker must register for *Sécurité Sociale* and make contributions that are extremely steep—sometimes up to 40 per cent of gross earnings; inquire at URSSAF. Some companies prefer to use a *travailleur indépendant* rather than hiring a full-time employee, thus avoiding payment of high benefits. People considering working independently should therefore determine the amount they will be required to pay out from their gross earnings before setting their fees.

LOOKING FOR A JOB

Make sure your resumé is translated into French. Some companies test for aptitude and personality, as well as a foreigner's fluency in French. An advertisement may ask for an applicant's *prétentions*, meaning the salary desired. It is best to find out the salaries being paid for comparable positions before responding.

Open positions may not be publicly advertised. *Cooptation* (networking) is increasingly important for the more skilled positions, and *piston* (personal influence) plays a part when it can. Cultivating contacts, networking and knocking on doors may be as effective as any other means of finding a job. Sometimes a favoured person may be *parachuté* (dropped into) into a particular job without going through the application process.

Know Your Rights

The current standard work week is 35 hours, and no one may be required to work on Sunday. Five weeks is the minimum vacation allowance, and there are 11 national holidays. Vacation accrued is calculated as of 1 May.

THE JOB SEARCH IN PARIS

In addition to the above, EU nationals and those with a work permit may use the public employment service Pôle-Emploi ANPE de Paris, which has branches throughout the city (www.pole-emploi.fr/accueil). Some specialise in particular professions, including *cadre* positions (see overleaf). Paris also has a free service posting both offers and inquiries for jobs (www.paris-emploi.paris.fr), and a cyber network (www.cyber-emploi-centre.com). *Le Figaro* publishes an important jobs supplement every Monday and *Le Marché du Travail* is also a job publications.

Cadres are people with higher education degrees or with managerial experience. They may use the resources of APEC (l'Association pour l'Emploi des Cadres); (tel: 0 809 361 212; www.apec.fr). For *cadre* and technical positions, there are several job boards:

- www.cadremploi.fr
- www.cadresonline.fr
- www.monster.fr
- www.leboncoin.fr

Americans may deposit their resumés with the American Chamber of Commerce, which keeps them for two months as a resource for its corporate members.

TEACHING

French public universities may hire foreigners as visiting professors or lecturers, but only French citizens may teach in French public schools; exceptions are made for teaching assistants. There are also a variety of English-speaking private universities in Paris to explore (see Chapter 5).

Teaching in an international elementary or secondary school is a possibility. Applications must arrive no later than January for the following September. You should have a college degree, teaching certificate and proof of experience. Organisations such as International Schools Services (ISS) hold recruiting fairs (US tel: 1-609 452-0990; www.iss.edu).

Teaching English privately is a possibility, but non-EU citizens will have a hard time finding a position in a language school. This is a popular occupation for young people from the EU, who arrive in droves with official credentials for teaching English as a Second Language (ESL). WICE, a non-profit anglophone organisation offers a TEFL certificate course (www.wice-paris.org).

STUDENT WORK PERMITS

Students from the EU do not need work permits. In certain cases, registered students from outside the EU may obtain an *autorisation provisoire de travail* (temporary work permit) and be allowed to work part-time during the school year and full-time between semesters. To apply, you'll need a valid student *carte de séjour*, student identification cards from the previous and current year, a statement from the school confirming student status and a written promise of employment from the company. (This does not apply to first-year students, who must prove that they have sufficient funds for the first year of studies.) Students at institutions that do not provide *Sécurité Sociale* medical care coverage are not eligible to work. And, students under 18 years of age must have authorisation from their parents.

Students may work for a maximum of 20 hours per week during the school year and up to 35 hours during the three-month summer vacation (between June and October). All earnings are taxable under the French tax system. Student jobs are often found by word-of-mouth, but looking in the agencies and other outlets is also helpful, as well as the Internet (http://erasmusu.com/en/erasmus-paris/student-jobs).

Full-time students from American and some non-EU countries may work in France during vacations through a Work Abroad Programme approved by the French government. In the United States, contact Council on International Educational Exchange (CIEE) at 300 Fore Street, Portland ME 04101 (US tel: 1-207 553-4000; www.ciee.org).

AU PAIR WORK

EU nationals only need a valid passport and not a pre-arranged position in order to come to France to work as an *au pair*. Non-EU nationals, however, must have applied for a *visa de long séjour* and obtained a *declaration d'engagement* with a French family. The contract must detail the hours, tasks and remuneration, and the family must declare the *au pair a stagiare aide familiale*, which permits health coverage. All *au pairs* must register and take French lessons during their contract.

Au pairs generally take care of children in exchange for room and board, sometimes with a slight stipend. Other options exist, such as receiving room and board in exchange for light housework. *Au pairs* must be unmarried and between the ages of 18 and 30. The contract cannot exceed 18 months. *Au pair* positions are monitored by the Ministry of Labour. For agencies that handle *au pair* positions, put "au pair France" into your browser and several will appear.

Think carefully before accepting an *au pair* position. The work, which consists of taking care of children full-time, usually includes some housework as well, and days off are few. Although it is an economical way to live in Paris, such a position may not correspond to the experience of living in Paris you had in mind before coming.

FAST FACTS

CHAPTER 10

'Paris France is exciting and peaceful.'
—Getrude Stein

Official Name
Paris

Flag
The flag of municipal Paris consists of a vertical band of blue (on the left) and one in red (on the right), the traditional colours of the city. In the centre is the city's coat of arms.

Time
Greenwich Mean Time plus 1 hour (GMT + 0100) in standard time; plus 2 hours (GMT + 0200) during summer.

Telephone Country Codes
Country Code for France: 33
Prefix for Paris: 01
Prefixes for cell phones: 06 and 07
Non-geographical prefix: 09

Land Area and Highest Point
105 sq km (40.5 sq miles)
Top of Montmartre hill (130 m/426.5 ft)

Climate
Mainly temperate, with the warmest temperatures during July and August. The coldest period is during December and January. This generalisation holds true even in this period

of climate change, although there are more extremes in temperatures throughout the seasons.

Population
66.26 million in metropolitan France, 2.34 million in Paris, with another 10 million in the surrounding suburban towns.

Ethnic Groups
Eighty per cent of the Greater Paris populace is born in Paris or from other French provinces. Foreign immigrants (primarily from North African countries—which had once belonged to France) make up about 20 per cent. It is forbidden by law for the official census to ask questions about ethnicity or religion.

Religion
Some 80 per cent of the populace is nominally Catholic, although less than 20 per cent is religiously observant. With five million Muslims in France (about 9 per cent of the population), Islam is the second most important religion.

Official Language
French

Government Structure
The city of Paris is the only city in France that is a single Department (75). It operates as a municipal entity, with an elected mayor and council. Each of the city's 20 districts (*arrondissements*) has its own council with representatives on the Paris city council, and its own mayor. The suburban communes in the Paris region each have their own municipal governments.

Currency
Euro (€)

Gross Domestic Product (GDP)
France: US$2.8 trillion (2014)
Paris: US$650 billion (2014)

Industries
Manufacturing, service and tourism

Airports
The two principal Paris airports are Charles de Gaulle International (northeast), which serves most intercontinental flights, and Orly (south), which handles most domestic and some international flights.

Measurements
1 kilogramme = 2.2 pounds
100 grammes = 3.5 ounces
One litre = 1 quart, 2 ounces; about 4 cups
One litre = 0.26 gallons (US liquid); 0.22 gallons (Imperial)
One teaspoon dry measure = about 7 grammes
One tablespoon = 14 grammes
One stone = 6.35 kilogrammes

1 centimetre = 0.39 inches
1 metre = 3.3 feet
1 kilometre = 0.62 miles
1 mile = 1.6 kilometre

0° Centigrade = 32° Fahrenheit
37° Centigrade = 98.6° Fahrenheit
100° Centigrade = 212° Fahrenheit

Women's Dress Sizes
American	8	10	12	14
French	38	40	42	44
British	10	12	14	16

Men's Suit Sizes
American	38	40	42
French	48	50	52
British	36	38	40

FAMOUS PEOPLE
Charlemagne (742–814)
King of the Franks and Holy Roman Emperor. Seen as the father of France, Germany and Belgium, and of modern Europe.

Joan of Arc (1412–1431)
Devout girl who followed 'voices' to lead the French in defeating the English at Orléans during the Hundred Years' War. Captured and delivered to the English, she was convicted of heresy and was burnt at the stake at age 19. Made a saint by the Church.

René Descartes (1596–1650)
Known as the founder of modern philosophy, whose most famous saying was "*Cogito ergo sum*" ("I think, therefore I am").

Louis XIV (1638–1715)
The 'Sun King' who fought wars to extend the power of France. Reigned for 72 years and built the opulent Chateau of Versailles. His last words were, "I am going away, but the State will always remain."

Voltaire (1694–1778)
Influential poet, playwright and satirist. He spoke out for social reform and defended civil liberties and religious freedom. His play *Candide* is still widely read.

Louis XVI (1754–1793)
An ordinary man, depressed and indecisive, he roused the ire of a nation in debt and a people mired in poverty, leading to the French Revolution. His Austrian wife Marie Antoinette (1755-1793) was also hated by the people. Put on trial during the French Revolution, both died by the guillotine.

Gilbert du Motier, Marquis de La Fayette (1757–1834)
A 'hero of two worlds', La Fayette fought on the side of the colonists against the British in the American Revolution. A

reformer at home, he also took part in the French Revolution a decade later.

Napoléon Bonaparte (1769–1821)

Corsican soldier and military strategist, his successes in broadening the lands of France led him to become Emperor. He instituted social, legal and administrative reforms, but disastrous military campaigns forced him into exile. After a triumphant return of 100 days, he was defeated by Wellington at Waterloo, and died eventually on the remote island of Saint-Helena.

Alexandre Dumas (1802–1870)

A writer popular worldwide, Dumas' most famous novels are *The Count of Monte Cristo* and *The Three Musketeers*.

Louis Pasteur (1822–1895)

Father of modern medicine whose discoveries are credited with lengthening the human lifespan. Developed a method to eliminate contaminated milk (pasteurisation) and immunisations to combat disease.

Georges Auguste Escoffier (1846–1935)

Elevated French cooking to an art, creating what is known as *haute cuisine*.

Jean Moulin (1889–1943)

Leader of the French Resistance against the Nazi invaders during World War II. Betrayed, Moulin was arrested and tortured, but gave no information to the Nazis. He died on the way to a concentration camp and has become for the French an enduring symbol of the Resistance.

Maréchal Henri Philippe Pétain (1856–1951)

French hero of World War I, Pétain headed the collaborationist puppet government of Vichy during World War II. He was tried as a traitor and sentenced to life imprisonment.

Général Charles de Gaulle (1890–1970)
Leader of Free France during World War II, he inspired resistance to the Nazi occupiers and collaborationist government in Vichy. He returned to Paris in triumph in 1945 and became President of Fifth Republic from 1958–1969.

Jean-Paul Sartre (1905–1980)
Proponent of 'existentialism', which argues that people are basically alone in a universe with no moral order, and that individuals themselves determine what is right and wrong and are accountable for their decisions and actions. A prominent figure among the Left Bank intellectuals.

Edith Piaf (1915–1963)
'The Little Sparrow' was one of France's greatest and most beloved singers. It is said that her funeral was the only time that traffic in all of Paris came to a complete stop.

François Mitterrand (1916–1996).
French President (1981–1995). A Socialist who brought greater internationalism to France and improved French relations within the EU. He oversaw domestic decentralisation and a series of *Grands Projets* (Great Works) that revitalised Paris.

Johnny Hallyday (1943–)
France's most famous rock'n'roll star, influenced by Elvis Presley.

Anne Hidalgo (1959–)
The current mayor of Paris. Socialist and forward-looking.

Zinédine Zidane (1972–)
Football player of strength and elegance. A sports hero to the French.

THE USE OF ABBREVIATIONS

The French are enthusiastic users of initials, acronyms and abbreviations both in speaking and writing. When looking in the telephone book for a number, if you can't find a listing under its full name, try its initials (RATP, SNCF, FUAJ, etc.). Below are a few commonly used abbreviations.

BHV   Bazar de l'Hôtel de Ville: major department store
BNP   Banque Nationale de Paris: major national bank
CB   Carte Bleue: Credit/debit card
CNI   Carte Nationale d'identité: French identity card
DOM-TOM Départements/terretoires d'outre mer: French overseas holdings
EDF   Electricité de France: biggest electric company
FUAJ   Fédération Unie des Auberges de Jeunesse: a youth hostel organisation
FUSAC   France-USA Contacts: a helpful online publication for Anglophones in Paris
GDF   Gaz de France: gas company
HT   Hors tax: before sales tax
PMU   Paris Mutuel Urbain: offtrack betting
RC   Rez-de-Chaussée: ground floor
RATP   Régie Autonome des Transports Parisiens: the public transport system.
RDV   Rendezvous: meeting or date
RER   Réseau Express Régional: commuter train
RF   République Française: The French Republic
RIB   Relevé d'Identité Bancaire: official identification of a bank account
RV   Rendez-vous: appointment
SIDA   Acronym for AIDS
SNCF   Société Nationale des Chemins de Fer: the national railroad
TGV   Train à Grande Vitesse: the express train
TTC   Toutes Taxes Comprises: all taxes included
TVA   Taxe sur Valeur Ajoutée: the sales tax (VAT)
VF   Version Française: a foreign film dubbed in French
VO   Version Originale: film in its original language
WC   Water Closet: the toilet

CULTURE QUIZ

SITUATION 1

You bought five handles for your kitchen cabinets in a Parisian hardware store. When you get home, however, you see that one is damaged, and besides, it turns out you needed only four. You go back to the store with the receipt to return the unwanted item, politely explaining the situation to the salesman. He is not at all accommodating, saying you should have noticed the problem before you left the store and that there's nothing he can do. He points to a sign on the wall that says 'no returns'. You:

- **Ⓐ** Agree, saying, "*oui, monsieur*", you understand that, in general, nothing should be returned, but this item was defective. You add that you do not wish to be difficult but hope to continue patronising his shop in future.
- **Ⓑ** Realise that the salesman's arrogant attitude is just a show, which can easily be overturned once he realises that he may lose your business. Thus, you tell the salesman that you will never again patronise his shop and, what's more, you will advise your foreign friends to do likewise, if he doesn't comply with your reasonable request.
- **Ⓒ** Ask to speak to his manager or supervisor, as Parisian salespeople have must not the power to make any decisions.
- **Ⓓ** Politely tell the salesman that where you come from, all respectable shops abide by the motto 'the customer is always right', and firmly request that he reimburse you for the defective item.

Comments

Although it may take a longer and probably more stressful exchange with the salesperson than you would have expected, **Ⓐ** is the way to go about it in Paris. Standing your own ground, while reassuring the salesperson that you wish to maintain friendly relations with the store, is the best way to get French salespeople to acquiesce, albeit grudgingly, to your requests. Answers **B** and **D** will be of no use as the French do no react well to patronising or threatening talk. Asking to see his superior, as in **C**, will only leave you with the chore of having to do another round of lengthy negotiations, as the French attitude towards customer service is basically the same from the top to the bottom of the hierarchy. While in France, and especially Paris, never assume that the customer is always right. It pays to be meticulous in what you buy, checking everything before you leave the store. Get used to the French notion of customer service, which will hopefully change. In any case, quiet persistence usually works. The above notwithstanding, the concept of customer service is actually beginning to be understood in some places and at some times. Don't expect it, but when you get it, be extremely appreciative.

SITUATION 2

You have entered a boutique, said *"Bonjour, madame"* and indicated that you are just looking, at least for the moment. You browse and find a dress that you like, so you take it off the rack to hold it up in front of the mirror. The salesperson rushes to you, whisks the item away and asks politely whether you would like to try it on. You are annoyed (although you say nothing), for you had not finished browsing yet. So you:

A Indicate that you would like to look around some more. Thus you continue to browse and take a few other dresses off the rack, handing them to the salesperson to bring to the fitting room for you.

B Feel intimidated by the salesperson's controlling attitude and walk away from the boutique, heading for the more impersonal shopping centres.

C Whisk the item back from the salesperson and firmly tell her to please leave you alone, as you have not finished browsing yet.

D Follow the salesperson to the fitting room and try on the dress. If it doesn't fit, ask the salesperson to show you other similar outfits.

Comments

Both answers **A** and **D** are correct, if you intend to get any shopping done at the boutique, although **D** is the better option. In a small shop, customers generally do not remove items from the rack themselves. This is the domain of the shopkeeper, whose job is to help you. (This holds true of fruit markets as well—let the *marchand* or shopkeeper pick the fruit for you. Unless a sign says *libre service* (self-service), do not help yourself or paw through the fruit.) If you want to be left alone while you are browsing, go to a department store, as in answer **B**, where there are fewer salespeople per customer and where the personnel have a less personal attitude. Answer **C** will work against you if you eventually need the salesperson's help in finding or trying on an outfit, or if you plan on coming back to this store again.

SITUATION 3

There is a group of people standing haphazardly at one of the vegetable stalls at the *marché* (market). Someone approaches the stand, pushes to an empty spot closer to the front and winds up being served before you. What do you do?

A Stand your ground. As no one seems to be doing anything about it, the vendor will probably allow others to jump queue as well, so you better speak up and point out the injustice.

B Do nothing. The person who has jumped the queue has disrupted the order of service for the others as well; if there's anything to say, let someone else do it.

C Gently say to the *marchand* as he finishes his transaction and before he serves the client who has not queued, "*Je pense que c'est à moi, monsieur*", reminding him that it is now your turn.

D Look out for any empty spots near the front and quickly position yourself behind the person being served. In Paris, unless you assert yourself, you will never get served.

Comments

This is a good opportunity to learn how to be patient. Making a fuss will get you nowhere nearer to being served, so answer **Ⓐ** is of no use. First try **Ⓑ**, letting others in the line complain for you. But if that doesn't work and it looks as though you are being totally ignored for some reason, try **Ⓒ**. **Ⓓ** will just compound the problem and make you no friends, so don't even consider it.

SITUATION 4

You are at a *traiteur* in your new neighbourhood, and the spread of dishes looks so delicious, you think you might like to patronise the shop regularly. After ordering, you realise that the slice of meat you have been given has too much gristle and fat for your taste. When you politely say so to the *vendeuse* (saleslady) and ask her for another slice, you notice that her lips are pursed and her demeanour has turned frigid. What might you have done differently?

Ⓐ You could have taken a look at the slices of meat and, after noticing that they were fatty, leave the shop and look for another *traiteur*, where the meats sold are leaner.

Ⓑ Nothing. It is your right as a customer to choose the items you wish to buy, and it is the *vendeuse*'s job to give you what you choose. If she is not happy about this, that is her problem, not yours.

Ⓒ Instead of saying that you didn't like her original selection, you might have said, "Oh, I'm so sorry to bother you, but might I have that slice to the left instead? Thank you so much, that's very kind."

Ⓓ In your best French, you could have explained to the woman that fatty foods are harmful to one's health, which is why you stopped eating oily food years ago. She would have surely understood then—after all, who isn't concerned about health issues these days?

Comments

By asking the *vendeuse* to exchange the piece she had given you for another one, you probably made her feel that her initial choice was not good enough—this is not acceptable to the French. If you want to have any of the items exchanged, you needn't explain or put the woman in the wrong. Thus, **D** would not work. The best way to go about it is to, firstly, apologise for any inconvenience caused, then ask politely if you might have a different piece, as in **C**. **A** and **B** are possible, but they will not help you in adapting to Parisian life. This situation should remind you to be vigilant: you could have pointed out in advance the slice you wanted, thus avoiding disappointment on your part and offending the *vendeuse*.

SITUATION 5

You have been invited by a French couple you have recently become friends with, to dine in a restaurant they have chosen. From the way your friends live and knowing that one of them is not working, you realise that their current financial situation may not be all it should be. Thus, you:

A Tactfully suggest a different, less expensive restaurant that you know they like.

B Accept their invitation, and after the lovely meal, offer to contribute to the bill.

C Find a good excuse to decline their invitation, suggesting that you wish to make up for it by asking them to a nice meal some time soon.

D Accept their invitation graciously but remind yourself to reciprocate at the earliest appropriate opportunity.

Comments

Except for **D**, all of the above choices would either annoy or offend your friends. In **A** and **B**, you would have indirectly brought up their personal financial situation by suggesting a less expensive restaurant or by offering to pay the bill, and referring to money is not done. Your friends had chosen a restaurant they thought you would like, and it is not up to you to change the plan. In addition, they would not have suggested an evening that would put them in the workhouse. Lastly, since your friends are taking the trouble to invite you to a restaurant, you should be gracious enough to accept their hospitality, and not decline their invitation or suggest that you treat them instead, as in **❻**. So, **❶** is best.

SITUATION 6

A colleague has invited you to his home for dinner. You want to make a good impression, so you dress carefully and bring along a nice box of chocolates. You arrive 20 minutes late, as is the standard, only to find that you are the first one there. It is clear that your host and his wife are busy in the kitchen. Your colleague shows you into the living room, which is large and beautifully decorated, with several other intriguing rooms opening off to the sides. Your host gestures to the couch and says to make yourself comfortable. You:

❹ Sit down and stay there until either other guests arrive or your host indicates otherwise.

❺ Take a quick peek into the other rooms, which look so beckoning, then sit down.

❻ Roll up your sleeves and offer to help in the kitchen.

❶ Browse around the living room, helping yourself to the aperitifs and snacks that are sitting on a table nearby.

Comments

First of all, please be assured that you have done nothing wrong by arriving 20 minutes late. You made an effort to conform to the cultural norms of your French hosts; unfortunately, even though you arrived late, it wasn't late enough. This is one of those situations where you just have to make do. Once you have arrived at your colleague's home, however, you should sit down where indicated and stay put. You may look at books on the coffee table (if any), the view or the pictures on the wall (and comment about them nicely afterwards), but you should not help yourself to any food or drink unless you have been asked to do so. Thus **❹** is the best answer. The important thing to remember, no matter what you do, is to respect the privacy of your hosts. Answers **❺**, **❻** and **❶** would, as a result, make you seem intrusive and ill-mannered.

SITUATION 7

At the home of an acquaintance, you accidentally brush up against a case holding some beautiful china figurines. One of them falls and breaks. Naturally, you apologise...

Ⓐ ... profusely throughout the entire evening, in order to convey to your hostess how truly sorry you feel.

Ⓑ ... sincerely once and then drop the subject immediately. Who wants to ruin an otherwise lovely evening?

Ⓒ ...once in private, and then help pick up the pieces. You mention nothing about paying for the figurine, as the French are sensitive about issues relating to money. Instead, you send a bouquet of flowers to the hostess the next day.

Ⓓ ... once sincerely and publicly, help pick up the pieces and tell your hostess you are going to look for a replacement or to pay for one. You add that you will call your insurance company to alert them that there might be a claim. Nevertheless, you still send a bouquet of flowers to your hostess the next day.

Comments

Only **Ⓓ** is acceptable in this difficult situation. Your apologies should be sincere and profound, but you don't have to bring it up all evening, spoiling everyone's enjoyment of the event. Apologise, help repair the damage, offer to pay for the replacement, then drop the subject, but do send flowers the next day. Remember that in France, everyone has *multi-risque* (multi-risk) household insurance, so offering to pay for the repair or replacement of the item is both courteous and responsible.

SITUATION 8

You and some American friends from home have eaten quite well in a crowded restaurant, but now it's time to pay the bill and go home. Since the waiter is obviously occupied, one of your friends takes out his credit card and puts it on the corner of the table, assuming that the waiter will see it, take it, then bring it back to the table with the bill. Nothing happens and the waiter doesn't come. After about 10 minutes, your friend starts to get annoyed. Finally you catch the waiter's eye, and when he comes over, your friend points to his credit card but says nothing. Both your friend and the waiter are clearly annoyed. He brings the bill with the little credit card machine, the bill is paid, and everyone leaves, slightly uncomfortable that a pleasant evening has ended on an awkward note. Your friend grumbles about the French being anti-American, as surely the waiter should have seen the card on the table. So why didn't the waiter just proceed from there?

Ⓐ Your friend is right: some French waiters just have a natural aversion towards Americans in general.

Ⓑ Your friend should have called the waiter's attention by either politely calling out or signalling.

Ⓒ Your friend should have called over the restaurant host and asked him for the bill.

Ⓓ French waiters are proud. Your friend should have walked over to the waiter and handed him his credit card directly.

Comments

This is clearly a case of cultural assumptions colliding. Americans, especially, are used to the bill appearing automatically—usually just after dessert and coffee have been served—but French waiters are used to verbal cues or hand signals, or even a smile and a nod. Just putting a card on the table and expecting the waiter to jump to it, so to speak, is rude and does not show respect for the waiter. In France, being a waiter is a lifelong trade like any other; it is not a stopgap position for someone who is training for another career. As to anti-Americanism, there's much less of this than purported. People who make an effort to conform to the French sensibilities of *politesse* and respect will be treated in the same manner. Only **Ⓑ** is correct.

DO'S AND DON'TS

So here you are in Paris. Your belongings have arrived, your children are in school, you've most likely started to work at a job with new colleagues—even your dog has made friends in the park! What comes next? That's clear: building your life in Paris so you can enjoy what the city has to offer, with a minimum of 'culture shocks' that will make you feel like an alien from an unknown planet. Some cultural pitfalls can be sidestepped, so here are some tips to give you some confidence in starting your new life in Paris.

DO'S

- Do be polite to people. The most important thing to understand about the French is their reliance on manners and formality (although harried people anywhere can sometimes be rude). French codes of behaviour and mannerly rituals are strictly adhered to, and they are actually quite pleasant, once you get used to them.
- Do greet people whenever you can. When meeting someone for the first time, say "*bonjour* (or *bonsoir*) *madame*" or *bonjour monsieur.*" (Do not say "*enchanté*" or repeat the person's name.) When you board a bus, say "*bonjour, monsieur/madame*" to the driver, and to a chauffeur in a taxi before you say where you want to go. Say "*au revoir et merci*" when you get out of the cab. (You can't do this on the bus, because you must exit from the rear doors.) Greet, too, your local merchants and *restaurateurs*. Upon entering a small shop, say "*bonjour, madame*" to the salesperson, even if you just want to look around and aren't ready to buy. If in a larger office or store you need to get someone's attention—a person who, for whatever reason, has not looked up from behind the desk or counter as you approached—manners will do the trick. Say "*Excusez-moi de vous déranger, monsieur, mais...*" ("Excuse me for bothering you, sir, but..."), and when the person looks up, ask for what you need.

- Do observe good manners with both strangers and friends. Speak in a manner appropriate to the situation. If you are on a crowded bus or *métro* and an older person boards, offer to give up your seat. (This also holds true for pregnant women or those carrying small children.)

- Do excuse yourself if you happen to bump into someone while walking. "*Pardon*," you might say, or "*Pardon, monsieur/madame*."

- Do address women as "*madame*". Women should note that being called *madame*, even if you're young or unmarried, is not an insult. If you look to be over 30 years of age, you're called *madame* out of respect, so you should do the same when speaking. If a woman is clearly quite young, you may say *mademoiselle*, although officially this is frowned upon.

- Do shake hands. The French shake hands a lot—the physical contact reinforces their feelings of amity and respect. Shake the hands of acquaintances or colleagues you meet on the street. At a restaurant you patronise frequently, the owner may shake your hand to signal that he knows you are a 'regular'. (For the staff, however, a smile and "*bonjour, monsieur*" will do. French waiters are not chummy and do not introduce themselves by their first name. Treat them with respect.)

- Do greet your friends with a kiss—the French are great kissers. Once you have made a French friend, you will no doubt move from shaking hands to kissing. Generally this involves a slight kiss on each cheek upon greeting and later, upon saying goodbye.

- Do respect people's sense of domain. At the market, do not pick out the fruit or vegetables yourself, unless there is a sign that says *libre service*; wait instead for the merchant to help you. In a shop, don't let your kids run wild and touch everything. At the office, always knock before entering other people's offices.

- Do dress appropriately for the occasion. Appearance counts when you're out and about. If you're in a casual situation, you should still dress neatly, and if you're in a situation that calls for you to dress up, do so. Although young people wear jeans around town, older people don't.

And if you look at those young people, they still look put together, jeans or otherwise.

■ Do remember who you are. Even after living in Paris for years and speaking what you think is fluent French, never try to pass for a native. Don't assume that just because you speak French, the merchants are friendly to you and you have close French friends, that you will be considered French. This will never happen.

DON'TS

■ Don't use people's first names from the start. Using first names is not automatic; if your colleagues want you to call them by their first names, they will let you know. If invited to dinner with friends, you will most likely be on a first-name basis with your hosts and the other guests, but this does not apply to dinner at the home of your boss or the more senior professional acquaintances.

■ Don't move from using the *vous* form of address to the familiar *tu* unless given the green light; even when you are on a first-name basis with your friends. Wait until your friend indicates a desire to *tutoyer* (use the *tu* form) or listen carefully to hear whether there hasn't been a subtle move toward this intimate term of address.

■ Don't ask personal questions. The French guard their privacy and do not volunteer much personal information. With acquaintances, don't ask what they do for a living, how they voted, or where they've bought the clothes they're wearing—even if you'd like to visit that shop sometime. Let them make the first move.

■ Don't speak loudly. Be alert to how loudly you're talking on your phone while on the bus, in a crowded restaurant or in a museum. Don't give a belly laugh or guffaw (except while watching a funny film). Keep a low profile.

■ Don't show impatience, ever. Not everything always goes your way, but it is ill-mannered to show impatience, whether to strangers or friends. Even if there is no orderly queue at a shop or stall at the market, generally the merchant knows who's next. If not, just wait until you are called upon to give your order.

- Don't start any encounter with an 'attitude'. Just because French people—especially the older generation—don't smile, don't assume they're rude or even unfriendly. If a salesperson in a store is busy with another customer, do not interrupt, even just to ask directions to the department you're looking for; wait patiently until it is your turn.

- Don't insist on getting apologies from the French. The French have developed a need to be right—or at least not to be wrong—and if you can get by without upsetting this 'rule', everyone will be better off.

- Don't always be on time! Be punctual for professional meetings and for dates with friends or colleagues in restaurants. If for some unforeseen reason you are delayed, call the person's mobile phone, apologise and say when you will arrive. But don't ever (ever!) be early or punctual for dinner at a French person's home. If you arrive early, find a café nearby, order a drink and wait until 20–30 minutes after the time agreed upon.

- Don't talk about money. Money is one of those subjects that is pretty much taboo with the French, at least on a personal level. You can mention where you've seen items on sale and you can complain about how expensive life is in general, but don't translate this into talking about your personal situation with money, or anyone else's.

- Don't get too graphic. Avoid details such as your own health or that of your family, problems with your in-laws, or even specific problems with the bank or tax bureau. And don't go into long personal anecdotes.

DINING ETIQUETTE AT A RESTUARANT
Do's

- Do order a cup of coffee at the bar (or something else) first, if you're going into a café just to use their restrooms.

- Do place the napkin on your lap immediately upon sitting down.

- Do rest the hand that does not hold your fork on the table, not in your lap. Don't rest your elbow on the table.

- Do spread your butter bite by bite. Don't take a huge pat and put it on your plate.

- Do eat everything you can with cutlery, not with your fingers. This includes fruit, cheese, even French fries.
- Do place your knife and fork neatly and diagonally, across the top of your plate when you have finished eating.
- Do inform a waiter of your dietary needs (no butter, etc.) by asking how a dish has been prepared. But if a waiter says that a dish would be ruined without a particular ingredient, don't argue. Order something else.
- Do close your menu and put it on the table, when you are ready to order. If you keep looking at it (even just out of curiosity), the waiter will assume you are still deciding and will not approach the table to take your order.
- Do ask for the bill (*l'addition*) when you are ready to leave. The waiter waits for your cue.
- Do leave a small tip—about five per cent of the bill—in cash on the table, if the service has been acceptable. A basic gratuity of 12–15 per cent is included in the bill.
- Do ask your neighbours if smoking bothers them, even on an outside patio where smoking is permitted. Most people are accommodating, especially if they are in a smoking section.

Don'ts
- Don't cut your lettuce leaves. If the salad has large pieces of lettuce, fold them with your fork and knife.
- Don't mop up gravy with bread in your fingers, use a knife and fork. Don't mop at all, unless you're with friends.
- Don't ask for coffee before the end of a meal. Coffee is served after the dessert, not with it.
- Don't talk business immediately at a business lunch or dinner. Catch up on the news before you zoom in; follow your colleagues' cues.
- Don't pour the wine yourself—the waiter, host, or sommelier will do it. But you pour your own water.

DINING ETIQUETTE AT SOMEONE'S HOME
Do's
- Do follow all the above general guidelines meticulously.
- Generally, if invited for dinner, it is customary to arrive

around twenty minutes later than specified. For an invitation to lunch, however, arrive about on time.

■ Do bring something nice, but don't bring anything that requires the hostess to divert her attention from the dinner. For instance, don't bring flowers for which she might first have to find a vase and then have to arrange. Chocolates, given discretely to the hostess are always appropriate.

■ Do take only as much as you will eat if platters are passed and you are to serve yourself. It is a terrible gaffe to take or ask for more than you can eat.

■ Do take some more if you are offered seconds and you are still hungry, but not of the soup or cheese courses.

■ Do follow the shape of each cheese, when helping yourself to the cheese course. Don't cut off the point of a triangular cheese, but slice a thin slice off the side, so everyone will get a good part.

■ Do close the door after you have used *les toilettes*.

Don'ts

■ Don't bring wine, which heretofore has been taken as a suggestion that the host's wine selection might not be up to your standards. However, this is slowly changing, so if your own country excels in producing a particular wine, you might bring a bottle as a novelty.

■ Don't talk about money, religion, politics or someone's health problems (even your own); take your cue from your hosts or the others. Travels, art exhibitions or good films, a new restaurant to try—these are always enjoyable topics.

■ Don't help yourself, unless it is a buffet. The host or hostess will notice when your plate or glass is empty.

■ Don't leave when others are still lingering with coffee, but don't stay when it is clearly time to move on.

GLOSSARY

Even if you don't speak a word of French, you should have no trouble finding your way in Paris if you stay on the tourist track. Nonetheless, it's still a good idea to have a basic vocabulary, for the French appreciate visitors who try to speak their language—it is their country, after all.

All this said, if you don't have any French in your repertoire, the one most efficient sentence you might consider learning is "*Pardonnez-moi monsieur (madame), parlez-vous anglais?*" which means "Excuse me sir (ma'am), do you speak English?" And if you do speak some French, but have difficulty understanding someone, you can always say, with an apologetic little smile, "*Parlez lentement, s'il-vous-plaît*", and most people will oblige by speaking slowly.

If you are here to stay for while, however, you should learn at least enough French to get by. It will be helpful in daily life, no matter how short your stay. Take some lessons to get you started. Most schools offer short-term courses, which can be fun as well as instructive. See Chapter 8 for language schools and for some hints on French pronunciation.

NUMBERS

Zero	*Zéro*
One	*Un*
Two	*Deux*
Three	*Trois*
Four	*Quatre*
Five	*Cinq*
Six	*Six*
Seven	*Sept*
Eight	*Huit*
Nine	*Neuf*
Ten	*Dix*
Eleven	*Onze*

Twelve	*Douze*
Thirteen	*Treize*
Fourteen	*Quatorze*
Fifteen	*Quinze*
Sixteen	*Seize*
Seventeen	*Dix-sept*
Eighteen	*Dix-huit*
Nineteen	*Dix-neuf*
Twenty	*Vingt*
Thirty	*Trente*
Forty	*Quarante*
Fifty	*Cinquante*
Sixty	*Soixante*
Seventy	*Soixante-dix*
Eighty	*Quatre-vingt*
Ninety	*Quatre-vingt dix*
Hundred	*Cent*
Thousand	*Mille*

DAYS OF THE WEEK

Monday	*Lundi*
Tuesday	*Mardi*
Wednesday	*Mercredi*
Thursday	*Jeudi*
Friday	*Vendredi*
Saturday	*Samedi*
Sunday	*Dimanche*
The week/ The month	*La semaine/ Le mois*

MONTHS

English-speakers should recognise the names of months , for they all bear some relation to the names of the months in English: *Janvier, Février, Mars, Avril, Mai, Juin, Juillet, Août, Septembre, Octobre, Novembre, Décembre.*

TIME

In writing, for timetables, television programmes, films and making reservations in a restaurant, etc., the French express time using the 24-hour clock. In speaking, however, many people say 8:00 pm rather than 20 *heures*.

1:00 pm	13h
2:00 pm	14h
3:00 pm	15h
4:00 pm	16h
5:00 pm	17h
6:00 pm	18h
7:00 pm	19h
8:00 pm	20h
9:00 pm	21h
10:00 pm	22h
11:00 pm	23h
midnight	*minuit*

COMMON EXPRESSIONS

Good day/ hello, sir (ma'am)	*Bonjour, monsieur* (*madame*)
Good evening	*Bonsoir*
Good night	*Bonne nuit*
How are you?	*Comment allez-vous?*
Very well, thank you.	*Très bien, merci.*
Yes, no, maybe	*Oui, non, peut-être*
Please	*S'il-vous-plaît*
Thank you; you're welcome.	*Merci; je vous en prie*
Good luck!	*Bonne chance!*

BEING POLITE

The French pay great heed to *la politesse*. Here are some standard phrases which the French use in daily life.

Goodbye and thank you	*Au revoir et merci*
Yes, please	*Oui, s'il-vous-plaît*
No, thank you	*Non, merci*
Thank you very much	*Merci beaucoup*
You're welcome	*Je vous en prie*
Pardon me (if you bump into someone)	*Pardon*
Excuse me (if you are apologising)	*Excusez-moi*
I'm sorry, but I don't understand	*Excusez-moi, mais je ne comprends pas*
Yes, I understand, thank you	*Oui, je comprends, merci*
Sorry to bother you, but...	*Pardonnez-moi de vous déranger, mais...*
OK or I agree	*D'accord*
Have a nice day	*Bonne journée*
Have a nice evening	*Bonne soirée*
You, too	*A vous aussi*

EMERGENCIES

Emergency!	*C'est urgent!*
Help me, please!	*Aidez-moi, s'il-vous-plaît!*
Call the fire department/ the police!	*Appelez les pompiers/ la police!*
My name is	*Je m'appelle*
The building code is	*Le code de l'immeuble est*
Where is the pharmacy?	*Où se trouve la pharmacie?*

OUT AND ABOUT

The street	*La rue*
The pavement	*Le trottoir*
The metro	*Le métro*

The metro station	*La station de métro*
Where is the closest metro?	*Où se trouve le métro le plus près?*
Entrance	*L'entrée*
Exit	*La sortie*
Metro/ train transfers	*La correspondance*
Platform	*Le quai*
Bus	*Le bus*
Bus stop	*L'arrêt de bus*
Map	*Le plan*
Transport ticket	*Le ticket*
Ten bus/ metro tickets	*Un carnet*
Where is the bathroom?	*Où se trouve les toilettes? / Où sont les toilettes?*

MONEY TERMS

I don't have any cash	*Je n'ai pas d'argent*
Automatic cash dispenser	*Distributeur*
Is there a bank nearby?	*Y-a-t-il une banque près d'ici?*
Do you accept credit cards?	*Acceptez-vous les cartes de crédit?*
How much is this, please?	*C'est combien, s'il-vous-plaît?*
It's (not) expensive	*C'est (pas) cher*
It's a little too expensive for me	*C'est un peu trop cher pour moi*
I'm going to pay in cash	*Je vais payer en espèces*

LE SHOPPING

A department store	*Un grand magasin*
The pharmacy	*La pharmacie*
A book shop (a book)	*Une librairie (un livre)*

Dress, blouse, skirt	Robe, chemisier, jupe
Jacket, raincoat, hat	Veste, impermeable, chapeau
Gloves, scarf	Gants, écharpe
Shoes, socks, pantyhose	Chausseurs, chaussettes, collants
Shirt, tie, suit	Chemise, cravate, tailleur (for women)/costume (for men)
I'm just looking for the moment, thank you	Merci, je regarde pour le moment
Thanks, anyway	Merci, quand même
May I look around?	Puis-je jeter un coup d'œil?
I take size 10	Je fais un quarante
May I try it on?	Puis-je l'essayer?
It's too large/small.	C'est trop grand/petit
I'll take it	Je le prends
On sale	Soldé

ON THE TELEPHONE

Who's calling?	De la part de Qui?
Please speak more slowly.	Parlez lentement, s'il-vous plait.
May I leave a message?	Puis-je laissez un message?

DINING OUT

Waiters in most centrally located and well-known restaurants generally know enough English to interpret what you are saying. If you are adventurous in your restaurant searches, however, it's best to have at least a little knowledge of 'restaurantese'. When calling for the waiter, always say "monsieur" or "madame," never "garcon," as you might have been taught in school.

| I'd like to book a table | Je voudrais réserver une table |

For two/three people	*Pour deux/trois couverts*
At eight o'clock	*A vingt heures*
The menu	*La carte*
The fixed-price meal	*Le menu*
The napkin	*La serviette*
The cloakroom	*Le vestiaire*
The waiter/waitress	*Le serveur/la serveuse*
The tip	*Le pourboire*
The bill, please	*L'addition, s'il-vous-plaît*
Breakfast	*Le petit déjeuner*
Lunch	*Le déjeuner*
Dinner	*Le dîner*
The snack	*Le casse-croûte, le snack*
The first course	*L'entrée*
The main course	*Le plat/plat principal*
Dessert	*Le déssert*
A pitcher of tap water	*Une carafe d'eau*
Mineral Water	*Eau minerale*
Still/fizzy	*Plate/Gazeuse*
It's very good, thank you	*C'est très bon, merci*
What is the special of the day?	*Quel est le plat du jour?*
A little more, please	*Encore un peu, merci*
To your health	*A votre santé*

RESOURCE GUIDE

This section first lists telephone numbers that are important to have handy in case of emergencies. Two-digit numbers may be dialled without charge, while those starting with 01 are charged as local calls. Numbers that start with 08.00 are also free. Others that start with 08 (08.92, for instance) or those that have only four- or six-digit numbers (such as for SNCF or France Télécom) incur a number of *centimes* per minute—the cost per minute is announced at the beginning of the connection.

For information on activities in Paris, go to the Paris Tourist Office or access its website, which has extensive information on all facets of Paris life (www.paris-info.com) The *mairie* (town hall) of your *arrondissement*, or the Hôtel de Ville (City Hall), should have brochures for residents that describe the services, programmes and even sports facilities sponsored by the city. See below for detailed information.

Toward the end of this chapter are some well-known networking resources in Paris, for both professional and social contacts.

EMERGENCIES & HEALTH
Emergency Numbers
- Police   17
- Pompiers (Fire Department)   18
- Gas Emergencies   0800 47 33 33
- Emergencies anywhere in Europe   112

Dire Health Emergencies
- Fire Department Paramedics   18
- SAMU (Medical services and Ambulance)   15

24-hour Medical Help
- Urgences Médicales de Paris   01.53.94.94.94
  (house calls)
- S.O.S. Médecins (house calls)   3624;
                                                 01.47.07.77.77
- Anti-poison Hotline   01.40.05.48.48

- Burns (Adults) Hôpital St-Antoine — 01.49.28.20.00
- Burns (Children) Hôpital Trousseau — 01.44.73.74.75
- Urgences Funéraires (Deaths) — 08.00.88.00.88
- SIDA (AIDS) Support (24-hr daily) — 08.00.84.08.00
- SOS Ecoute Gay — 01.44.93.01.02
- Association des Medecins Gaies — 01.48.05.81.71
- Alcoholics Anonymous — 01.46.34.59.65
- Dental Emergencies: Hôpital de la Pitie-Salpêtrière — 01.42.16.00.00
- American Hospital (English-speaking) — 01.46.41.25.25
- SOS Vétérinaires de garde (pets) — 01.47.46.09.09

24-hr Hospitals
See the section on Health starting from page 124.
- American Hospital (does not accept pediatric emergencies; call SAMU instead)
  63 boulevard Victor Hugo, Neuilly-sur-Seine
  Tel: 01.46.41.25.25
- Hôtel Dieu
  Place du Parvis Notre Dame (Ile-de-la-Cité)
  Tel: 01.42.34.82.34
- Hôpital Necker (Children's Hospital)
  149 rue de Sèvres, 75007
  Tel: 01.44.49.40.00
  For children's dire emergencies, first dial SAMU: 15

24-hr Pharmacies
Pharmacies identify themselves by a green cross outside; when it is lit, the pharmacy is open. Pharmacists fill prescriptions, offer advice on medications, sometimes offer such services as blood pressure, bandaging cuts, etc. For English-speaking pharmacies and those that carry British or American products, see pages 134–135. To find a pharmacy in your own area that is open outside normal business hours (la pharmacie de garde), check online (www.3237.fr).
- Pharmacie les Champs (8ᵉ)
  84 avenue des Champs-Elysées; Tel: 01.45.62.02.41
- Pharmarcie Européenne (9ᵉ)
  6 place de Clichy; Tel: 01.48.74.65.18

- Grande Pharmarcie Daumesnil (12e)
  6 place Félix Eboué; Tel: 01.43.43.19.03
- Pharmacie de la porte Maillot (17e)
  68, avenue de la Grande Armée; Tel: 01.45.74.17.31

PRACTICAL INFORMATION ONLINE

- U.S. State Department information about France:
  www.state.gov/r/pa/ei/bgn/3842.htm
  www.state.gov/p/eur/ci/fr
- Brittish Expat Guide
  www.britishexpat.com
- American Embassy Information for Expats in Paris
  http://france.usembassy.gov
- Préfecture de la Police
  www.prefecture-police-paris.interieur.gouv.fr
- Public sector links
  www.service-public.fr
- Tourist Office Information in English
  http://en.parisinfo.com
- More Paris Information
  www.paris.fr
- Paris Ile-de-France Tourism
  http://en.visitparisregion.com
- 24-hour Post Office
  www.laposte.fr
- Weather Report
  http://france.meteofrance.com
- For young people
  www.jeunes.gouv.fr
- For students
  www.etudiantdeparis.fr

Hôtel de Ville (City Hall)

Place de l'Hôtel de Ville, 75004
Tel: 01.42 76.40.40; Helpline: 3975; www.paris.fr
Open Mon–Sat, 10:00 am–7:00 pm; Sun, 2:00 pm–7:00 pm

- For the *mairie* of your *arrondissement*, insert "www.*mairie*"
  and then your *arrondissement*, followed by ".paris.fr"—for
  1e: www.mairie1.paris.fr; for 2e: www.mairie2.paris.fr, etc.

Orange Télécom
- Customer Service   1014
- Helpline in English   09.69.36.39.00
- Repair hotline   1013
- Les Pages Blanches (residential listings)   118 012
- Les Pages Jaunes (business listings)   118 008
- Telephone numbers online: www.pagesjaunes.fr

Transportation
- RATP (Buses, Métro, RER)
  Tel: 3246; www.ratp.fr
- SNCF (Trains)
  Tel: 3635; www.sncf.com
- Eurostar (to London and Lille)
  Tel: 08.92.35.35.39; www.eurostar.com
- Thalys (to Amsterdam, Brussels, Cologne)
  Tel: 3635 (say 'Thalys'); www.thalys.com

Lost & Found
The train stations and airports have lost and found departments. If you lose something on the *métro*, go to the terminus of that line within 24 hours. And for items lost on trains, go to the station having to do with that line. The city's own Lost and Found Department is
- Bureau des Objets Trouvés
  36 rue Morillons, 75015; tel: 08.21.00.25.25

Lost Credit Cards
- American Express   01.47.77.72.00
- MasterCard, Maestro   08.00.90.13.87
  Cirrus, Eurocard
- Visa   08.00.90.11.79

MAKING FRIENDS
General Networking
The large English-speaking community in Paris offers a variety of support and welcome groups, both formal and informal, as do other international interest groups. Most embassies have community liaison offices for their citizens

in Paris, which may be able to supply specific contacts in Paris. The groups below can be helpful. Note that some are run by volunteers and hours may vary.

- **The American Church in Paris**
  65 quai d'Orsay, 75007
  Tel: 01.40.62.05.00; www.acparis.org
  Christian religious and social gathering venue for the entire Anglophone community. Each October, the Women of the American Church sponsor the excellent 'Bloom Where You Are Planted' acclimatisation programme for English-speaking newcomers, providing a helpful booklet on living in Paris.

- **Association of Americans Resident Overseas (AARO)**
  4, rue de Chevreuse, 75006
  Tel: 01.47.20.24.15; www.aaro.org
  Represents the interests of Americans overseas on issues such as taxes, Social Security, etc. Good for making friends with people of like concerns.

- **Association of American Wives of Europeans (AAWE)**
  34 avenue de New York, 75016
  Tel: 01.40.70.11.80; www.aaweparis.org
  Addresses current issues faced by American wives and promotes contacts and friendship.

- **Association Irlandaise Paris**
  59, avenue Gabriel Péri 93400- Saint Ouen
  (Métro 13, Garibaldi)
  Tel: 01.47.64.39.31; www.association-irlandaise.org
  Open to all who are interested in Ireland and its culture.

- **American Women's Group**
  4 rue de Chevreuse 75006
  Tel: 01.42.73.36.74; www.awgparis.org
  Social and cultural activities promoting Franco-American friendship, such as luncheon meetings, courses, tours.

- **British Commonwealth Women's Association**
  151 rue du Faubourg-St. Honoré 75008
  Tel: 01.47.20.50.91; http://bcwa.paris.online.fr
  Facilities such as clubrooms and a library; organises social and cultural activities, 'at-homes' and publishes a monthly newsletter.

- **Canadian Women's Group**
  5, rue Constantine 75007 Paris
  Tel: 01.44.43.21.03; www.canadiennesaparis.org
- **France-Amérique**
  9–11 avenue Franklin-Roosevelt, 75008
  Tel: 01.43.59.51.00; www.france-ameriques.org
  Discussions, lunches, etc. to improve cultural and economic
  relations between France and the Americas.
- **American Club of Paris**
  4, rue de Chevreuse 75006
  Tel: 01.47.23.64.36; americanclub paris.net
  Promotes Franco-American ties and friendship, plus
  opportunities for meeting Americans and other nationalities,
  with events and cultural programs.
- **Lions Club International**
  295 rue Saint-Jacques, 75007
  Tel: 01.46.34.14.10; www.lions-france.org
  International service organisation.
- **Rotary Club of Paris**
  40 boulevard Emile Augier, 75116
  Tel: 01.45.04.14.44; www.rotaryparis.org
  International service organisation.
- **The Standard Athletic Club**
  Route Forestière du Pavé de Meudon,
  92360 Meudon-la-Foret
  Tel: 01.46.26.16.09; www.saclub.org
  Prestigious British club, which also includes members from
  various international communities.
- **Toastmasters**
  www.toastmasters75.org
  Meet friendly people and improve your self-confidence and
  public speaking skills. Check website for dates and venues
  around Paris.
- **WICE (WICE Institute of Continuing Education)**
  10, rue Tiphaine 75015
  Tel: 01.45.66.75.50; www.wice-paris.org
  A wide-ranging organisation, offering a variety of English-
  language courses on living in France, French culture and
  politics. Special events.

Gay and Lesbian Networking

The gay and lesbian communities in Paris are among the most accepted in Europe. Some years ago, the French government instituted the *Pacte Civil de Solidarité*, commonly known as PACS, a 'contract of social union' that gives unmarried cohabiting couples—straight or gay—the same financial rights as married couples. Surprisingly, the majority of those who did so were not gay. Since 2013, however, same-sex marriage is legal in France, and some 2400 marriage were performed in the first year. Paris is an open and tolerant city—for the most part. There are scores of gay-friendly hotels, restaurants, bars, discotheques and shops. Every year, Paris hosts the largest Gay, Lesbian, Bi, Trans March on the continent. For some gay venues, see pages 271–273.

- **Les Mots à la Bouche**
  6 rue Ste-Croix de la Bretonnerie, 75004
  Tel: 01.42.78.88.30; www.motsbouche.com
  English-language books, gay guides, films, magazines and information. Open daily (Sundays 1:00–9:00 pm).

- **Centre Lesbien, Gay, Bi & Trans**
  63 rue Beaubourg
  Tel: 01.43.57.21.47; www.centrelgbtparis.org
  Extensive resource centre for gays and lesbians: information about the community and ongoing events, plus a library and meeting place for activities of various groups. Currently, some 80 "related" associations are members.

- **INTER**
  5 rue Perée 75003
  www.inter-lgtbt.org
  An umbrella group for dozens of LGBT organizations, sponsoring activities of its own, including the popular Paris Printemps. Access the website for news, current activities, and links to other LGBT sites.

- **Maison des Femmes**
  163 rue de Charenton, 75012
  Tel: 01.43.43.41.13; http://maisondesfemmes.free.fr
  Locale that offers information on a variety of feminist and lesbian groups. Also houses Les Archives, Recherches,

Cultures Lesbiennes (ARCL), an important documentation centre open on Tuesday evenings (www.arcl.fr)

- **Melo' Men: The International Gay Choir of Paris**
  63, rue Beaubourg 75003
  www.melomen.com
  Well-known gay choir with performances in Paris and elsewhere.
- **www.gaybox.fr**
  A dating and meeting Internet site.
- **www.parismarais.com**
  Information about the Marais and gay/lesbian resources in Paris.
- **www.tetu.com**
  Formerly a magazine, now a website for the gay community

WORSHIP IN PARIS

Since the 6th century, the history of Paris has been intertwined with Christianity (see Chapter 2). However, for the last 100 years, there has been an official separation of church and state in France. Although some 90 per cent of the population claims Catholicism as its religion, it is said that only about 12 per cent are active worshippers. In addition to the 200 Catholic churches found in Paris, there are opportunities for worship in just about whichever denomination and religion you choose— and in the major languages of the world. Religions other than Catholicism are called 'cults'.

- **Anglican/Episcopal**
  American Cathedral in Paris
  23 avenue George-V, 75008;
  Tel: 01.53.23.84.00; www.americancathedral.org
- **Catholic**
  Neighbourhood churches open about 8:00 am and generally hold three masses daily. For masses and music at the Cathedral of Notre Dame, access its website (www.notredamedeparis.fr). Services in English can be heard at St. Joseph's Church at 50 avenue Hoche, 75008 (tel: 01.42.27.28.56; www.stjoeparis.org).

- **Christian Science**
  First Church of Christ, Scientist
  36 boulevard Saint-Jacques 75014;
  Tel: 01.47.07.26.60; www.tfccs.com
- **Interdenominational Protestant**
  The American Church in Paris
  65 quai d'Orsay 75007;
  Tel: 01.40.62.05.00; www.acparis.org
  'For all people of all nations', one of the focal points of the
  Protestant community in Paris.
- **International Christian**
  Saint Michael's
  5 rue d'Aguesseau 75008;
  Tel: 01.47.42.70.88; www.stmichaelsparis.org
- **Islam**
  La Grande Mosquée
  Place du Puits-de-l'Ermite 75005;
  tel: 01.45.35.97.33; www.mosqueedeparis.net
  Call for worship times and information on other mosques.
  Inquire also at the Institut du Monde Arabe at 1 rue des
  Fossés Saint-Bernard, 75005; tel: 01.40.46.84.62.
- **Judaism**
  Divided into *Non-Consistoire* (ultra-Orthodox), *Consistoire*
  (Orthodox), *Massorti* (traditionally Conservative)
  and *Libérale*.
  Consistoire: Rothschild (Grand) Synagogue;
  44 rue de la Victoire, 75009
  Tel: 01.40.82.26.261
  Libérale: Kehilat Gesher (with services in English);
  7 rue Léon Cogniet, 75017
  Tel: 09.53.18.90.86; www.kehilatgesher.org
- **Presbyterian**
  The Scots Kirk
  17 rue Bayard, 75008;
  Tel: 01.48.78.47.94; www.scotskirk.com

FURTHER READING

The books listed here should all be available at the American Library of Paris. You can also check the bookshop W.H. Smith or others for new or used books. See pages 229–300.

HISTORY

How Paris Became Paris Became Paris: The Invention of the Modern City. Joan Dejean. New York: Bloomsbury, 2014.

- An interesting look at how Paris emerged from its medieval surroundings becoming the modern yet traditional city it is today.

The Greater Journey: Americans in Paris. David McCullough. New York, Simon and Schuster, 2011.

- American artists of all sorts, intellectuals and many others who were inspired by Paris.

And the Show Went On: Cultural Life In Nazi-occupied Paris. Alan Riding. New York: Knopf, 2010.

- Cultural life did not stop in Paris, even when it was occupied by the Nazis in World War II, as artists and intellectuals struggled to maintain themselves under adverse conditions.

The Jews of France: A History from Antiquity to the Present. Esther Benbassa. Princeton, New Jersey: Princeton University Press, 1999.

- The turbulent history of the Jews in France, including during World War II.

Paris After the Liberation: 1944-1949. Antony Beevor and Artemis Cooper. London: Penguin Books, 2004.

- How Paris was shaped by the war and how it recovered.

Paris Noir: African Americans in the City of Light. Tyler Stovall. New York: Houghton Mifflin Company, 1996.

- Interesting and detailed history of blacks in Paris.

The General: Charles de Gaulle and the France He Saved. Jonathan Fenby. New York: Skyhorse Publishing, 2012.

- A national hero who inspired the resistance in World War II and went on to lead France into modernity afterwards; this book gives a readable and well-researched understanding of the man and his times.

Paris Reborn: Napoleon III, Baron Haussmann and the Quest to Build a Modern City. Stephane Kirkland. New York, St. Martin's Press, 2013.

- A detailed understanding of the most famous urban renewal project—its controversies, debacles, and ultimate successes.

FAMOUS ACCOUNTS OF PARIS

Walks in Hemingway's Paris. Noel Riley Fitch. New York: St. Martin's Press, 1990.

- Quotes and anecdotes about the writers and artists who lived in Paris during the 1920s and 1930s, and suggested walks to show their haunts.

Autobiography of Alice B. Toklas. Gertrude Stein. Modern Library, 1993.

- Stein's classic book of expatriate life in Paris.

A Moveable Feast. Ernest Hemingway. New York: Touchstone Books, 1992.

- Hemingway's ever-popular book about life in Paris.

A Place in the World Called Paris. Steven Barclay. San Francisco: Chronicle Books, 2002.

- Quotes from people who have loved Paris.

WALKS IN PARIS

Time Out Book of Paris Walks. Andrew White. UK: Penguin Books, 1996.

- Thirty-two walks around Paris, accompanied by informative and chatty descriptions.

Around and About Paris: Volumes 1–3. Thirza Vallois. London: Iliad Books, 1995.
- Important reference to keep on your shelf. Sprinkled with anecdotes, relates the history of Paris through recommended walks in every district, street by street.

Permanent Parisians. Judi Culberton and Tom Randall. Chelsea, Vermont: Robson Books, 2000.
- Places where famous people are buried in Paris. Famous cemeteries in Paris—especially Père Lachaise—are popular Sunday strolls for Parisians.

FOOD

French Cheeses: A visual guide to more than 350 cheeses from every region of France. London, Dorling Kindersley, 1996.
- A visual guide to more than 350 cheeses from every region of France.

French Wines: The Essential Guide to the Wines and Wine Growing Regions of France. Robert Joseph. London: Dorling Kindersley, 1999.
- Everything you want to know about French wines.

PRACTICAL READING

French Toast. Harriet Welty Rochefort. Montreuil, France: Anglphone s.a, 1997.
- Helpful, chatty look at living in France, with much insight and wit.

French or Foe? Getting the Most out of Visiting, Living and Working in France. Polly Platt. London: Culture Crossings, 1995.
- Witty and informative book about living in Paris.

Paris, Moi, and the Gang: A Memoir of Sorts. Frances Gendlin: Paris, Summertime Publications, 2010.
- A fictionalized memoir of one year of the author's life in Paris.

Paris: The Novel. Edward Rutherford. New York, Doubleday, 2013.

- A novel about the history of Paris, through the eyes and actions of the characters.

Angels of Paris: An Architectural Tour Through the History of Paris. Rosemary Flannery. New York, Random House, 2012.

- A charming look at the history of Paris through the sculptures of angels that dot the streets—from the Middle Ages to the Twentieth Century.

INDEX

ABOUT THE AUTHOR

Fran Gendlin has held leadership positions in both magazine and book publishing. She was Editor and Publisher of the magazine *Sierra*, and was the Sierra Club's Director of Public Affairs. As Executive Director of the Association of American University Presses, she helped foster the interests of scholarly publishing worldwide. Through her own business, The Right Word, she helped writers with their projects and taught English and business writing to foreign professionals. In 1997, she wrote *Living & Working Abroad: Rome*, and in 2001, *Living & Working Abroad: San Francisco*, two widely read guides to understanding and living in those cities. *CultureShock! Paris* also has had several new editions over the years, as important changes occurred.

While she was growing up, her family moved several times to different areas of the United States, each with its own characteristics and culture, climate and cuisine. This has led her to appreciate new cultures, to wonder about their differences and similarities, and to seek to understand them. All her life she has enjoyed travel and new adventures, meeting people she might otherwise not have done, and making new friends.

Fran has lived in Paris for more than a decade, and life there is just as agreeable as she has conveyed in his book. Her fictional memoir, *Paris, Moi, and the Gang: A Memoir...of Sort*s can be ordered at bookshops, on amazon.com, and on other online sites. Currently she also spends winter months in Puerto Vallarta, Mexico, and is pleased with the sunny climes.

L'AS DU FA

SOUS LE CONTROLE DU BETH-

FALLAFEL

L'AS du FALLAFEL

פלאפל

שאַוארמא

RUE DES ROSIERS ◆ PARIS

toujours imité   jamais égalé

NOS SANDWICHS
@Pita a Emporter

Fallafel Special   (vegetarien)
Schawarma   (Viande Agneau)
lamb and turkey

Mixte viandes de Poulet Grille   (burguini)
Grilled Chicken Steak
Escalope de Poulet   Pané

Schnitz

Escalope Poulet Grille
Grilled Chicken Steak
Pav et Saute Au Carré
Chicken Turkey

Saute de Viandes
           mixed d

Morgane de Boeuf
           Saussages
Boulettes de Kft

FALAFEL

**TOUJOURS IMITE
JAMAIS EGALE**
MAISON FONDEE EN 1979

MAISON FONDÉE E

Salle de
110 Places Assises
A L'interieur
Selon Le Controle de Beth Din De Paris

KOPHER

שר

L'AS du FALLAFEL

toujours imité jamai

There's always a crowd here in the Marais at l'As du Falafel, waiting for their order of delicious Middle-East specialties. Take-away dishes, food trucks, and storefronts selling crêpes to eat on-the-go, speak to a younger, more casual generation of Parisians.

Titles in the CultureShock! series:

Argentina	France	Portugal
Australia	Germany	Russia
Austria	Great Britain	San Francisco
Bahrain	Hawaii	Saudi Arabia
Beijing	Hong Kong	Scotland
Belgium	India	Shanghai
Berlin	Ireland	Singapore
Bolivia	Italy	South Africa
Borneo	Jakarta	Spain
Brazil	Japan	Sri Lanka
Bulgaria	Korea	Sweden
Cambodia	Laos	Switzerland
Canada	London	Syria
Chicago	Malaysia	Taiwan
Chile	Mauritius	Thailand
China	Morocco	Tokyo
Costa Rica	Munich	Travel Safe
Cuba	Myanmar	Turkey
Czech Republic	Netherlands	United Arab
Denmark	New Zealand	Emirates
Ecuador	Pakistan	USA
Egypt	Paris	Vancouver
Finland	Philippines	Venezuela

For more information about any of these titles, please contact any of our Marshall Cavendish offices around the world (listed on page ii) or visit our website at:

www.marshallcavendish.com/genref